THE BOOK OF
KNOWLEDGE
ANNUAL 1960

THE BOOK OF KNOWLEDGE

ANNUAL 1960

THE FIFTIETH ANNIVERSARY OF THE CHILDREN'S ENCYCLOPEDIA

GROLIER INCORPORATED · NEW YORK
GROLIER SOCIETY OF CANADA LIMITED · TORONTO

CONTENTS

Nature

Sports

Activities

Transportation

Men at Work

Gardens

Art and Entertainment

Index

Contributors

ROBERT G. ALBION   *Travel and Transport, page 222*
Gardiner Professor of Oceanic History and Affairs, Harvard University; author, FORESTS AND SEA POWER; SEAPORTS SOUTH OF SAHARA.

CLINTON P. ANDERSON
The Atom Keeps House, page 177
United States Senator from New Mexico; Chairman, the Joint Congressional Committee for Atomic Energy.

GEORGE ARMSTRONG   *Pope John XXIII, page 105*
Writer; correspondent, North American Newspaper Alliance.

MARIUS BARBEAU   *Grizzly Bears, page 277*
Folklorist for the Canadian Government, National Museum of Canada.

CARLETON BEALS   *Latin America, page 65*
Author and lecturer; contributor, HARPER'S, SATURDAY EVENING POST, SATURDAY REVIEW.

ARNOLD C. BRACKMAN   *South Asia, page 46*
Staff writer, The News of the Week in Review, The New York TIMES; contributor, CHRISTIAN SCIENCE MONITOR, London ECONOMIST.

WILLIAM BRIDGES   *Tiger Cubs, page 273*
Curator of Publications, New York Zoological Society; author, ZOO EXPEDITIONS, ZOO DOCTOR.

WALTER BRIGGS   *The Far East, page 53*
Special correspondent, The New York HERALD TRIBUNE; contributor, COLLIER'S, THE NEW REPUBLIC.

ERWIN J. BULBAN   *Aviation, page 334*
Southwest Editor, AVIATION WEEK.

BRYAN BUNCH   *Science Highlights, page 197*
Assistant Editor, THE ENCYCLOPEDIA YEAR BOOK.

FRANCES F. CLINGERMAN   *4-H, Good Citizens, page 319*
Home Economics and Youth Information Specialist, Federal Extension Service, United States Department of Agriculture.

PADRAIC COLUM   *Hawaii, page 149*
Poet, critic and dramatist; author, THE BRIGHT ISLANDS, STORIES OF HAWAII.

BOSLEY CROWTHER   *Motion Pictures, page 234*
Film Critic, The New York TIMES; author, THE LION'S SHARE.

PAUL DE KRUIF   *Medicine and Health, page 210*
Author, THE MICROBE HUNTERS, LIFE AMONG THE DOCTORS, MEN AGAINST DEATH; contributor, THE READER'S DIGEST.

JAMES DUGAN   *Underwater Swimming, page 304*
Secretary, United States Liaison Committee for Oceanographic Research; author, MEN UNDER THE SEA.

ESMOND S. FERGUSON   *Middle East, page 41*
Investment Manager, Lord, Abbet & Company; former Deputy Administrator of the finances of Iran.

PATRICK FERRY   *Yankee Bat Boy, page 311*
Bat boy for the New York Yankees.

THOMAS M. FRANCK   *Africa, page 32*
Associate Professor of International Law, New York University; contributor, PARLIAMENTARY AFFAIRS, CENTRAL AFRICAN EXAMINER.

PAUL GARDNER   *Sports Review of the Year, page 291*
Former sports writer for the New York JOURNAL AMERICAN.
GLENN GARRISON   *Terminals for the Jet Age, page 340*
Associate Editor, AVIATION WEEK.
SONDRA GORNEY
        Girl Scouts' Adventure in Television, page 318
Director, Magazine Services, Girl Scouts of the United States
of America.
GEOFFREY L. GRIFFITH   *Australia, page 28*
Editor, Maitland MERCURY; author, A GUIDE TO LAW COURT
REPORTING.
DOROTHY C. HAMILTON
        Girl Guides at Home and Abroad, page 320
International Commissioner, The Girl Guides Association.
PHILIP T. HARTUNG   *Movies in Review, page 406*
Motion picture critic, the COMMONWEAL and SCHOLASTIC.
PAUL F. HEALY   *Christian A. Herter, page 117*
Washington correspondent, New York DAILY NEWS; contrib-
utor, SATURDAY EVENING POST.
D. P. HERRON   *Making the Titan, page 351*
Director, Information Services, The Martin Company, Den-
ver.
R. H. HOBSON   *Rescue in Rhodesia, page 157*
Federal Information Officer, Federation of Rhodesia and
Nyasaland; journalist.
JOHN TASKER HOWARD   *Music, page 392*
Retired Curator, American Music Collection, New York
Public Library; author, OUR AMERICAN MUSIC, THE WORLD'S
GREAT OPERAS.
EDWARD HUMPHREY   *Fission and Fusion, page 186*
Executive Editor, THE BOOK OF KNOWLEDGE.
JACQUES ANDRE ISTEL   *Sport Parachuting, page 308*
President, Parachutes Incorporated; contributor, FLYING,
INFANTRY JOURNAL, PARACHUTIST.
LOREN F. KAHLE   *Ocean-going Oil Tankers, page 346*
Transportation Coordinator, Standard Oil Company (N. J.);
contributor, OIL AND GAS JOURNAL, WORLD PETROLEUM.
H. V. KALTENBORN   *Berlin, page 140*
Independent news analyst; columnist, General Features
Syndicate; author, IT SEEMS LIKE YESTERDAY, FIFTY FABU-
LOUS YEARS.
PHILIP J. KLASS   *Satellites at Work, page 162*
Avionics Editor, AVIATION WEEK.
ELIZABETH W. LESLIE   *Camp Fire Jubilee, page 322*
Writer, Camp Fire Girls, Inc.
CLAUDIA LEWIS
        Young People's Books of the Year, page 314
Specialist in children's literature, Bank Street College of
Education, New York City; author, STRAPS THE CAT.
WILLY LEY   *The Exploration of Nearby Space, page 170*
Rocket expert, lecturer and technical advisor for TV; author,
ENGINEER'S DREAM; ROCKETS, MISSILES AND SPACE TRAVEL.
HERBERT W. LUNN
        Boy Scouts' Safety Good Turn, page 324
Assistant to the Director, Editorial Service, National Coun-
cil, Boy Scouts of America.
LOUISE McDOWELL   *Gardens of the World, page 365*
Editor in Chief, THE BOOK OF KNOWLEDGE ANNUAL.
GEORGE H. McMURRAY
        Producing a TV Special, page 382
Press representative for Hallmark Hall of Fame TV series.

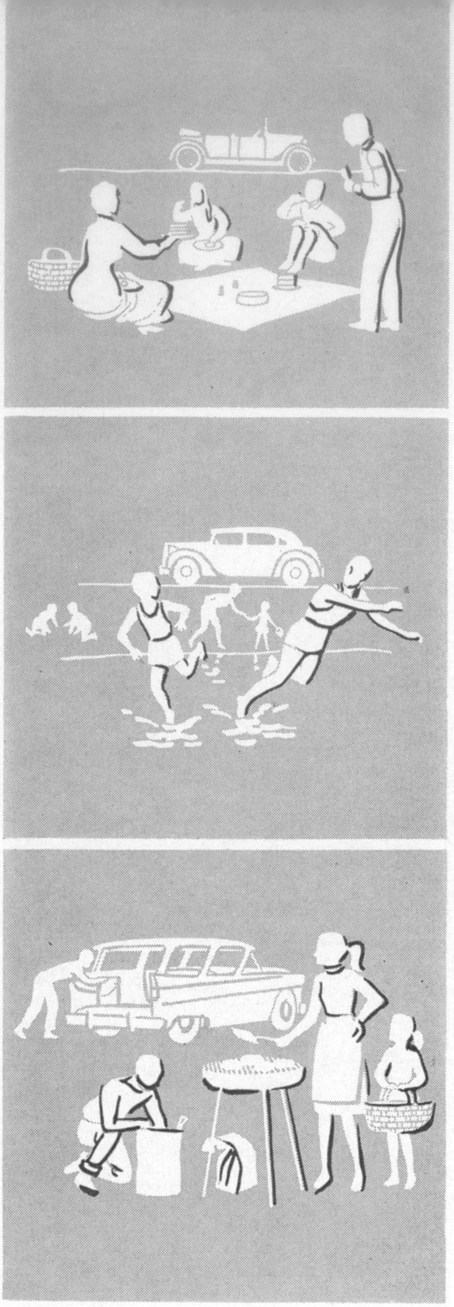

R. D. HILTON SMITH *Canada, page 59*
Antiquarian bookseller; former Deputy Chief Librarian, Toronto Public Libraries; consultant editor, ENCYCLOPEDIA CANADIANA.

I. D. W. TALMADGE *Western Europe, page 71*
Editor, WORLD WEEK.

LEONARD B. TENNYSON
The European Community, page 134
Director, The European Community Information Service, Washington, D. C.

LOWELL THOMAS, JR. *Tibet, page 153*
TV film producer; author, OUT OF THIS WORLD; OUR FLIGHT TO ADVENTURE; SILENT WAR IN TIBET.

MARIE TORRE *Television during the Year, page 388*
TV and radio columnist, The New York HERALD TRIBUNE.

L. A. VINCENT *Fire, the Great Destroyer, page 325*
General Manager, National Board of Fire Underwriters.

IRIS VINTON *Boys' Club Amateur Cooks, page 321*
Director, Publications Service, Boys' Clubs of America; author, JOHN PAUL JONES; LONGBOW ISLAND.

LEWIS W. WALKER *Owls, page 287*
Associate Director, Arizona-Sonora Desert Museum; contributor, TIME, LIFE, NATIONAL GEOGRAPHIC, NATURE, NATURAL HISTORY.

RUTH WARREN *Cyprus, page 129*
Writer; traveler in the Middle East.

JOHN S. WILSON *The Revival of Ragtime, page 397*
Jazz reviewer, The New York TIMES; conducts radio program The World of Jazz, WQXR, New York.

SALEM'S ACCOUNT OF THE INTERVIEW WAS PUBLISHED IN AL GU

JG719AES

A74

   WIREPHOTO ADVISORY

   UPCOMING: SYRACUSE FOOTBALL STAR GERRY SCHWEDES AND TEA

SHARE STUDY P

CLEARS HURDLE

SQUABBLE, A33

   AP

      NOV. 10

A90DN

   SUB INTRO

   HOUSTON, N

BY TUG BOAT C

ABOARD THE S.S. AMOCO VIRGINIA SUNDAY THAT KILLED SEVEN ME

INJURED 25 WAS CAUSED BY A "HUGE POOL OF FIRE WHICH SWEPT

   THE CAPTAIN OF THE TUG "PAN VI" TOLD NEWSMEN HE TESTIFI

COAST GUARD PRELIMINARY INVESTIGATION AT PORT ARTHUR THAT

DID NOT START "NEAR OUR BARGES, TUG, OR THE AMOCO VIRGINIA

   CAPTAIN HODGES SAID X X X PICKING UP THIRD GRAF.

   MM749ACS A NM

A93

   PARIS, NOV.10 (AP)-NATO REPRESENTATIVES TODAY AGREED TO

HOLD A SPECIAL MEETING OF THE ALLIANCE'S FOREIGN MINISTERS

DEC.22 TO HEAR RESULTS OF THE WESTERN SUMMIT MEETING.

   PERMANENT REPRESENTATIVES OF THE 15 MEMBERS OF THE NORT

ATLANTIC TREATY ORGANIZATION DECIDED AT THEIR WEEKLY MEETI

AHEAD WITH THE ANNUAL FOREIGN MINISTERS MEETING IN PARIS I

AS ORIGINALLY PLANNED.

   BUT THE REPRESENTATIVES ALSO AGREED TO ANOTHER MINISTER

GATHERING FOLLOWING THE WESTERN SUMMIT TALKS, WHICH BEGIN

PARIS DEC.19, A NATO SPOKESMAN SAID.

   THE DECISION TO HOLD A SECOND MINISTERIAL MEETING WAS A

IN WASHINGTON YESTERDAY. THE NATO MEETING TODAY FIXED THE

   B905AES

A94

   AMMAN, JORDAN, NOV.10 (AP)-KING HUSSEIN LEFT IN HIS PRI

PLANE TODAY FOR A VACATION IN EUROPE. AFTER A STOP IN BEI

TOP
of the
NEWS
By STEPHEN RUDDY

JANUARY

CASTRO TAKES CUBA

In Cuba, Fidel Castro overthrew the government of General Fulgencio Batista. Since 1956 Castro and his revolutionaries had waged guerrilla warfare against Batista's army from mountain hideouts. In 1958 they succeeded in paralyzing Cuba's vital sugar industry. The threat of economic ruin finally turned the tide against Batista, whose rule was opposed by many Cubans. In November 1958 the Government launched an all-out offensive to crush Castro's rebellion. Castro led his forces from hiding to fight, and won a crucial four-day battle. Castro arrived triumphantly in Havana and announced, "My only aim is to bring democracy to Cuba."

A smiling and friendly Anastas Mikoyan visits a factory on his coast-to-coast tour of the United States, the first such trip by a high Soviet official since the war.

MIKOYAN VISITS THE UNITED STATES

The Soviet Union's First Deputy Premier Anastas I. Mikoyan landed at Idlewild, New York, for a tour of the United States. In Washington he conferred with Secretary Dulles, Vice-President Nixon and President Eisenhower. Mikoyan also met and impressed American business leaders, and seemed himself to be impressed by American business. Everywhere Mikoyan went he urged the United States and Russia to "settle their differences in the interests of world peace." But although his speeches were friendly, Mikoyan offered no new proposals for ending the cold war. Experts guessed that he came to promote a summit meeting between Nikita Khrushchev and President Eisenhower, and to act as a spearhead for a Soviet "peace offensive" on the future of Germany.

EUROPE UNITES

Six nations of Europe—Belgium, France, Italy, Luxembourg, the Netherlands and West Germany—were joined by treaties in two new economic units. These units had different aims. The Economic Community was designed to bring about a large Continental market where trade could flourish free of tariffs and restrictions of almost all kinds (as within the United States). Euratom's main aim is the joint European development of nuclear energy to meet the growing power shortage in each nation. Together with the successful European Coal and Steel Community these new organizations are solid steps toward an eventual European union.

FEBRUARY

MACMILLAN IN MOSCOW

Britain's Prime Minister Macmillan flew to Moscow to talk informally with Soviet Premier Khrushchev on issues dividing the East and West. Macmillan's ten-day visit was aimed at finding out the Russians' attitude to the future of Berlin, Germany and Europe in general. Western diplomats felt that the British Prime Minister "held the

17

banner high" in the face of calculated rebuffs by Premier Khrushchev. Typical of these was Khrushchev's nationwide radio speech (during Macmillan's absence) in which the Soviet leader bluntly rejected the West's proposal for a foreign ministers' meeting. The visit produced no major agreement. But it was felt that Macmillan's firsthand reports to the United States, France and West Germany would be of use as the basis for future moves by the Western Alliance.

CYPRUS SOLUTION

As a result of an agreement signed in London the republic of Cyprus was "created." Since 1955 terrorist civil warfare had raged on this small, eastern Mediterranean island. The Greek Cypriote majority fought the British to enforce their demands for union with Greece, while the Turkish minority pressed for partition of the island. Britain rejected all plans on which Greeks and Turks disagreed. Finally, all parties compromised. Cyprus would become an independent republic in which Greeks would hold 70 per cent, Turks 30 per cent of the seats in the legislature, and Britain would keep her strategically important bases on the island.

DULLES AILING

John Foster Dulles, United States secretary of state for six years, was stricken with a recurrence of cancer. Undersecretary Christian A. Herter took over Mr. Dulles' duties. His illness posed crucial problems for the Administration, since President Eisenhower had a uniquely close relationship with Mr. Dulles, called him "indispensable" and delegated to him a great deal of decision-making on foreign policy. Mr. Herter therefore had immediately to pick up the threads of the strategy Mr. Dulles had personally created for the Western Alliance, while also facing the challenge of new Soviet cold-war pressures.

● MARCH

HAWAII—THE 50TH STATE

Congress passed a measure to make Hawaii the fiftieth state. Although official statehood would not come for several months, Hawaii had won its 60-year struggle to join the Union. The fiftieth state consists of a group of 20 beautiful islands covering 6,423 square miles, located in mid-Pacific Ocean about 2,090 miles from San Francisco. The population of the islands, which numbers over 600,000, includes Americans of Chinese, Filipino, Portuguese, German, Japanese and Puerto Rican ancestry. Annexed by the United States in 1898, Hawaii became an American territory in 1900. During World War II the islands were the chief Pacific outpost for the operations of United States forces in the fight against Japan.

TIBET REVOLTS

Long discontent flared into an anticommunist rebellion. When the revolt was savagely suppressed by Chinese troops, the young Dalai Lama, spiritual leader of Buddhist Tibet, fled Lhasa, the capital city, with a retinue of loyal guards. He escaped Chinese paratroops in the wild Himalaya Mountains and eventually arrived at the Indian frontier. There he was granted asylum by Indian Prime Minister Nehru. In India the Dalai Lama firmly denied Peking's charges that he had been "kidnapped." His former coruler in Tibet, the Panchen Lama, was appointed puppet ruler by the Chinese Communists who now openly ruled Tibet. The brutal suppression of the Tibetan revolt caused a sharp change in Asian opinion about China.

PROJECT ARGUS

Washington confirmed that in August and September 1958 a series of three high-altitude atomic explosions had thrown a temporary shell of man-made radiation around the world. Four thousand miles out in space, this shell lay between two girdles of intense natural radiation, one 1,400 to 3,400 miles, the other 8,000 to 12,000 miles from the earth. Known as Project Argus, the man-made radiation shell was detected by rockets, the Explorer IV satellite and ground stations of the IGY.

● APRIL

SECRETARY OF STATE HERTER

After radiation treatments, Secretary Dulles had flown to Florida for a rest. On April 12, unexpectedly, he returned to Washington for further medical observation. Later the State Department announced that his cancer might have spread. President Eisenhower announced that Secretary Dulles would submit his resignation. Acting Secretary Herter was nominated for his post. The Senate unanimously confirmed Herter's appointment, and the next day he was sworn in as the fifty-fourth secretary of state. The President gave Mr. Dulles an official commission as special consultant to the President. At month's end, Secretary Herter was representing the United States at the Paris conference with Britain, France and West Germany.

THE ASTRONAUTS

The National Aeronautics and Space Administration introduced the "Mercury Astronauts" to a crowded press conference. One of these seven young flying officers, chosen from the Air Force, Navy and Marines, will be the nation's first space pilot. After more intensive training, the chosen astronaut will be sealed into a capsule and shot into space by an Atlas missile. He will rise 125 miles and circle the earth three times at about 18,000 miles an hour, communicating his observations to earth by radio. He will fire braking rockets to end the flight and will make a "splash landing" in the Atlantic.

Colonel Grivas, Cypriote guerrilla leader (in sweater), is greeted at Athens airport.

The Dalai Lama of Tibet blesses a crowd in India, where he is living in exile.

The seven Astronauts: one of them will be the first American space explorer.

19

The flag from the casket of John Foster Dulles is presented to his widow. President and Mrs. Eisenhower stand with the family.

Able and Baker meet the press after their 1,500-mile flight. Holding them is Dr. Don Stullkey.

ROYAL WEDDING IN JAPAN

Crown Prince Akihito, heir apparent to the Japanese throne, married Miss Michiko Shoda, daughter of a Tokyo businessman. The new Princess Michiko will be the first commoner to be empress in the more than 2,000-year history of the Japanese imperial family. The national day of celebration was marred by a youth who hurled a rock at the open carriage in which the Crown Prince and his bride were riding. Neither one was injured. The marriage—performed with traditional Shinto ritual—was popular with the great majority of the Japanese people. They saw in the royal family's revolutionary move proof that Japan's postwar democratic social trend will be continued and encouraged.

● MAY

DULLES DIES

John Foster Dulles, secretary of state and close personal friend of President Eisenhower, died after about four months of illness. For many years a student of foreign affairs, international lawyer and State Department emissary, Mr. Dulles had dedicated himself to the task of preserving peace since becoming secretary in 1953.

To do so, he vastly expanded American world alliances and dealt personally with the leaders of other nations. On February 10, 1959, he entered Walter Reed Army Hospital for surgery that revealed a recurrence of the cancer he had developed in 1956. When, in April, Mr. Dulles learned that treatment had failed he resigned his post. Pneumonia soon complicated his condition and on Sunday, May 24, he died.

ABLE AND BAKER

Two specially trained monkeys, Able and Baker, were dressed in protective suits, wired for physiological reactions and placed in separate compartments in the nose cone of a Jupiter rocket. The Jupiter thundered into the skies over Cape Canaveral, then hurled its payload 300 miles into space at 10,000 miles an hour. The cone plunged back into the atmosphere 1,700 miles away, near Antigua, in the South Atlantic. Checked by the atmospheric brake, then by parachute, the cone drifted into the sea, whence it was promptly recovered by United States Navy patrol ships. Although the flight had lasted fifteen minutes, Able and Baker were both in perfect physical condition; only a slight variation from normal heartbeat and breath-

Queen Elizabeth II and Prince Philip are joined by President and Mrs. Eisenhower on the deck of the royal yacht Britannia after the ceremonies that officially opened the St. Lawrence Seaway.

ing was recorded. Their dramatic journey showed that someday man could withstand space travel.

 **JUNE**

GENEVA TALKS RECESSED

The Geneva conference, between the British, French, Soviet and United States foreign ministers (with West and East German representatives also attending), recessed until mid-July after forty-one days. The Russians had continued to insist that the West quit Berlin within eighteen months. United, the Western powers refused and said they would not negotiate under threats. Moscow, still determined to call a summit meeting, said the talks showed "progress." The Western allies, except for Britain, disagreed. President Eisenhower said that he refused to consider a summit meeting unless some preliminary progress was made toward a general European settlement.

ST. LAWRENCE SEAWAY OPENED

Queen Elizabeth II and President Eisenhower formally dedicated the St. Lawrence Seaway in a joint ceremony at St. Lambert, Quebec. The seaway, a 400-mile waterway studded with a series of locks and canals, has opened central North America to ocean shipping. A joint project of Canada and the United States (cost: $475,000,000), the seaway was opened for traffic April 25. During May almost 2,500,000 tons of cargo moved through. After the dedication the Queen cruised on in her yacht, Britannia, to join Vice-President Nixon and New York's Governor Rockefeller in dedicating the St. Lawrence power plant at Massena, N. Y., and Cornwall, Ont. This plant was a joint effort of Ontario and New York State (cost: $650,000,000).

THE ADENAUER-ERHARD DISPUTE

Last spring, West German Chancellor Konrad Adenauer decided to give up his powerful post and run for president. His party, the Christian Democratic Union, chose Dr. Ludwig Erhard, Adenauer's Economics Minister, as their candidate for chancellor. In May, Adenauer decided to remain as chancellor. He then made a series of statements to his party and the press to the effect that Erhard was unfitted for the chancellorship. Erhard threatened to resign unless Adenauer apologized and retracted the statements. Adenauer did apologize but later made another similar statement. Erhard again threatened resignation. By the end of June the feud was publicly patched over, and the stage was set for Dr. Adenauer's hand-picked candidate, Dr. Heinrich Luebke, to be elected as West Germany's new president.

● JULY

SOVIET FAIR IN NEW YORK

Soviet First Deputy Premier Frol R. Kozlov (a leading prospect to succeed Premier Khrushchev) arrived in the United States to open the Soviet Exhibition of Science, Technology and Culture in New York's Coliseum. After escorting President Eisenhower and Vice-President Nixon around the fair, Kozlov departed on a coast-to-coast tour, proclaiming Russia's peaceful intentions to all Americans he met. In his formal speeches he also pleaded for more trade between the United States and the Soviet Union (1958 total: $21,-000,000). However, in a White House talk with the President, Kozlov told of Soviet determination to oust the West from Berlin; appearing before the National Press Club and the Overseas Writers he said, "force will be met with force if war is unleashed" over Berlin. Washington felt that Kozlov's friendly words were aimed at influencing world opinion while his threats

United States Secretary of Defense Neil H. McElroy looks over a model of the Soviet atomic icebreaker Lenin at the Soviet trade exhibition in New York.

were an attempt to wring concessions from the West, a standard Soviet diplomatic maneuver in the past.

NIXON VISITS RUSSIA

On July 23, Vice-President Richard Nixon and Mrs. Nixon, accompanied by more than sixty United States newsmen, flew into Moscow to open the United States fair, a glittering collection of consumer goods, designed to show America's high standard of living to Russians. Despite a cool official reception and much antifair propaganda Muscovites showed enthusiasm both for the Nixons and for the fair; the latter attracted fifty thousand visitors a day. As Nixon escorted Khrushchev around on opening day the two statesmen engaged in an astonishing duel of words— Soviet aims versus American—in which Nixon more than held his own. He continued to state the American point of view in conference with Khrushchev, in a radio-and-TV speech to the Russian people and, despite hecklers, throughout his grueling trip through Russia.

DEADLOCK AT GENEVA

In their seventh week of conference at Geneva the Big Four foreign ministers found they could not agree on long-range plans for either Germany or Berlin. Britain, France and the United States tried to negotiate a truce that would preserve the existing status of Berlin and to discuss a long-range settlement for Germany. Gromyko offered an eighteen-month truce but refused to say whether the existing status in Berlin would continue after that time. He also insisted that a Berlin truce depended upon an all-German committee to discuss Germany's future. Gromyko then rejected all Western substitute suggestions. But when the West began to talk of breaking off the talks, Gromyko showed indications of conciliation and it was decided to continue the conference.

With hands held high, President Eisenhower acknowledges the cheers of a French crowd in front of Paris' town hall. Beside him is President de Gaulle of France.

● AUGUST

STEEL STRIKE

The steel industry and the United Steelworkers of America were deadlocked in the costly ($10,000,000 a day) steel strike which started July 15. Both sides poured out statistics to justify their positions. The union pointed to record steel profits and wage increases of 7 to 10 cents an hour in other industries. The steel industry answered that their workers were paid more than the national average (average weekly steel wage $127.10) and argued that any wage increase would cause inflation. Nobody questioned the statistics; nobody could or would interpret them. Government fact-finder Secretary of Labor

James P. Mitchell refused to recommend any settlement formula. And President Eisenhower emphasized his reluctance to have the Government intervene.

EISENHOWER RALLIES THE WEST

On August 26 President Eisenhower flew to Bonn, Germany, on the first lap of a ten-day visit to America's major European allies. The trip's purpose was to unify the West before Soviet Premier Khrushchev's visit to the United States and to calm fears that Western European interests would be neglected during the informal United States–Soviet talks. After a rousing German reception and successful talks with Chancellor Adenauer, Eisenhower flew to London to an even greater reception from the British. Following his visit with Queen Elizabeth II at Balmoral Castle in Scotland, the President and Prime Minister Macmillan spent two days in conference at Chequers, the Prime Minister's country home. The next stop was London where the President and the Prime Minister gave an informal TV-radio report that outlined their basic agreements and common aims. At month's end the President prepared for the most difficult part of his mission—the Paris meeting with France's President de Gaulle.

WEDDING IN SOEGNE

On August 22 the Cinderella courtship of Anne Marie Rasmussen, 21-year-old daughter of a grocer, and Steven C. Rockefeller, 23-year-old son of an American multimillionaire, ended in their marriage at Soegne, Norway. Blonde Anne Marie first met Steven when, on a trip to the United States to perfect her English, she worked as a maid in the home of his father, New York's Governor Nelson A. Rockefeller. Soegne (population 4,000), a small town mainly supported by its fishing industry, was invaded by hundreds of photographers and sightseers for the occasion

23

The wedding took place in the Lutheran church where Anne Marie had worshiped all her life, and was attended by both families. Commented the bridegroom's mother, "It was a beautiful, beautiful service."

● SEPTEMBER

KHRUSHCHEV IN THE UNITED STATES

From September 15 through September 27, Soviet Premier Nikita Khrushchev toured the United States. In a hectic ten days of dinners, speeches, handshaking and sight-seeing, he saw a great variety of the country, and he met and was seen by many Americans.

His trip in outline: arrival in Washington with his wife, Nina, family and a large party; talks with the President; tour of Washington; two state dinners and a National Press Club speech and interview. In New York he saw the city, attended receptions, spoke at the Economic Club and gave a speech on disarmament at the United Nations. Then on by jet to a stormy stay in Los Angeles where he saw a film-in-the-making and toured the city. In San Francisco the moods of both the hosts and guests lightened and relaxed despite a rough debate with some American labor leaders. From there on Khrushchev saw more and gave a warmer impression of himself. In the Des Moines area the highlight was hybrid corn; in Pittsburgh, factories. Then back to Washington for two days of talks with President Eisenhower at Camp David in Maryland.

The fast and furious ten days were a vivid series of dramatic, comic and deadly serious meetings between the ruler of the Soviet Union and the people of the nation he has sworn to overtake. The main impression he gave America and America seemed to give him was the acknowledgment of each other's strength and peaceful intentions.

Roswell Garst shouts at newsmen crowding his guest, Nikita Khrushchev, on their tour of Iowa cornfield.

This sober yet hopeful mood carried over into the two-day, face-to-face conference at Camp David. The President and the Premier discussed the main problems between the East and West. When the talks ended both stated they had talked frankly on all world issues and had agreed that disarmament was the key problem to be solved. The talks over, Khrushchev flew back to Moscow.

SOVIETS HIT THE MOON

At 5 A.M. (EST) on September 12, close to the second anniversary of the first sputnik's launching, Soviet Russia fired a multistage rocket. At 4:02 P.M. (EST) on September 13, Lunik hit the moon, only 84 seconds behind schedule. Few details of Lunik's construction were released. Those that were, revealed that Lunik's last stage weighed 2,466 pounds without fuel, and that the 858-pound sphere containing scientific and radio-technical equipment had been sterilized to avoid contaminating the moon with earthly microorganisms. Scientists manning Britain's giant radiotelescope at Jodrell Bank confirmed Moscow's reports on the flight; at the instant of impact, said Jodrell Bank, Lunik's signals ceased. The rest was guesswork. Scientists reasoned that Lunik needed an initial thrust of from 600,000 to 800,000 pounds to catapult it along its 236,875-mile journey, and that the scientific purpose of the trip was to analyze conditions in the space between earth and moon and to collect data on cosmic rays, magnetic fields, and radiation belts.

● OCTOBER

THE BRITISH ELECTION

On October 8 almost 79 per cent of Britain's 34,000,000 voters returned the Conservative Party to power with a landslide majority: 365 seats in Parliament. It was the first time since 1868 that any British party had won three elections in a row and was a crushing defeat for the Labor Party, which captured only 258 seats. The Liberal Party made a surprising showing. Although it held only its six seats it nearly doubled its total popular vote over the last election (1955). Macmillan's victory was attributed to his economic policies, which have lifted Britain to prosperity, and to his efforts to arrange a summit conference. Labor's defeat resulted from an internal split between its moderate and left-wing factions and popular disapproval of the old-fashioned Labor call for nationalization of key industries. Macmillan's post-election comment: "It has gone off rather well."

THE SUMMIT POSTPONED

France's President Charles de Gaulle upset plans for an early summit conference by inviting Premier Khrushchev to visit Paris at about the time Washington and London had expected to hold the Big Four meeting. He also insisted that a summit conference should try to solve more than the issues of Berlin and disarmament. American and British observers saw De Gaulle's move as a time-gainer to make France an atomic power and generally increase its prestige. Moscow quickly capitalized on the West's differences. After De Gaulle's statement, Khrushchev announced that a summit conference was necessary, the sooner the better. The net result of all these moves was that any summit meeting was put off until spring of 1960 and was expected to produce modest results—at best a postponement of the Berlin issue and a speed-up of disarmament negotiations.

KHRUSHCHEV IN PEKING

From September 29 to October 4, Premier Khrushchev visited Peking to attend Communist China's tenth anniversary celebrations, report on his Camp David talks with President Eisenhower and co-ordinate

Britain's Prime Minister rides in an election motorcade through the streets of west London.

strategy with Mao Tse-tung. On arrival he made a speech that Western observers interpreted as a "lecture" to the Chinese to ease up on their aggressive tactics in the Far East. The Chinese reaction was ambiguous. Official newspapers "accorded warm response and support" to the United States-Soviet aim of thawing the cold war. But the same issues carried articles calling for "an unrelenting fight against American imperialism." It looked as though Peking would pay lip service to Moscow for her annual $200,000,000 in Soviet aid but continue to create tension to "justify" continued sacrifices by the Chinese people.

NOVEMBER

THE QUIZ-SHOW SCANDAL

When a New York grand jury first investigated charges in 1958 that TV quiz shows were rigged, about 150 witnesses, including college professor Charles Van Doren, testified under oath that they had won ther huge prize monies honestly. This month Van Doren (who won $129,000) admitted to the House Special Subcommittee on Legislative Oversight that he had been given answers to questions on the

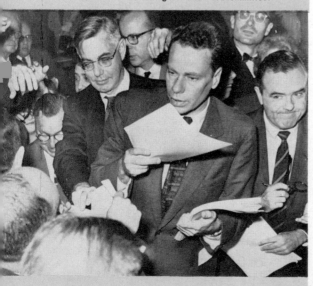

Charles Van Doren hands reporters copies of his statement to Congressional subcommittee.

quiz show Twenty-one. Columbia University accepted Van Doren's resignation; NBC canceled his $50,000-a-year contract. Public reactions varied between congratulations because he had confessed and condemnation because he had betrayed the cause of education and scholarship. It was revealed that of the 150 other witnesses "maybe fifty told the truth." Perjury prosecutions were recommended; so was the house cleaning of the entire TV industry. The scandal was called "a national fraud."

THE STEEL STRIKE—80-DAY BREAK

After 116 days of idleness most of the 500,000 steel strikers returned to work when the terms of an 80-day Taft-Hartley injunction were upheld by the Supreme Court. The act stipulates that "the duty of the parties [is] . . . to make every effort to . . . settle their differences . . ." Despite President Eisenhower's plea that both sides "recognize their responsibilities to the United States," leaders of the United Steelworkers union and management continued in deadlock over the value of wage and benefit increases (present average wage $3.10 an hour) and the changing of plant working rules. If the strike, one of the worst in United States history, is resumed on January 26, the President will submit proposals to Congress for dealing with the situation. Any legislation on the steel issue would probably cause revision of present laws dealing with major strikes. Whatever the final outcome, the strike had been a bad blow to the nation's economy.

THE INDIAN-CHINESE BORDER DISPUTE

India's Prime Minister Jawaharlal Nehru, long an exponent of neutralism in the East-West struggle, was finally forced to take a stand against Communist China. The issue —China's claim and partial occupation by force of 40,000 square miles of Indian territory along the Indian-Chinese border. Under strong domestic pressure Nehru

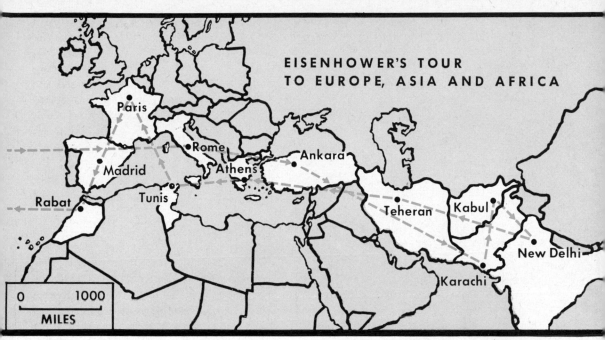

EISENHOWER'S TOUR
TO EUROPE, ASIA AND AFRICA

0   1000
MILES

warned China that India (army, 550,000) would resist aggression by China (army, 3,000,000) "by all means available." China's Premier Chou En-lai proposed talks and a mutual withdrawal of forces for 12½ miles in the disputed areas. New Delhi said this would still leave the Chinese Communists well within Indian territory. Soviet Premier Khrushchev surprisingly urged settling the matter by negotiation, a move, observers said, designed to conciliate the West and hold in check his increasingly powerful Chinese ally.

● DECEMBER

EISENHOWER ON TOUR

"Frankly, I am hoping to build in that region of Asia and I hope in many other parts a better understanding of the United States and a good will for us."

President Eisenhower

With these aims the President set out December 3 on a venture in personal diplomacy that took him 22,000 miles in nineteen days, during which he conferred with leaders of more than thirteen countries and Pope John XXIII. His program included stops in Italy, Turkey, Pakistan, Afghanistan, India, Iran, Greece, Tunisia, France, Spain and Morocco. This was the first time a United States president in office had visited Asia. On December 19-21 Mr. Eisenhower attended the Western summit conference in Paris. On December 22 he returned home: his epic trip was over.

ANTARCTIC TREATY

Argentina, Australia, Belgium, Chile, France, Japan, New Zealand, Norway, the Union of South Africa, the Soviet Union, the United Kingdom and the United States agreed that the frozen continent of Antarctica be made into a preserve for international research. They also agreed that there should be no nuclear testing or dumping of radioactive material there and that an open inspection system should be set up for the entire continent.

AUSTRALIA

By GEOFFREY L. GRIFFITH
Australian Journalist

IN the southwestern Pacific—only a few air hours from Asia—the Australians are trying to create a large, powerful nation based on the great institutions and traditions of the English-speaking world.

Australia's island-continent is now capable of feeding two or three times the present population of 10,000,000 without changing its present mode of agriculture. With diversified farming it could feed many millions more, and could employ an almost indefinite number if its industries were expanded.

Australia, in 1959, was experiencing a long boom greater than that experienced by the United States between 1850 and 1910. Rural productivity rose and secondary industry strengthened its self-sufficiency. And, as the highlight of the year, the population of Australia in March 1959 passed the 10,000,000 mark, having increased by 3,000,000 in the last decade.

With costs and prices rising alarmingly, industries are flourishing. Employment in factories rose by more than 20,000 in twelve months and the value added to raw materials by the process of manufacture increased from about $2,800,000,000 to $3,000,000,000.

In the last ten years, Australian industries have invested more than $80,000,000

overseas. More than seventy Australian companies have established plants in other countries and the current Australian investment abroad is now at the rate of $20,000,000 a year. The bulk of investment is in New Zealand but recently more has been flowing toward the United States, Africa and the Far East.

The future may be even more promising: the oil industry plans to spend about $120,000,000 on developmental works in Australia in the next two years. (In 1959, $210,000,000 was already invested in oil exploration in Australia, New Zealand and the rest of Oceania.) Airlines, including Qantas Empire Airways, Australia's national airline, have launched a $60,000,000 re-equipment program. (Seven four-jet Boeing 707 aircraft, each carrying ninety passengers, were delivered to Qantas in 1959.) Australia's meat production—beef and lamb—will be greatly increased. An interesting side light on the Australia–United States meat trade was the successful experimental shipment of 40,000 sheep on the vessel Delfino from Sydney to California.

Although restricted in less than three years of existence to Sydney and Melbourne, television made great advances in 1959. It has spread more rapidly in its early

THE
SNOWY
MOUNTAINS
SCHEME

Giant segment of pipeline is hauled into position up a mountainside.

Workers and equipment are dwarfed by a giant water-diversion tunnel.

Preparing to blast out the rock face for Munyang powerhouse.

Workers and material use this shaft to reach a 14-mile tunnel through mountains of the Australian Alps.

stages than in any other country. In the next two years (with country TV stations established), television will be within reach of more than 75 per cent of the population. At the end of 1959, more than 800,000 TV licenses had been issued in Australia.

United States investment is considerable; a total of 920 American firms have invested more than $1,400,000,000 in Australia and, of these, 200 have established Australian subsidiaries or are affiliated with Australian companies. The plow-back into Australian industry of undistributed profits in 1959 amounted to nearly $40,-000,000. A trade mission comprising some 25 leading executives of Australian manufacturing, primary industry, exporting, banking and commercial interests visited the United States in 1959.

On the tenth anniversary of the Snowy Mountains Hydroelectric Scheme (July 1959), two of the major projects of the $700,000,000 scheme were completed.

One is the Tumut One underground power station, from which electricity is now available for commercial use in New South Wales. The other is the 14-mile tunnel that diverts waters of the Eucumbene River, the largest tributary of the Snowy, to the Murrumbidgee Valley.

The Snowy River scheme involves the construction of 7 major dams, 15 power stations (most of them underground), 83 miles of tunnels, more than 350 miles of race lines or aqueducts along mountainsides to pick up streams, shafts of up to 1,100 feet in depth and hundreds of miles of mountain roads. The scheme will divert water from the Snowy River (which at present runs down to the well-watered southeast coast) through the Great Dividing Range westward to the Murray and Murrumbidgee rivers where it can be used to irrigate dry and parched land.

Interest in the search for uranium, both by companies and individual prospectors,

TO FILL A CONTINENT, NEW AUSTRALIANS (1947–1960)

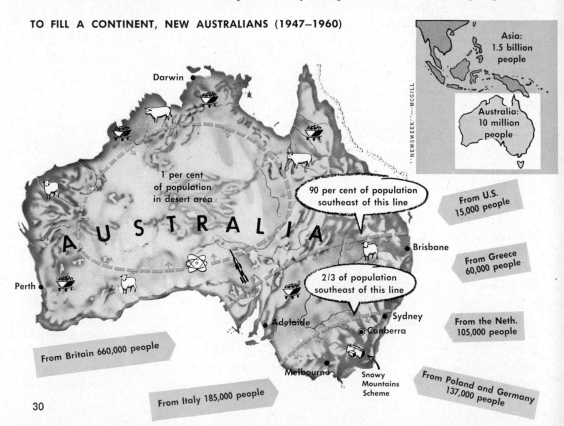

30

Princess Alexandra on the bridge of HMAS Warramunga sailing through the waters of the Great Barrier Reef.

declined in 1959. The Rum Jungle laboratory continued research into uranium recovery and the Australian Atomic Energy Commission's research establishment at Lucas Heights (opened in 1958), New South Wales, continued to expand.

An international symposium on Antarctic weather was held in Melbourne in 1959. The symposium had special value for Australia because Antarctic atmospheric processes have a direct relationship to weather in the Southern Ocean and to forecasting in the Australian region.

The Liberal-Country Party coalition remained in control of the Federal Government in 1959, with Mr. Robert G. Menzies as prime minister. During the year, Mr. Menzies completed a four-month good-will tour of the United States, Canada, Europe and Asia.

Princess Alexandra of Kent, cousin of Queen Elizabeth II, came to open the Queensland centenary celebrations and made an informal tour of all of the states.

In one of the most thrilling contests in tennis history, Australia won back the Davis Cup from the United States. Neale Fraser was the star, winning both his singles and joining with Roy Emerson in a doubles victory. Later, Fraser established himself as the world's leading amateur by winning the United States national singles title.

Australian territories in Oceania— Papua and New Guinea—made good progress in 1959, with concentration on primary education. About 125,000 of the estimated 400,000 native children of school age in Papua–New Guinea are enrolled in government and mission schools.

During the year, investigations were made into the possibility of harnessing volcanic natural steam under pressure, a source of power already being used extensively in New Zealand. Its aim was to drive turbines for electric-power generation in the Rabaul (New Guinea) area.

Native-owned coffee plantations in the Pacific islands produced more than 35,000 tons of dry beans in 1959 and the rising profit is a potent incentive to investment.

New Zealand sent a trade mission to Australia and relations between the two Commonwealth nations were most cordial.

Australia is on the threshold of great internal development but only the future can tell whether she can remain in isolation from Asia.

AFRICA

By THOMAS M. FRANCK
New York University

THE year 1959 was one of nation building for Africa. Like the Americas in the eighteenth century and Asia in the 1940's, Africa was shedding its European rulers and learning to look after itself.

Nowhere was this process more spectacular than in the giant French African empire. Until General de Gaulle's resumption of power in 1958, the countries of that empire had been making slow progress toward independence, generally against the wishes of the French. Only two states—Tunisia and Morocco—had actually been able to break away from the French African empire.

With the bloodless revolution of General de Gaulle and especially after the vote on September 28, 1959, when a new constitution for France and its empire (or overseas territories) was put into force, things changed with great speed. France suddenly awoke to the fact that the rights of all Frenchmen—liberty, equality, fraternity—would have to be extended also to French Africans, even if it meant allowing them to choose no longer to be Frenchmen.

During 1958 and 1959, thirteen new African states were brought into existence by the agreement of France and the leaders of its African territories following a free popular referendum:

1. Malagash Republic
2. Sudanese Republic
3. Republic of Senegal
4. Republic of the Chad
5. Republic of Gabon
6. Republic of the Congo
7. Islamic Republic of Mauritania
8. Central African Republic
9. Republic of Dahomey
10. Republic of the Ivory Coast
11. Voltaic Republic
12. Republic of Niger
13. Republic of Guinea

Of these, the Republic of Senegal, the Sudanese Republic, the Voltaic Republic and the Republic of Dahomey at once joined in a loose union called the Mali Federation, though the Voltaic and Dahomey republics later dropped out. To the surprise of the extremists both in Africa and in France, only one of the thirteen states—Guinea—chose to cut all its ties with France.

The other twelve joined with France to form what is called the French Community,

Drilling for samples of tin ore near Jos, in the high plateau region of Nigeria. The ore is often found close to the surface. It is dug out by modern mining machinery.

which jointly administers the foreign relations, justice, currency and defense of each state but which leaves all other matters up to their independent governments.

After long seeking liberty and national equality, why did these twelve nations now freely prefer to establish a close new fraternity with France? There are many reasons. Some are economic. The African countries, by and large, are not poor, but they do not have the available funds to explore and develop their natural resources. For this they have traditionally looked to France, who in her colonial past opened mines, built railroads, modern cities, schools, and hospitals throughout Africa.

Countries, like people, need money to make money, and by close association with France the new African states hope to benefit through continuing French eco-

33

The airport at Kano, Nigeria, is equipped with graceful modern buildings; the arrival of a plane is announced in romantic fashion by the blowing of a long, slender trumpet.

nomic help. Moreover, France has persuaded the other nations of the six-member European Economic Community (Germany, Italy, Belgium, the Netherlands and Luxembourg) to help the new states of France's former African empire. Despite the quarrels of the past, most of the new states would rather continue to get help from the French, whom they know and understand, than from the Russians, the British or the Americans.

Guinea, the exception, entered into a so-called federation with neighboring Ghana. This seemed to mean little more than that Ghana would provide aid and credit to Guinea. Since Ghana is part of the British Commonwealth, Guinea seemed to be saying that it was not prepared to forgive and forget the colonial past and would look to the British rather than to the French community of nations for its help and guidance. Since that early impetuous decision, Guinea has had sober second thoughts and may reconsider its future relation with France.

That the other twelve nations preferred to look to France for aid is evidence that French rule in Africa was far from being all bad. French culture, in particular, has had a great attraction for Africans. The French language is widely spoken, and Africa has produced some top-rate poets and writers in the French language. Africans have always been treated as equals in France itself. A native of the Ivory Coast, M. Félix Houphouet-Boigny, is a secretary of state in the De Gaulle cabinet. There has been relatively little racial discrimination between French and Africans in the former colonies. There appears, in short, to be a greater affinity between African and Gallic culture than between Africans and other European societies.

It is, however, to be expected that the present relationship between the states of the French Community is only a transitional phase. The African states, as they are able to digest it, will probably ask and receive a greater helping of independence, while still retaining some ties to France.

In keeping with its new attitude toward African nationalism, France has also decided to give independence to two territories, French Cameroons and French Togoland, that it has been administering as wards or trusteeships, of the United Nations. French Togoland is a tiny splinter

34

of land on the borders of Ghana, and its Premier, Sylvanus Olympio, is British-educated and oriented. It is likely, therefore, that Togoland, like Guinea, will in the future tend more to align itself with Ghana and the British Commonwealth. This is particularly probable because a very large number of Togolese already live in Ghana.

In regard to Algeria only was French policy still controlled by the colonial past, by a desire to hold Africans in close union with the mother country, by force, if necessary.

There are two special reasons for this. The first is that more than a million Frenchmen (*colons*) actually live in Algeria.

Cities like Algiers and Oran are, at least in many districts, difficult to distinguish from towns like Lyon or Marseilles in France. The sentiment in these Algerian coastal towns and in the farm belts around them is, obviously, very much in favor of a close integration between France and Algeria. It was here that the revolution began which put De Gaulle into power in 1958 with the battle cry "Algeria is French." Indeed, so dominant has the role of these Algerian *colons* in French politics become that their cry might better be "France is Algerian."

The other reason is the discovery of huge oil reserves in the Algerian Sahara. A pipeline carrying this wealth to Algerian ports is already in operation and France bases its dreams for a return to the status of a great power on the wealth to be derived from the Sahara. Anti-Western feeling is rampant in the Middle East, Western Europe's source of oil, and, therefore, the basis of its industry. Thus there is danger that oil supplies may be cut off unless a convenient alternative source can be developed. The French hope and believe such a source is theirs in Algeria.

De Gaulle realizes, even if some of the *colons* do not, that the riches of Algeria can be developed only with the consent of the nine million other inhabitants of the territory who are Muslims of Arabic culture. Accordingly, on September 16, 1959, the French President set forth certain proposals that may become the basis for an Algerian solution. De Gaulle's plans call for a cease-fire in the civil war, following which a free referendum (open to observers from all over the world) would allow all Algerians to vote on three choices: complete independence (secession), complete integration with France (complete "franciscation") or internal self-govern-

Ashanti boys of Ghana weave the robes of *kenti* cloth worn by the legislators at Accra, the capital. A robe 3 yards by 4 sells for about $280.
CHARLES MAY

35

STEPHANIE DINKINS

In the shade of a straw parasol, a cloth dyer dips a length of material in a vat of indigo dye. Kano, Nigeria, is an important center of the cloth and indigo industries.

ment within the French Community. A cooling-off period of up to four years between the cease-fire and the referendum would allow all parties to campaign peacefully for Algerian support.

Thus the time appears near when Algeria will be allowed to make the same free choice as the other French African territories. Who knows whether the outcome, then too, will be favorable to France?

While the French were thus beginning to assist the nationalist movements in their parts of Africa, Britain was continuing its policy of helping the development of new self-governing states in British Africa. Nigeria had become fully self-governing in all domestic matters and was slated to become independent also in foreign relations and defense in 1960. Thereafter, it would continue, like Ghana, to remain within the British Commonwealth—an association of states comparable to but less formal and looser than the French Community. Queen

CHARLES MAY

Elizabeth II under the new constitution of Nigeria would be the queen of the Federation just as she is the sovereign of the United Kingdom, Canada, Australia and four other realms of the Commonwealth.

To prepare the way for independence, a new, enlightened criminal code was enacted in the Northern Territory of the country, the province that contains more than half Nigeria's population. Unlike the Christian and pagan south, the north is predominantly Muslim. These Nigerian Muslims are among the most orthodox in the world. Until 1959 their only criminal laws were the strict and sometimes brutal rules of the religious courts. It is an interesting comment on the British imperial system that the new Nigerian code is essentially the one drafted by Britain for Sudan, which in turn was borrowed from the colonial government of India. Many concessions to Muslim feelings are made by the code. It is, for example, a serious criminal offense to consume alcoholic beverages.

To greet the new day of freedom, Nigeria adopted a national anthem:

STEPHANIE DINKINS

Members of Parliament (right) at Accra, Ghana, wearing their gorgeous robes made of *kenti* cloth, a speciality of the country.

The Government of Ghana builds for the future as well as the present. The new post office at Accra (below) is an example.

ALFRED ZULLIGER, SHOSTAL

Peanut production is the chief industry of Kaolak, Senegal. Here the nuts are brought to be separated from the chaff in hand-operated machines. Then, packed in stout bags, the peanuts are shipped to many foreign countries.

Nigeria, we hail thee,
Our own dear native land,
Though tribe and tongue may differ,
In brotherhood we stand,
Nigerians all, and proud to serve
Our Sovereign Motherland.

A prize of $2,800 has been offered for the best music to those words.

In Tanganyika as well, independence loomed peacefully just around the corner—probably in four or five years—as African, European and Asian citizens worked with a minimum of discord in the newly elected legislature.

In British Africa, as in French, the principle of Africa for the Africans was accepted except in those regions where there are large white settlements or economic interests. While France had its Algerian cross to bear, Britain had trouble in Nyasaland.

Serious rioting occurred in Nyasaland in February and March of 1959. The territory consists of some 2,500,000 Africans and 8,000 whites. Without the consent of the Africans, Britain in 1953 federated Nyasaland with two neighboring British African possessions: Northern Rhodesia and Southern Rhodesia. The latter have larger white communities (some 300,000 Europeans altogether) and much European investment. They also practice a modified version of South Africa's policy of white supremacy. Britain has maintained that Nyasaland, a poor country, would benefit by association with the richer Rhodesias. The Nyasaland Africans, however, prefer to remain poor but proud. They fear that to accept Rhodesian economic aid would also mean the acceptance of Rhodesian racial policies.

All this feeling boiled over in 1959. Dr. Hastings Banda spoke for most Nyasalanders when he swore "to break this stupid and hellish federation."

CHARLES MAY

Harvesting pineapples near Kindia, Guinea Republic. Pickers fill the rack with fruit ready for market. Then the rack is carried to the end of the row where other workers unload the fruit.

THREE LIONS

Tobacco, especially small-leaf Turkish varieties, is one of the important exports of the Rhodesias. Here long strings of the aromatic leaves are being hung on stakes to dry.

38

Outdoor classwork at a village school in Northern Rhodesia. The native African children are eager to learn.

Hastings Kamazu Banda was born in Nyasaland fifty-four years ago and went to a Presbyterian mission school. So strong was his thirst for learning that he walked one thousand miles through country almost without trails, let alone roads, to Johannesburg, in South Africa. Here he worked for eight years in a gold-mine compound for a few cents a day and attended night school, until, in 1926, with some savings and the aid of a Methodist bishop he was able to come to the United States to study. He worked at odd jobs and as a Sunday-school teacher until he had earned a medical degree, after which, in 1941, he went to Edinburgh, Scotland, where he practiced medicine and became a Presbyterian elder. Next he went to London where he built up a large and well-known practice, largely of white English patients.

By this time the fame of the man who left Nyasaland on foot at the age of twelve and who spoke no African language had become a legend in Africa. Representatives of his people came to London to plead with him to return, almost as a savior. His decision to do so in 1959 was the occasion for wild rejoicing and even wilder state-

ments. Banda called on his followers to "reject moderation," "fight for freedom" and "fill the prisons."

As a result, in February and March, large parts of Nyasaland were in the hands of rioters. Troops had to be flown in from Southern Rhodesia and Tanganyika to put down the outbreak. Fifty-two persons, all Africans, lost their lives, many were injured and nine hundred persons were jailed.

The disturbances failed to win independence for Nyasaland. They did, however, arouse British public opinion to the Nyasalanders' complaints. One immediate benefit was the appointment by Britain of the first two Africans to the Nyasaland Executive Council, or cabinet.

Nevertheless, by the end of 1959, Dr. Banda was still in jail. A British newspaper carried a perceptive cartoon that showed Banda being placed on a pedestal with such leaders as Prime Ministers Nehru of India and Nkrumah of Ghana and Archbishop Makarios of Cyprus, all at one time arrested for opposing British colonial rule.

39

Rioting also occurred, during January 1959, in the Belgian Congo. The result was that this colony was given a charter promising its rapid development toward freedom. After this development, Spain and Portugal became the only European countries to retain their faith in old-fashioned African colonialism.

Not all the events of Africa during 1959 concerned the states struggling to become independent. Problems were also being faced by states that were already free. It was rapidly being learned by the African people that to be free of colonial rule does not necessarily mean that all the benefits of democracy are theirs. Sudan, for example, had no sooner gained its independence in 1956 than corruption and chaos began to create the conditions that led to the establishment of a military dictatorship on November 17, 1958.

Ghana, too, appeared to be inching further away from liberty. Since its independence in 1957, Ghana's leaders have become ever more sensitive to criticism. A Preventive Detention Act permits arrests without trial for as long as five years. A Deportation Act permits persons to be sent out of the country permanently even though they may be Ghanian citizens. A Press Law of 1959 threatens newspaper editors with jail for printing "false" information about the authorities and the False Reports Act of 1959 makes it a crime for Ghanians to report "untruths" about their Government while visiting other countries.

According to Prime Minister Nkrumah, the explanation for these laws is that there is a danger of conspiracies to overthrow the Government. Their effect, however, has been to make it very difficult to oppose the Government of Ghana by open, democratic means, and to increase opposition in the form of secret plots and revolution.

Fishing fleet at Accra, Ghana. The fish brought in by most of the boats has been sold, and a late-coming craft attracts a crowd anxious to bargain for perhaps the last catch of the day.

40

CHARLES MAY

MIDDLE EAST

By ESMOND S. FERGUSON
Specialist in Iranian Affairs

WEARIED and exhausted after several years of revolution and riots, the countries of the Middle East were relatively calm during 1959. But it was little more than a surface calm. These countries are frequently referred to as "underdeveloped countries." They are not only economically underdeveloped, but with their feudal social systems they are politically "backward countries."

Yemen is an extreme example. When the ruling absolute monarch, Imam Ahmad, went to Rome for medical treatment, his son, Crown Prince Muhammad al-Badr, who had been educated in the West, tried to introduce some modern ways into the country's affairs. But his moves created tension and the possibility of revolt. The old Imam returned to his country to find a state of unrest. He immediately "restored order" by threatening to behead those who sought to bring about any change.

In Saudi Arabia the reform movement made a better showing than in Yemen. There, Emir Faisal is trying to bring order into government finances and other areas of administration. He has a difficult task. Despite the tremendous income from the sale of oil, the royal family and the court spend such huge sums of money that debts of millions of dollars have to be paid.

Around the Persian Gulf there were many boundary disputes. These were especially important since oil might be found in the disputed areas. All the countries around the Persian Gulf as well as Britain and the United States, who hold the major oil concessions in the area, are involved in these disputes. Claims and counterclaims are being made to islands in the Persian Gulf, to offshore lands between Bahrein and Saudi Arabia, to Qatar boundaries, to the Buraimi oasis and to Oman. The various disputes have gone on for years, but any one of them could flare up into a serious problem at any time.

In Kuwait the reform movement makes little headway because the country is immensely wealthy from oil revenues and there is no unemployment. At the first sign of any unrest Sheik Abdullah Mubarek rounds up all foreigners from nearby lands and deports those of questionable loyalty.

Iran is another Middle East country where there is a race between successful reform and revolution. The Shah's difficulty is greater than that of the Arab rulers. There are more complications from powerful groups, including the very backward landowners of the country. Unhappily, it is to this group, the Army and some of the tribal chieftains that the Shah has had to

Using a housetop as platform, Premier el-Kassem of Iraq addresses crowds in Baghdad streets during the revolt of some army units.

WIDE WORLD

A street in Baghdad, ancient city of the Arabian Nights and capital of present-day Iraq. A new and very modern office building rises next door to the mosque.

UNITED NATIONS

look for his main support. Eventually land reform must come, either by steady steps or by violent upheaval. The Shah is pressing for steady reform but is meeting with opposition from the groups on which his support rests. For example, he had to dismiss Abol Hassan Ebtehaj, the man in charge of the Seven-Year Plan Organization, when Ebtehaj quarreled with Prime Minister Eghbal, who represents the conservative landowners. Had he done otherwise there would have been a government crisis that the Shah was not prepared to meet. The Shah relies heavily on aid from

the West. Although military aid from the United States is substantial, the quality of the Iranian Army still remains doubtful.

Early in the year an Iranian–United States defense pact was signed. The United States also signed military agreements with Turkey and Pakistan. At the same time, Iran denounced those articles of an earlier treaty that gave Russia the right to move troops into Iran under certain conditions.

The only major outbreak of violence in the Middle East during 1959 was an abortive revolt in Iraq. Early in March army forces under the leadership of Colonel Ab-

Premier Ben-Gurion being welcomed by the Druse community. On either side of him are members of the Knesset, the Israeli parliament.

Sacks of Israeli cement unloaded from a Danish ship at Port Said after Egypt banned Israeli cargo from Suez Canal. Later the shipowners stopped the unloading.

del Wahab Shawaf revolted against the government of Premier Abdul Karim el-Kassem. The revolt occurred in Mosul, the largest city in northern Iraq. The leaders of the revolt claimed that the Baghdad Government was violating Arab solidarity by giving more power to Communists. It was also believed that the revolt had the backing of supporters of President Nasser of the United Arab Republic. This revolt opened a wide breach between the two Arab leaders, Premier el-Kassem of Iraq and President Nasser. The latter called Premier el-Kassem a communist agent, but

the Premier refrained from speechmaking as he put down the revolt, in which Colonel Shawaf was killed. El-Kassem's quick success in stopping the revolt and maintaining control greatly enhanced his prestige and correspondingly lowered that of President Nasser.

At the time of the revolt, Iraq had a mission in Moscow. With the ending of the revolt, Moscow and Baghdad announced that they had reached "complete unity of views," on economic and technical co-operation. The agreement called for substantial Soviet loans ($137,500,000) at low

43

interest rates, as well as technical assistance in housing, industry and agriculture. Premier Khrushchev told the Iraqi mission, "You have selfless and reliable friends who are ready to come to your aid any time you are in trouble." At the same time, he warned President Nasser that his attacks on communism were futile.

It is believed by some that the Iraqi Communists are tightly controlled by Moscow. It is not to their advantage to take open control of the Government, for then they would be directly responsible for the improvement of the nation's living standards. This the communist leaders know no one can do quickly enough to satisfy the public. They therefore prefer a "popular front" type of government with the responsibility placed on someone else.

In July a procommunist revolt flared in the Kirkuk oil center in northeastern Iraq. It was quickly brought under control with a statement from Premier Kassem that he would "settle accounts" with the mutineers.

In September, thirteen Iraqi army officers were executed by the Baghdad Government for their part in the Mosul rebellion. In both Cairo and Damascus the executions were used as a pretext for attacking Premier Kassem and accusing him of a "red dictatorship."

A real upheaval is taking place in Iraq. It is a revolt against the landowners, a revolt that may spread to any Middle Eastern country. So far Premier el-Kassem has not allowed the situation to get out of control. If he succeeds in his social and agrarian reforms in Iraq, the country will become an example for the Arab world and other countries in the Middle East, particularly Iran.

The extent to which Iraq succeeds will place a corresponding pressure upon President Nasser of Egypt and the Shah of Iran to solve their nations' problems.

The United Arab Republic resumed relations with Jordan during the year. There

was also a definite attempt on the part of other Arab leaders, especially Arab League Secretary General Abdel Kalek Hassouna, to bring Arab rulers into more friendly relationship. These Arab leaders were fully aware of the significance of developments in Iraq. A closer Arab relationship with the West began to take place when President Nasser realized how isolated his position was becoming. His experience with Russian trade practices had been a lesson. Soviet-bloc countries reexported Egyptian cotton to Western countries substantially below market prices. The United States met President Nasser halfway by extending loans for the purchase of locomotives.

There have been second thoughts in Syria over the union with Egypt. Nearly all the difficulties that confront Syria are now blamed on the union. Trade disturbances, suppressed political activity, poor harvests, general discontent are all thought to be due to union with Egypt. There are reported to be dissident elements in Syria ready to join Iraq.

Jordan is even more poorly situated than other Middle Eastern countries. It has survived only because the United States and Britain have been willing to lend money for that purpose. In 1959 the fear that President Nasser might try to unseat King Hussein of Jordan vanished. Where the voice of Cairo had called for the assassination of King Hussein there were now friendly meetings between the two.

Israel has stated that an outside attack on Jordan would not go unnoticed, which means probable Israeli annexation of the west bank of the Jordan River. Although Egypt is in no position to invade Israel across the Sinai desert, it does not prevent her continued harassment of Israel. The outstanding example of this is the seizing of all merchandise destined to Israel that goes through the Suez Canal. President Nasser does this on the pretext that a state

of war still exists between Egypt and Israel. Because of this blockade Israel had to ship a torpedo boat overland from Haifa to Elath, a tortuous 249-mile route.

Calm also prevailed in Lebanon, though there was no great confidence that anything had been settled by the civil strife of the previous year. Some progress was being made toward restoring the democratic system that prevailed before the outbreak of civil war. In September of 1959 Premier Rashid Karame of Lebanon visited President Eisenhower. After the visit Mr. Karame said that Lebanon's policy of "nonalignment" with Eastern or Western blocs "does not contradict our sincere desire to co-operate and make friendships with all countries, especially with this great country of yours." Lebanon's future is to a large degree united with that of Syria. Now Syria is becoming more and more a battleground for the opposing camps of Premier el-Kassem and President Nasser.

The role of the Soviet Union in the Middle East is of great importance. Should the communist position in Iraq be stabilized great pressure would be placed upon Syria to bring about a union with Iraq. Such a move would mean the downfall of President Nasser and the firm establishment of the Soviet Union as a leader of Arab nationalism. Since President Nasser is well aware of this he will now have to turn more to the West. He cannot do so openly, so a quiet *rapprochement* without speeches or threats against the West can be expected.

Against this background Senator James Fulbright, chairman of the United States Senate Foreign Relations Committee, called for a new long-range American policy in the Middle East. He asked for a more mature and realistic understanding of the area's problems. His point was that the United States should cease to adopt the attitude of a parent with a wayward child. Rather, its attitude should be that of one friend helping another.

Middle East Strong Men

Muhammad al-Badr, the crown prince of Yemen, advocates modern ways.

Emir Faisal is trying to reform the administration of Saudi Arabia.

Sheikh Abdullah Mubarek, deputy ruler of Kuwait, called Eagle of the Gulf.

45

SOUTH ASIA

By ARNOLD C. BRACKMAN
Staff Writer,
The News of the Week in Review
The New York Times

SOUTHERN Asia is bounded on the west by the Arabian Sea, on the south by the broad Indian Ocean, on the north by the snowy peaks of the Himalayas and on the east by the emerald chain of islands known as Indonesia and the Philippines.

The area contains more than 600,000,-000 people—one fifth of mankind. The people are of diverse religions, ethnic background, languages and customs. Some are Buddhist as in Burma and Cambodia, some Hindu as in India and others Muslim as in Indonesia and Pakistan. Some south Asians prefer to wear saris (Indians), others sarongs (Malays) and still others the *ao dai* (Vietnamese), a style of dress similar to the Chinese. The people of this vast region speak hundreds of different languages and dialects. With few exceptions they study English as a second language. Most of the peoples of southern Asia share a delight in a diet of rice and highly seasoned dishes.

At the end of World War II the only independent nation in this area was Thailand, whose name means "land of the free." Today, however, virtually every nation is independent. The remaining Western dependencies are: the British territories of northern Borneo; a few small Portuguese territories, such as Timor in the East Indies; and Netherlands New Guinea, a disputed territory which Indonesia claims and calls Irian Barat. The list of new nations is impressive—India, Pakistan, Ceylon, Burma, Laos, Cambodia, North and South Vietnam, Malaya, Indonesia and Singapore. The last became a self-governing state only last year.

Most of these young states are militarily weak, politically unstable and economically poor. With few exceptions these countries mistrust the Western world—the bitter legacy of a century of Western colonial rule. All, however, are concerned with the problems of maintaining independence, establishing stable governments and raising living standards. With the exception of North Vietnam, all are republics or kingdoms that aspire to representative government and personal liberty. North Vietnam is the only communist state among them, a dictatorship on the Moscow-Peking model.

In this region, many observers believe, the decisive battle in the communist assault upon the noncommunist world may be fought. In 1959, communist pressure on the area was intensified. The pressure came from without and from within. From without, there was Communist China casting an ominous shadow across the face of the region. From within, there were the disciplined, well-organized local communist parties operating in each country to exploit political and economic unrest. In some countries, the Communists sat in the parliament (as in India), or were outlawed (Burma and the Philippines), or sat in the highest councils of the state (Indonesia) or waged guerrilla war (Laos and Malaya).

During the past year events in southern Asia moved swiftly. For the first time since the end of World War II, the people of the region became acutely aware of the communist threat to their independence and way of life. Communist pressure centered partly on India, the biggest nation in southern Asia.

India—The icy peaks and wind-swept plateaus of the Himalayas divide India from China, the two most populous nations in the world: China with 680,000,000 people, India with 400,000,000. The border between them stretches for 2,500 miles, follows the crest of the Himalayas and is dotted with three small Buddhist states. In the northwest is Tibet, formerly a semi-independent country which the Chinese Communists invaded, conquered and occupied in 1950. In the northeast, extending for 800 miles, is the disputed McMahon

line. The line has been a source of tension between India and China for years. In 1956, however, the Chinese said that although they contested the line, they would recognize it because of custom and usage.

Since then, China has revived her old claims to the frontier area and has circulated maps to show that the 35,000 square miles of Indian territory near the line are really hers.

In 1959 the border disputes flared into the open when the Tibetans rose in revolt against communist misrule. Peking crushed the rebellion. Incensed, India and the nations of south Asia denounced China's action in Tibet as "Asia's Hungary." The Dalai Lama, revered by the Tibetans as a living god, fled from Tibet with more than 13,000 refugees and found sanctuary in India. During the summer the friction between India and China continued to mount. The Chinese crossed into India, fired on Indian frontier guards and seized several miles of Indian territory. Prime Minister Jawaharlal Nehru announced that the Communists had also penetrated India's frontier at several other points.

India was also jarred by communist pres-

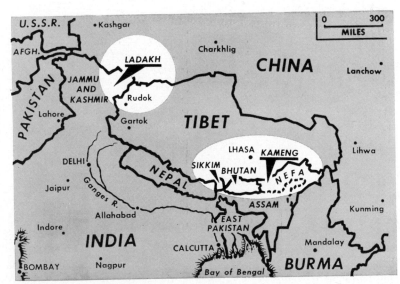

India and China share a border of 2,500 miles. The Chinese claim large sections of Indian land as part of China. There have been clashes near Ladakh and Kameng.

sure from within. During the summer there were growing disorders in the state of Kerala (which means "the land of the coconut"). Although the Communists won only 35 per cent of the Kerala vote in 1957, they were able to form a minority government because the other political parties were disunited. Last year, however, the overwhelming majority of Kerala's fifteen million people demonstrated against the local communist government. They were aroused by the government's attempt to control the state's Roman Catholic and other private schools. Mr. Nehru was forced to step in and dissolve the local government—the only communist provincial regime India has had—to avert, he said, "a civil war." The Communists retaliated by staging riots in Calcutta, India's largest and poorest city. Order was finally restored only when Mr. Nehru dispatched the Army to the scene.

Pakistan—The conflict between India and China served to bring India and Pakistan closer together. When both countries won independence from the British, in 1947, Muslim Pakistan was carved out of predominantly Hindu India. Since then, however, India and Pakistan have been feuding—over religious differences, divided Kashmir (a province both claim) and other issues including the difficult problem of water rights.

Last year Mr. Nehru met President Mohammed Ayub Khan of Pakistan for the first time and the two countries came nearer to a settlement of their water-rights dispute.

In Pakistan, 1959 was a year of reform. Only the year before, General Ayub, the commander in chief of the Pakistan Army since 1951, had seized control of the country. "I came to the conclusion that the country was going to the dogs," General Ayub explained. He was referring to the bureaucratic red tape, corruption and economic dislocation that had gripped Paki-

stan since independence. In 1959 the General launched a land-reform program and other economic measures. He also pledged constitutional reform and free elections as soon as the nation was restored to "good health." His efforts won him wide approval both inside and outside Pakistan.

Laos—While the communist pressure on India grew and Pakistan and India moved toward better relations, the Communists struck again in southern Asia—this time in Laos. Again, the pressure came from within and without. Laos is a Buddhist kingdom of about 91,000 square miles, dotted with jungle-clad peaks and tiny villages. Laos is the "land of a million elephants," according to legend, and has about two million people.

In 1957 the Laotian Communists, who maintained a private army, agreed to integrate their forces into the Royal Laotian Army. By 1959, most of them had been absorbed, but a battalion of 800 guerrillas balked and dug in along the Laotian frontier with communist North Vietnam. In July, under cover of the rainy season, they launched surprise attacks on the Royal Army's positions. Because of poor communications, outside knowledge of the exact situation was hazy, but the Royal Government accused North Vietnam of aiding the rebels. Laos appealed to the United Nations for help, and the Security Council, over the objections of the Soviet Union, sent a team of observers to study the situation. Laos' strategic position in southeast Asia made the communist activity in Laos especially threatening. It shares common frontiers with six states—two communist, China and North Vietnam; two neutralist, Burma and Cambodia; and two allied to the West, Thailand and South Vietnam. Whatever eventually happened to Laos, therefore, would have serious effects elsewhere in southeast Asia.

Burma and Cambodia—The communist pressure on Burma and Cambodia was the

The first of several thousand Tibetans flee across the Indian frontier after an unsuccessful rebellion against Chinese forces that invaded their homeland.

In the streets of Changanacheri, demonstrators support the widespread effort of the opposition to oust the communist government of Indian state, Kerala.

Indian Prime Minister Nehru and President Mohammed Ayub Khan of Pakistan meet in an effort to improve their countries' relations.

UPI

stronger because both are neutralist. South Vietnam and Thailand, which are allied to the West, can always look to the United States for immediate, direct military assistance in defense of their independence.

Both Burma and Cambodia are rice baskets. While Burma has 20,000,000 people, Cambodia has only a scant 4,500,000. While Cambodia has enjoyed relatively internal stability, the situation in Burma the past year has been like that in Pakistan.

Last year the Burmese Parliament renominated General Ne Win, the commander of the Burmese Army, as Premier. Since then he has undertaken a vigorous program of reform, resettling squatters, trimming the cost of living, launching a reconstruction program and opening a drive against corruption. During 1959, Burma took a long step toward greater stability. Here again, there was always communist pressure—from within and without. In the spring the Chinese Communists violated Burma's border twice. The Burmese Communists, who have been fighting against the Government since Burma became independent in 1948, continued to harass the country from their jungle lairs.

Indonesia—During the past year important events occurred in Indonesia, the most populous Muslim nation in the world (86,000,000). Indonesia proclaimed its independence on August 17, 1945, two days after Japan's surrender in World War II. Then a provisional constitution was hastily drawn up, giving President Sukarno almost dictatorial powers. Within a few weeks this constitution was replaced by a multiparty parliamentary system on the French model with the President's powers sharply curtailed. The change was made to placate many people who mistrusted Sukarno's personal ambitions.

Since 1945 Indonesia has been in turmoil, racked by military, economic and political disorders. Three years ago President Sukarno blamed Indonesia's troubles on

Laotian soldiers, equipped with American rifles, look for communist infiltrators.

Right, the late Prime Minister of Ceylon, Solomon Bandaranaike. Below left, his successor, Wijayananda Dahanayake, standing beside his twin brother.

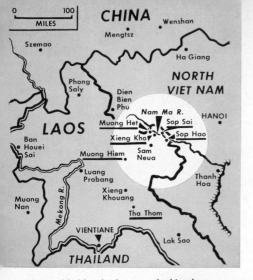

The troubled border between the kingdom of Laos and communist North Viet Nam.

Burma's Premier, anticommunist General Ne Win.

Cambodia's King and Queen narrowly escaped assassination by communist foes.

In Singapore large Chinese crowds attend a meeting of the People's Action Party.

parliamentary democracy and called for "guided democracy." The President was vague about what "guided democracy" means. The upshot, however, was a return to the 1945 constitution. Thus, last year, Mr. Sukarno proposed a new cabinet with himself at the head to rule for five years "without interference from the opposition." The Constituent Assembly, freely elected by the Indonesian people in 1955, refused to accept his plan. With army support, President Sukarno dissolved the assembly and put his plan into operation by decree. While his action was clearly dictatorial, the situation inside Indonesia had become so grave that most Indonesians backed the President. They hoped a return to the revolutionary spirit of 1945 would restore national unity and enable the country to overcome its mounting political and economic problems.

Malaya and Singapore—In 1959 Malaya gave further evidence that she was the most stable and prosperous nation in southern Asia. At the same time, Singapore embarked on self-government, though Britain retained control of its defense and foreign affairs. Its official name is the State of Singapore.

Comprising nine princely states and two former British settlements, Malaya became independent in 1957. Rich in raw materials, producing one third of the world's rubber and tin, it has a population of 3,000,000 Malays, 2,300,000 Chinese and about 700,000 Indians. Since 1948, Malaya has been the scene of a communist guerrilla war. Under communist pressure the Chinese, Malayan and Indian communities of Malaya have worked together. Last year, in the country's first national election as a sovereign state, the Alliance Party received a strong mandate to govern Malaya for the next five years. The Alliance won 73 out of 104 seats. The Alliance consists of the United Malay National Organization, the Malayan Chinese Association and the Malayan Indian Congress. The prospect is that the moderate Alliance, representing the country's three major ethnic groups, will continue to guide Malaya's destiny for a long time.

The outlook is not so rosy in Singapore, the crossroads of the East. Singapore is a tropical island twenty-six miles long and fourteen miles wide linked to Malaya by a causeway. It is a British military bastion and a key trading post astride the shipping routes between Europe and the Far East. About 75 per cent of Singapore's 1,500,000 people are Chinese.

In 1958 the British yielded to nationalist pressure and, as a step toward Singapore's eventual complete independence, agreed to grant the island internal self-government while they retained control over defense and foreign affairs. Last June, Singapore went to the polls and elected its first home government. The People's Action Party, a left-wing grouping with many communist members, scored a landslide victory, winning 43 out of 51 seats. Many Chinese voted for the PAP under pressure from Communist China. The PAP promptly declared that its victory paved the way for an "independent, democratic, noncommunist, socialist state." At the end of the year the big question was whether the Communists in the PAP would submit to the relatively moderate PAP program or would challenge the leadership of the party in an open bid for power.

Ceylon—This island, at the tip of India, has about nine million people, including a large Indian minority. Ceylon is rich in rubber, tea and semiprecious stones. Since gaining independence in 1948, the country has had many problems: a difficult economic situation; language and racial tension between Ceylonese and Indians; and sharp interparty rivalries. Last year these difficulties were increased when Prime Minister S. W. R. D. Bandaranaike was shot and killed.

THE FAR EAST

By WALTER BRIGGS

Far East Correspondent
New York Herald Tribune

CHINA, the colossus of 680,000,000 people, dominated the Far Eastern scene in 1959. In China it was a year of economic slowdown, of backing down from production claims for 1958, of a change in national leadership—and of a campaign to quell smoldering discontent in Tibet. Outside China the Chinese Communists waged aggressive propaganda warfare, their troops violated the frontiers of India and adjacent border states, and they certainly played a part in the communist uprising in Laos. These events overshadowed all others in Asia during the year.

Late in 1958 the Chinese Communist Party's powerful Central Committee announced that sixty-six-year-old Mao Tsetung soon would step down as chairman —roughly, president—of the national Government. The National People's Congress "election," in April 1959, of Liu Shao-chi as Mao's successor came as no surprise. Liu, a theoretician and party organizer, long had been rated No. 2 in the Chinese Communist hierarchy. Mao remained chairman of the party and as such continued to be responsible for all major decisions in China. Having rid himself of ceremonial and day-to-day administrative chores, he would now be able to devote himself to "direction, policy and line of the party and of the state" and to pursuit of "theoretical work in Marx-Leninism." Among Mao's concerns would doubtless be the "people's communes," the "basic new unit" of Chinese society.

Six months after the communes had been set up on a nationwide basis in mid-1959, 99 per cent of China's peasants—four fifths of the population—had been herded into them. Then, late in the year, the cadres —workers for the party—were ordered to take their time about separating children from parents, husbands from wives; in enforcing communal dining; in seizing all personal possessions. Communal regimentation was still the goal. It was to be gradually extended to the cities. For the time being, however, the peasants had to be mollified, for their passive resistance was resulting in lower farm yields than had been anticipated.

The year 1958 was to have been the beginning of a "big leap forward" in production of all kinds. One Chinese goal was to "surpass Britain" in total (not per capita) output within fifteen years. However, by early 1959 Peking was admitting that railroad transport had broken down, especially under pressure of hauling coal, iron ore and steel. Much of this freight was needed to supply hundreds of thou-

CHINA REVISES ITS CLAIMS AND GOALS				
	Original 1958 Claims	Revised 1958 Claims	Original 1959 Goals	Revised 1959 Goals
Grains	375	250	525	275
Cotton	3.35	2.1	5	2.3
Coal	270	270	380	335
Steel	11	8	18	12

(All figures are millions of tons)

sands of back-yard "steel mills." Most of the output of these primitive mills admittedly turned out to be unusable.

Meanwhile, there were numerous hints that all was not going well. Food rations had to be cut, despite boasts of a 102 per cent increase in grain harvest for 1958 over 1957. Government spokesmen blamed this on the ravages of flood, drought and locusts. See chart above.

A party communiqué containing these admissions blamed the false figures on "lack of experience in assessing and calculating output."

China's "leap forward" was more of a hop. The Government was hard put to raise production to keep up with the nation's 15,000,000-a-year population growth.

Chinese Communist troops had invaded Tibet in 1950. Gradually, revolts broke out at remote points in this huge Himalayan fastness. So resentful were the populace of Chinese intrusion that Peking eventually announced it would postpone communization there for some years. Early in 1959 there were fresh outbreaks. A group of the most militant Tibetans feared that the Chinese meant to seize the Dalai Lama, the region's god-king. Spiriting him out of his palace, they escorted him over a long and

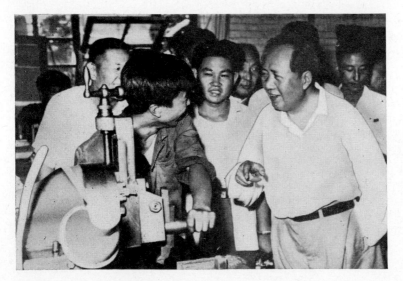

The leader of Communist China, Mao Tse-tung, chats with students working in their school's factory.

tortuous trail, evading Chinese interceptors, to safety in India.

More than 13,000 Tibetan refugees have joined the Dalai Lama in India. Latecomers reported that as many as 80,000 Tibetans may have been killed by the Chinese, and that thousands of Lamaist monks had been forced into labor camps. The Chinese meantime installed the Panchen Lama, Tibet's second-ranking leader, as the country's nominal ruler. He was later reported under arrest. The Dalai Lama appealed to the United Nations for assistance, declaring that the "suffering of my people is beyond description."

The Chinese Communists, irritated by the protection given the Dalai Lama, opened a propaganda campaign against India. Meanwhile, having cut off all trade with Japan (as an ally of the United States) in 1958, they continued to assail Japanese Premier Nobusuke Kishi and his Government for "hostility" toward Red China.

In August, Indian officials disclosed that Chinese forces had occupied Indian outposts and had also invaded the tiny northern states of Bhutan and Sikkim.

At the same time it became clear that Peking was backing a communist uprising in the tiny Indochinese Kingdom of Laos. Some of the Laotian Communists were trained in neighboring communist North Vietnam. Arms supplied to the rebels by North Vietnam had come originally from Red China. Moreover, Ho Chi-Minh, the Vietnamese communist leader, had visited

Peking (and Moscow) just before the communist uprising.

What does Peking expect to gain by acting in this way? Perhaps to impress the world with its stature as a great power. Perhaps to direct the attention of China's people away from the suffering they are forced to endure.

The reasons, whatever they are, must be compelling. Otherwise, the Chinese Communist leaders would not have risked alienating Asian sentiment. As it was, they did just that; India's Prime Minister Jawaharlal Nehru said harsh things about them for the first time, and the Japanese began to take a second, more realistic look at goings on across the Yellow Sea.

Japan—This Japanese attitude was reflected in the voting at an election June 3 for the upper house of the Diet (parliament). A few weeks before the election a high-ranking delegation of the Japan Socialist Party, visiting Peking, had gone down the line with Premier Chou En-lai's criticisms of Premier Kishi. Inajiro Asanuma, the party's secretary-general, had called the United States an "enemy" of his people. However, Japanese voters elected only 38 Socialists to 71 Liberal-Democrats. The Socialists lost nearly 1,000,000 votes —the first such drop in ten years.

Of widespread political interest in Japan was the Liberal-Democrats' intention to revise the nation's military-security agreement with the United States. They also wanted greater "equality" for Japan in determining where American forces and equipment were to be stationed inside the country. The Socialists meanwhile demanded outright ending of the treaty, and the assumption of a neutralist posture backed by security guarantees from Red China and the Soviet Union.

Premier Kishi, who previously had visited the United States and made two swings through southeast Asia, spent five summer weeks in quick calls on countries in Europe

Japan's Premier Kishi, leader of Social Democrat Party.

55

and South America. The Premier sought to persuade other peoples that Japan has cast aside all expansionist aspirations and is now eager to expand trade, economic co-operation and cultural interchange.

Probably the most important development of 1959 in Japanese foreign relations was persuading the International Red Cross Committee, with headquarters in Switzerland, to agree to oversee the repatriation of Korean residents who wish to return to communist North Korea. President Syngman Rhee (of South Korea) insisted that most of these have been coerced by Korean Communists into reaching this decision. Japan replied that such repatriation must be permitted on humanitarian grounds.

Overshadowing all events in 1959 was the April wedding of twenty-five-year-old Crown Prince Akihito to a commoner. It was the first time in Japan's history, which according to legend stretches back 2,620 years, that the heir to the throne had married outside the royal circle. The prince's bride, Miss Michiko Shoda, was a charming, twenty-four-year-old daughter of a wealthy flour miller. Except for a handful of Imperial Household traditionalists, the Japanese were almost universally delighted with Akihito's choice. Some essayists described his move as a long step toward tearing down the "chrysanthemum curtain" separating Emperor Hirohito and the imperial family from the Japanese people. After the wedding, Japan began to enjoy

Stamp issued on the wedding day of Prince Akihito and Michiko Shoda.

what some newspapermen have called the "Michi boom" in honor of the Princess.

In a galloping recovery from the 1958 recession, the nation was heading toward its most prosperous year in history. By August the Government's Economic Planning Agency was speculating that economic growth would reach 10 per cent for the year (earlier estimates had been 5.5, then 8 per cent), leading some official economists to predict a doubling of the gross national output within ten years.

Exports for the year were expected to top $3,000,000,000, an all-time high, and to exceed imports for the first time since the war. Japan's exports to the United States (its best single customer) were soaring, despite restrictions on such imports as cotton textiles, and tableware.

Japanese farmers enjoyed bumper crops for an unprecedented fifth straight year. The average city worker's pay bounded to the monthly equivalent of $84.25 per household—exceedingly high for Asia. Prices held steady. Television antennas made a jungle of city rooftops; electric washing machines showed up even in remote villages. Prosperity was so great that the Finance Ministry warned that the economy might become "overheated" in 1960.

Republic of Korea—Seoul's irritation over the Japanese repatriation move was heightened by President Rhee's continued hostility toward Japan. Denouncing Premier Kishi as a "Communist," the Koreans cut off all trade with the Japanese. Negotiations to "normalize" relations between the two countries, on and off for years, were resumed later but promised little. Mr. Rhee's unwillingness to forgive the Japanese for thirty-five years of occupation is the main obstacle to a new friendship that would benefit both countries.

The eighty-four-year-old Mr. Rhee has been the republic's only president. In June he announced that he would accept his Liberal Party's nomination to run for a fourth straight four-year term. His chief opponent in the election, to be held in May or June 1960, will probably be Vice-President John M. Chang. A leader of the Democratic Party, Mr. Chang lives in semiseclusion because of attempts on his life.

South Korea, with help from the United States, was recovering from wartime ravages and making notable advances. Industrial output had risen 70 per cent since 1955. Inflation had been checked, bank deposits were rising, and tax revenues had greatly increased. Korea's per capita income is about $100 a year, the average for Asia.

South Korea could have recovered even faster but for the need to maintain huge military forces. To defend the 144-mile-long truce line that roughly follows the thirty-eighth parallel there are eighteen Korean and two American divisions.

President Rhee would like to reunite his country by force, but the United States has refused to let him attack North Korea. United Nations and Korean and Chinese Communist negotiators continue to meet periodically at the historic truce site of Panmunjom.

Defectors from North Korea continue to tell harrowing tales of the grim life there. The North Korean Communists are setting up agricultural organizations very much like Red China's rural communes. In industry, Pyongyang has concentrated on heavy manufactures, as is the communist pattern, and cut down on the production of consumer goods. Despite such production "successes" for 1958 as almost 9,000,000 tons of coal and 870,000 tons of steel, the people of North Korea still lack many of the commodities that are regarded elsewhere as human necessities.

Taiwan—The year was one of comparative quiet in the Formosa Strait. The Chinese Communists only sporadically fired on the Nationalist-held offshore islands of Quemoy and Matsu. It was generally expected that Peking sooner or later would again take the offensive against the Nationalists, as it did with its forty-four-day bombardment of the Quemoys in 1958.

The Chinese Nationalist Assembly of Taiwan (Formosa) decided to amend the constitution, which allows for only two terms, to permit seventy-two-year-old Chiang Kai-shek to serve another term as president. President Chiang's second six-year term is to end in May 1960. The assembly's decision, supported by the ruling Kuomintang (Nationalist Party), assures that the leader will remain in power.

Syngman Rhee, president of the Republic of Korea, breaks ground for South Korea's first reactor.

In August, Taiwan was visited by typhoon-triggered floods that were the worst in the island's recorded history. Police reported over 1,000 persons dead or missing, and one fourth of Taiwan's cultivated land under water. A severe earthquake that caused extensive damage to several towns followed soon after.

Despite these calamities, Taiwan continued to prosper. Prices held steady. The Government predicted that the industrial output between 1956 and 1960 would show an increase of 100 per cent. Exports

57

of processed sugar and pineapples, textiles of many descriptions, small manufactures and handicrafts were increasing.

The Philippines—The immediate future of President Carlos P. Garcia's ruling Nacionalista Party was clouded by many defeats in November's elections for eight Senate seats and for many local offices. Arsenio H. Lacson, a bitter foe of Garcia, won a third term as mayor of Manila.

Jesus Vargas   Carlos Garcia

The islands' economy was in bad shape as the year ended. Unemployment exceeded 2,000,000 (among about 20,000,000 people). Many businesses were stagnating. The country's meager foreign-exchange reserves were dropping. Officials hoped for an economic revival from such measures as raising taxes and import levies, plus imposition of a 25 to 40 per cent surcharge on foreign-exchange sales—which amounted to devaluation of the peso.

Charges of corruption were openly voiced. Typically, the independent weekly Philippines *Free Press* declared that "there is more grafting and thieving in our government today than there ever was in previous administrations . . ." At mid-year, President Garcia dismissed the defense secretary, Lieutenant General Jesus Vargas, who in the past had used the Army to enforce honest elections, and appointed a member of his own party.

So seriously do many Filipinos view conditions that there has been talk of revolution—or a military *coup d'état*. In fact, the Army tried—and cleared—an officer

charged with having been involved in planning such a coup.

All parties claim to be pro-American, but the Nacionalistas appeared to be using the United States as a whipping boy, blaming it for present bad conditions. Many Nacionalista Party leaders sought to exploit popular feeling to give the Philippine Government increased criminal jurisdiction over American servicemen. They also pressed for United States payment of financial claims ranging to $900,000,000. But despite all this talk, anti-American criticism seemed to be gaining little sympathy in the provinces.

The Filipino Communists have all but given up the guerrilla terror tactics of the Huk movement that was quelled by the late President Ramon Magsaysay. But they continue to feed on mass discontent, increasing hardship and Filipino nationalism, and they were gaining strength in the labor unions, in the schools and among the large Chinese community.

The Philippines remained a stanch member of the Southeast Asia Treaty Organization. When Laos was threatened, Filipinos were among the first to recommend that SEATO accept its obligation to defend the country against communist expansion.

Hong Kong—It was an uneventful year for the nearly 3,000,000 population of this British crown colony, nearly half of whom are refugees from nearby Red China. The colonial government continued during the year to push its $70,000,000 housing program. So far, 275,000 refugees have been accommodated in new seven-story apartment buildings. Hong Kong's fledgling industries continued to boom, though they met with some opposition in the United States, Europe and South Africa because of their low prices. Most of Hong Kong's residents (99 per cent of them Chinese) continued to hope and believe that Peking would keep hands off.

CANADA

By R. D. HILTON SMITH
Author, Critic and Librarian

Aɴʏ record of the chief happenings in Canada in 1959 is bound to be at the same time a record of the royal tour. Queen Elizabeth II and Prince Philip saw more of Canada in forty-five days than most Canadians see in a lifetime.

It is not possible to do justice here to the picturesque details of the royal tour —the trooping of the colors planned by various famous regiments, the naval and air reviews, the plays and concerts the Queen attended and the many other events that were crowded into the program. All in all the royal visitors saw a great many representative aspects of Canadian life.

By air, by water and by land the royal couple traveled 15,000 miles. Their course took gigantic zigzags from the Atlantic to the Pacific and from the United States border to the last frontiers of development in the far north. They visited 115 towns and villages and shook countless thousands of hands. In every kind of weather and under a variety of conditions they carried out their official duties.

The travelers saw a different Canada from the country they had traveled through more briefly in 1951. This was especially true of Newfoundland and Quebec. In Newfoundland the Queen visited small, primitive logging centers and also opened a vast jet-age installation at Gander. In Quebec she saw much that was ancient, quaint and picturesque but also much of that province's recent and amazing industrial expansion.

When the royal party went to the St. Lawrence River port of Seven Islands, for instance, they found a town of 10,000 people, bustling with new industries, in what had been a small, remote mission settlement. At Schefferville the Queen went down an iron mine. Ten years ago Schefferville did not exist; today it is a town of 4,500 population, reached from Seven Islands by a railway built across 350 miles of bog and wilderness in the face of almost incredible difficulties.

Among other places they visited were the world's largest aluminum plant, at Arvida, and the world's largest papermaking center, the town of Trois Rivières. These are only random examples of the development going on all over Quebec. During the year about 150,000 men were employed in the province on construction projects estimated to cost $1,000,000,000.

One of the main objects of the royal visit was the official opening of the St. Lawrence Seaway. It had been unofficially

THE QUEEN'S VISIT

PHOTOS, NATIONAL FILM BOARD OF CANADA

A farm couple stop their work to wave at the royal yacht Britannia as it sails to Montreal.

The Queen sees evidence of Quebec's industrial growth at a modern aluminum plant in Arvida.

opened in April, with ships entering the seaway at the rate of one ship every forty-two minutes since then. The gala occasion on June 26 went off splendidly. The star that day was HMY Britannia. That sleek and beautiful vessel drew admiring comments from all onlookers as it led the procession into the waterway.

An interesting event of the royal visit to Montreal was a meeting of industrialists and labor leaders, called together by Prince Philip to plan for a conference to be held in Canada. It will study the problems of developing natural resources and will try to pool the experience of different Commonwealth countries for the benefit of all. Canada was selected as the meeting place because of her long experience in huge projects connected with such resources as minerals, lumber and water power.

The old and pleasant custom of making gifts to visiting royalty took a new turn last year. The Queen and Prince Philip did receive many beautiful personal gifts, but the national gift took a different form: the Government established the $1,000,-000 Queen Elizabeth Fund for research into childhood diseases. Several of the

provinces followed the national example and set up medical-research centers, special scholarship and bursary funds, and funds for helping the old and the poor in the Queen's name.

After the seaway opening and visits to several centers in eastern Canada, the royal party steamed across Lake Michigan on the Britannia to the only American destination of their itinerary. At Chicago, 2,500,000 people turned out to give them a rip-roaring welcome.

The royal journey through the Prairie Provinces included a view of the famous Calgary Stampede. Here the visitors saw the noisy, dusty and exciting chuck-wagon races. They then went on to British Columbia for the official opening of the Deas Island Tunnel. This novel tunnel links Vancouver by road with the lower Fraser Valley and the United States border. It was built ashore in rectangular cross sections, which were floated into position and then sunk into a dredged trench. The only other tunnel like it is in Holland.

For their three-day stay in Victoria, capital of British Columbia, the Queen and Prince Philip were the guests of the Lieu-

The Queen and Prince Philip inspect an iron-mine plan at Schefferville in north Quebec.

The Queen talks with a group of young patients while visiting Montreal's Children's Hospital.

tenant Governor at the new Government House, recently opened. It was built to replace the one that was burned down a few years ago. This striking 51-room house, said to be the finest official residence in Canada, is surrounded by 35 acres of beautiful grounds. From her bedroom window the Queen had a magnificent view of the Strait of Juan de Fuca, which separates Vancouver Island from the state of Washington on the United States mainland.

The next stage in the journey was northward. It was unique, for never before had a reigning monarch visited the Yukon. This is the region immortalized by Robert W. Service in his poems of the northland, and the visitors were reminded of him at nearly every step. They visited the McBride Museum to see relics of the stirring times Service wrote about. They saw the old stern-wheelers that used to ply the waters in gold-rush days. They met several old-timers, and they were greeted everywhere in the free-and-easy style of the area (probably a welcome change from the more formal atmosphere elsewhere).

From the Yukon the royal party headed southeast to take in several of the more northerly centers across the prairies and eastern Canada. Meantime, Prime Minister Diefenbaker had summoned his cabinet to a meeting at Halifax, Nova Scotia, to coincide with the Queen's presence there on August 1, just before the end of the tour. After this meeting it was announced that Canada's new governor general would be Major General George P. Vanier. He succeeded the Right Honorable Vincent Massey, who retired after seven and a half years of outstanding service.

On September 15, General Vanier took three oaths—of allegiance to the Queen, of office, and of keeper of the Great Seal of Canada. "I do, *je le jure,*" General Vanier replied to each oath as he became the first Roman Catholic and French-Canadian governor general of Canada. The new Governor General is a famous soldier-diplomat, descended from one of the original Quebec families. Now seventy-two years old, he lost a leg in the first World War. After the war he gave up practicing law to start a new career in diplomacy. He had been Canadian ambassador to France for only a short time when World War II started. On the fall of France in June 1940, he escaped the German invaders by taking a fishing boat out into the Bay of Biscay, where his party was picked up by a British destroyer. During the war he served in London as Canadian ambassador to several governments in exile. Twelve days after the liberation of France he was re-appointed as ambassador there and filled the post for nine years.

Canada's 17,500,000 people had a good year, as the national economy boomed again after its sharp dip the previous year. Industrial production in the first six months of 1959 was nearly 8 per cent higher than in 1958, department-store sales were up by about 10 per cent and in June the export figure reached an all-time peak of $519,900,000. Employment figures also broke new records at midyear, with nearly 6,250,000 men and women working. The yield from all forms of taxation continued to exceed the minister of finance's earlier estimates.

The Government helped to boost exports by taking a more active part in trade fairs all over the world. Last year Canadian goods were on display at more than twenty important fairs in Europe, North and South America, the West Indies, South Africa, Japan and Australia.

The hum of increased business and the jingle of the cash registers could be heard in most kinds of trade and industry. However, each section of the nation had problems to face. The Maritime Provinces were hit rather severely by cutbacks in iron and coal production, but the development of mines, mills and air bases on the Atlantic seaboard is bringing in new wealth to the area, and with it hope for a brighter economic future.

In the Prairie Provinces the experience of Alberta is typical. Production of natural gas rose to 67,000,000 cubic feet in just the first two months of the year. At the same time, farm income went up in nearly the same proportion. It is clear that this region's agriculture has nothing to fear from industrial development.

Perhaps the outstanding event of the year in national politics was the Government's bold decision to scrap the Arrow fighter plane. This Canadian-designed plane, said to be the fastest and most advanced fighter in the world, had cost $340,-000,000 to develop. Its existence was a matter of national pride, and its continued construction would keep one of the biggest plants in the country busy. Nevertheless, Mr. Diefenbaker and his cabinet de-

The modern airport at Gander, Newfoundland, is used by a quarter of a million passengers a year; twenty air-traffic controllers handle the take-offs and landings of jets.

WIDE WORLD

A spectacular view of the Trans-Canada Highway running through Banff National Park in Alberta.

cided that it was already out of date in this missile age. This difficult and far-reaching decision caused a tremendous uproar at first, but few doubt today that it was necessary.

In March, Sidney Smith, minister for external affairs, died suddenly. He was succeeded by Howard Green, and this was the only major change in the cabinet. Another famous Canadian who died last year was Edward Johnson, former manager of the Metropolitan Opera Company and in his younger days a noted opera singer. The death of Maurice Duplessis in the fall removed a controversial and colorful figure from the political scene in Quebec, where he had been premier for many years.

Several provincial elections were held, mostly resulting in the mixture as before. In Manitoba, Premier Dufferin Robbin's Conservative Party became the first Conservative majority government to hold office since Robbin's own grandfather's government resigned in 1915. In Alberta, the Social Credit government gained 24 seats to give them all but 4 of the 65 seats in the legislature and to return Ernest Manning for his sixteenth year as premier.

The Canada Council continued its good work of aiding the arts by means of grants to universities, symphony orchestras, theater and ballet companies and art galleries. Also, of course, this government-sponsored group makes grants to talented men and

UPI

Governor General Vanier and Mrs. Vanier. He
is the second Canadian to hold this high post.

women who are likely to contribute to
Canadian cultural development—schol-
ars, artists, writers, composers and others.
Among the Canadians who made a particular mark abroad was Lynn Seymour.
This twenty-year-old Alberta girl became
the star of England's Royal Ballet and the
youngest prima ballerina ever to appear at
Covent Garden.

During the year new centers of learning were started in different parts of the
country. In Newfoundland, construction
began on a new Memorial University to
replace the old, temporary buildings. Four
thousand miles away the University of British Columbia was building its $2,800,000
medical-science center. Lord Beaverbrook,
who has made many fine gifts to his native
province of New Brunswick, announced
during the year that he would provide an
archives building for the province to house
the precious records of its past.

Canadians subscribed the entire cost of
the new law-faculty building for the He-
brew University of Jerusalem. The board-
room furniture includes a chair once used
by Sir John A. Macdonald—the gift of a
Toronto newspaper publisher.

If one were asked to guess what nation
produces the biggest talkers, how many of
us would answer "Canada"? Yet, if statis-

tics can be believed, Canadian men and
woman, girls and boys, are the most loqua-
cious people on earth. For the fourth consecutive year, Canada topped all other
countries in the number of telephone con-
versations. They reached the astonishing
average of 497 per head of population
per year.

Debate continued on the question of a
national flag. Many Canadians must be interested in it, because so far the Government has on file 1,347 different designs
for a distinctive national flag.

Another subject of general interest has
been the completion of the Trans-Canada
Highway. During the year, construction
was busily under way to close the few remaining gaps or to improve existing sections. About three quarters of the 4,487-
mile highway has already been paved. All
the rest of the route was open to traffic
except for two sections of about sixty miles
each—one to the northeast of Lake Superior and the other in British Columbia. By
the time these words appear in print, this
old dream of a highway stretching from
coast to coast will be a dream come true.

Maurice Duplessis was premier of Quebec
1936-39 and 1944 until his death in 1959.
He also founded the National Union Party.

WIDE WORLD

LATIN
AMERICA

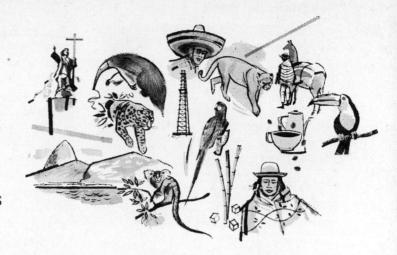

By CARLETON BEALS
Author and Lecturer

Cuba continued to hold the spotlight in Latin American affairs throughout 1959. A few hours before dawn on January 1, Cuban President Fulgencio Batista fled by air from Cuba to the Dominican Republic. After several years of armed struggle, young Fidel Castro, leader of the July 26 Movement, and his *barbudos*—bearded ones—rode into Havana on tanks that had been captured from Batista's forces in running battles across the land. The crucial three-day battle for Santa Clara, the central sugar city of the island, brought victory. Dr. Manuel Urrutia Lleo, a former Santiago judge, was recalled from exile and sworn in as provisional president.

After a quick good-will flight to Caracas, Venezuela, where he was warmly received by President Romulo Betancourt (who had recently replaced General Marcos Perez Jimenez), Castro embarked on a tour of the United States to explain his revolution and its aims. He flew on to Canada, then south to the Inter-American Conference at Buenos Aires. Castro told the conference that the United States should embark on a ten-year plan of financial aid to Latin America totaling at least $30,000,000,000.

By then the peace of the Caribbean had been disturbed by the first of a series of "rowboat invasions." A small armed band, mostly Cubans, landed at Playa Colorada in the jungles of Panama. The landing had been masterminded by the Panamanian diplomat Roberto Arias.

The next day the United States Government provided President La Guardia of Panama with arms. Two days later an investigating commission of the Organization of American States (OAS) flew south. Within a few days, Arias' wife, the leading dancer of the Royal Ballet of London, was captured, Arias took refuge in a foreign embassy, and the expeditionaries surrendered. After a few weeks they were sent back to Cuba.

By May, trouble struck Nicaragua. Three plane-loads of invaders landed at two strategic points. The blow was timed to coincide with a business strike in Managua, the capital. President Luis Somoza Debayle, who had inherited his father's power, and his brother, head of Nicaragua's armed forces, moved swiftly. The invaders soon surrendered. Various would-be invaders from Cuba were later arrested in Honduras, some in Mexico.

Then on June 14, some sixty armed Dominicans flew into the Dominican Republic to attempt to overthrow the thirty-year Trujillo dictatorship. Ten days later three hundred more tried to come in by sea. Both invasions were quickly crushed. Trujillo brought charges before the OAS that the invasions had been instigated by the governments of Venezuela and Cuba.

Denying the charges, both Cuba and Venezuela countercharged that Trujillo was hiring mercenaries in Spain and elsewhere for the invasion of their countries. Trujillo dropped the charges, and the OAS took no action other than calling a foreign ministers' meeting in Santiago, Chile, in August to consider peace and other pressing matters.

Meanwhile Castro had taken over the post of head of the cabinet and was moving ahead with his program. His chief effort was directed toward land reform. A beginning was made of distributing government-owned lands. A nationwide crusade was started for funds to provide seed, animals and tools to the new settlers. The pub-

lished land decree put limits on the size of all holdings. Excess acreage had to be sold within a year to private owners or to the Government at assessed valuation. No sugar refinery could own land, and foreign ownership of agricultural land was forbidden. Since 60 per cent of all Cuban arable land was owned or controlled by United States corporations, this was bad news for many American investors. The United States State Department advised the Cuban Government that payment for land with interest-bearing bonds would not be considered adequate compensation, only payment in cash would be. The Cuban Government rejected this, saying it would be the same as having no land reform.

The land reform set off a number of conspiracies instigated by cattle and tobacco and other landholding interests. These were quickly squelched. In July a rift over the

Castro addresses a rally on the Government's policy toward war criminals.

Roberto Arias and his wife, Margot Fonteyn. Panama charged him with revolutionary activities.

Invaders, mostly Cubans, surrender to Panamanian troops at Nombre de Dios. Arias was said to have planned the invasion.

NEW YORK TIMES

POLITICAL PICTURE IN LATIN AMERICA

UNITED STATES

Castro faces economic and social problems.

CUBA

MEXICO

DOM. REP.

HAITI

Caribbean rulers fear Castro will aid rebels.

VENEZUELA

GUATEMALA
EL SALVADOR
HONDURAS
NICARAGUA
COSTA RICA
PANAMA

GUIANAS

COLOMBIA

ECUADOR

Pacific Ocean

PERU

BRAZIL

BOLIVIA

PARAGUAY

Government puts down revolt by Right Wingers.

CHILE

URUGUAY

ARGENTINA

Atlantic Ocean

Strikes and rumors of plots beset Frondizi.

■ Under military dictatorship
▨ Now or recently in ferment
▨ Stable

67

A bed-sheet flag of truce signals collapse of brief rebellion in Nicaragua.

land policy and other matters led to the ousting of President Urrutia, who was replaced by Osvaldo Dorticos, author of most of Castro's reform laws.

Chile, in 1959, was staggered by a catastrophic drop in copper and other raw-material prices, hit by disastrous inflation, troubled by unemployment and by a violent strike. She began moving back to stability through the efforts of able, newly elected conservative President Jorge Alessandri. Aided by $135,000,000 in United

States private and governmental loans, Alessandri began a strict program of economy which increased employment.

In Bolivia, President Hernan Siles Zuazo was faced with strikes, student uprisings, riots and armed revolts. Deep-seated ill feeling toward the United States broke out violently on March 2, sparked by an article in an American news magazine. The article quoted an unnamed American Embassy official as allegedly saying that the only solution for Bolivia's ills was to divide its

President and Mrs. Lopez Mateos of Mexico in Washington. The guests sit in front of their host so they can wave to crowds.

Arturo Frondizi
of Argentina

Hernan Siles Zuazo
of Bolivia

Jorge Alessandri
of Chile

ALL PHOTOS, WIDE WORLD

O Palacio da Alvorado (Palace of the Dawn), official residence of the president in Brasilia, the beautiful new capital of Brazil.

69

territory up among its neighbors. A crowd burned the American flag and stoned the United States Embassy, forcing the entire staff to take refuge in the suburbs for four days under heavy armed guard. The United States Information Service offices in La Paz, Cochabamba and Oruro were also attacked.

No government in Latin America has survived more stormy events than that of Intransigent Radical President Arturo Frondizi in Argentina. Frondizi is the first elected president since Juan Peron's ten-year rule and three subsequent years of army rule. He was elected with the help of Peron forces, who control most of the labor movement and who probably accounted for at least 40 per cent of his vote. However, he failed to take Peronists into his cabinet as was expected and has faced strikes and disorders ever since. He crushed one general strike and in September was faced with another general strike, of forty-eight hours, that tied up most of the country. A sugar strike in Tucuman ended in armed revolt. The Communists have also been active in opposition. Army, Navy and Air Force conspiracies have required repeated arrests of high officers. The Vice-President headed one conspiracy and was ousted.

Part of Frondizi's trouble has been caused by his oil concessions to United States interests, made in the hope of ending Argentina's expenditures for imported fuel oil and gasoline. This was one of the chief causes of Peron's downfall also. The Navy, in particular, and most of the Army consider oil a sacred Argentine resource that should be developed only by the government-owned oil corporation. Labor is also opposed to Frondizi's oil concessions. Repeated strikes have resulted, even though Frondizi tried to soften the deal by giving minor concessions to British and European interests and to the Soviet Union. But at one time, the head of the Navy de-

manded his resignation; at another time Frondizi put twenty top naval officers under arrest. Thus far Frondizi has risen above all his trials.

In Brazil, President Juscelino Kubitschek completed five years of his six-year term. He has steered his country through a coffee crisis, bad inflation, labor disputes, serious financial and trade difficulties—all with a minimum of disorder and a maximum of civil liberties. The powerful Communist Party, outlawed for more than ten years, has been legalized.

This vast country was larger than the United States until the admission of Alaska to statehood. It has a bigger population than any country in Europe except the Soviet Union. Brazil has continued the upward spiral of its agricultural and industrial development. There has been a steady expansion of the steel and tool industries. This has caused inflation and serious economic and cultural dislocations, but it has also provided full employment and the expansion of public works, services and communications.

On April 21, 1960, the Government will move to its new capital, Brasilia. In the wilderness on the interior plateau, where the climate is more equable and salubrious than in Rio de Janeiro, homes for 500,-000 people are being built. When completed, Brasilia will be the most modern and dramatic of all the world's capitals. Magnificent buildings have already been constructed—the Presidential Palace; twin domes and twin twenty-five-story skyscraper towers for the Senate and Chamber of Deputies; sky-floating hotels; skyscraper apartment houses; and hundreds of one-family homes. Brazilian architecture is a world leader, and the originality and functional brilliance that is characteristic of so much of Brazil's modern construction has been surpassed in the new city. The newborn capital is a symbol of the spirit of modern Brazil.

WESTERN EUROPE

By I. D. W. TALMADGE
Editor of World Week

THROUGHOUT 1959 Western Europe continued to be the center of the East-West conflict. The major issues of the cold war were focused on Berlin, the reunification of Germany, and European security. As the year progressed, there was a growing feeling among West European leaders that they had been left on the side lines, that the future of Western Europe would be determined not by them but by the outcome of the struggle between two "outside" powers—the Soviet Union and the United States.

This feeling spurred renewed efforts to patch up differences among the West European countries and to create a more powerful and unified Western Europe.

The year began auspiciously with two significant moves toward Western European unity. On January 1, 1959, the European Economic Community and the European Atomic Energy Community came into force.

The European Economic Community (popularly known as the Common Market) is aimed at the gradual meshing of the national economies of six Western European countries into a single trading community. The six countries are France, West Germany, Italy, Belgium, the Netherlands and Luxembourg. (These countries already pool their coal and steel resources through the European Coal and Steel Community.)

The object of the Common Market is to tear down the many economic barriers (such as export-import duties) that have long divided Western Europe and obstructed the free flow of trade.

In the past, there have been many economic walls between the nations of Western Europe. Germany, for example, protected its Volkswagen automobile against competition from similar types of automobiles manufactured in France. The protection was given by German tariffs that made the French imported cars more expensive in Germany than the Volkswagen. Similar protective measures were taken by French automobile manufacturers against Germany.

All this is now due to change. Under the Common Market, trade restrictions will eventually be removed on all commerce *within* the six-nation bloc. All tariffs between the participating countries will be scrapped, and the six nations will maintain a common tariff in their trade with the outside world.

The Common Market will be achieved by a gradual, step-by-step process. The six countries started by cutting their tariffs against one another by 10 per cent. There will be further reductions in succeeding years until all tariffs are eliminated. Although this may take twelve to fifteen years, in the end, raw materials, manufactured goods, man power, and funds for capital investment will move as freely among the six member nations of the Common Market as they do now among the fifty states of the United States or the ten provinces of Canada.

The result will be increased trade, increased output and a higher standard of living for the 173,000,000 people in that area. The creation of the Common Market marked the beginning of a new era in the economic life of Western Europe.

Equally significant was the birth on January 1 of the European Atomic Energy Community (known as Euratom). The purpose of Euratom is to promote nuclear research and to share atomic know-how among the same six nations.

Euratom is vital to the economy of the countries of Western Europe. It has taken on even more importance because of the continuing unrest in the oil-rich Middle East. Oil is the one mineral that Western Europe lacks and needs desperately. The Suez crisis in 1956 was a reminder of Western Europe's critical dependence on Middle Eastern oil. By planning ahead the six countries may be able to use the atom to make up for this energy shortage.

Furthermore, because the present cost of producing electric power in Western Europe is so high, atomic power may soon become commercially feasible.

The supervision of both the Common Market and Euratom is entrusted to three supranational (supergovernment) bodies: a Council of Ministers, representing each member government and empowered to make policy; a Legislative Assembly with advisory powers, now chosen by the parliaments of the member countries, later to be chosen by direct vote of the peoples in

Greek Prime Minister Karamanlis meets Colonel Grivas, commander of Cypriote nationalist group.

those countries; a Court of Justice to mediate disputes that may arise among the member nations.

The year 1959 saw the settlement of a three-sided squabble over the control of Cyprus, a rocky, mountainous island, lying in the eastern Mediterranean.

Cyprus has a population of 530,000, of whom four fifths are of Greek descent, and one fifth of Turkish descent. For four years, the Greeks, the Turks and the British quarreled bitterly over who should govern the island. While diplomats traded notes and threats, Cypriote terrorists and British soldiers fired bullets at one another, and about 450 persons were killed.

The Greek Cypriotes, backed by the Greek Government, demanded *enosis*— union of Cyprus with Greece. The Turkish Cypriotes strongly opposed this plan, fearing that as a minority they would be badly treated under Greek rule. The British were reluctant to leave Cyprus because the island had become in recent years their most important military base in the strategically vital eastern Mediterranean.

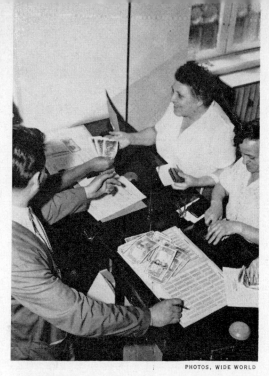

Saarlanders exchange their French francs for marks as the Saar rejoins West Germany.

NATO (the North Atlantic Treaty Organization) was caught squarely in the middle of this tangled dispute. Britain, Greece and Turkey are all members of this fifteen-nation defense alliance.

The quarrel over Cyprus finally threatened to disrupt the alliance. Eventually cooler heads prevailed. From February 5 to 11, the premiers and the foreign ministers of Greece and Turkey quietly met in neutral Zurich, Switzerland, and finally broke the diplomatic log jam. In a spirit of friendship and compromise that surprised the world, they reached an accord on Cyprus. Later this accord was also approved by Britain and the Cypriotes.

Following are the principal provisions of the agreement:

1. Cyprus would become a republic, with its independence guaranteed by Greece, Turkey and Britain.

2. The new nation would have a Greek Cypriote president and a Turkish Cypriote vice-president. The latter would have the right to veto any legislation affecting the Turkish minority.

3. The national assembly would be two-thirds Greek and one-third Turkish.

4. Britain would retain her military bases on Cyprus. Greece and Turkey would set up a combined NATO force of troops on the island.

A few months later another thorny dispute was ended in free Europe. This was the centuries-old quarrel between France and Germany over the possession of the Saar basin.

The Saar—with a population of 996,000 —is one of the richest coal-and-steel regions in the world. The Saarlanders speak German and are closely tied in culture and custom to Germany.

Situated between France and Germany, the Saar has changed hands several times in recent history. After Germany's defeat in World War II, France gained control of the Saar. However, since most Saarlanders resented French rule, France put forth a plan to set up the Saar as a partly independent state. But this plan was rejected by the Saar voters in 1955.

A year later, France yielded to the inevitable and agreed to the return of the Saar to Germany. It was to be accomplished in two stages—Germany was to take over (a) political control of the territory on January 1, 1957, and (b) economic control on January 1, 1960.

On July 5, 1959—six months ahead of the deadline—the customs posts were moved from the Saar-German border to the Saar-French border. The Saar had become, once more, a political and economic part of Germany. France, however, retained special rights of access to Saar coal and special privileges in the Saar market.

The accords on Cyprus and the Saar removed two major obstacles to solidarity in Western Europe. They also showed the world that disputes among democratic nations can be settled peacefully.

While during most of 1959 all of Western Europe was living under the shadow of the Soviet ultimatum on Berlin, important national developments were taking place. Under the leadership of General Charles de Gaulle, who assumed the presidency on January 8, France had a year of political stability and economic growth.

For the first time in many years, the French people had confidence in their future. They had a strong government with a strong man at the helm. There were none of the political disorders and cabinet crises that had plagued France since the end of the war. One of the achievements of President de Gaulle was to convince most Frenchmen that a democracy can function best under a strong, stable government.

Through a series of bold financial and currency reforms, the De Gaulle Government revitalized France's national economy. The flight of capital out of France was halted. More than a billion dollars in "fugitive capital" flowed back into the country from abroad. Industrial production was at an all-time peak. Inflation was checked. Since De Gaulle came to power, prices have gone up less than 4 per cent—thus virtually ending a fourteen-year inflationary trend. France's exports during the first six months of the year exceeded its imports. The total economic picture of the nation was never brighter.

In foreign relations, De Gaulle strove to gain for France a greater say in the councils of the Western alliance. In order to increase his country's weight in military matters, he pressed ahead with the development of French nuclear weapons and planned to test an atomic bomb in the Sahara Desert. His main objective was to have France join the "nuclear club," at present limited to the United States, Britain and the Soviet Union.

De Gaulle introduced a new era in colonial affairs. To all France's colonies in Africa (except Algeria), he offered a choice: (a) self-government while remaining members of a new "French Community," or (b) complete independence. Of the thirteen colonies, only Guinea at first selected independence. Later, on September 14, 1959, two other territories—Senegal and the French Sudan—informed President de Gaulle that they, too, wished to become fully independent. Earlier these two and the other ten territories—with a population of more than 20,000,000—had voted to join the French Community. As members of the Community, they have complete control over internal affairs, but such matters as foreign policy, defense and currency are jointly controlled with France.

However, the greatest challenge to De Gaulle was the problem of Algeria—the very problem that had brought him to office. This North African territory—with an area about four times the size of France—is inhabited by 8,600,000 Muslims and about 1,000,000 Europeans (mostly of French descent). For the past five years, the Muslim nationalists have been waging a hit-and-run guerrilla war against the French. Their goal is complete independence from France. The rebellion in Algeria has cost thousands of lives and has been draining the French treasury at the rate of $3,000,000 a day.

Ever since De Gaulle came to power he has been trying to find a solution to the Algerian problem. Finally, on September 16, he unveiled his plan for ending the Algerian conflict. This plan called for the Algerians to decide their own future by "ballots, not bullets."

President de Gaulle spelled out these choices to the Algerians: (1) Secession, in which case France would pull out of Algeria and cease financial aid. (2) Integration. Algeria can become a fully integrated part of France, whereby Algerians could live and work in their homeland or in France and enjoy precisely the same political, economic and social rights as mainland Frenchmen. (3) Internal self-government. Under this choice, the Algerians would

Shaped like a giant A the new NATO headquarters in Paris is shown as it neared completion.

Charles de Gaulle, president of France, takes a salute with his predecessor, René Coty.

A 31-story tower dominates this new business and residential development, Westminster, London.

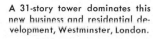

Heinrich Luebke, new president of West Germany, and his wife, center, are entertained in Bonn by the Federal Republic's first President, Theodore Heuss.

75

New Italian racing car of unique low design.

run their internal affairs completely but would receive French help in economic, educational, defense and foreign affairs.

But he insisted that first the rebellion must cease. De Gaulle promised to fix the date for voting on the three proposals "at the latest, four years after the restoration of peace."

For Britain 1959 was a year of unusual prosperity. For the first time in this century, the British earned more from exports than they spent on imports.

A Treasury report on Britain's economic health in mid-1959 showed gains in industrial output, exports, employment, consumer buying and worker productivity. Automobile production reached record levels. Despite these gains, there were no signs of inflation. Wages and prices remained stable. "It is clear," the Treasury report concluded, "that the economy is growing and that this expansion is likely to continue."

During the first eight months of 1959, the most popular sport in Britain was to guess the date of the national election. On September 8, Britain's Prime Minister, Harold Macmillan, ended this game. He announced that he had set October 8 as the date for the voting.

Under British law, national elections must be held at least every five years. But they may be held sooner if the prime minister so desires. The preceding election took place on May 26, 1955. Thus the following election could have been postponed until as late as May 26, 1960. However, Prime Minister Macmillan felt that October 8, 1959, was a more "convenient" time —that is, more convenient for his Conservative Party.

In Britain, as in the United States, there are only two major parties. They are the Conservative Party and the Labor Party. In the recent past, the lines between the parties were clearly drawn. The Labor Party stood for nationalization (govern-

ment ownership) of industry, and a wide program of social welfare. During their period in power, from 1945 to 1951, the Laborites nationalized coal, railways and other undertakings. They also increased social security and introduced a tax-supported national medical service.

It is an old Conservative habit to take over the opposition's program. In recent years, the Conservatives have adopted most of the Labor Party's welfare state and have even enlarged on it.

The Labor Party, for its part, has found that there is little "vote appeal" in further nationalization of industry when jobs are plentiful and wages are rising.

In international affairs, both parties support the Western alliance—but the Labor Party seemed to favor several "new" approaches in dealing with international problems.

The campaign in the 1959 election was waged mostly on domestic issues. The Conservatives "pointed with pride," while the Laborites "viewed with alarm." It all boiled down to the usual fight between the outs and the ins.

When the ballots were tallied on the night of October 8, it was found that the British people had given Prime Minister Macmillan a smashing personal triumph in one of the most decisive political battles of the postwar era. The Conservatives won their third straight victory. In 1951 and 1955 their margin had risen; this time they doubled their majority in the House of Commons. The party standings after the election were: Conservative 365, Labor 258 and Liberal 6.

West Germany continued to amaze the world with its spectacular prosperity.

Steel output—a rough measure of economic health—was at an all-time high, 10 per cent above the 1958 figure. Total exports were 5 per cent over 1958. Wages, too, were on the increase while the cost of living remained stable.

Prince Albert, heir presumptive to the Belgian throne, smiles at his bride, Italian Princess Paola, at their wedding in Brussels.

With more money in the consumer's pocket, retail sales continued to soar. Ownership of TV sets doubled in one year. The general prosperity of the country was also reflected in the money spent on foreign travel. During the first six months of 1959, West German tourists spent a billion marks (about $238,000,000) on vacations abroad—a 30 per cent increase over 1958.

What's more, West Germany was one of the few countries in the world with a labor *shortage!* Set against the 193,349 registered as jobless were 350,000 vacant jobs!

West Germany's problems were external—the Soviet threat to Berlin, the Soviet refusal to permit the reunification of West and East Germany.

On the domestic scene, there was one major political crisis in 1959. This was when President Theodor Heuss completed the two terms allowed by the West German constitution. Eighty-three-year-old Konrad Adenauer, who had been chancellor (prime minister) since the country became self-governing in 1949, announced on April 7 that he would resign from his office and seek election as president. (In West Germany the presidency is a ceremonial post.) Later, on June 5, he reversed his decision. Dr. Adenauer explained that the international situation was so tense that he preferred to remain chancellor.

Dr. Adenauer's change of mind caused a rift in his Christian Democratic Party. However, differences were soon patched up, and the party united on the candidacy of Dr. Heinrich Luebke, agriculture minister in Chancellor Adenauer's cabinet.

On July 1 the electoral college met in West Berlin and chose Dr. Luebke as president. He took office on September 15.

In Italy on February 6, Antonio Segni, sixty-eight, a Christian Democrat, succeeded Antonio Fanfani as premier. In the Netherlands the Catholic People's Party won a small margin over the Labor (Socialist) Party in a general election held on March 12. A few weeks later, Premier Jan Eduard de Quay, of the Catholic People's Party, formed a new coalition cabinet. It was the first Netherlands cabinet in twenty years to exclude the Labor Party.

In Ireland, New York-born Eamon de Valera, seventy-seven, was elected President on June 17. For twenty-one of the past twenty-seven years, he had served as Ireland's Prime Minister.

Overshadowing these developments in the various Western European countries was the crisis of Berlin—which threatened the peace of all Western Europe.

The crisis had begun the year before, on November 27, 1958, when Soviet Premier Nikita Khrushchev served notice on the

Western powers to withdraw their troops from West Berlin by May 27, 1959.

The West rejected Khrushchev's demand. For weeks East-West relations were tense. Then both sides agreed to hold a Big Four foreign ministers' conference to deal with West Berlin and the whole question of German reunification. United States Secretary of State Christian Herter, British Foreign Secretary Selwyn Lloyd, French Foreign Minister Maurice Couve de Murville and Soviet Foreign Minister Andrei Gromyko met in Geneva, Switzerland, on May 11.

The holding of the conference had one positive effect. The Soviets allowed their deadline of May 27 for the withdrawal of Western troops from West Berlin to pass without taking any action.

During the talks at Geneva, the West presented a plan that would unite West Berlin and communist East Berlin by free elections. Then, free elections in *all* Germany (both West Germany and communist East Germany) would unite the country. These elections would decide what kind of government a reunited Germany would have.

The Soviets, on their part, demanded that West Berlin become a "demilitarized" city and that Western troops be withdrawn. They insisted on separate peace treaties with East and West Germany and that the two German governments themselves decide on how and when—if ever—to reunite the country.

The West refused to accept the Soviets' plan. It would leave the two million people of West Berlin at the mercy of the Soviets and give the East German communist regime the power to block the formation of a united, democratic Germany.

The Soviets rejected the West's plan. They realized that under that plan Moscow would lose control of East Germany because, given the choice, the East Germans would vote against the Communists and in favor of a more democratic government.

The conference in Geneva went on for five weeks, recessed for three weeks and met for another three weeks. It finally broke up on August 5—without reaching an agreement.

But in its closing days a dramatic development occurred. It was announced on August 3 that Premier Khrushchev would visit President Eisenhower in the United States in September and that the President would later visit Khrushchev in the Soviet Union.

To allay any misgivings in Western Europe, the President made it clear that his talks with Khrushchev would be "exploratory rather than any attempt at negotiation" and that he would not commit Western European allies of the United States to any courses of action.

Prior to Khrushchev's arrival in the United States on September 15, President Eisenhower crossed the Atlantic for nine days of face-to-face talks with Chancellor Adenauer in Bonn, Prime Minister Macmillan in London, and President de Gaulle in Paris. The result was the forging of a unified Western position for dealing with the Soviets.

It was announced in early November that President Eisenhower would go to Paris after he completed a short tour of the Middle East and south Asia. On December 19 he would meet again with Macmillan, De Gaulle and Adenauer. The President's trip was considered necessary to ensure agreement by the major Western allies on the important issues before the summit meeting with Premier Khrushchev and before the President set out on his visit to the Soviet Union sometime in the spring.

As the year drew to a close there was a cautious feeling of optimism in Western Europe. It was hoped that perhaps the exchange of visits between Eisenhower and Khrushchev would prevent a war and lead to the easing of world tensions.

SOVIET EUROPE

By HARRISON E. SALISBURY
Correspondent, The New York Times

In the communist world of the Soviet Union and Eastern Europe the big event of 1959 was the beginning of a new pattern in relations between East and West.

It was a year that began in crisis with a Soviet ultimatum over Berlin. Before it closed, an extraordinary series of events had occurred, suggesting, as President Eisenhower phrased it, that the ice in the cold war had begun to melt a little.

The stage was set for the year's drama by Soviet Premier Khrushchev when he sent joint notes to the United States, Great Britain, France and East and West Germany calling for an end to the occupation status of Berlin.

The notes were sent off from Moscow on November 27, 1958. They fixed a deadline of six months in which action must be taken to end the "abnormal" status of Berlin. If action were not taken within that time period the Soviet Union threatened to sign a separate peace treaty with the East German Government and turn over all its rights, privileges and responsibilities in Berlin to the East Germans.

This action by Mr. Khrushchev was regarded in the Western countries as an ultimatum designed to oust the Western occupation forces from Berlin and a threat to West Berlin. Since West Berlin is an island within communist East Germany, access to and from the city has been guaranteed since the end of World War II by Allied four-power agreements. These agreements permit the West to use highways, railroads and air corridors to move in and out of West Berlin through East Germany.

The threat raised by Mr. Khrushchev hung over the world for months, although the Soviet Premier insisted that it was not an ultimatum. Some of the tension began to relax as negotiations went forward through diplomatic channels and finally culminated in a conference of the foreign ministers at Geneva.

During this period there was little of international note going forward in the East European communist countries.

Such countries as Rumania and Bulgaria seemed to be almost completely out of the picture. They played no role in the interplay of relations between East and West that centered around Berlin and Germany, and little of consequence occurred in their domestic relations.

For Bulgaria the event of the year was the resumption of diplomatic relations with the United States after a lapse of nine years. The United States had broken with Bulgaria in 1950 because Bulgaria falsely asserted that the United States Minister,

Donald Heath, was involved in a Bulgarian "purge" case. With the passing of the Stalinist era, the Bulgarians had publicly admitted that the charge was a false one and for several years had been seeking to restore relations with the United States. The agreement to resume relations was signed in March 1959, and official missions were re-established in July.

For Albania, a country with which the United States still does not maintain relations, it was also a year of comparative obscurity, marked only by a long visit by Premier Khrushchev of Russia in June. He traveled all over the country, originally scheduling himself to spend a fortnight there. He used his visit and Albania's nearness to Italy (just across the Adriatic Sea) and to Turkey and Greece (just to the east and south) to deliver sharp warnings to these countries about permitting the establishment of NATO rocket launching bases. He threatened that if the rocket sites were placed in such locations the Soviet Union would be compelled to establish counterbases. He implied that the bases would be in Albania, although he also noted that Soviet rockets have such range that there is great flexibility in choosing launching installations.

The Soviet Premier cut short his visit in Albania for a few days in order to stop off in Budapest and confer with Premier Ferenc Münnich. It was thought that Mr. Khrushchev hoped also to have a private meeting with Marshal Tito of Yugoslavia. But, whether or not this was his intention, the meeting did not come off.

Soviet relations with Yugoslavia through the year remained cool but correct. This was not true of relations between Albania and Bulgaria, on the one hand, and Yugoslavia, on the other. Yugoslav-Albanian relations deteriorated almost to the point of severance of diplomatic contacts. Abusive language was exchanged constantly between the Bulgarian and Yugoslav press.

For Hungary, too, the year was a quiet one. All of the Eastern European countries concentrated on domestic affairs. This brought about a slow but definite rise in the standard of living and in the total output of industry and agriculture. The improvement of living conditions was particularly marked in Czechoslovakia, where extensive efforts were made to increase exports of high-quality consumer goods, machine tools and heavy machinery. These sales were made not only to communist Eastern countries but also to the West.

During the year the Soviet Union made a special effort to improve and strengthen its relations with Poland. Because of her strategic location between Germany and Russia, Poland is always especially sensitive to any changes affecting Germany. The crisis over Berlin and Germany, provoked by Mr. Khrushchev, aroused alarm in Poland because Poland has large areas that were formerly German territory—for example, Silesia and part of East Prussia. (After World War II these were given Poland as compensation for eastern Polish regions ceded to the Soviet Union.) Poland deeply fears that a resurgent Germany will seek to recover these lost eastern territories. In an extensive midsummer tour of Poland, Mr. Khrushchev sought by means of personal diplomacy to assuage Polish fears and to establish a firmer and more friendly basis for Soviet-Polish relations. He made speeches throughout the country, both in industrial cities and in farming areas, stressing the durability of Soviet-Polish friendship, the reliability of Soviet guarantees to Poland and the superiority of the communist farming system.

The Khrushchev trip appeared to ease some of Polish Premier Gomulka's concern over the German situation. However, the Polish farmers were not enthusiastic about Soviet farming methods. Poland continued to be one country in the communist system where individual farming is the rule and

WIDE WORLD

Vice-President Richard Nixon receives an enthusiastic welcome from Polish crowds as he arrives in Warsaw for a short stay after his tour of the Soviet Union.

SOVFOTO

Soviet Premier Nikita Khrushchev and his host, Polish communist leader Wladyslaw Gomulka, view a new automatic mine-control system on their tour of mines in Silesia.

81

socialized farming is a rare exception.

Polish relations with the United States warmed as Vice-President Nixon visited Poland on his way home from his trip to Russia. His reception was almost hysterically enthusiastic, contrasting sharply with the stolidity and lack of enthusiasm that the Poles had shown for Mr. Khrushchev during his visit.

Mr. Nixon had the longest conversation with Premier Gomulka that any foreigner has ever held, with the exception of Mr. Khrushchev. The two men spent about six hours together, carefully reviewing every facet of Polish-American relations.

Unfortunately, the good feeling of the Nixon visit evaporated somewhat in a dispute that arose in the United Nations concerning elections to the Security Council.

The candidacy of Poland was advanced for a seat that had been held by Japan. The Western nations, including the United States, supported Turkey. The Poles contended that the seat had originally been allocated to Eastern Europe and that it rightfully belonged to that area. The United States disputed the Polish contention. Despite the United Nations controversy, however, over-all Polish-American relations showed marked improvement.

Against the backdrop of these events in Eastern Europe, affairs in the Soviet Union took a dramatic turn. Despite the continuing crisis over Berlin and Germany, a steady movement was evident in the policies of both the United States and Russia to ease in some way the harsh tension of the long cold war.

A view of the giant new furnace of the Lenin metal works at Diosgyör, Hungary.

A giant robot thrills a crowd of Russian children at a Moscow fair.

This was first made evident by the growing number of exchange visits on both sides in recent years. These exchanges were originally confined to professors, specialists and artistic groups. For example, the Bolshoi Ballet company of Moscow and the violinist David Oistrakh visited the United States, and the *Porgy and Bess* company, the New York Philharmonic and the pianist Van Cliburn toured Soviet cities.

A vast extension of this movement took place in 1959. The United States and the Soviet Union agreed to exchange national exhibitions. These were held in New York and Moscow during the summer. There was a marked increase in the importance and number of officials from each side visiting the other's country. First Deputy Premier Anastas Mikoyan toured the United States in January 1959. During the summer, First Deputy Premier Frol R. Kozlov came to the United States and Vice-President Nixon went to the Soviet Union for short but extensive tours.

Within the Soviet Union there was a marked relaxation of tension. The economy was working better, food crops improved, consumer goods were more plentiful and the activities of the police were sharply curtailed.

The Soviet Union was subjected to a virtual invasion of American tourists. More than fifteen thousand went to Russia during the year, the largest number to visit that country since the early 1930's.

All this tended to ease relations between Russia and the United States despite the fact that the foreign ministers, meeting in

American tourists stand in front of Leningrad's Hermitage museum.

Premier Khrushchev claps along with audience applauding one of his speeches.

Geneva, found themselves unable to work out any solution of the Berlin question.

At this point President Eisenhower invited Premier Khrushchev to the United States and agreed, himself, to make a return visit to the Soviet Union. With the announcement of the exchange of visits at the highest level there occurred a letup in Soviet propaganda against the United States. During Mr. Khrushchev's visit to America, for the first time in more than ten years, the Russian-language transmissions of the Voice of America were permitted to be heard in the Soviet Union without interference.

Mr. Khrushchev's visit to the United States was treated in the Soviet Union as a great success. His discussions with Mr. Eisenhower, their agreement on a possible summit conference, their decision that the President would go to Russia in the spring of 1960, their agreement on procedures for the Berlin Question—all were presented to the Soviet people as clearing the way for a basic reduction of world tension.

Reducing tension was a major preoccupation of Mr. Khrushchev's throughout the year because only by bringing the cold war to an end can he turn Soviet production to satisfying the urgent need and desire of the Russian people for better living.

The theme of overtaking and surpassing America in production, in standards of living, in "peaceful competition" was stressed again and again in this period. At the same time there was more emphasis upon the necessity for maintaining peace and for settling international disputes without force.

The year was marked by the meeting of the 21st Soviet Communist Party Congress. This meeting, however, produced none of the sensations or revelations of the 20th Congress, in February 1956, when Mr. Khrushchev made his famous speech exposing the crimes of the Stalin era. The congress devoted its attention chiefly to the new seven-year economic plan. One of its goals is to catch up with the United States in the production of meat, milk and dairy products. Another is the expansion of heavy industry to a point at which it would be fairly close to that of the United States on a quality basis, even if it still lagged far behind on a per capita basis.

These new lines of Soviet policy had an enthusiastic reception among the Soviet people, who, after more than forty years of hardship, sacrifice and threat, felt that they were beginning to draw nearer to a better day.

However, the outline of the new Soviet goals appeared to put some strain on Russia's relations with her great Far Eastern associate, China, which was carrying on a much more aggressive and inflexible policy in both domestic and foreign affairs.

The Soviet seemed to be using its influence to tranquilize the Chinese and to induce them to a more peaceable line of conduct. Russia offered to mediate in the border flare-up between India and China. Mr. Khrushchev promised to try and intervene with the Chinese regarding Americans still held prisoner there. When Mr. Khrushchev visited Peking after his tour of the United States his declarations were notably more peaceable and less aggressive than those of his Chinese comrades.

Of great long-range importance were new Soviet successes in the field of space exploration. Russia launched new space rockets. She hit the moon for the first time and then launched a satellite that orbited the moon and earth. Despite the energetic efforts of the United States, Russia was maintaining her lead in this field.

In domestic policy, in foreign policy, in scientific development and in international living standards much progress was made during 1959. The Soviet and its Eastern European satellites may well mark the year as their most successful and satisfying since the end of World War II.

THE
UNITED
STATES

By ALAN HARVEY SMITH
Associate Editor
The Americana Annual

For the United States the year 1959 was a difficult one to appraise. Many of the year's most important news stories concerned international matters and had to be written without endings. In most cases the endings could not even be accurately predicted. The answer to the crucial question of our time—whether the world would disarm itself or destroy itself—was not even in sight. Nevertheless the fear of mankind's self-destruction weighed heavily on world leaders in both the East and the West.

Throughout 1959 the United States sought the same basic foreign-policy goals as it had since the end of World War II. It strove to continue building the industrial and military might of free nations everywhere. For that purpose Congress furnished $3,255,000,000 for another year's foreign aid.

American foreign policy, President Eisenhower said in his State of the Union message of January 9, aimed at substituting the rule of law for rule by force. To be prepared, however, to meet the use of force, the United States continued to build its military attack and defense forces. At the same time the nation was seeking effective means to disarm itself and other nations of the world.

In one of these efforts the United States had, on October 31, 1958, joined Britain and the Soviet Union in a conference at Geneva, Switzerland. They sought to reach political agreement on prohibiting nuclear-test explosions. The discussions moved slowly into 1959 but fell short of success. In over a hundred sessions the conference hammered out seventeen of two dozen proposed articles for a treaty on the subject. The meetings eventually bogged down. Russia was unwilling to accept a proposal that would allow Western representatives to inspect her territory to detect whether nuclear explosions were taking place. Finally, on August 20, with no final success in sight, the meetings were recessed. Earlier in the month the three nations and France agreed to set up a new ten-nation group to attempt to achieve disarmament.

One hopeful sign was that none of the Big Three powers set off nuclear-test explosions during the year. The Soviet Union pledged not to conduct any tests so long as the West did not do so.

During Premier Nikita Khrushchev's visit to the United States the world looked forward to a speech he was to make to the United Nations on September 18. It was hoped that he would offer a workable solution to the problem of over-all disarmament. His remarks formed a sweeping proposal for complete disarmament of the nations of the world within four years. Because his plan was so broad and contained no practical provisions for enforcement, most Western observers were highly doubtful of its worth. They were, however, willing to study the proposals closely.

Another conference at Geneva was even more of a failure. This was a meeting of the foreign ministers of France, Britain and Russia, and of American Secretary of State Christian Herter. These diplomats met May 11 to search for a settlement of the Berlin crisis. This crisis had arisen out of a demand made by Soviet Premier Khrushchev on November 27, 1958. He insisted that the Allies pull their troops out of West Berlin. The Allies refused, fearing that the Soviet Union was preparing the way for West Berlin to become part of Communist East Germany. When no progress was made toward a solution of this problem, the meetings were recessed on June 20. After reassembling on July 13 the conference ended on August 5. The only agreement reached was that the talks had been "useful."

There was a significant improvement in relations between Russia and the United States in 1959. This was the growing exchange of visits between United States and Soviet citizens. Some fifteen thousand American tourists saw the U.S.S.R. in 1959. A large number of Soviet citizens

Russian dancers in wild moment of New York variety show.

visited the United States as members of cultural and scientific groups which were exchanging visits with similar American groups.

In the area of cultural exchanges the most distinguished Soviet offering was the famous Bolshoi Ballet which opened its American tour on April 16 at the Metropolitan Opera House. New York critics were enraptured with the great Russian ballerina Galina Ulanova. In July a Russian Music and Dance Festival was staged at Madison Square Garden in New York.

A major American triumph in Russia was the New York Philharmonic, conducted by Leonard Bernstein. Attracting enthusiastic praise, it completed its tour of Russia in mid-September. The most offbeat development in the cultural exchanges between the two nations was an unscheduled one. Two American Negro jazz-men tourists, Dwight Mitchell and Willie Ruff, staged an impromptu concert in Moscow's Tchaikovsky Conservatory. Featuring piano and bass fiddle, the two instrumentalists brought down the house with the hottest music yet heard in Russia.

The most important exchange visits were those between Russian and American political leaders. The first trip to the United States by a major Soviet official was that of First Deputy Premier Anastas I. Mikoyan in January. Six months later another First Deputy Premier, Frol R. Kozlov, arrived in New York to open the Soviet Exhibition of Science, Technology, and Culture on June 29. Both Russian leaders toured the nation. Each had personal talks with President Eisenhower and other American leaders about Russian-American relations.

Vice-President Richard M. Nixon in turn went to the Soviet Union in July to open the United States National Exhibition in Moscow. At the fair's official opening, on July 24, Soviet Premier Khrushchev and Nixon broke into an unplanned, vigorous, informal debate over the relative merits of

President Eisenhower meets Premier Nikita Khrushchev in Washington at the start of the Soviet leader's two-week, coast-to-coast tour.

THE NEW YORK "TIMES" BY GEORGE TAMES

the Russian and American ways of life. Their arguments delighted fairgoers and captured international headlines.

During his stay, Nixon visited five Russian cities and traveled 8,500 miles. He met with Khrushchev at various times for a total of over a dozen hours. He also delivered a Moscow address on television. Before his return to the United States he flew to Poland for a two-day visit.

But the biggest news story for Americans was the visit to the United States of Soviet Premier Nikita Khrushchev. A vigorous man, he took on the challenge of a grueling tour from September 15 to 27 with zest. He made East Coast stops in Washington and New York. On the West Coast he visited Los Angeles and San Francisco. Returning eastward he stopped in Iowa at Des Moines and on the Roswell Garst farm at Coon Rapids. There he renewed his acquaintance with Democratic leader Adlai E. Stevenson in a long talk. He then proceeded to Pittsburgh, Pennsylvania, where

he received the most cordial welcome of his trip. Finally at Camp David, Maryland, Khrushchev entered into two days of discussion with President Eisenhower and other American leaders. He left for Moscow on September 27.

On tour, Khrushchev delivered numerous major speeches, including one before the United Nations. He also engaged in frequent verbal fireworks at luncheons and dinners with newspapermen, businessmen, labor leaders and government officials.

At first, Americans received Khrushchev courteously but coldly. But after a chilly and confused reception in Los Angeles which seemed to anger him, he and the Americans he met warmed up. Generally Americans were curious about both the man and his views. He claimed constantly that he and the Russian people were interested only in peace. The Soviet Union, he insisted, wished above all to thaw out the cold war with the warmth of an era of peaceful competition between the United

States and Russia. His faith in communism was as granite. He was powerfully persistent that the Soviet economic and political system would ultimately triumph on a world-wide scale.

At short range the principal outcome of the Khrushchev visit was that tension between the Soviet Union and the United States was lessened. Although his discussions with President Eisenhower did not solve any outstanding issues between the two nations, they brought hope for an eventual solution without war. The Berlin problem remained a sore point. But the Soviet Premier seemed willing, for the time being, to forget his order for the Allies to leave the city. Negotiations were to be reopened on the future of the city and of divided Germany. There would likely be a summit conference of the American, Russian, British and French heads of government near the end of 1959 or early the following year. Another outcome of the meetings with President Eisenhower was an agreement that the President would return Khrushchev's visit and travel to the Soviet Union in the spring or summer of 1960.

Before receiving Khrushchev in Washington, President Eisenhower met in Europe with British, French and West German leaders to reassure them that no final agreements would be reached independently between the United States and the Soviet Union. On his ten-day tour of the Allied capitals, President Eisenhower achieved a personal triumph. He was warmly received by the leaders and people of each of the three nations. What he achieved in terms of specific understandings or agreements was unknown. It was, however, necessary for the President to reassure West German Chancellor Konrad Adenauer that the United States would not falter in supporting a free Berlin and West Germany. In France, Eisenhower faced the difficult task of persuading President Charles de Gaulle to raise his nation's contributions to the Western alliance to their former level. At the same time it was necessary for President Eisenhower to resist France's demand for a stronger voice in NATO (North Atlantic Treaty Organization). In Britain the President explained to Prime Minister Harold Macmillan his unwillingness to agree to a summit conference unless some good could be expected from it.

A hopeful international development of the year was the relative calm in most of the Middle East. To help preserve such stability the American Government on March 5 signed separate defense treaties with Iran, Turkey and Pakistan. In these accords the United States promised to "take such appropriate action, including the use of armed forces, as may be mutually agreed upon" to protect any or all of the nations against an attack. Besides assurances, these three Central Treaty Organization (formerly Baghdad Pact) nations received approximately half a billion dollars in economic aid from the United States during the year.

In the Far East, Chinese Communist guns pointing in the direction of Nationalist Chinese Taiwan were for the most part silent. But Chinese intervened in Tibet to overthrow the existing Government despite a treaty pledge not to do so. They also moved troops menacingly to and over India's borders.

But the most serious disturbance in Asia was a revolt in the kingdom of Laos. There communist rebels were seriously harassing government forces. The Laotian Government reported that the rebels were being furnished guns and were helped by troops from the bordering communist-controlled country of North Vietnam. The United States charged in the United Nations that Communist China, along with the Soviet Union, was co-operating with North Vietnam in these aggressive moves.

Starting in late August the American Government began airlifting military supplies to Laos in response to that country's request. Not long afterward a subcommittee representing the United Nations Security Council flew to Laos to investigate whether North Vietnam was guilty of aggression.

United States relations with its Western Hemisphere neighbors seemed generally to improve during the year.

President Eisenhower flew to St. Lambert, Quebec, to join Queen Elizabeth II in ceremonies dedicating the St. Lawrence Seaway on June 26. The next day the Queen and Vice-President Nixon dedicated the St. Lawrence hydroelectric power project at Massena, New York.

In Latin America the United States sped its efforts to build good will. Congress approved participation by the United States in the establishment of an Inter-American Development Bank. This institution, long desired by Latin American nations, would provide funds for the industrial and commercial growth of the area. The United States agreed to contribute slightly under half of the starting sum of one billion dollars to this fund.

During President Eisenhower's visit to Mexico in February, he and Mexican President Adolfo Lopez Mateos announced that the two countries would share in building Diablo Dam on the Rio Grande. The Mexican leader visited the United States in October.

The American space-satellite program went forward falteringly. Soviet engineers and scientists were still ahead of their American rivals in the rush to conquer

CRAWFORD IN THE NEWARK "NEWS" (N. J.)

MR. KHRUSHCHEV SEES THE U. S. A.

The Soviet Premier received the most extensive press coverage ever given a foreign visitor to the United States.

The new state of Hawaii's Representative Daniel K. Inouye is sworn in by Speaker of the House Sam Rayburn.

One of Hawaii's new senators, Oren Long, is welcomed to Washington by Nevada's Alan Bible and Alaska's Ernest Gruening.

space. The country's industrial machine, after picking up speed in the latter months of 1958, moved along through 1959 with growing rapidity. In the fall it threatened to slow down because of a strike in the steel industry.

An outstanding development of the year was President Eisenhower's more vigorous role in steering a course for the nation. Three factors contributed to this shift. One was the Chief Executive's restored physical vitality in a year free of any serious illness. Another was the resignation of Presidential Assistant Sherman Adams. With Adams gone the President found it necessary to exert his influence directly on domestic matters. The third was the death of Secretary of State John Foster Dulles, following which the President took full command of foreign policy.

Congress began its 1959 session on January 7. Democrats controlled 64 seats in the Senate to 34 for the Republicans. In the House there were 283 Democrats against 153 Republicans. Later in the year, after Hawaii held its first election as a state, Democrats picked up an additional seat in each branch and Republicans gained one Senate seat.

When Congress assembled, many observers expected that the big bloc of newly elected Democrats would work with liberal Republicans to take full charge of lawmaking and that President Eisenhower would have less influence on Congress than in previous years.

However, as the year moved on, the Democrats and their leaders increasingly followed, willingly or not, many of the President's wishes. The program finally legislated bore the conservative stamp of the Chief Executive.

The President constantly insisted on economy in the bills passed. He backed his stand for economy with vetoes of several measures. At other times he threatened to use a veto. In this manner he was able to force Congress to cut back some of its spending proposals before bills were finally written. Congress itself reduced some spending proposed by the President, while in other cases it succeeded in raising spending beyond his wishes.

Congress found it necessary to vote a record $82,000,000,000 for all government operations and programs during the year beginning July 1, 1959. Almost half of the voted total funds, or $40,000,000,000, went for defense purposes.

A number of measures that the Democratic majority had been expected to produce fell by the wayside. A long-awaited bill for Federal aid to education was never passed. Also defeated or sidetracked were measures approved for Federal financial help to "depressed" economic areas of the nation. Increased unemployment payments, higher minimum wages and further Social Security changes were sidetracked.

The major piece of social legislation that Congress succeeded in passing was a housing bill. President Eisenhower refused to sign two housing measures because he thought they were too expensive. He finally approved a revised bill which provided for 37,000 public-housing units to be built in a forty-year period. The law also continued for another year financial help for removal of slums and for improvement of city areas.

However, the President lost a fight with Congress in connection with another spending bill. He twice refused to sign a measure that proposed spending over a billion dollars on river and harbor improvements and other construction projects. He objected because the measure provided for sixty-

seven new projects for which the Administration had not budgeted. Congress mustered the required two-thirds vote to pass the measure over the President's second veto. For the first time a bill became law without Eisenhower's signature. Since taking office in 1953 he had vetoed 145 bills and had made every one of his vetoes stand.

One of the chief measures that Congress approved during the year was the Labor Reform Act of 1959. The need for a labor law in this field was dramatically unfolded by a Senate committee headed by John McClellan of Arkansas. After months investigating labor-management relations the committee turned up shocking evidence of corruption, lack of democracy, and violence in several labor organizations.

The Democratic leaders in Congress had expected to pass a labor bill introduced by Senator John Kennedy of Massachusetts and passed by the Senate. The House of Representatives preferred a tougher meas-

This simplified chart, based on one released by the Bureau of the Budget, shows where the Federal Government obtains revenue ($82,000,000,000 in 1959) and general areas where it is spent.

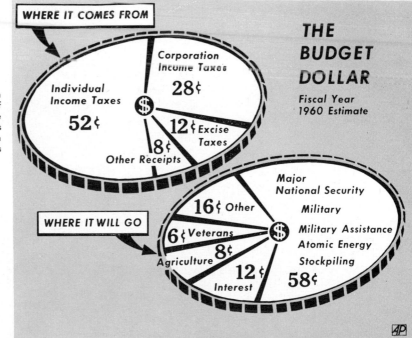

WHERE IT COMES FROM

THE BUDGET DOLLAR

Fiscal Year 1960 Estimate

Corporation Income Taxes 28¢

Individual Income Taxes 52¢

12¢ Excise Taxes

8¢ Other Receipts

WHERE IT WILL GO

16¢ Other

6¢ Veterans

Agriculture 8¢

12¢ Interest

Major National Security
Military
Military Assistance
Atomic Energy
Stockpiling
58¢

Senators on the Labor Rackets Committee; seated, from left, Sam Erwin, John McClellan, John Kennedy. Standing, on left, Carl Curtis, and right, Barry Goldwater.

ure of its own called the Landrum-Griffin bill. President Eisenhower went on radio and television asking the public to back the House measure. After a deadlock occurred in Congress, a fourteen-man Senate-House conference committee wrote a compromise very much like the stiffer House measure. The Senate passed the final bill with only two opposing votes and the House by a count of 352 to 52. The measure was the first major law dealing with labor since the Taft-Hartley Act of 1947.

The new law requires labor organizations to file regular financial reports and to reveal information as to how they operate. It forbids former convicts to hold union positions. A bill of rights written into the act is designed to protect workers in the ranks from abuses by their leaders. The law also places certain limitations on union activities during strikes.

Another major action of Congress was its approval of statehood for Hawaii. On March 11 the Senate voted 76 to 15 for admission of the territory to the Union. The next day the House gave its approval, 323 to 89. Residents of Hawaii voted overwhelmingly for statehood on June 27. President Eisenhower on August 21 formally declared Hawaii to be admitted to the Union. Alaska, which had gone through the formal

Former Atomic Energy Commissioner Lewis L. Strauss testifies before Commerce Committee of the Senate.

requirements for admission in 1958, was officially proclaimed a state on January 3, 1959. The first bill introduced in Congress to admit Hawaii to statehood dated back to 1921. The first for Alaska went back to 1916.

Congress increased the gasoline tax by a cent a gallon to help pay for the building of interstate superhighways. It went along with the President's request to raise the ceiling on the national debt to $295,000,-000,000.

Two bills were of interest to veterans or future veterans of the armed services. One set up a new schedule of payments for all disabled veterans and their dependents. Another extended the military service program for another four years.

Congress showed its greatest independence of the President's influence in acting on his appointments. In June the Senate refused to accept the appointment of Lewis L. Strauss as secretary of commmerce after a long bitter fight.

Two important rulings by the Supreme Court redefined earlier decisions that had aroused strong criticism. One ruling seemed to indicate that the court was not going to keep as tight a rein on Congressional investigations as had been expected. A second judgment assured state governments that they had the right to pass laws against sedition. (Sedition is the advocating of resistance to government authority to such a degree that it may lead to revolution.)

In another ruling the court struck down a Federal security program. The court reasoned that the program deprived accused persons of certain protections that neither Congress nor the President had indicated should be denied them.

The most sensitive social problem of 1959 continued to be the question of mixing Negro and white pupils in schools.

At the start of the 1959 school year fifteen additional school districts were permitting Negroes and whites to attend the same classes. One of these districts, however, was the first in Florida to do so. Only five states now remained in which all public schools were segregated. These were Alabama, Georgia, Louisiana, Mississippi and South Carolina.

The year's major victories for school integration were won in Virginia and Arkansas. In Virginia the movement of "massive resistance" to the integration of public schools crumbled. In Arkansas two of Little Rock's high schools were opened to classes of both whites and Negroes. Local police authorities were able to handle the resulting disturbances.

In another civil-rights development, Congress extended the life of the Federal Civil Rights Commission for two years.

In 1959 the United States moved away from the recession of the previous year. The nation's economy was brought to high levels in early summer. Only the long strike in the steel industry slowed it down.

An indication of good times was that Americans were, by summer, spending their earnings at a record rate. One of the principal items they were buying was an automobile. Automobile output reached an annual rate of 6,135,000 cars and 200,-000 trucks in the first seven months of 1959. This production rate was substantially up from 1958 levels.

Ford's Falcon at the end of its assembly line. It competes with GM's Corvair, Chrysler's Valiant, Studebaker-Packard's Lark and American Motor's Rambler in the compact-car field.

Another sign of prosperity was the increased amount of building. In the first half of 1959, 690,000 new homes were started, compared with 515,000 in the similar period of 1958. Large sums of money were also spent on new factories and office buildings and on new equipment.

Employment took a big spurt from mid-March to mid-April and continued to rise. The number of employed workers in July reached 67,594,000. This all-time high was above the July 1958 total by 2,415,000. Unemployment, however, remained a disturbing problem. It was estimated that in the fall seven of every hundred persons who had lost jobs during the bad times of late 1957 and early 1958 were still out of work.

The general improvement in the economy did not extend to farmers. At harvest-time, crop output for the year was expected to come near the record 1958 high. Nevertheless, farm earnings were expected to drop since farm prices were down 4 per cent from 1958 levels.

Living costs held fairly steady from the spring of 1958 through March 1959. In early autumn, families were paying $1.01 for goods that sold for $1.00 a year earlier.

Just as the nation seemed to be pushing on toward new prosperity, a number of strikes broke out that noticeably hurt the nation's economy. Walkouts hit steel and glass manufacturing plants; copper, lead, and zinc mines; and East and Gulf coast ports. In early October over a million workers were on strike, including 500,000 steelworkers.

The steel and shipping strikes were the most serious. When dock workers quit their jobs because of dissatisfaction over wages and fear of greater use of automation on the docks, cargo ships could not be loaded or unloaded. Because the thickly populated eastern-coast areas depend heavily on water commerce for their food, President Eisenhower took emergency action on October 6, five days after the strike started. He used a provision of the Taft-Hartley Act to start procedures that would return workers to their jobs for eighty days while further attempts at settlement were made.

The steel strike began on July 15 and remained unsettled in October. The steel union sought a substantial rise in wages and other benefits. Management wanted greater control over factory-work practices to improve efficiency. After months of off-and-on-again bargaining between the two sides, President Eisenhower became dissatisfied with the lack of progress. He launched Taft-Hartley proceedings to return the workers to their jobs and to revive needed production of steel.

Striking longshoremen watch a liner leaving its berth. Their strike tied up all Atlantic and Gulf Coast ports until a court ordered an eighty-day cooling-off period.

On November 9 the Supreme Court decreed that the Taft-Hartley Act could be brought to bear on the strike. The court upheld an injunction ordering the 500,000 steelworkers back to their jobs for eighty days.

Despite the Supreme Court's action there was concern that the strike that had lasted 116 days already would be continued in January when the eighty days were over. There was no sign that the union and the majority of the steel companies were even near an agreement. They were still disputing the steel companies' demand for greater control over local work rules (scheduling of relief periods and the size of work crews for particular jobs). Whatever the ending the nation was the loser.

As a presidential election lay ahead, professional politicians and public-opinion polls agreed that Vice-President Nixon was most likely to be the Republican candidate in 1960 for president. His nearest rival was Governor Nelson Rockefeller of New York.

In Democratic ranks public-opinion polls showed Senator John Kennedy of Massachusetts to be leading for his party's nomination. Other leading candidates were Senators Stuart Symington of Missouri, Lyndon Johnson of Texas and Hubert Humphrey of Minnesota. Adlai Stevenson indicated that he did not want to run for a third time, but some observers felt that, willingly or not, he would emerge a contender before the conventions were held.

Strike break: Nickolas P. Veeder of Granite City Steel and David McDonald of the United Steelworkers after signing new pact.

Kaiser Steel workers go back to work at the Fontana, California, plant. Most of rest of the steel industry remained strikebound.

New Flags of the World

By STEPHEN RUDDY

SINCE the end of the second World War many areas have achieved independence and become nations. One of the important signs of their new status is the flags that fly over them.

These new banners are symbols of great political and social changes. The changes have brought independence to more than 600,000,000 people; they have also swept countless other millions into communist rule.

Here is a brief run-down by regions of how the twenty-seven flags you see here came into being.

Europe. Although Iceland was considered a sovereign state from 1918 it remained united with Denmark through the Danish crown until 1944.

North America. Ten British Caribbean island colonies joined in a federation called the West Indies in 1958.

The Middle East. The United Arab Republic was formed from the union of Egypt and Syria in 1958. The state of Israel came into being in 1948 after years of effort by Jews all over the world. The tiny desert kingdom of Jordan was formed out of the British mandate of Trans-Jordan in 1946. Lebanon, a French mandate, achieved independence in 1944.

Asia. The great European empires broke up after the war. The British Empire based on the Indian subcontinent became a series of independent nations that, save for one (Burma), freely stayed in the Commonwealth of Nations. India, Pakistan and Ceylon became independent in 1947-48; Burma in 1948; The Federation of Malaya

in 1957. The French Empire split into four units after the cruel and inconclusive war fought in Indochina. French Indochina was divided into North Vietnam (communist-ruled) and South Vietnam. The rest of the territory became the independent kingdoms of Cambodia and Laos. Korea, occupied by Soviet and United States troops after World War II, split along the Korean war armistice line into North and South Korea. The Dutch Empire (Netherlands East Indies) became the Republic of Indonesia in 1949 after a hard-fought war stopped by the United Nations. The Philippines, after more than forty years of rule by the United States, became a republic in 1946. Mongolia, the ancient home of the Mongols of Kublai Khan, became a Soviet-sponsored state, the Mongolian People's Republic, in 1945.

Africa. The tides of nationalism that ended colonialism in Asia were not long in coming to Africa. The French protectorate of Morocco became sovereign in 1956 as did Tunisia. Libya was formed from Italy's former north African empire in 1951. Sudan after being under Anglo-Egyptian rule became independent in 1956. The Federation of Rhodesia and Nyasaland was formed from a self-governing British colony and two British protectorates. Although not fully self-governing it hopes to become so by 1961. On Africa's west coast two Negro nations have emerged. Ghana, which was formerly the British Gold Coast, became free in 1957; and Guinea, in 1958 after voting not to join the new French Community.

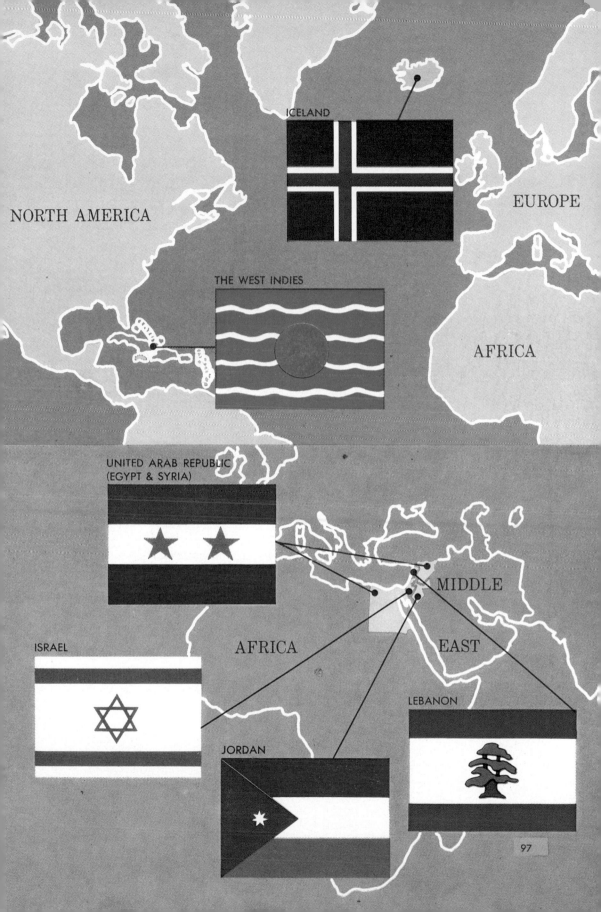

NORTH AMERICA

EUROPE

AFRICA

ICELAND

THE WEST INDIES

UNITED ARAB REPUBLIC
(EGYPT & SYRIA)

MIDDLE

EAST

AFRICA

ISRAEL

JORDAN

LEBANON

97

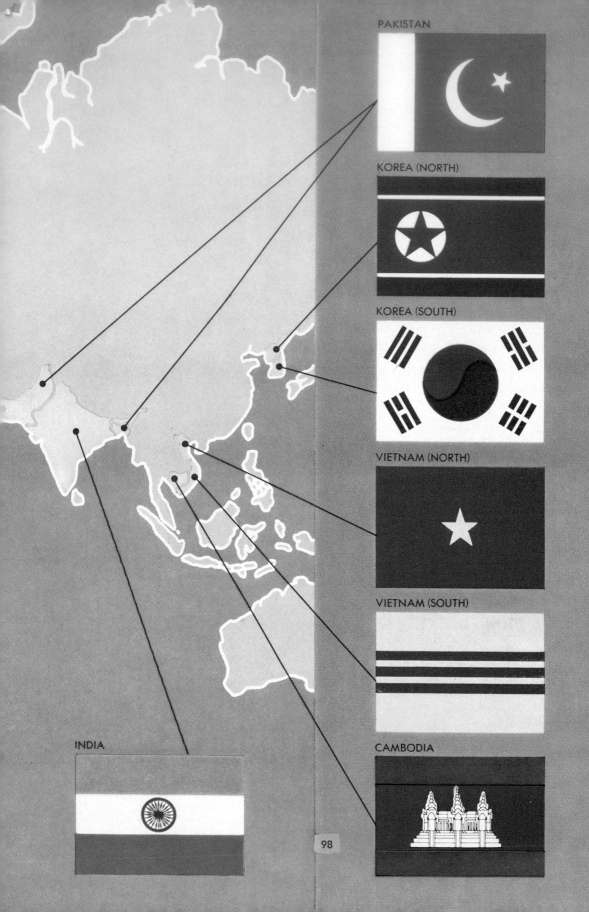

PAKISTAN

KOREA (NORTH)

KOREA (SOUTH)

VIETNAM (NORTH)

VIETNAM (SOUTH)

INDIA

CAMBODIA

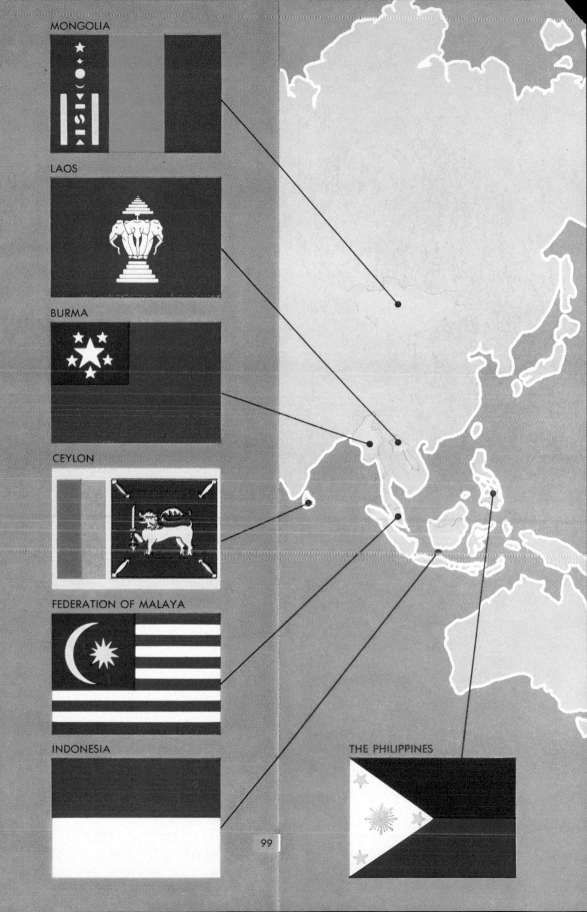

MONGOLIA

LAOS

BURMA

CEYLON

FEDERATION OF MALAYA

INDONESIA

THE PHILIPPINES

99

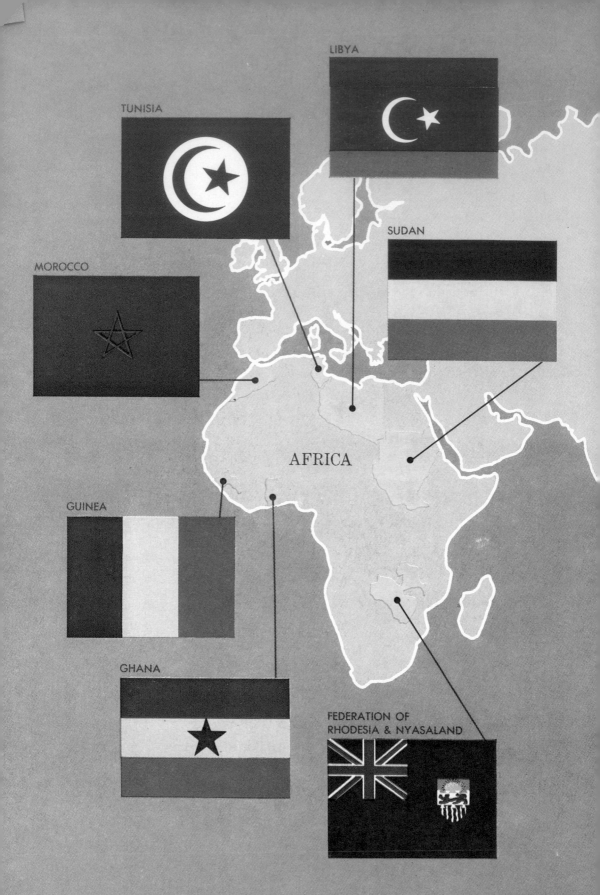

LIBYA

TUNISIA

SUDAN

MOROCCO

AFRICA

GUINEA

GHANA

FEDERATION OF
RHODESIA & NYASALAND

J.E.D.Stuve

BLAU-PIX

Prime Minister Macmillan

By ROBIN MILLER

Author and Journalist

W HEN Harold Macmillan drove to Buckingham Palace on January 10, 1957, to be offered the post of prime minister and first lord of the treasury by Queen Elizabeth II, Britain was facing her most serious national and international crisis since the war. With the notable exception of Winston Churchill in 1940, no British prime minister of recent times has taken up his appointment under less favorable circumstances.

Macmillan's predecessor, Sir Anthony Eden, had just resigned amid a storm of criticism over the Anglo-French invasion of the Suez Canal. At home the opposition Labor Party was making political hay out

of the uproar which had split the Conservative Party. Even more serious, the attack had caused a rift between Britain and the United States, damaged Britain's prestige throughout the world and temporarily crippled her delicately balanced economy.

With the exception of Lord Privy Seal Richard Austen Butler (who aroused violent opposition in some quarters), Macmillan was the only possible candidate. Even so, many people considered that the combination of his notoriously acid tongue and Edwardian appearance would hamstring the new prime minister and eventually prove another disaster for the Government.

Today, only three years later, Harold Macmillan has turned possible disaster into a series of triumphs. Under his leadership Anglo-American co-operation has been re-

101

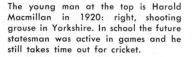

The young man at the top is Harold Macmillan in 1920: right, shooting grouse in Yorkshire. In school the future statesman was active in games and he still takes time out for cricket.

stored and has seldom been closer; British policy has regained its prestige; the pound sterling is now almost freely convertible into hard currencies, including dollars; and the United Kingdom's standard of living has soared.

Much of this success can be attributed to Macmillan's confidence in the face of disaster. He has always had this quality. As a young Grenadier Guards lieutenant in World War I Macmillan was wounded in no man's land. At dawn, when the stretcher party found him, he was calmly reading Horace in the original Latin. Nearly forty years later, in 1951, as Conservative minister of housing and local government he announced that he would build 300,000

houses a year. The Labor Party declared that his goal was impossible. Macmillan proved them wrong by building even more.

When Macmillan became prime minister, he tackled the formidable job of putting Britain's house in order with the same confident spirit. No government of recent times, Conservative or Labor, has dared such politically unpopular moves. In 1958, for instance, Macmillan pushed the long overdue repeal of the Rent Act through Parliament. Although there was great opposition to this from organized tenant groups, it finally removed rent controls set in 1939 from one million homes, allowing landlords to charge realistic rents and improve their properties. As chancellor of the exchequer,

The Prime Minister dances with his wife, Lady Dorothy, at a party for Young Conservatives.

The P.M.'s Diplomatic Travels

In Bermuda with President Eisenhower.

In Paris with President Charles de Gaulle.

In Moscow with Premier Nikita Khrushchev.

his credit squeezes and cuts of government expenditure earned him the nickname of Mac the Knife. Recently, his budgets have provided tax relief for all income groups to encourage free enterprise.

Macmillan has kept a good balance between the welfare state to which the great majority of Britons are committed and the encouragement of an economy free from government controls which is the basis of his party's policy. He has instituted a vigorous campaign for building better schools and training new teachers. And he has pushed Britain's urgently needed nuclear-power program ahead at full speed. Possibly Macmillan's most revolutionary move was his recent (1958) campaign urging workers to buy shares in their industries. These forward-looking policies anticipated most of Labor's claims for the next elections. A pre-election British cartoon showed Hugh Gaitskell, leader of the Labor Party, looking sourly at posters showing Macmillan as the star of a one-man revue. The caption read: "I hate his program— but I wish it was mine."

In foreign policy Macmillan has adopted the usual British policy of trying to coexist with powerful hostile powers. Although he has ranged Britain firmly alongside the United States on major issues, he has left no stone unturned in his efforts to meet the Russians halfway wherever possible. His trip to Moscow in 1959 and his subsequent visits to confer with President Eisenhower, President de Gaulle, and Chancellor Adenauer laid the foundations for the foreign ministers' conference at Geneva in May 1959. Macmillan's greatest diplomatic successes so far have been rebuilding cordial relations with President Eisenhower and other United States leaders and the compromise settlement of the difficult Cyprus problem.

Part of his ability to get along well with Americans may be due to the fact that, like Churchill, Macmillan is half-American by birth. His mother, Helen Artie Belles, was a native of Spencer, Indiana. In Paris she met Maurice Crawford Macmillan, a successful publisher and son of a once poor Scottish tenant farmer. Harold Macmillan was born on February 10, 1894.

Young Macmillan won scholarships to Eton and Balliol College, Oxford, where he emerged as a brilliant orator. After World War I he served briefly as aide-de-camp to the Duke of Devonshire, then governor general of Canada. In 1920 he married one of the Duke's daughters, Lady Dorothy Cavendish. They have one son and three daughters. This marriage connected Macmillan with the politically powerful Cecil and Cavendish families, many of whom were—and still are—diplomats and members of Parliament.

Macmillan's subsequent career was the best possible training for the prime ministry. In 1924 he was elected Conservative member of Parliament for Stockton-on-Tees and represented that constituency 1924-29 and 1931-45. From 1940 to 1945 Macmillan also held successive appointments as parliamentary secretary to the ministry of supply, parliamentary undersecretary of state for the colonies, British resident minister at Allied headquarters in northwest Africa and diplomatic representative with the French Committee of Liberation. He was also British member and chairman of the Advisory Council for Italy (he was present with General Eisenhower when the Italian armistice was signed) and secretary of state for air.

In 1944 Macmillan supervised negotiations to settle the Greek civil war and, since the end of World War II, he has been active in furthering European unity and co-operation. In 1955 he was appointed Anthony Eden's foreign secretary. In December of the same year he became chancellor of the exchequer, and thirteen months later he succeeded Anthony Eden as prime minister.

Since his appointment Macmillan has done a remarkable job of selling his aims and methods, and those of his party, to the British people. The high degree of his success became strikingly apparent in the general election of October 1959. The Conservative Party was returned to power with a nearly doubled majority in Parliament.

Today, there is no doubt about Macmillan's personal popularity. The man who used to be dubbed Old Mothballs is now known affectionately as Mac from John o'Groat's to Land's End.

The first impression of Macmillan as a dandified, sleepy-eyed aristocrat of the old school has given way to that of a vigorous, progressive and inspiring leader.

Pope John XXIII

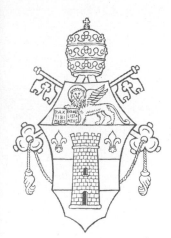

KARSH, OTTAWA—PIX; COAT OF ARMS, WIDE WORLD

By GEORGE ARMSTRONG
Rome Correspondent

O N October 28, 1958, around six in the evening, Nicola Cardinal Canali appeared on the balcony facing St. Peter's Square. In Italian-accented Latin he proclaimed to the thousands of people waiting below: "We have a Pope, and he is to be called John the Twenty-third!" Then Angelo Giuseppe Roncalli appeared, to greet the crowd and to give it his first papal blessing.

To the thousands in the square and to the millions then watching him on television, the new head of the Roman Catholic Church appeared to be short, plump and easygoing. To the dozens of writers and diplomats who specialize in Vatican affairs the new Pontiff seemed a Pope "of transition and compromise."

By "compromise" they meant that Roncalli, who was not one of the leading candidates at the beginning of the three-day conclave, had apparently been elected as a compromise choice. In speaking of "transition," they were referring to Roncalli's age (seventy-six at the time of the election). It was presumed that the pontificate could not be a very long one. The aged Pope would be a sort of stand-by, largely inactive, holding the position for a successor who might happily come to the throne at a less critical moment of the world's history.

The people in the square that night did not know that after Cardinal Roncalli said his "Accepto" (I accept) he had made four decisions that showed the Sacred College of Cardinals that behind his affable manner was a knowledge of church history, a readiness to command, and a willingness to thrust church machinery into high gear.

He has said that he chose the name of John because it was his father's name and

Student priest   Army sergeant

because he was baptized in St. John's Church in his home town of Sotto il Monte, near Bergamo. But he also knew that a fifteenth-century antipope (pretender to the papal throne) had called himself John XXIII. For a real pope to bear the name would not only set the record straight but restore the sturdy, straightforward name to good standing.

Pope John's second decision was to restore a tradition that his four immediate predecessors had allowed to lapse. As he removed his cardinal's zucchetto to replace it with the white papal cap, he put his cap on the head of Alberto di Jorio, the priest who was serving as secretary of the conclave, making him a cardinal on the spot.

His third decision was to inform the cardinals that the conclave was to be maintained until the following morning despite the discomfort of the makeshift conclave lodgings. This decision made it clear to all that the new Pope intended to start at once his active service.

His fourth decision was important for the future administration of the Holy See. John announced that he would resume the regular audiences with the heads of the various congregations (similar to cabinet ministers in a lay state). Since the illness of Pope Pius XII in 1954, these audiences had been suspended.

Pope John was born November 25, 1881. He is the son of a sharecropper. His three surviving brothers now own and still work their father's farm in Lombardy. The Roncallis were not impoverished but there was never an abundance of anything when

Angelo was a child. Pope John has said "There are three ways for a man to ruin himself: women, gambling, and farming. My father chose the most uninteresting of the three." The Pope has some eighteen nephews and nieces who, altogether, form a typical lower-middle-class Italian family: one is a priest, two are nuns, one is unemployed, one is married to a Communist. Though the family has been received in the papal apartments since "Uncle Angelo" became Pope, all have returned to their former work. This will be the first time in recent church history that a new pope's relatives have neither borne nor been given noble titles.

At the age of eleven, after receiving his early education from the parish priest, Angelo Roncalli was admitted to the seminary in Bergamo. He was bright enough to be invited to Rome to complete his studies and was ordained there in 1904. He returned then to Bergamo where Bishop Radini-Tedeschi took him on as secretary. The Bishop was famous in Italy for his active part in the budding labor movement, and Father Roncalli's political character was probably formed in those years. He holds the memory of Radini-Tedeschi in great admiration and has written a five-hundred-page biography of the Bishop.

In 1915 the young priest was drafted into the Italian Army, given sergeant's stripes and assigned to the medical corps. The next year he was promoted to lieutenant and was made a chaplain.

After the war, he began to make a name for himself by organizing the first student

Preparing for an official picture, Pope John listens to some instructions given him by famous Canadian photographer Karsh.

Newly elected Pope

The Pope among His People

He visits a jail on a tour of Rome.

Blessing a helicopter in the Vatican.

He greets a young missionary student.

107

hostel (Casa dello Studente) in Italy and one of the first Catholic women's clubs.

In 1921, Roncalli was ordered to Rome to work with the Sacred Congregation for the Propagation of the Faith, and four years later Pius XI saw him consecrated bishop and gave him the appointment of apostolic visitor to Bulgaria. He began there his twenty-eight-year career as a Vatican diplomat, the major part of which he spent in non-Roman Catholic areas.

In 1935, he was transferred to Ankara and given the title of Apostolic Delegate to Turkey and to Greece. He remained there until 1944. It was during these years that the future Pontiff acquired his knowledge of the Eastern Churches, knowledge that he will find useful when he convokes an Ecumenical Council in 1961. The announced purpose of this council, the first to be called since 1869-70, is to seek the "reunion of separate Christian bodies."

Archbishop Roncalli was recalled to Rome in 1944 and given the difficult post of Papal Nuncio to Paris. This assignment required considerable diplomacy because the previous nuncio had been accused in some French circles of undue friendship with the Vichy government. When he left Paris in 1953, a cardinal, the Catholic hierarchy had regained the esteem of the French people, and Roncalli had restored good relations between the Vatican and Paris.

From 1953 until his election as Pope, Cardinal Roncalli was Patriarch of Venice, his first pastoral post. Any Venetian will tell you that it was a role that suited him well. Romans have found their new Pope a good pastor, too. In the first year of his reign he left the Vatican more often than any pope since 1870. There are few Romans who cannot claim to have seen the new Pope touring through the city and the countryside, on his way to visit the city jail or an orphanage or a sick friend.

Though Pope John has shown himself an observer of church tradition, he does not consider himself bound by all the laws of his predecessors (and theoretically is not). Sixtus V (1585-90) ruled that there should never be more than 70 cardinals and there never were until 1958. Two weeks after his coronation Pope John nominated 22 new cardinals, giving the College a plenum of 75.

The only representative from a Soviet-dominated country to come to Rome for the 1958 conclave was the Polish Cardinal, Stefan Wyszynski. At John's request, Wyszynski stayed behind in Rome for several months, the two men meeting on a number of occasions. Wyszynski, who had been imprisoned for several years by the Communists, is considered an advocate of coexistence between the church and the Polish communist Government. For this reason, he has been regarded with some suspicion in certain quarters. However, Polish Catholics enjoy more freedom than those in other countries of the Soviet bloc, and when Wyszynski left Rome he left with praise from the Pope for his peacemaking work.

The situation of the Catholic Church in China and in Hungary, on the other hand, caused the Pope to make his strongest remarks of his first year, even using the dreaded word "schism" to describe the efforts of the two communist governments to appoint their own clergy.

Italian politics, by geography and by tradition, have been the concern of all popes. Pope John's election was regarded with warm approval by many liberal Catholics. Italian Socialists recall that during their party's annual convention, held in Venice three years ago, Cardinal Roncalli had welcoming proclamations hung on every church door in his diocese. Since then the Pope has shown he will hew to no one political line. Now that he has become "pastor to the whole world" (to use his own words), the world has seen John XXIII to be a warm, shrewd and tolerant shepherd to his flock.

Dr. Thomas A. Dooley

By HOWARD A. RUSK, M.D.
Associate Editor, The New York Times

Tom Dooley was a St. Louis, Missouri, boy with a dream—a dream that has grown so large that some day it may help to relieve the suffering of millions of people all over the world.

When Tom Dooley was a high-school student, he selected medicine as a career because he felt that that was the most direct way in which he could help other people. At the age of seventeen he became a Navy medical aide. His two years of service intensified his determination to become a doctor.

After his discharge from the Navy, Tom Dooley completed his premedical training at the University of Notre Dame and studied for a while at the Sorbonne in Paris. In 1953 he was graduated from the St. Louis University School of Medicine and rejoined the Navy for his internship as a lieutenant, junior grade. It was at this time that he had the experience that set the future course of his life.

After the French fortress of Dien Bien Phu in North Vietnam fell to the communist invaders from the north, Dr. Dooley was assigned by the Navy to a refugee camp in Haiphong. Through this camp more than 600,000 persons escaped from communist North Vietnam to freedom in South Vietnam.

Accustomed only to the high standards of health and medical care of the United States, Dr. Dooley was shocked by the amount of preventable disease that plagued the refugees.

He threw himself into the task of treating the sick with such extraordinary effect

109

Dr. Dooley, Dwight Davis and Earl Rhine leave Bangkok on the long journey to the village of Nam-tha, to set up a clinic for 40,000 Laotians.

that he became the youngest officer in the history of the medical corps to receive the United States Legion of Merit decoration and he was given South Vietnam's highest award by President Ngo Dinh Diem.

Released from the Navy in 1956, he returned to the United States. Meanwhile, he had written his first book, *Deliver Us from Evil,* which was a best seller and was condensed by the *Reader's Digest.*

For Tom Dooley the thought of settling down to a prosperous private practice at home was now impossible. He had seen the sick and the dying in southeast Asia and he knew that his place was with them. Using his own funds, contributions and the generous help of United States drug companies, he returned to southeast Asia to build a village hospital in the Kingdom of Laos. With the help of his three former corpsmen he proved to the Laos people deep in the jungle what men of good will and skill could do to prevent sickness and death.

He came back to the United States, in 1957, to raise more money for his jungle hospital. On this trip he met Dr. Peter D.

Comanduras, a Washington specialist and medical professor. Dr. Comanduras had seen the medically underprivileged in other lands and had the idea of starting an organization that would send American doctors, technicians and drugs to any part of the world where medical treatment was needed. Together Dooley and Comanduras, who became its secretary-general, formed MEDICO (Medical International Cooperation Organization) in February 1958. Within a year and a half, MEDICO was operating or supporting hospitals and providing specialists for eight countries.

The idea of MEDICO, a nongovernmental and nonsectarian organization, has already been tested and proved successful by Dr. Albert Schweitzer, in Africa, and Dr. Gordon Seagrave, "the Burma Surgeon." There are hundreds of millions of people in Asia, Africa and Latin America who, in the normal course of events, would never see a doctor. In some of these areas the ratio of doctors to people is one to 200,000.

More than one thousand American doctors have offered to go overseas for MED-

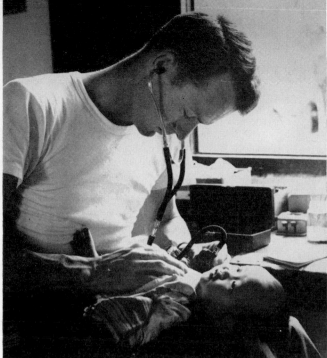

Tom Dooley and MEDICO are saving the lives of many babies in the remote villages of Laos.

The doctor, convalescent after his operation, looks at a photo of rebel prisoners in Laos.

ICO and many more thousands can, undoubtedly, be enlisted.

In 1957 Dr. Dooley remained in the United States raising money for MEDICO and writing a second book, *The Edge of Tomorrow*. He then returned to Laos to open his third hospital. The two others he had set up were turned over to the Laos Government for operation by people Dooley had trained.

To appreciate Dr. Dooley's devotion to his self-appointed task we must keep in mind all that he gave up to do it. The son of a family in comfortable circumstances, his personality, intelligence and drive could have brought him prominence and wealth as a doctor in the United States, with all the comforts and luxuries that go with such a position.

Dr. Schweitzer, the medical missionary whose work in Africa is known throughout the world, has long been an inspiration to Dr. Dooley. Of Schweitzer he has written, "One of Doctor Schweitzer's most important concepts is that of the Fellowship of Those Who Bear the Mark of Pain. I and my men have found this Fellowship wherever we have gone. Who are its members? Doctor Schweitzer believes the members are those who have learned by experience what physical pain and bodily anguish mean. These people, all over the world, are united by a secret bond. He who has been delivered from pain must not think he is now free, at liberty to continue his life and forget his sickness. He is a man whose eyes are opened. He now has a duty to help others in their battles with pain and anguish. He must help to bring to others the deliverance which he himself knows."

Dr. Dooley considers himself a privileged man to be able to turn his back on the comforts of civilization and to show kindness to people who have almost forgotten what it is. In one of his letters from Laos he wrote, "Keep your ears tuned to the 'still sad music of humanity.' Count your blessings . . . the blessings of America. My thanks to the hundreds who write to me. How fortunate I really am. I know why I am here. The essence of a man, the sheer justification for his existence is to be found in his consideration of his fellow man . . . his love of his brother. The whole concept of our world is based on this. You remind me of this. And my heart easily finds it morning."

He has constantly voiced his deep appreciation to those who have helped him and the whole MEDICO program. His appreciation of the work of his colleagues in Laos is enormous.

They may not yet have mastered the language of Laos; they have not yet learned all about medicine; but the language of their compassion, understood by all, pours forth its unconscious eloquence. They give much and do not know that they give at all.

His is a sublime confidence that the brotherhood of man will triumph. In another letter from Laos he writes, "I am positive that the human spirit can rise supreme; that man can develop the feeling of oneness with other men. All beings of blood and breath are brothers, here to help one another."

Dr. Dooley returned to the United States for surgery in August 1959, when it was discovered he had cancer of the chest. After his operation and a nationwide speaking tour he returned to Laos about the middle of December 1959.

Dr. Dooley has been widely cited for his great work. In 1956 he was named by the Junior Chamber of Commerce as one of the ten outstanding young men in America; he has received a Man of the Year Award from the Catholic Youth Organization, the Christopher Award for literature and the Mutual of Omaha Criss Award for his services to humanity. In addition, he has been given two honorary degrees.

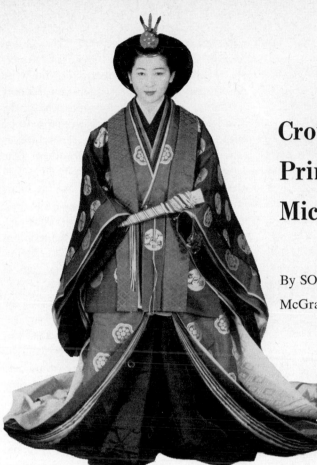

Crown Princess Michiko

By SOL SANDERS
McGraw-Hill World News, Tokyo

CROWN PRINCESS MICHIKO, the young lady who will one day be empress of Japan, was born a commoner. She will be the first empress in the history of the Japanese royal family (which according to legend goes back more than 2,500 years) who was not a member of the nobility.

Michiko-san was born in October 1934 and is the elder daughter in the family of Hidesaburo Shoda, a wealthy flour-milling company executive. Michiko (which in Japanese means "daughter of beauty and wisdom") has four brothers and one younger sister. The family is a distinguished one. An uncle of the Crown Princess is president of Osaka University, another is a professor at Tokyo University, a third is an officer of the Mitsubishi Bank.

Michiko-san is 5 feet 4 inches tall and weighs 114 pounds. Her heavy, black hair is naturally wavy and she usually wears it cut short. Her complexion is very fair and she uses little make-up. She generally wears simple clothes, preferring suits with white blouses, and modest accessories. Her favorite colors seem to be small black and white checks, or charcoal blues and grays.

Michiko-san has enjoyed many of the privileges of a Japanese upper-class family. She went to a private primary school in Tokyo. Then after World War II, when her family left the bombed and burned-out city, she attended elementary school at Kamakura and Karuizawa, both fashionable artists' colonies near Tokyo. In 1947 Michiko-san, who is a Buddhist,

113

Baby Michiko at the seaside in sun hat and playsuit, happily digging in the sand. Left, a portrait taken at the age of seven, just before she began primary school.

PHOTOS, BLACK STAR

schools all over the world. This was a natural climax to her career at Sacred Heart where she was elected president of the student body during her senior year.

Michiko-san has a reputation for being a hard worker and a young woman with a strong sense of responsibility. For example, other girls at Sacred Heart prepared their final thesis in handwriting, then had someone type it for them. But Michiko-san taught herself to use a typewriter. She learned so well during her summer vacation that she typed the essay herself and presented it for her diploma.

Michiko-san's school record was good but not outstanding. She excelled in athletics, was an excellent runner and general all-around sportswoman. She is also interested in motion pictures and music. She speaks English well and French passably. She learned both languages at Sacred Heart, and her lessons are now being continued with a private tutor.

It was Michiko-san's athletic skill that first attracted the attention of Crown Prince Akihito. She is an excellent tennis player, so well known for her game that in the Sacred Heart yearbook she was put down as the "Queen of Tennis." Her tennis specialty is the long volley rather than the smash. And this tactic has proved successful in many a game—including her singles matches with the Crown Prince when she has often won in spite of his own skillful game.

It was at Karuizawa, a favorite cool mountain retreat from Tokyo's very hot summers, that the couple first met. Crown Prince Akihito has spent several summer vacations as a visitor at the Karuizawa Lawn Tennis Club. Because the club membership includes a large number of foreigners and upper-class Japanese, it was possible for the Crown Prince to move about there with a minimum of the formality and the complicated protocol that usually surround the Japanese royal family.

entered the Junior High School of Sacred Heart Institute, a French Catholic school in Tokyo, which is one of Japan's most fashionable schools. She continued at Sacred Heart College and was graduated in 1957. She majored in English literature and her graduation thesis, required of all students, was an essay on Galsworthy's *Forsyte Saga*.

In 1958 Michiko-san went to Brussels as the Japanese representative at a meeting of alumni from the Sacred Heart

Still, the courtship of the Crown Prince and Michiko-san was carried on largely through third persons. After their first game during a tournament at the club, the Crown Prince told a mutual friend that he admired Michiko-san's game—and the girl herself. The following day he invited Michiko-san to a party, but she refused because of the traditions that set Japanese royalty apart from other people.

It was not until both returned to Tokyo that they met again, on a tennis court at the Tokyo Lawn Tennis Club. At this meeting the Crown Prince photographed Michiko-san. He later gave her a print of the photograph and mounted another for display at the Palace.

Michiko-san continued to refuse to meet the Crown Prince at Japanese tea ceremonies, flower-arrangement sessions and other social occasions that might have brought two ordinary Japanese young people together. Instead they had a weekly tennis match!

Prince Akihito's fiancée and her parents leave the palace after a ceremonial visit to the Prince.

UPI

BLACK STAR

The Crown Prince and his bride pause to talk with one of her classmates at the Sacred Heart.

While all this was going on, the Imperial Household Agency (the ministry of the Japanese Government set up to manage the affairs of the royal family) and the Council of the Imperial Household (the leading members of the family and the Government) were considering the question of the Crown Prince's bride. Traditionally the emperor's bride was always selected from the kuge (noble) families. Although titles of nobility were abolished after World War II, it was generally believed that Akihito's bride would be chosen from one of these families.

In choosing the bride the council considered several points. The girl must come of a respectable family with a good health record. A strong argument against selecting the bride from the nobility was the tremendous amount of intermarriage that has taken place over the centuries among the few noble families. The present Emperor and Empress, for example, were related by blood ties before their marriage.

The council also felt it necessary to consider the Crown Prince's wishes. Prince Akihito has a reputation for earnestness and a deep respect for the responsibilities of his position.

It is believed that a list of candidates was drawn up for the Crown Prince and that Michiko-san's name was on it. In August 1958 a representative of the Imperial Household Agency approached Michiko-san's parents with a proposal for her marriage. They declined the honor, in the traditional Japanese fashion, many times before finally accepting on November 13. On November 27 the Imperial Household Council met and approved the engagement which was announced the following day.

The announcement won almost unanimous approval among all Japanese circles. Most newspapers and public commentators said it was a choice in keeping with the spirit of the new postwar Japan.

A round of preparations and festivities then commenced which were climaxed by the wedding of the young couple on April 10, 1959. The Crown Prince and Michiko-san were married in the traditional Japanese Shinto ceremonies in a shrine on the Imperial Palace grounds. Both wore the formal robes of imperial office. Michiko-san was attired in an elaborate set of kimonos which had been worn by the Crown Prince's mother, Empress Nagako, at her wedding. The Crown Prince and his bride then made ceremonial visits to the Emperor and Empress and to the Shrine of Ise, one of Japan's most important national monuments, where they reported their marriage to the royal family's ancestors.

In August it was learned that the Crown Prince and Princess will have a child early in 1960. The royal couple are now living in a palace completed last year for them some distance from the Imperial Palace compound in central Tokyo. They have announced that their children will be reared in their own family household instead of being removed to a court nursery in the age-old tradition of the Japanese royal family.

It is generally believed that this departure from royal custom is one of many that will characterize the couple's future private and public life. Both the Japanese royal family and the Imperial Household Council are known to feel that the royal family —which was continued after the war against considerable opposition—will increasingly have to conform to the new, more democratic character of Japanese society. The emperor is "the symbol of the state" in the postwar Constitution of Japan rather than the god-figure that had been built up through the centuries. His family is likely to become more and more like the royal families of Britain and Scandinavia. In that new role, Crown Princess Michiko will play an important part.

Christian A. Herter

By PAUL HEALY
Washington Correspondent
New York Daily News

Oₙ April 21, 1959, the nomination of Christian Herter to be secretary of state was confirmed by the United States Senate with almost unprecedented speed. The Senate Foreign Relations Committee questioned Herter briefly, approved him unanimously and then rushed the nomination directly to the Senate floor without observing the customary six-day waiting period. One hour later the Senate approved the nomination on a roll-call vote of 93-0.

There were two principal reasons for such swift and enthusiastic acceptance. Mr. Herter was taking over at a crucial time from the ailing John Foster Dulles. Of even greater importance was the fact that he was uniquely qualified for the post. Foreign Relations Committee Chairman J. William Fulbright, an Arkansas Democrat, said: "This man is qualified to be leader of the Department of State in nearly every respect I can think of." The Senate noted that Herter had had long experience in government as a state legislator, congressman, governor of Massachusetts and, more recently, as undersecretary of state. Senators were also happy that the President had appointed a man who had begun his career as a State Department attaché to the nation's number-one diplomatic post.

Six feet, four inches tall, and slender, Mr. Herter is slightly stooped from arthritis. Although he supports himself with canes and it tires him if he walks or stands for long periods, his condition has not cost him a single day of work in the State Depart-

117

Christian Herter as a page boy. When he was twelve his artist father used him as a model in a painting of the Magna Carta signing. It now hangs in the Supreme Court building in Madison, the capital of Wisconsin.

ment. He has a small-boned, patrician face, a soft voice and, in general, the aristocratic look and bearing that used to be more common than it is now among diplomats.

Lacking outward dynamism, Herter's sincerity and earnestness make him effective as a public speaker. In international negotiations he is firm without being stubborn; he speaks easily without being talkative. He is refreshingly candid with the press and has a quick sense of humor.

Christian Herter was born on March 28, 1895, in Paris, the son of American artists Albert and Adele (McGinnis) Herter, who were studying painting there at the time. The family returned to New York City when he was nine and he entered Harvard at sixteen. He was graduated *cum laude* from Harvard in 1915, the youngest man in his class.

Though young Herter then began the study of architecture, he yearned for more excitement. Within a year he secured appointment as an attaché at the United States Embassy in Berlin through a former classmate who was already working there. Six months later, Herter was transferred to Brussels, Belgium. He was there when the United States broke off diplomatic relations with Germany. He tried to enlist in the Army but was rejected for physical reasons.

Herter, in 1917, married the former Mary Caroline Pratt, granddaughter of a founder of the Standard Oil Company. They have four children: Christian, Jr., a

Boston lawyer and former aide to Vice-President Nixon; Adele, who is married to a research pathologist in Concord, Massachusetts; Miles, employed by a Boston cable manufacturer; and Frederic, a Dobbs Ferry, New York, surgeon.

In 1918 the State Department sent him to Switzerland as assistant commissioner on the Allied commission that negotiated a prisoner-of-war agreement with the Germans. The following year he served as a special assistant on the American staff at the Versailles peace conference.

A year later he became executive secretary of the European Relief Council headed by future president Herbert Hoover. In this job Herter made an inspection tour of Russia. When Hoover became secretary of commerce in 1921, Herter was appointed his special assistant and remained with him until 1924.

Still seeking a satisfying career, Herter successively published a small political weekly newspaper in Boston, tried gentleman farming and lectured on international relations at Harvard. In 1930 he ran for political office and was elected to the Massachusetts House. He was re-elected for six consecutive terms, serving the last two terms as speaker.

In 1942 Herter ran for the United States House of Representatives and was elected to the first of his five terms there. In 1947 he proposed and then headed a special House committee which made an on-the-spot investigation of European economic

John Foster Dulles and Christian Herter. Assistant secretary under Dulles, Herter became secretary after Dulles was stricken with his fatal illness.

President Eisenhower looks on as Christian Herter takes the oath as secretary of state.

Secretary of State Herter confers with West Germany's Konrad Adenauer and others.

119

conditions. The work of this committee helped pave the way for the Marshall Plan and the present foreign-aid program.

Herter was elected governor of Massachusetts in 1952, defeating the late Paul A. Dever, the Democratic incumbent. He was re-elected to a second term two years later. When that term ran out in January 1957, President Eisenhower appointed him undersecretary of state.

In April 1959, when Herter took over the State Department, its size and many responsibilities could hardly have been imagined by Thomas Jefferson, the first secretary of state. Besides advising the president on foreign policy and negotiating treaties, the secretary of state presides over 76 embassies and 200 other posts scattered around the world. These posts range from the large and glittering embassy in London to the tiny advisory mission on Okinawa.

Herter directs the work of 76 United States ambassadors, who in turn direct the complex activities of their embassies. Attached to them are numerous Americans engaged in nondiplomatic missions, which deal with atomic-energy matters, military assistance, naval research, and Air Force

bases. The State Department itself has 6,889 employees in the United States, almost as many Americans stationed abroad, and another 9,337 locals who are hired abroad. To run his department the secretary is given approximately $220,000,000 a year. Under the law, the secretary of state sets the policy for the administration of the foreign aid program, and the global United States Information Agency, including the Voice of America.

The secretary of state is a key member of the National Security Council, the president's board of advisers on international strategy. Here he has an important voice in deciding on moves that could mean peace or war.

His department has various other responsibilities, such as issuing passports to millions of Americans who go abroad every year and visas to the foreigners who wish to come to the United States as immigrants or visitors.

The secretary of state is the top-ranking member of the cabinet. He is fourth in line to succeed to the presidency after the vice-president, speaker of the House and president pro tempore of the Senate.

WIDE WORLD

Secretary and Mrs. Herter relax in their Washington home with their pair of cairn terriers.

Princess Beatrix of the Netherlands chats with children in Dutch costumes as she arrives for a visit in New York City.

Mrs. Khrushchev's warm smile and friendly manner pleased all who saw her during her visit through the United States.

SNAPSHOTS
1959

Famed architect Frank Lloyd Wright stands beside a model of his controversial design for the Guggenheim Museum of modern art.

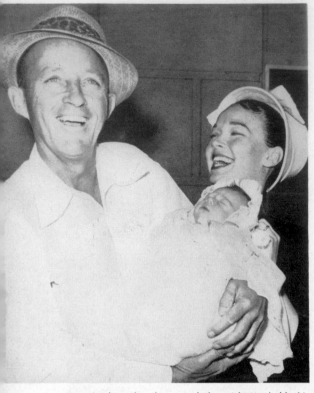

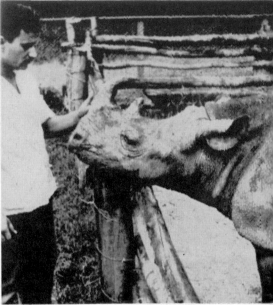

Bing Crosby takes home a baby girl. He holds his first daughter, Mary Frances; Mrs. Crosby looks on.

Steven Rockefeller and Anne Marie Rasmussen together a short time before they announced their wedding plans in Kristiansand, Norway.

Lord Beaverbrook gives $3,000,000 art collection to his home town.

Elected a councilman by the citizens of Sao Paulo, Brazil, as a protest against local politicians: Cacareco (Skinny), a rhinoceros at their zoo.

"Queen" Ethel Barrymore of America's royal family of the theater; an actress for more than sixty years.

In her seventy-sixth year, Mrs. Roosevelt carries on with zeal and efficiency her work for the United Nations.

Deep in thought, Bernard Berenson, authority on Italian Renaissance art, judges a painting of the period.

Snapshots: 1959

STEVEN AND ANNE MARIE ROCKEFELLER

On August 22 the son of New York's Governor and an heir to the great Rockefeller fortune married Anne Marie Rasmussen in the little Norwegian town where she lived. While working in his family's home she met her future husband.

PRINCESS BEATRIX

The twenty-one-year-old heiress to the throne of the Netherlands was invited to take part in New York's celebration of the 350th anniversary of Henry Hudson's voyage up the river named for him. With the land around it he claimed it for the Dutch.

MRS. NIKITA KHRUSHCHEV

Nina Petrovna Khrushchev, second wife of the Soviet Premier and mother of his youngest child, was the best-liked of the visiting Russians by the American public. A former teacher, she speaks several languages, is fond of books and music.

FRANK LLOYD WRIGHT

World-famous for his revolutionary ideas on architecture, Wright designed the earthquake-proof Imperial Hotel in Tokyo, a house over a waterfall in Pennsylvania and other unusual buildings. Born in Wisconsin in 1869, he died April 9 in Arizona.

HARRY LILLIS CROSBY

Known to most of the world as "Bing," he has been a star of radio, screen and TV for the past thirty years. He is also a baseball magnate, amateur golfer and racing enthusiast. He has five sons; the four oldest are now in show business themselves.

LORD BEAVERBROOK

The Beaverbrook Art Gallery, on the banks of the St. John River at Fredericton, New Brunswick, was formally opened on September 16. The painters range from Reynolds to Winston Churchill. An endowment fund is part of the gift.

ETHEL BARRYMORE

The beloved actress, who died June 18, was born in 1879 to Maurice and Georgiana Drew Barrymore of the acting family. A niece of John Drew and the sister of Lionel and John Barrymore, she had a long career in theater, TV and movies.

MRS. FRANKLIN D. ROOSEVELT

A tireless traveler and worker in the cause of human rights, Mrs. Roosevelt reached her seventy-fifth birthday October 11. In her long career she has probably met and talked with more people in more places than any other woman of her time.

BERNARD BERENSON

Born in Lithuania and graduated from Harvard, Berenson's outstanding knowledge of Italian art benefited countless museums and private collectors. On October 6, he died at ninety-four in his Tuscan villa which he left to Harvard University.

New Nations
in French West Africa

By CHARLES PAUL MAY

Senegalese guard
on duty.

SINCE the end of World War II, nationalism has swept through Asia and Africa. The tide has been so strong that it has broken up most of the old European colonial empires. In the place of the once great British, French and Dutch empires have come a score of new nations, either completely free or loosely linked with their former rulers.

From the British Empire have emerged the new states of India, Pakistan, Ceylon and the Federation of Malaya in Asia, and Ghana in Africa. They are all joined in a voluntary Commonwealth with Britain, Canada, Australia, New Zealand and the Union of South Africa. Burma alone of the former British possessions has gone its own way outside the Commonwealth.

Unlike the British, the Dutch fought bitterly to hold on to the Dutch East Indies.

Two views of West African life: in Labé, Guinea, a small boy teaches his sister to read; in the market place of Timbuktu, Sudan, vendors sell tobacco and peanuts.

SCHWAB-PIX

This struggle ended in the complete break-away of the new Republic of Indonesia.

The French have followed a path somewhere between those of the British and Dutch. They fought to keep Indochina and lost the entire area. In Algeria they are still fighting the Muslim independence movement. However, in the areas of former French West and Equatorial Africa they have tried to come to terms with nationalism by granting the people complete internal freedom within the framework of a new French "community."

After Charles de Gaulle won control of the French Government in 1958, he went through the territories of French Africa to ask the peoples to vote for his new constitution. If they voted for it they could become republics within the new French Community. If they voted no, they could be completely independent.

Only one region, Guinea, voted for complete independence. It did so largely because of the efforts of the dominant political party, led by Sékou Touré.

All the other territories voted to join the Community. These regions took new names: Republic of Senegal, Republic of the Ivory Coast, Republic of Dahomey, Islamic Republic of Mauritania, Sudanese Republic, Voltaic Republic and Republic of Niger. These names may change, however, as alliances are formed with neighbors, so let us look at them under their old names.

Senegal, although small in area, 76,-124 square miles, is more fortunate than some of her neighbors. Dakar, her largest city, is one of the major ports of the continent. A fine harbor has been developed, with tanks for petroleum storage, warehouses for storing goods, and generous dock space. Because it is the most westerly of Africa's major ports, ships coming across from the Americas, down from Europe and up from South Africa stop there. As air traffic has increased throughout the world, Dakar's position has given it considerable prestige. Many airlines make regular use of Dakar's international airport.

From the time the French created French West Africa, the center of government was at Dakar. It was the capital of all French West Africa. Saint-Louis was capital of Senegal. It was also the governmental headquarters for Mauritania, which is to the north. Now, however, Senegal's government has been shifted to Dakar, and Mauritania has its own capital—Nouakchott.

Senegal has a climate that is bearable most of the year, though July, August and September are hot and humid. The winter months are quite pleasant, with dry, warm days and cool nights. Consequently, Senegal has attracted most of the tourist traffic

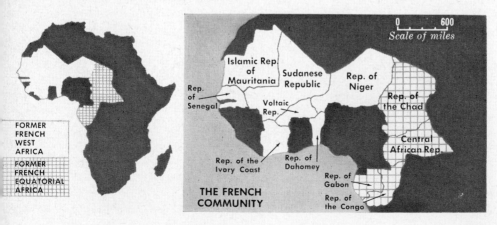

FORMER
FRENCH
WEST
AFRICA

FORMER
FRENCH
EQUATORIAL
AFRICA

Islamic Rep. of Mauritania
Sudanese Republic
Rep. of Niger
Rep. of Senegal
Voltaic Rep.
Rep. of the Chad
Rep. of the Ivory Coast
Rep. of Dahomey
Central African Rep.
Rep. of Gabon
Rep. of the Congo

0   600
Scale of miles

THE FRENCH COMMUNITY

SCHWAB-PIX

WIDE WORLD

SÉKOU TOURÉ,
President of Guinea

FRENCH CULTURAL SERVICES

HOUPHOUET-BOIGNY,
Ivory Coast leader

In Mauritania, a teacher
helps a student with his
French.

of former French West Africa. The fact that Dakar has developed into a city with a European atmosphere has helped too. Foreign visitors who feel at home there seldom care to travel beyond it. It is not surprising that Dakar has grown to be a city of 230,000 people (a tenth of the total population of Senegal).

One major crop is grown in Senegal—peanuts. Many of the industries of the region, such as making peanut oil, are based on this crop. Near Dakar there are also plants for making palm oil and canning foods. Phosphate deposits also contribute to Senegal's economy.

The Ivory Coast has an area of 124,503 square miles and a population of 2,485,-000. It is a rich region, for its rain forests supply valuable woods—mahogany, ebony, rosewood, teak. Bananas, coffee, cocoa and palm oil are also exported. Here there are important deposits of manganese, and diamonds are found in the interior.

Abidjan, the capital, is a rapidly growing city, though its population at present is only 128,200. A channel was cut through the sandbanks that separate a deep lagoon around the city from the Gulf of Guinea.

Now ocean-going vessels can come right to the docks of Abidjan. What is left of the sandbanks makes the city one of the well-protected ports of the world. Abidjan is Dakar's greatest rival among western African ports. However, it still lacks cranes to help in handling cargoes, and its warehouse facilities need improvement.

Because its climate is hot and sticky the Ivory Coast draws few casual tourists. People who are not there on business do not stay long. Air conditioning helps, though only one of the hotels is equipped well enough to give real relief.

Dahomey is a small region—44,696 square miles—with a population of 1,713,-000. It is squeezed in between Togoland and Nigeria. Porto-Novo (31,500) is its capital as well as its main port. Being on the Gulf of Guinea, it must compete with Lagos, Accra, Takoradi and Abidjan.

The Negroes, who make up all but about 150,000 of the population, are farmers or herders. They produce just enough to keep themselves alive. However, there is some export of palm kernels, palm oil, coffee and cotton.

Although Mauritania has the advantages

127

of an Atlantic Ocean coast line, its development has lagged. It is one of the larger sections of West Africa, with an area of 419,229 square miles, yet it has the smallest population—624,000 people, most of whom are Muslims.

Sudan, Upper Volta and Niger are all inland. Sudan has a population of 3,708,-000 in an area of 464,873 square miles. It is the largest of the eight divisions. Next largest is Niger, with 458,993 square miles and 2,415,000 people. Upper Volta is small by comparison, 105,839 square miles. Yet it has more than 3,326,000 people, almost all Negro tribesmen.

If it were not for railways connecting the inland sections with Dakar and Abidjan, these areas would have had little chance of development during the past half century. Niamey, capital of Niger, is on the Niger River, so it has not had to depend entirely on railways. During the past decade it has gained importance as an international airport. Bamako, capital of Sudan, is also on the Niger and is also developing as an airline center.

The people of these countries raise livestock and grow corn, rice, cotton and peanuts. These inland sections are economically the weakest ones. They are therefore the most interested in federating with each other.

What of Guinea, the one area that broke free? It did not take her leader Sékou Touré long to find that his move for complete independence may have been a mistake. He had hoped that freedom from France would give him more chance to sell tropical fruit and bauxite to iron-curtain countries such as Poland and Czechoslovakia. Touré at first intended to send all French officials home. Then he saw that his Government would not run smoothly without them. He offered to let them stay at considerably less than their original salaries and with no guarantees that payment would be made regularly.

For a time Touré turned all his diplomatic efforts on Ghana. He even considered the possibility of a union with that African member of the British Commonwealth. However, Kwame Nkrumah, Ghana's prime minister, did not want outside influences to gain ground in his country. Besides, Guinea is still keyed to a franc economy, while Ghana does business in pounds—union would disrupt the trade of both.

Although Touré kept his people out of the French Community, it seems he may try friendship with France once more. He does not want to join the Community, but he may wish to regain some of the stability that comes with being part of a group of nations. As long as Guinea's position remains unsatisfactory the other new republics are not likely to want to leave the French Community.

Abidjan, capital of the Ivory Coast, is one of the fastest-growing cities of West Africa.

CHARLES MAY

CYPRUS

By RUTH WARREN
Free Lance Writer

Turk

Greek

Briton

CYPRUS is the third largest island in the Mediterranean, covering an area of 3,572 square miles, about the size of Puerto Rico. Its chief cities are Nicosia, Famagusta, Limassol, Larnaca and Kyrenia.

Cyprus is a sunny island for most of the year. Oranges, lemons, grapefruit, olives and grapes grow in abundance. You can ski during the short winter season on mountain slopes. You can swim in summer in the blue-green Mediterranean. You can go camping and hiking in Cyprus' two mountain ranges, the northern range rising to some 3,330 feet, the southwest range, which is green and wooded, rising to 6,406 feet.

Near Cyprus are many exciting and interesting places to visit. In from one to three and a half hours you can fly to the Pyramids of Egypt, the Parthenon at Athens, Jerusalem and Bethlehem, the crusader castles of Syria, the temple of Jupiter in Lebanon, the famous and beautiful mosques of Istanbul.

Cyprus' closeness to her neighbors puts her in a particularly strategic position.

About 250 miles away as the crow flies is the Suez Canal; the Dardanelles lies about 500 miles away; and the important Soviet, Black Sea port of Odessa is about 875 miles away.

World powers have viewed with great concern the past five politically stormy years in Cyprus. Though Cyprus was a British crown colony between 1925 and 1959, about 80 per cent of its 549,000 population are Greek-speaking people, who long wished to unite with Greece. The Turkish-speaking population, comprising approximately 18 per cent, favored partition of the island between Greece and Turkey. Britain, meanwhile, was reluctant to relinquish her strategic military bases on Cyprus.

In 1959, peace at last came to Cyprus. After long negotiations the governments of Britain, Greece and Turkey and the leaders of the Greek and Turkish Cypriotes together worked out and signed an agreement. Under the terms of this pact, signed in London on February 19, 1959, Cyprus became a republic exactly one

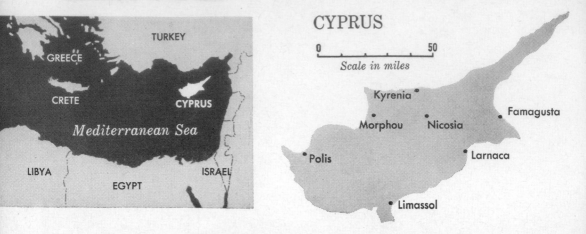

year later. It has a Greek-Cypriot president, a Turkish-Cypriot vice-president, a legislature 70 per cent Greek, 30 per cent Turkish, and security guaranteed by Greek, Turkish, and Cypriot forces. Britain continues to maintain sovereignty over her military bases on the island.

The livelihood of the majority of the people comes from agriculture. Wheat, olives, almonds, lemons, grapefruit, oranges, grapes, grains and potatoes are the chief crops. There are also many manufacturing plants on the island. They make candies, canned fruits and jam, grape juice, wine, macaroni, cigarettes, textiles, clothing, leather goods, soap, plasterboard and asbestos sheets. The chief exports are oranges, wine, potatoes, asbestos, cupreous (containing copper) concentrates, cupreous pyrites, iron pyrites, copper, cement and gypsum.

Mining was an important industry in Cyprus four thousand years ago when its copper mines were already being worked. These mines must have been famous, for Cyprus gave its name to copper—*cyprium aes* in Latin.

Cyprus entered the pages of history about 1500 B.C., when Egyptian scribes recorded the island's conquest by Pharaoh Thutmose III. From then on Cyprus changed hands again and again. It passed from Egypt to Assyria, again to Egypt, to Persia, to Alexander the Great, to the Ptolemies of Egypt, to Rome, to the Byzantine Empire, to the crusaders, to the Venetians and finally to the Ottoman Turks, who ceded the island to Great Britain in 1878.

Zeno, founder of the Stoic school of philosophy, is one of Cyprus' famous sons. He was born at Citium, a Phoenician colony, in about 300 B.C. St. Barnabus was born in Salamis, and it was he and St. Paul who introduced Christianity to Cyprus in A.D. 46.

Gibbon tells us that Mark Antony presented Cyprus to Cleopatra, and proclaimed her its queen.

St. Helena, mother of Constantine the Great, is said to have founded the monastery of Stavrovouni and to have presented this monastery with a piece of the true Cross which she brought from Jerusalem. St. Hilarian, who introduced monasticism into Palestine, died in Cyprus in A.D. 371. Richard the Lion-hearted stopped at Cyprus, on his way to the Third Crusade, to marry Berengaria of Navarre, on May 12, 1191.

The legacy that people and passing centuries have left behind on the island of Cyprus includes medieval walled cities, seemingly impregnable sea castles, tower-

130

GEORGE E. PICKOW, THREE LIONS

THREE LIONS

Workers check a wagonload of asbestos at a plant in Amiandos.

The main square of Nicosia, the capital of Cyprus and center of the island's industry and commerce.

BRITISH INFORMATION SERVICES

The Abbot of the monastery of Kykko feeds his pet mouflon, a wild sheep with horns.

Cypriot farmers load wheat. Agriculture is still the islander's main occupation.

CAMERA PRESS-PIX

The sturdy ruins of the ancient Greek temple of Apollo at Curium; the graceful Gothic arches of the Bella Pais Abbey; the camel

ing Gothic churches with graceful pointed arches, whitewashed monasteries hidden in wooded mountains, ruins of temples, theaters, forums, aqueducts and the fairy-book mountaintop castle of St. Hilarian.

A good way to become acquainted with Cyprus is to take a leisurely drive around the island's coastal road and spend a long relaxing week end in the mountains.

Nicosia, Cyprus' capital, lies almost in the center of the island in a plain between the two mountain ranges. Nicosia is the island's seat of government, commerce and of many manufacturing plants. It is a modern city with comfortable hotels and good restaurants. In it are shops that sell almost any kind of merchandise you need or want to buy, including the beautiful lace and embroidery done by village women.

Nicosia is said to have been founded before 280 B.C. You can explore its ancient walls, three miles in circumference, thrown up by the Venetians when they rebuilt the city's fortifications in 1567. You can also visit St. Sophia, now a mosque but once a church built by Lusignan kings who came to the Middle East as crusaders and ruled the island almost three hundred

years. If you are looking for even more ancient mementos of Cyprus' past, you may examine in the Cyprus Museum the treasures turned up by archaeological excavations.

The road across the island from Nicosia to Famagusta, Cyprus' chief seaport on the southeastern coast, crosses the fertile Messaorian plain. You will see men and women working in the fields everywhere. They may be cultivating or harvesting oranges or lemons, or pruning grape arbors, or winnowing wheat by the age-old method of tossing it up into the wind so the chaff can fall away from the grain.

Famagusta has fifteenth-century walls, built by the Venetians, that are particularly well preserved. As you walk through the entrance gate, you will see the Gothic cathedral of St. Nicholas, now a mosque with a minaret flanking its tower.

Modern Famagusta has spread out beyond the walls. It is a busy seaport city with tree-shaded streets and a long sandy beach. Cyprus' southern coast has two other seaports. Larnaca has a palm-tree-shaded water front, crowded with many out-of-door coffee shops overlooking its

EUROPEAN

caravan preparing for a journey in Nicosia; all show the imprint made on Cyprus by the different peoples that have lived there.

harbor. Beyond lies Limassol, where Richard the Lion-hearted was married to Berengaria.

One of Cyprus' most scenic towns is Kyrenia, which lies on the island's northern shore. A massive sea castle with crenelated walls guards its harbor, and inland is a dramatic background of mountains. An unforgettable landmark of Kyrenia is the silhouette of St. Hilarian's castle on its craggy hilltop overlooking the sea. A short drive and a half-hour's climb up winding steps brings you to the royal apartments at the top of the castle.

Another of Kyrenia's heritages from the past is Bella Pais Abbey. It stands on a cliff in the foothills of the mountains, overlooking a green valley of orange groves and beyond the sea to the Turkish coast. The church and cloisters are delightfully mellowed with age and surrounded by flower gardens.

To people from the Middle East, used to deserts, treeless plains, treeless hills, the green, wooded mountains of Cyprus are perhaps the island's most exciting attraction. Cyprus' mountains are a very popular summer resort with people of the eastern Mediterranean. Prodhromos is the topmost village in the island and lies some 4,600 feet above sea level. Mount Olympus (not the Mount Olympus of the Greek gods) rises above the village on the south, while on the north is a long succession of valleys leading to the sea. At Prodhromos and at nearby Pano Platres are summer hotels, camps, cottages.

On your way to Prodhromos from Nicosia, a three-hour drive, you can take time out to visit some of the island's monasteries which are tucked away in wooded hills. Kykko is a famous one. Here a black-robed monk in tall black brimless hat will show you the church that has an icon of the Blessed Virgin said to have been painted by St. Luke.

When in Cyprus you should try to visit with the people of the island. A good way to make friends is to stop for a cup of Turkish coffee at a village coffee shop. You may even be invited to someone's home and asked to taste the delicious jam which is offered to guests and for which the island is famous. But best of all you'll be sure, always, of a warm welcome from Cyprus' friendly people.

133

The European Community

By LEONARD B. TENNYSON

Director, The European Community Information Service
Washington, D. C.

THE European Community is a group of six nations. They have joined in several organizations for the purpose of economic and, eventually, political union. Belgium, France, the Federal Republic of (West) Germany, Italy, Luxembourg and the Netherlands are bound by treaties by which they have given up certain national rights to the Community's organizations. Their aim is to bring about a free flow of trade and commerce within a single Continental market.

The organizations of the European Community are: the European Coal and Steel Community (ECSC); the European Economic Community (the Common Market, or Euromarket) and the European Atomic Energy Community (Euratom). Each has a separate executive branch responsible to a single European parliament and to a single European court of justice.

A United States of Europe has been a dream of statesmen, philosophers and kings since the time of Charlemagne. But until now, neither force nor fiat was able to unite nations that had warred against each other for centuries. Only in the common effort to repair the ravages of World War II did a real chance arise for Europe to unite freely.

On June 5, 1947, Secretary of State George Catlett Marshall proposed that the United States extend help to war-torn Europe through a program of direct economic aid. At the time, Secretary Marshall urged the European nations themselves to band together to make the utmost of American assistance by co-operating in a common effort of reconstruction. On April 16, 1948, sixteen nations of Western Europe heeded Marshall's urging and joined in the Organization for European Economic Cooperation (OEEC). Shortly thereafter the great flow of aid from the United States to Western Europe began.

Through working together in the OEEC, the free nations of Europe came to realize how vitally the economic condition of one nation could affect another. In the process of reconstruction, Europe learned the value of economic co-operation. The OEEC made an invaluable contribution toward European unity. Yet it lacked real power.

On May 9, 1950, the first step toward European federation was suggested by the French Government. Robert Schuman, then France's foreign minister, proposed that Europe's coal and steel economies be interwoven to provide a solid foundation for building a federal Europe. The plan was based upon an idea advanced by Jean Monnet, author of France's Reconstruction and Modernization Plan.

M. Schuman suggested that the first step be limited to coal and steel—the two most basic industrial materials. He declared that if the entire Franco-German production of coal and steel, along with the production of other free European countries, was placed under a common authority, it would create an economic fusion that would make any future war between France and Germany "not only unthinkable but materially impossible." This was received favorably.

Less than a year later, on April 18, 1951, six nations signed a treaty giving effect to the Schuman proposals. On July 25, 1952, the treaty was ratified by the six parliaments. By August 10, 1952, the organization of the Coal and Steel Community began work in the city of Luxembourg. The first step toward unity had been taken.

The Coal and Steel Community brought into existence a permanent common market of 165,000,000 people for coal, steel, steel products, scrap and iron ore.

The treaty that brought the Coal and Steel Community into existence set the stage for several far-reaching economic and social steps. They would affect every person who lived in the six-nation Community. Its treaty, and its constitution, brought into existence Europe's first antitrust laws; pro-

vided Europe's first labor passports—enabling coal miners and steel workers to move freely within the Community to take jobs of their own choosing. It also established European regulations to insure free competition within the common market; provided aid to workers who became unemployed because of the pressures of new competition; provided funds for low-cost workers' housing; established a loan fund from which industries could borrow at low rates of interest to modernize their plants and compete in the common market; standardized transport rates among nations and abolished expensive terminal charges at national frontiers.

Since the creation of the Coal and Steel Community eight years ago, the steel production of its members has increased from

ECSC: The European Coal and Steel Community.

Euromarket: The European Economic Community.

Euratom: The European Atomic Energy Community.

42,000,000 metric tons to 58,000,000 tons. Intra-Community trade in iron and steel products increased 171 per cent and trade in scrap almost tripled. Production of iron ore climbed from 65,000,000 metric tons to 87,000,000 tons. During the same period, however, coal production in Europe's mines increased by only 3 per cent.

Of great importance to Europe's eventual political unity were the federal institutions created under the Coal and Steel Community treaty. The principles that guided the drafters of the United States Constitution were followed in setting up these new institutions. They provide for a clear separation and balance of powers distributed among an executive, parliamentary and judicial branch.

Europe's first federal executive is a nine-man body known as the High Authority. Its members do not represent the countries from which they come. They cannot, in fact, accept or solicit instruction from *any* national government including their own. Members of the High Authority are appointed for six-year terms (no more than two from each member nation). They are responsible for carrying out the terms of the treaty which is also the Community's constitution.

The parliamentary body of the ECSC was called the Common Assembly. Its seventy-eight members were elected from and by the parliaments of the member nations. The Common Assembly possessed no real lawmaking powers under the treaty but had the power to oust the executive branch by a two-thirds vote if it disapproved of its actions and policies. Within two years after the Assembly's establishment a notable change occurred. Then members, who at first had seated themselves according to national blocs, grouped themselves according to European political parties. For example, Italian Socialists joined Belgian and French Socialists in one group. At the same time Liberals and Christian Democrats from

Luxembourg is the headquarters for the High Authority of the Coal and Steel Community.

these and other member nations joined in their own groupings. An awareness of a common European political purpose was born. The Common Assembly of the ECSC was dissolved in February 1958 and re-constituted as the European Parliamentary Assembly, a 142-man body serving all three Communities. However, its responsibilities with respect to the High Authority remain the same as those of the Common Assembly.

Europe's first federal judiciary established under the ECSC treaty was called the Court of Justice. It was a seven-man body of jurists appointed from the member nations. It was the only judicial body to which individual industries, associations, governments or individuals could appeal from decisions taken by the High Authority. Its jurisdiction supplanted that of the national courts of member countries and its judgments were final.

On October 7, 1958, the Court of Justice was re-established as the Court of Justice for the ECSC and the two new Communities. Distinct authority was given to it by the treaties concerning each Community.

In addition to the federal government established by the ECSC treaty, there is a fourth institution, the Council of Ministers, which includes one representative from each member state. The chief function of the Council of Ministers under the ECSC treaty is to assure harmony between the federal or European policies of the Community and the national economic policies of member states.

The achievements of the Coal and Steel Community prompted Europe to try another move to closer union in the form of the European Defense Community. The EDC would have set up a European army and also federal institutions with considerably more authority than possessed by the ECSC. However, the EDC treaty, though ratified by four of the six Community nations, died on August 30, 1954, in the French National Assembly.

Because of the failure of the EDC, European leaders realized that the next steps toward federation would have to concentrate on economic integration.

Meeting in Messina, Sicily, June 1-3, 1955, the foreign ministers of the Six

137

agreed to study proposals put forth by the Benelux nations (Belgium, the Netherlands and Luxembourg) for a treaty that would further join their national economies. A year later, at Venice, Belgium's Foreign Minister Paul-Henri Spaak presented to the foreign ministers a draft of two treaties. One was for a European atomic community and the other for a general economic community. Both were to share with the Coal and Steel Community a common parliament and court.

On March 25, 1957, after nearly ten months of negotiations among the Six, the European Atomic Energy Community Treaty and the European Economic Community Treaty were signed in Rome. On January 1, 1958, they came into effect.

The chief goal of the Atomic Energy Community, or Euratom as it is more popularly known, is the rapid development of atomic power to meet Europe's increasing demand for energy for its expanding economy. Studies made in 1956 and 1957 indicated that without new sources of energy Europe's imports of oil, coal and so forth might reach 45 per cent of total need by 1975 and cost about six billion dollars. Since nuclear power programs are costly, no single European nation alone could develop economic nuclear power. However, six nations working together, pooling skills and resources, would be able to meet the technical challenge and the high cost of nuclear development.

The Euratom Commission, the five-man executive of the Atomic Energy Community, is responsible for developing atomic power and also for safeguarding the health of workers and the general population against atomic hazards. It is solely responsible for all fissile materials, maintains title to all such materials and insures that they are not diverted from their intended (peaceful) use.

Apart from the financing of the research, investment and supply budgets, the operational expenses of Euratom are currently met by the Community's member states. Each contributes in the same proportions as it does to the Common Market. In time these contributions will be replaced by a Community tax.

In addition to co-ordinating and encouraging the development of nuclear power in the Community countries, the Euratom Commission is also responsible for relationships with nations outside the Community in the field of atomic energy. Thus, it was Euratom's executive branch that signed an agreement with the United States for a joint nuclear power program. This program aims at completing by 1965 full-scale atomic power plants in the Community that could produce a total of one million kilowatts of electrical energy. Euratom has also signed an agreement with the United Kingdom for co-operation in the nuclear power field. Agreements with other countries are under consideration.

A far more complex undertaking has been the creation of the European Economic Community, familiarly referred to as Euromarket, or the Common Market. The Economic Community is responsible for the full integration of the economies of the six nations. The process is to be a gradual one. Many industries in Europe are protected indirectly by subsidy, special tax privileges and other supports—as well as protected directly by tariffs and quotas. Therefore, the Common Market treaty provides for periods of transition during which tariffs between the Six are to be gradually reduced and quotas gradually enlarged. The total transition period to a full common market will take twelve years and under no condition can it take longer than fifteen years. After that period, tariffs and quotas between the Six as well as other restrictions to the free flow of trade will be abolished.

Another feature of the treaty is that overseas areas (mostly in Africa) associated with France, Belgium and Italy are given free access to the Common Market. The treaty provides a fund of $582,000,000 to be invested by the six member countries in these territories during the first five years of the Economic Community's existence.

Another part of the Economic Community structure is the European Investment Bank. Set up under the treaty, it is capitalized at a billion dollars. Its chief purpose is to lend funds to Community industry and agriculture for modernization.

The federal agencies of the European Community are recognized officially by other nations as the beginning of a federal government of Europe. Eleven nations, including the United States and Britain, sent ambassadors and accredited representatives to Luxembourg to the Coal and Steel Community after its founding. Now diplomatic representation has been extended to the new executives of the Common Market and Atomic Energy Communities. The

United States has appointed a full-time representative with personal rank of ambassador to all three Communities.

In Luxembourg, first capital of Europe, on the cornerstone of the new European School built there in 1956, these words are inscribed in Latin: "Young pupils educated in contact with each other, freed from their earliest years from the prejudices that divide one nation from another, and introduced to the value and beauty of different cultures, will have a growing sense of their common solidarity. Retaining their pride in, and love for, their own countries, they will become Europeans in spirit ready to complete and consolidate the work that their fathers have undertaken for the advance of a united and prosperous Europe."

The European Community represents the first steps toward the realization of this ideal. If it succeeds, it will be a great achievement for the people of Europe and for the entire free world.

Steel production and trade figures show the Community's world economic importance.

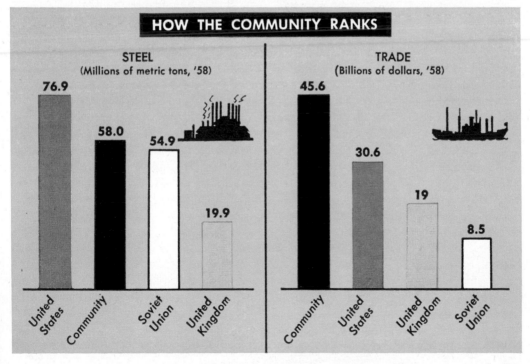

HOW THE COMMUNITY RANKS

STEEL
(Millions of metric tons, '58)

76.9 — United States
58.0 — Community
54.9 — Soviet Union
19.9 — United Kingdom

TRADE
(Billions of dollars, '58)

45.6 — Community
30.6 — United States
19 — United Kingdom
8.5 — Soviet Union

BERLIN

By H. V. KALTENBORN
News Analyst

EAST GERMANY · Berlin · Poland · Denmark · Baltic Sea · Netherlands · WEST GERMANY · Belgium · Luxembourg · Czechoslovakia · France · Austria · Switzerland · 0 100 Scale of miles

OUTPOST OF THE WEST

In 1959 Berlin was a focal point of world tension and concern. Located near the center of Europe, in the northeastern part of Germany, this third-largest city in Western Europe (after London and Paris) has been a "free island in a communist sea" since 1945.

The Berliners refer to themselves as "the islanders." They live 110 miles behind the iron curtain. The city is now divided into free West Berlin with 186 square miles under the protection of the Western powers, and East Berlin with 156 square miles under communist domination.

The Russians would like to see all of Berlin swallowed up by the communist German Democratic Republic. The contrast between prosperous, rebuilt West Berlin and shoddy, impoverished East Berlin is too glaring to be tolerated.

From a military point of view, Berlin cannot be successfully defended. Russian troops could overrun the city and its small British-French-American garrison in a matter of hours. But since this would launch a major war, Soviet Premier Khrushchev continues to tolerate what he has

often described as "a bone in my throat."

The Russians, overrun by German troops in World War I and again in World War II, are desperately afraid of a rebuilt, remilitarized Germany. They will do anything they can to prevent Germany from again becoming a threat to Russia.

The Western powers are determined to continue Berlin's links with the Federal Republic of Germany, of which it remains the unofficial "capital city." Because West Berlin has been a showcase of Western achievement, the people under communist rule can see there what a free people can achieve in the way of reconstruction and economic progress. West Berlin also stands as a symbol of the United States commitment in Europe.

As for the people of West Berlin, who have been through so many crises, occupations and hardships over the centuries, they want above all else the restoration of their complete independence and freedom.

Today Berlin stands as a symbol to the Germans of their country's past achievements and future hopes. Since it was first established in the thirteenth century, Berlin

A CITY DIVIDED

THE BRANDENBURG GATE

GERMAN TOURIST INFORMATION OFFICE

has been a focal point in German history. The Hohenzollerns, rulers of Brandenburg, made Berlin their chief residence from the end of the fifteenth century. The Great Elector, Frederick William, who ruled from 1640 till 1688, stimulated the growth of the city. In 1701 it became the capital of the kingdom of Prussia. Frederick the Great further enhanced its size and importance.

As Prussia gradually assumed leadership and control of all Germany, Berlin increased in importance. When the German railway system was established, Berlin was made the center of the web of rail lines. A network of canals was built to connect the capital of Prussia with the other German states. In 1871, under the leadership of Bismarck, the German states were consolidated into one nation, and Berlin became

the capital of the new German Empire. As Germany grew in economic and political strength, Berlin continued to expand.

It was only natural that Adolf Hitler, who became dictator of Germany in 1933, would seek to build up Berlin as the capital of his Third Reich. By 1939, with 4,300,-000 inhabitants, Berlin had become the greatest commercial and industrial city in Europe. However, just as it had become the symbol of Hitler's conquests and power, in 1945 it became the symbol of his complete defeat. As the Allied armies swept across Germany from the west, the Russians conquered the city from the east.

The city was 70 per cent destroyed and 25 per cent of the population was killed. More than half the dwellings were left uninhabitable. This was the result of a com-

Mayor Ernst Reuter rallied West Berlin during hard days of 1948–49 blockade.

Mayor Willy Brandt is the symbol of West Berlin's determination to stay free.

141

SEEGER-PIX

ROSENTHAL-PIX

BRUNNER PIX
WIDE WORLD

West Berlin: strollers pass the sidewalk cafes on the fashionable Kurfürstendamm; cars and full shops are the mark of the Schlossstrasse, a typical shopping street.

bination of air raids and twelve days of artillery bombardment by the Russians.

The city fell to Russian troops on May 1, 1945. By the time Russia allowed the other Allied troops to enter Berlin to begin the agreed-upon joint occupation, the entire city had been plundered by Russian troops. Quantities of industrial equipment that remained after the Russian occupation began were shipped back to Russia as "reparations."

On June 5, 1945, the former capital of Germany was officially divided into four sectors of occupation among the British, French, Russians and Americans. But no provision was made for assuring free access for any or all of the Big Three from the west to Berlin, situated deep in Russian-controlled territory.

For a short time the whole of Berlin was administered jointly by the four Occupying Powers under an Allied *Kommandatura* which supervised uneasily the slow rebuilding of the destroyed city. The city was in desperate straits, crowded with war victims, refugees and unemployed. The only links between Berlin and the western part of Germany were a single-track railroad,

a highway and some canals, all under Russian control.

Repudiated decisively in city elections, the Communists did everything they could to restrict and hamper the work of the freely elected city government. The Russians aimed from the first to drive the Allies out of Berlin and absorb the entire city into the Eastern zone of Germany under communist control. This plan came to partial fruition on June 24, 1948, when the Russians, acting in defiance of previous agreements, proclaimed dissolution of the Four Power authority governing Berlin. The city was arbitrarily divided into two sections, West and East, with two rival military governments and two rival local governments. The Russians went one step further and clamped a blockade on the Western half of Berlin, hoping by that move to drive out the three Western powers.

The Allied answer was the Berlin airlift which successfully supplied the city by air for fifteen months. From June 26, 1948, till September 30, 1949, some 2,300,000 tons of food and coal as well as other goods and supplies were flown into Western Berlin. The people of Berlin were resolute in

142

East Berlin: the Leipzigerstrasse still carries the marks of wartime bombings; on another street, boots click again as the Communists stage a military parade.

their determination to resist Russian domination. Their resistance, a counter-blockade and the success of the expensive airlift eventually persuaded the Russians that their plan would not succeed. They abandoned their blockade.

Due to the blockade, Berlin's economic recovery lagged behind the rest of West Germany. The municipal authorities were further burdened with the ever increasing number of refugees who poured into West Berlin from the East Zone of Germany. As West Germany prospered, more and more Germans fled from the regimented life in East Germany into the prosperous West. The contrast between Berlin East and West remained a source of constant worry to the Russians.

On November 10, 1958, the Russians began another effort to drive the Western Allies out of West Berlin. In a foreign-policy speech delivered in Moscow, Soviet Premier Nikita Khrushchev denounced the Western occupation of Berlin. He declared his intention of transferring Russia's functions as an occupying power in East Berlin to the East German communist regime. In an effort to bolster the East German Government, Khrushchev proposed to the Western powers that they recognize and deal with it about their rights and interests in Berlin. He later gave the West until May 27, 1959, to adjust to the new situation.

During the long and inconclusive meeting of the foreign ministers of the United States, Britain, France and the Soviet Union in Geneva this Russian threat remained in force. However, shortly after the Geneva talks ended there began a series of moves by the heads of the great powers that seemed to mark a general thaw in the cold war and a particular lessening of the tension over Berlin. First, President Eisenhower visited Bonn, London and Paris. Then, Premier Khrushchev toured the United States. In December, Eisenhower, Macmillan, De Gaulle, and Adenauer met in Paris at a Western summit conference. Although the concrete results of these moves were slight, they did point toward an important meeting that might settle the outstanding questions between East and West. Only the future would tell whether they would bring a peaceful solution for the people of Berlin.

143

Dwight D. Eisenhower and Richard M. Nixon, the Republican winners in 1952 and 1956; Democratic loser, Adlai E. Stevenson.

THE BIG POLITICAL SHOWS OF 1960

By MERRIMAN SMITH
White House correspondent
for United Press International

THE scene is a vast hall, the center a great arena ringed by crowded tiers of seats much in the manner of the old Roman Colosseum. The air above the pit is choking with smoke and the humidity cast off by thousands of people. Signs proudly proclaim the names of the fifty states.

The noise is terrific. A bull-voiced loudspeaker system protrudes its horns out over the crowd and from it comes a flow of frequently unintelligible voices. On a huge rostrum at one end of the hall, high over the center pit, a sweating man pounds frequently with a polished wooden gavel. He turns occasionally to advisers behind him in an effort to keep track of what is hap-

144

pening far beyond his range of hearing and vision.

In this mixture of carnival and stock exchange, the American people through their two major political parties select their candidates for president.

Late in the summer of 1960, just when the baseball-pennant races are beginning to shape up, the Democrats and the Republicans will hold their national nominating conventions. The Republicans will meet in a vast arena beside the stockyards in Chicago, while the Democrats are going to be in a new exposition hall in Los Angeles.

Because of the travel expense involved for the many delegates who come from states east of the Mississippi, the big political parties rarely go to the Far West for their conventions. The Republicans did, however, in 1956 and the Democrats decided that they, too, would acknowledge the rising importance of the West by having their 1960 convention in California.

The Democrats also were motivated in their choice of Los Angeles by the fact that Vice-President Richard M. Nixon, a front-runner for the Republican nomination, is a Californian. In the 1958 Congressional elections in California the Democrats had great success and they want to take fullest possible advantage of their gains by convening there in 1960.

The so-called splinter, or minor, political parties have national conventions, too, but these smaller conventions usually do not receive the full-scale attention of the newspapers and the broadcasters. The reason is that comparatively few people are involved, public interest is limited and, more important, the minor candidates are going to get only a few votes.

The big show is between the Republicans and the Democrats. The many millions of people who have access to radio and television sets can follow the big conventions hour by hour. Television as an instrument of national politics has been a fine

thing for the country in that it brings the selection of a presidential candidate before the eyes of the entire nation. But there has been another result something less than desirable: some of the convention delegates are carried away by the thought of appearing on television. The result is that the casting of a routine vote often becomes a chance for the delegate involved to make the most of his brief moment in the coast-to-coast spotlight.

The great press associations and the major newspapers concentrate more man power on a national political convention than on most news events, even more than on the inauguration of a president or the coronation of a queen.

Because a convention is a large, unwieldy and frequently scattered affair, many important developments do not occur in the convention hall. Many important decisions are made in mid-town hotels of the city, where political bosses and managers of the various candidates meet to cajole, wheedle, pressure and otherwise influence the delegates.

Planning for a national political convention starts about two years ahead of the actual event. The advance planning is conducted by the powerful national committees of the parties. The Democratic and Republican national committees both have their headquarters in Washington where they can be close to the hub of political activity in the country—the Congress of the United States.

Through their executive committees and special-site committees the national organizations receive and consider bids from the larger cities. On rare occasions the Republican and Democratic committees consult with each other with the hope of getting together on a convention town and thus saving money. Such a city as Los Angeles, Chicago or Philadelphia is willing to pay a political party hundreds of thousands of dollars for a convention. This money comes

145

from the chamber of commerce, the trade development board and the merchants and hotelkeepers of the city who want to attract the delegates, the sight-seers, the reporters and photographers—and all the money they will spend.

Before the election, delegates and their alternates (each delegate has at least one alternate in case the delegate is away or ill) are chosen through a number of selective devices, varying with the state. In about half the states delegates are elected directly by the public. In the rest they are chosen by district or state conventions. The way the delegates are chosen within any state must conform with that state's primary laws. Some states have presidential preferential primaries in which the voters select slates of delegates who are committed to specific candidates. In some states the high candidate wins the entire state delegation of one party, for at least one convention ballot.

Most of the preconvention fireworks in 1960 will come in sixteen states, for these sixteen states have presidential preference primary laws by which the voters of each major party indicate their choice for the presidential nomination. They usually mark this choice on the same ballot on which they elect delegates to the national convention. In most cases, convention delegates are not required to abide by the choice of their state's voters beyond one or two convention ballots.

However, the value of a victory in a

series of these popularity contests is considerable, and defeat even in one of them can doom a candidate as having no popular appeal.

In the states where convention delegates are chosen by the party's organization in that state, the governor of the state usually heads the delegation of his party.

The number of delegates from each state varies according to the state's population. This means that the larger delegations come from California, New York, Illinois, Pennsylvania and Texas. Although it is possible for a presidential candidate to win a presidential election without all of the big states' electoral votes, it is exceedingly difficult to win nomination in a convention without their votes.

It would seem in these days of high political organization that the preliminary skirmishing for delegates would decide the result of a convention far in advance. Frequently this has been true, but there have been notable exceptions.

In 1940, for example, the late President Franklin D. Roosevelt let it be known in advance of the Democratic convention that he would try for a third term. This outraged many of his party's key figures, including the national chairman, James A. Farley. But as long as Roosevelt wanted the nomination, there was little doubt that he would get it—and he did.

The Republicans that year thought the dissension within the Democratic Party was giving them their first real opportunity in

Four senators who are in the Democratic nomination race; Hubert Humphrey of Minnesota, John Kennedy of Massachusetts, Stuart Symington of Missouri and Lyndon Johnson of Texas.

By contrast, the Democratic convention in 1952 was a study in confusion. In the preconvention developments, including some of the preferential primaries, Senator Estes Kefauver of Tennessee showed delegate strength. Adlai E. Stevenson, then the governor of Illinois, was showing strength, too, but said he would not seek the nomination actively.

It should be pointed out that presidents in office (like Truman in 1952) invariably go to great lengths to assure the public that, as far as they are concerned, the convention will be free and open, with no attempt by the president to dictate the nomination.

This is part of American political folklore. The man in the White House would be less than human if he failed to use some of his vast influence on the selection of a man who may be his successor. This certainly was true at the Democratic convention in Chicago in 1952. President Truman was operating over the long-distance telephone from Washington. At what he deemed the proper moment, he telephoned his Secretary of the Interior, Oscar Chapman, and told him to pass the word that he, Truman, was ready to "give 'em hell" in behalf of Stevenson. And, of course, Stevenson won the nomination.

From the spectator's point of view the conventions in 1956 were rather uninteresting since the renomination of Eisenhower and Stevenson seemed almost automatic. But watch out for 1960! It will take a large and complicated score card to tell the players and no one can guess the winners.

eight years to win the national elections. The so-called professionals—the men and women who make politics their life work—of the Grand Old Party had several favorites, among them New York's young governor, Thomas E. Dewey, and the late Senator from Ohio, Robert A. Taft. However, so-called amateurs took over the GOP convention and through not-so-amateur tactics stormed the delegates and nominated a virtually brand new political figure—Wendell L. Willkie. Even with war facing the United States, Willkie gave F. D. R. his toughest race up to that time.

In 1952 the conventions produced, at least in the Republican Party, a situation very like that in 1940. In the months leading up to the midsummer national convention, the GOP professionals were aligned in considerable depth behind Senator Taft. There were, however, many Republicans promoting the name of a national hero—General Dwight D. Eisenhower, who was in Paris at the time as commander of the North Atlantic Treaty Organization forces. The politically fresh name and image of Eisenhower—or Ike—caught on with the delegates. He came home from Paris in the late spring of 1952 to begin a series of speeches and firsthand meetings with state delegations. The Taft forces retained considerable strength as the convention got under way, but the contest within the convention itself was relatively brief and the Eisenhower forces swept to the nomination dramatically and powerfully.

Nelson Rockefeller of New York and Robert Meyner of New Jersey, two governors who are possible candidates.

147

As 1959 drew to a close, Vice-President Richard M. Nixon seemed to have the backing of the Republican professionals and the more conservative elements in the GOP. But a new face in Republican politics, Governor Nelson A. Rockefeller of New York, was, in the language of the race track, coming up fast on the outside.

The Democrats had a host of hopefuls. Their leading contenders were Massachusetts' Senator John Kennedy, two-time nominee Adlai Stevenson, Missouri's Senator Stuart Symington, Texas' Senator Lyndon Johnson and Minnesota's Senator Hubert Humphrey. Whoever finally wins the nomination, the Democratic convention fight is certain to be more complex and probably more entertaining than the Republican fight with only two major adversaries.

The gleaming glass eye of television will be watching for most of us at the 1960 ringsides in Chicago and Los Angeles. As they have done since 1952, when TV first offered blanket coverage of the proceedings, the party leaders are trying to streamline the convention proceedings to hold public boredom to a minimum. Although the words of an orator may sound exceedingly sweet to the speaker and his friends and relatives, they can be a frightful pain for millions of home viewers.

Meeting on the West Coast, the Democrats will have a special problem in commanding a large nationwide television audience. This is because of the three-hour time difference between California and the populous eastern half of the nation. The Democrats will have to do their big speaking early in the evening if they don't want to be blocked out of the living rooms by Jack Paar or old movies.

The Democrats have contributed some grand moments to national politics. Sadly, some of the more dramatic performances took place before the days of television, as when Henry A. Wallace first won the Democratic vice-presidential nomination at Chicago in 1940, and cheers for Wallace were piped into the convention hall. This led the anti-Wallace forces to label this sort of nonresident tub-thumping as "the voices from the sewer."

In the 1952 Democratic convention a fire broke out behind the South Carolina delegation at a point when the Southerners were threatening to walk out in a wrangle over the civil-rights plank in the party. This gave many newspaper correspondents a marvelous opportunity to tell how Southern tempers "went up in smoke."

A convention has the noisy, emotional aspects of a home-coming football game. Fist fights are not uncommon. Partisan banners, buttons and posters virtually hide the delegates from view. It is a mark of social station and worth to have box seats in the spectator section of a convention hall, and there is an enormous demand for them. The argument over distribution of tickets to the 1960 Democratic convention grew so heated in 1959—more than a year ahead of time—that, for a while, the national committee was thinking about moving the meeting out of Los Angeles.

The sound and fury of the floor proceedings are dramatic and entertaining, but it is important to remember that the show we will watch is much more than a show. A national convention, for all its surface foolishness and fun, is an important process of representative government. It is the way the political parties, and through them the people of the United States, select two men to run for the most important office in the world. As the crowds cheer and the votes are tallied we must remember that one of the two men who will emerge from the conventions will be the leader of the free world for four fateful years. What we shall see on our television screens may well shape the history of the world.

Outrigger canoes with brightly colored sails land on the world-famous beach of Waikiki near Diamond Head.

HAWAII

By PADRAIC COLUM
Author and Poet

ON March 18, 1959, President Eisenhower signed a bill that brought a fiftieth state into the Union. The new state is different from the other forty-nine in divers ways. It is made up entirely of islands; a majority of its people are of Eastern rather than Western origin; and before it became a territory of the United States it was first a monarchy and then a republic.

The Hawaiian landscape is full of contrast—snowy peaks, smoldering volcanoes, coral reefs, and blue lagoons fringed with coconut palms. There are no large rivers, but the green valleys sparkle with tiny lakes and streams, interlaced with countless waterfalls. Brilliantly hued flowers

A rich mixture of tropical flowers and lush vegetation on the island of Kauai.

149

Smoke rises from a burning field of sugar cane. All the useless foliage is removed by the flames but the sugar in the stems is unhurt if they are cut down right away.

bloom all the year round; many of them strange to visitors from the mainland. Although the archipelago lies on the Tropic of Cancer, it is cooled by the northeast trade winds.

The eight islands of the main group have a total area of more than 6,400 square miles and a civilian population of over 600,000. More than half of these people live in the capital city, Honolulu, on Oahu, the third largest island. The largest of the group is Hawaii (4,021 square miles), then in descending order come Maui, Oahu, Kaui, Molokai, Lanai, Niihau and tiny Kahoolawe, which is only 45 square miles in area and is uninhabited.

Westward from the main group a chain of atolls, reefs and shoals is scattered over a thousand miles of ocean. These are called the Leewards, and most of them form the Hawaiian Island Bird Reserve.

Like the rest of the United States, Hawaii is made up of many ethnic groups. According to one estimate about 2% are full-

blooded Hawaiians (Polynesians), and 16% are part Hawaiian. Americans from the mainland account for 25%; Puerto Ricans, 2%; Europeans, 1%; Japanese, 35%; Filipinos, 12%; Chinese, 6%; and Koreans, 1%. Working together, these people have built a prosperous and civilized community. Hawaii has good schools, a university which was founded more than half a century ago, music and theater groups and two famous historical and art museums.

There are few industries in Hawaii, partly because land is scarce and expensive and taxes are high. The state's greatest source of revenue is the huge defense establishment of the United States Army, Navy and Air Force. Next come sugar, pineapple products, the tourist trade, fisheries and animal products—the tourists bring in as much money as the last two industries combined.

The Hawaiian archipelago came into written history when, in 1778, Captain

Torch-ginger flower, one of the striking blossoms of the islands.
FRITZ HENLE, PHOTO RESEARCHERS

S. NADELMANN, SHOSTAL

WERNER STOY, PHOTO RESEARCHERS

Fishermen wade ashore with their nets to prepare for another day's catch.

On the island of Hawaii the firepit of Kilauea Crater showers fire and smoke in an eruption.

James Cook of the British Navy visited the islands. He named them the Sandwich Islands, after the Earl of Sandwich, then first lord of the Admiralty. The people Cook found living on the islands were the original Hawaiians, whose ancestors had left the mainland of Asia hundreds of years before. Through the slow centuries they had fanned out over the Pacific in their canoes, settling many islands—Tahiti, Samoa, New Zealand, Hawaii. The northernmost limit of the migration was Hawaii, a 3,000-mile voyage from Samoa.

The Polynesians were able to travel in canoes across the vast, unknown ocean because they knew the positions and move-

151

Women and machines team to pack pineapples in the world's largest cannery, in Honolulu.

ments of the sun and the moon and the stars. They observed the heavens minutely and continuously, and all that they learned was passed down from generation to generation in their long, rhythmic chants.

In Hawaii the voyagers settled near the beaches, for much of their food came from the sea. The only land animals they had were pigs, dogs and poultry, brought with them in the canoes.

When Captain Cook arrived, about 200,000 people were living in the islands— fishing, farming and building canoes. They were ruled by chiefs, who were believed to be descended from gods and who had divine powers known as *tapu*. All the land was owned by the chiefs, who received rent in the form of produce.

Cook's visit brought about great changes in the life of the people. Rough sailors

Flower leis hang ready for sale. Leis are woven from carnations, orchids and tuberoses.

and the offscourings of the seaports began to come in, bringing European diseases to which the Hawaiians had no resistance. For many years violent epidemics of smallpox, measles, influenza and other diseases steadily reduced the population.

In 1790, with the help of the foreigners' ships, one of the chiefs made himself monarch of the eight islands. This was Kamehameha I. He was a strong and able ruler, but his successors were weak and could not control the foreign element. A few enlightened Hawaiians, seeing that the social order was breaking down, appealed to the New England missionary schools; and in 1820 a group of Congregational missionaries made the long voyage round Cape Horn. They brought Christianity to Hawaii. They learned the Hawaiian language, reduced it to writing and printed books that the Hawaiians read with delight.

The result of this was that Hawaii, though still independent, came more and more under American influence. In 1893, when the last Hawaiian ruler was deposed, the provisional government applied for annexation to the United States, but President Cleveland was opposed to it. A republic was set up with Sanford B. Dole as president. Finally, in 1898, annexation took place. Two years later Hawaii became a territory of the United States, expecting eventually to be admitted to the Union. Today that expectation has at last been fulfilled; Hawaii is the fiftieth state.

A young Tibetan girl wearing a traditional striped apron.

TIBET

By LOWELL THOMAS, Jr.
Author and Explorer

DIDIER TAROT, PHOTO RESEARCHERS

Tibet, known for centuries as the Forbidden Land, is one of the most inaccessible places on earth. A country of 560,000 square miles, Tibet lies at an average altitude somewhere between 13,000 and 15,-000 feet and is almost entirely surrounded by massive mountain chains. In the south the mighty Himalayas separate Tibet from Nepal, Sikkim, Bhutan and India. In the west and northwest the Karakorams bend around Tibet in a gigantic arc, shutting out Kashmir and China's Sinkiang region. In the north the Kunluns link with the Karakorams. Only in the extreme east is there no lofty mountain barrier. Here the terrain undulates toward China in a series of rugged hills. The border between China and Tibet has always been ill-defined and a matter of dispute.

Within or near Tibet's borders rise seven of the world's great rivers—the Hwang Ho, Yangtze, Mekong, Salween, Brahmaputra, Ganges and, finally, the Indus.

Tibet has two major divisions. The Chang Tang plateau occupies the northern part of the country. It is a vast, bleak, frigid, wind-swept and forbidding wilderness. South of the Chang Tang plateau stretches the best part of Tibet—the warmer and more hospitable Valley of the Tsangpo (as the Brahmaputra is called by the Tibetans). Tibet's major cities—Lhasa, the capital, Shigatse and Gyangtse—are in the Tsangpo Valley. So is the best farmland.

There are about 1,300,000 Tibetans in Tibet. They would long since have been overrun and conquered had it not been for the protecting mountains around them. Behind this shield provided by nature, they have lived in security for centuries and developed a unique culture. They came to dislike foreign visitors as disturbers of their way of life. Their policy of seclusion has made Tibet the mysterious Forbidden Land of Western legend and romance.

Tibetans are not unfriendly as individuals. My father and I found them very cordial when we visited Lhasa in 1949. But they made no secret of their distaste for foreign customs and beliefs.

The society of Tibet is feudal. At the top are the aristocrats, who wear fine clothes, live in houses several stories high and enjoy all the honors and privileges of their rank. This aristocracy, however, is not a closed caste; other Tibetans often enter it when they become wealthy or influential enough. There is no middle class. The peasants do all the hard work. The great majority of Tibetans are farmers, who scratch a living from the soil of the Tsangpo Valley. The second largest group are nomads, who follow their herds and flocks. Many of these nomads escape to the Chang Tang plateau, where they become outlaws preying on the caravans bound for Lhasa.

The "work horse" of the Tibetan economy is the yak. This shaggy, patient, hardy and powerful relative of the buffalo performs an astonishing number of functions. The Tibetans ride yaks and yoke them to their plows. They use the hide and hair to make a whole array of articles, including boots, coats, beds, carpets and tents. Yak butter sweetens their tea and provides fuel for their lamps. Dried yak dung takes the place of firewood.

Many Tibetans grow rich in trade. From time immemorial, yak caravans have been plodding into Tibet with Chinese silk, Indian tea, and other articles to trade for Tibetan musk and yak tails.

An unusual thing about Tibet is that the people practice both polygyny and polyandry, that is one man may have several wives, or one woman several husbands, all at the same time.

DIDIER TAROT, PHOTO RESEARCHERS

Tibet has produced her share of poets, philosophers, artists and musicians. Her architecture alone is worth long study. The masterpiece of Tibetan architecture is the Potala, winter palace of the Dalai Lama.

The Potala is a towering structure built into the summit of a hill on the outskirts of Lhasa. The lower walls are whitewashed, those in the upper-central part painted red to show that they enclose the tombs of the Dalai Lamas. The roofs of these tombs glitter bright gold in the rarefied Tibetan atmosphere. In the Potala there are more than a thousand rooms, everything from dungeons to the private apartment of the Dalai Lama.

This wonderful building is a monument to the religious faith of the Tibetans. Their religion is Lamaism, a variant of Buddhism. The Buddhist creed came from China and mingled with the old pagan animism of Tibet called Bon Po. The result is a strange compound of metaphysical abstractions and very material gods and demons.

No people are more strict in performing

Dressed in the costume of an ancient Tibetan priest, a monk dances and mimes in an old play about a 9th-century Buddhist saint.

The Dalai Lama, head of both church and state in Tibet, was forced by the Chinese to flee his home and go into exile in India.

BALDEV KAPOOR, RAPHO GUILLUMETTE, PHOTO RESEARCHERS

their religious duties than the Tibetans. We saw prayer flags and prayer wheels in the meanest hovels in Lhasa. About a quarter of the male population goes into monasteries, of which one, Drepung, the largest in the world, houses 10,000 monks.

All Buddhists believe that some beings, having won the right to enter nirvana, choose instead to return to earth to aid suffering humanity. In Tibet these reincarnations are known as "lamas." Two are of special eminence—the Dalai Lama and the Panchen Lama.

The Dalai Lama is considered to be the god Chen-re-zi, the Lord of Mercy. Tibetans believe that when a Dalai Lama dies his spirit goes from his body to the body of his successor. Each successor is recognized in infancy by means of an elaborate ritual full of omens and soothsaying. After he is found, the Dalai Lama is escorted to

Lhasa and raised to be the god-king of Tibet, a theocrat who unites both church and state in his own person.

The Panchen Lama lives in the Tashi Lumpo monastery near Shigatse. He too is discovered by a complicated Lamaist ritual. Spiritually he is the equal of the Dalai Lama, for he is the Buddha of Boundless Light come down to earth. The really significant thing about the Panchen Lama is that he holds a purely religious office. The Tibetans revere him as a god

A Tibetan caravan pauses to set up a camp. Their camp is near the town of Kalimpong which is the terminus of the main trade route that goes between India and Tibet.

DIDIER TAROT, PHOTO RESEARCHERS

155

Palace, monastery and fortress, the towering Potala stands on the outskirts of Lhasa. Its lower walls are whitewashed, while the upper floors are red and the roof is gold.

incarnate, but they do not admit that he has any right to independent political power.

The reason for this is historical. The Dalai Lamas came first in the development of Tibetan Buddhism. They recognized the holiness of the lords of Tashi Lumpo, gave them status under the title of Panchen Lamas, and consulted them about religious affairs. The political supremacy of the Dalai Lama was taken for granted. There could be no question of rivalry between the two leaders until the Chinese decided to play the Panchen Lama off against the Dalai Lama.

Tibet had a taste of Chinese occupation before World War I. The then Dalai Lama, the Great Thirteenth who preceded the present one, fled to India rather than

submit. Peking set up the Panchen Lama as regent of Tibet and attempted to rule through him. The Tibetans, outraged by the indignities placed on their rightful leader, rebelled against the change. They were lucky that the Chinese Revolution of 1911, which overthrew the Manchu Dynasty and brought Sun Yat-sen to power, broke out at this time. Further Chinese occupation of Tibet became impossible and the Dalai Lama returned to Lhasa amid the rejoicing of his people.

In 1959 history seemed to repeat itself. Once again Chinese troops flooded over Tibet, bringing oppression and provoking resistance. The Fourteenth Dalai Lama reached safety in India after a daring escape from Lhasa, across Chinese-held territory, and through the Himalayas.

156

Rescue in Rhodesia

By R. H. HOBSON

Rhodesian Journalist

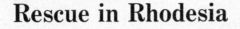

IN a hot, hidden valley in the heart of Africa, the great Zambezi River, which had flowed to the Indian Ocean slowly for millions of years, stopped in its course and began to spread north and south over its banks.

As the waters inched over the dry earth, millions of crickets crawled out of the sun-baked cracks and filled the air with their screeching. Small rafts of twigs and grass formed on the surface of the water, and scorpions, mice and shrews climbed on them. Millions upon millions of flying ants squeezed out of tiny holes and began their aimless fluttering flight. Overhead circled hundreds of egrets diving and swooping to catch them. Storks and plovers, lily-trotters, bee eaters and rollers gathered for the feast of insects.

In nine hours, the water in the narrow gorge rose six feet, and on the south bank, a row of islands quickly formed. Night fell and the croaking of thousands of frogs joined the chorus of crickets. In the tops of trees baboons crouched and shivered above the rising waters while puzzled antelope delicately picked their way to higher ground.

For the small group of men camped in tents on a rocky ridge overlooking the river, December 2, 1958, was the day for which they had been preparing for many

On an island in the rising waters, rescuers put up a camouflaged net to trap fleeing animals. They are then saved.

157

Behind the great wall of the dam the Zambezi steadily widens out, first creating, then swallowing islands. The force of all this water will eventually provide electric power for the entire federation.

weeks: the day on which they began a task that would not end for four years. It was the birth of Kariba, the greatest lake ever created by man, and it was the beginning of "Operation Noah," the task of saving the thousands of animals that would be trapped on islands and in trees as the waters spread over two thousand square miles.

"Operation Noah" is only part of the story of Kariba, and Kariba is only part of the story of the new Africa which in the last hundred years has outgrown its name of the Dark Continent.

The progress from darkness to light has been astonishing even to those who have lived through it. Nowhere has it been more astonishing than in that part of central Africa now called the Federation of Rhodesia and Nyasaland. This is an area of

nearly 500,000 square miles, divided into three countries: Southern Rhodesia, famous for its tobacco and gold; Northern Rhodesia, famous for its copper mines; Nyasaland, smallest and poorest of the three, but the most beautiful with its tremendous Lake Nyasa.

The development of these three countries was speeded seven years ago by joining them in a federation. The population grew, industries spread, and the need for a great source of electric power became urgent.

The answer lay in the Zambezi River, which runs from west to east as the natural boundary between Southern and Northern Rhodesia, passing through the narrow, rocky Kariba Gorge—though the name should really be Kariwa, the African name for a trap.

The legend is that many years ago a great lake existed where the new lake is now being formed. This lake broke through

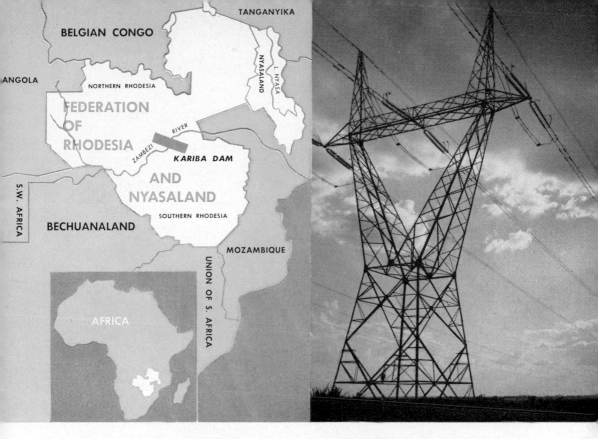

the present gorge, leaving a massive slab of rock, the Kariwa, suspended between the two walls of the gorge. The rock eventually collapsed. The legend of the lake is borne out to some extent by the finding of rounded pebbles far from the river's edge.

This gorge was a perfect place for building a concrete dam. When completed, the dam will have a curved wall rising to 420 feet, which will be higher even than Victoria Falls. The dam will cost, with all its machinery and buildings, about £114,-000,000 ($319,200,000) when it is finally completed.

When the river was stopped in its course it was a moment of drama for the engineers and builders and also for scientists—biologists, ecologists and anthropologists.

It was known that two thousand square miles of dry land would be covered by water. Before the dam wall was joined, thousands of Africans of the primitive Batonga tribe who had lived on the banks of

the river had been moved to high, safe land to begin a new life. The anthropologists and sociologists turned their attention to them to see how they would be affected by their new way of life. Down at the edge of the rising waters, other scientists watched to see the effect on mammal, insect, reptile and bird life, on fish that moved from a running river to a comparatively still lake.

Of even greater interest was the problem of the animals who would be trapped on islands and in trees as the water surrounded them and spread and surrounded other hills and rose over them and covered them.

They had to be rescued somehow, and this was the task of the game wardens, the men who look after the wildlife in the national parks and game reserves of the Federation. These men were ready on both banks of the river and, almost as soon as the first cricket was flushed from its crack in the dry earth, they were out in their boats to begin the job that soon be-

Rescuers Race the Rising Waters

A rescued vervet monkey starts its journey to the mainland.

Antelopes are hard to save, often dying of fright when they are caught.

PHOTOS, BRITISH INFORMATION SERVICES

came known as "Operation Noah." It was a new job, even to them, and they soon found that it had difficulties and dangers that no one had thought of. Dangerous snakes reared and curled in the trees; frightened baboons snapped at the friendly hands that sought to help them to safety; scorpions lurked in hundreds in the van of the advancing waters.

They gained experience quickly. A baboon in the water can be grasped by the tail and lifted out, seized behind the head and hind legs, and held safely. Small antelope, it was found, had to be treated with great care, or the extremely timid animals would die from shock and fear.

As the days passed and the waters rose higher, the numbers of animals saved grew bigger and bigger and rose to hundreds. They included bushbuck and duiker, im-

pala and kudu, wart hog and night ape, civet cats, monkeys, aardvarks, dassies, bush pigs, guinea fowl and even three domestic cats.

The game wardens learned that if land was not too far off the larger antelope could be driven into the water and across to safety. Zebra, they found, can swim about six hundred yards, kudu a mile, while the duiker soon tire in the water.

Four months after the lake began to form, it was so big that, at one point, water stretched to the horizon. Hundreds of animals had been rescued, and relatively few were known to have died. Many more, of course, reached safety by their own efforts.

But the story was only beginning. The lake will not be full until 1963. This means years of rescuing small animals, persuading and driving the larger ones—even ele-

A bush baby (galago) snatched from a treetop as it submerged.

Exhausted bush pig seems too tired to fight its rescuers.

Game ranger holding young doe antelope he has saved.

Bushbuck antelope swimming beside the game ranger's boat.

phant and buffalo—to swim to safety. Guns that fire a drugged dart are used so that the fear-stricken animals can be put to sleep and taken ashore quietly to recover. The deadly mamba snake has to be caught with a slip noose, which is drawn tight behind its head to prevent it from biting its rescuers. One of the more dangerous aspects of the rescue work is eluding the crocodiles that swim about in the lake.

Volunteers from many parts of the world have offered to help, but most have been turned away, since the work can be entrusted only to men with long experience with wild animals. The rescue operation has led to the collection of funds to provide more boats and equipment.

As you read this you can be sure that the boats are out on the waters of the lake and nosing into anchorages by the little is-lands. You can be sure that the sunburned game rangers and their African helpers are diving into the water to help a drowning impala or a struggling monkey, or netting a tiny duiker on an island, perhaps knocking a tree-bound lizard into the water to capture and rescue it.

They will travel farther and farther as the lake grows to its ultimate length of about two hundred miles. Rescue operations will go on long after the great turbines of the powerhouses have begun to turn and power passes down hundreds of miles of cable to the factories and mines of the cities and towns of the Federation.

There in the hot valley, far from civilization, "Operation Noah" will go on until the game wardens are sure that no mouse, no lizard, no elephant remains that can be brought to safety.

SATELLITES AT WORK

By PHILIP J. KLASS
Avionics Editor, Aviation Week

THE man-made satellites now in orbit around the earth are the forerunners of satellites that will perform many unusual and useful tasks for us all within the next ten to twenty years.

There will be meteorological satellites that will measure and report back on the earth's cloud cover (size and location of all clouds). Then weather forecasters can predict accurately storms and other weather conditions far in advance. With the increased knowledge gained from meteorological satellites, we may even be able to control our weather—at least to some extent.

The communications-relay satellite will make it possible to transmit television and telephone signals from any point on the earth to any other. By utilizing these satellites it will be possible to see important events taking place anywhere in the world, on the screen of a home TV set.

Still another type of satellite will serve as a navigation beacon to show the crews of airplanes, ships and submarines their precise position.

Work on these, and on other types of satellites designed to probe the unknown depths of space, is already under way in the laboratories of government and industry. The first of these new satellites are scheduled to be shot into orbit within the next few years.

Satellites are shot into orbit by powerful rocket engines. These lift them to an altitude of several hundred miles and give them speeds of approximately 18,000 miles per hour or more. Once in orbit, the satellite circles the earth.

Fired at very high speed, the satellite is restrained by the pull of the earth's gravity from going out into space.

The situation is similar to what would happen if you tied a rock to the end of a string, took hold of the other end of the string and started swinging it around your head. The rock tries to break free because of what is called centrifugal force but is kept from flying off by the string—which corresponds to the gravity pull of the earth on the satellite. The result is that the rock "orbits" around your head in much the same way a satellite orbits around the earth.

There is only one ten-billionth as much air at an altitude of two hundred miles as there is here on earth. However, this is enough to slow down a satellite ever so slightly with each revolution. The amount of drag on the satellite depends upon its orbital altitude. As the satellite loses speed it drops down to a slightly lower altitude. This increases the amount of drag, causing it to lose more speed and more altitude. Eventually the satellite reaches an altitude at which the air resistance (drag) is enough to heat up the satellite to the point where it burns up and disintegrates.

Although most satellites that have so far been launched have had a lifetime of only

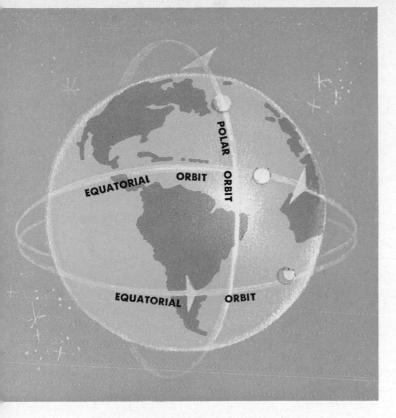

Polar orbit results when the satellite is shot in a north-south direction. Equatorial orbit results when satellite is shot in easterly direction.

a few months, the United States Vanguard I is expected to remain in orbit for more than one hundred years before it disintegrates.

While the satellite is revolving around the earth, the earth itself is rotating on its axis. This is why a satellite may be directly over New York City on one pass over the United States, while on the next orbit it may pass over Kansas City, and on the next over Los Angeles.

If the satellite originally is shot into space in a north-south direction, called a "polar orbit," it will pass over every portion of the earth twice a day.

Another type of satellite orbit is one in which the satellite is shot into space so that it circles the earth in an easterly direction around the earth's equator. If the satellite can be boosted up to an altitude of approximately 22,400 miles above the earth, it will be rotating at exactly the same speed as the earth is turning on its axis.

The result will be that both the earth and satellite will be revolving at the same speed, and the satellite will appear to be fixed with respect to the earth. Such a satellite could, for example, be made to hover over any desired spot on the earth's equator.

Dozens of factors influence our daily weather, many of them taking place thousands of miles away. The United States, Europe and other populated areas all over the world have extensive weather-reporting-station networks. However, for at least two thirds of the earth's surface, the area covered by water, relatively little weather information can be obtained. It is no wonder that forecasters have such a difficult time in accurately predicting the weather!

One very important factor influencing our weather is believed to be the location and extent of cloud cover over the surface of the earth. These clouds not only carry the moisture that produces rain and snow, but they also act as umbrellas to shield portions of the earth's atmosphere from the sun's warming rays. It is believed that if weather forecasters could get a continual and up-to-date picture of the size and location of the earth's cloud cover, they could learn more about the causes of weather and make more accurate long-range forecasts.

A satellite, which orbits above the earth's atmosphere and can look down on the world's cloud cover, would seem to be the ideal means of getting such information. With this purpose in mind, the satellite will be equipped with one or more tiny TV cameras able to discriminate between clouds and the earth. The cloud-cover picture taken by the TV camera will be recorded on a tiny tape recorder in the satellite. When it passes over a ground radio station set up to receive such information, the satellite will transmit to the radio station the cloud-cover picture it has recorded. Then it will go on to make a fresh picture on its next pass.

On earth, the radio signal will be recorded on tape. Later it will be used to produce a strip photo that shows the cloud cover above the area over which the satellite has just passed.

Before the satellites were created, the only way to transmit radio signals over distances of several thousand miles was to use what is called high frequency (abbreviated HF). Such HF radio signals are not always reliable. They can be interrupted, or even blacked out completely, by atmospheric disturbances. Furthermore, HF radio signals are not suitable for transmitting television programs.

On the other hand, radio signals transmitted at very high frequency (VHF) or ultrahigh frequency (UHF) are much more reliable. These signals can carry TV signals, but they cannot reach out more than about two hundred miles from the

HOW RADIO SIGNALS TRAVEL

BROADCAST BAND

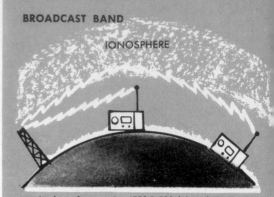

At these frequencies (550-1,500 kilocycles) waves curve around earth as far as 150 miles by day. At night, signals may bounce off ionosphere, electrically charged atmospheric layers 50-500 miles up, and carry as far as 750 miles.

SHORT WAVE

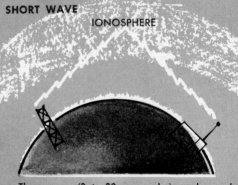

These waves (3 to 30 megacycles) are bounced back from higher in ionosphere, travel about 2,500 miles in one bounce, farther in repeated bounces. But ionosphere is unreliable reflector and signals often fade.

VHF AND UHF

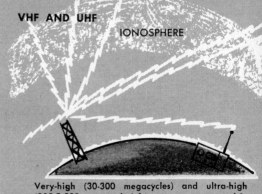

Very-high (30-300 megacycles) and ultra-high (300-3,000 megacycles) frequency waves travel in straight lines and do not bounce. These frequencies (used for TV, telephone relay and so on) are good only for line-of-sight transmission.

BOUNCING SIGNALS OFF A BALLOON

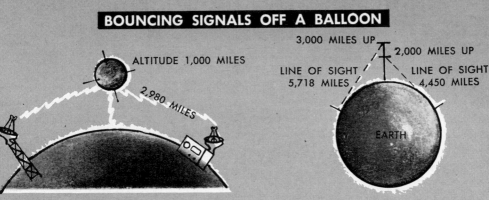

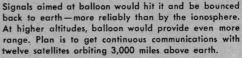

Because short-wave bands are crowded as well as un-reliable, National Aeronautics and Space Administration hopes to use satellite for long-range transmission of military, telephone-relay and possibly TV signals. A 100-foot plastic balloon is to be orbited 1,000 miles up.

Signals aimed at balloon would hit it and be bounced back to earth—more reliably than by the ionosphere. At higher altitudes, balloon would provide even more range. Plan is to get continuous communications with twelve satellites orbiting 3,000 miles above earth.

"HOVERING" SATELLITES TO COVER THE EARTH

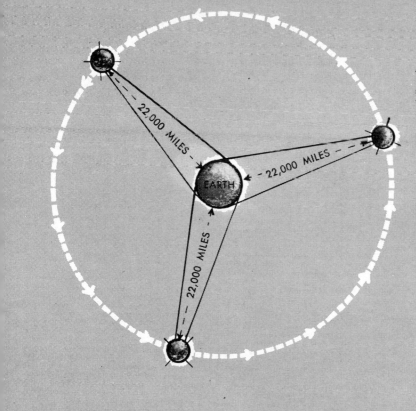

A more complicated project is planned that would make it possible to blanket the entire earth with a simultaneous signal. Three satellites would be orbited at 22,-000 miles, evenly spaced above the equator. At that height the velocity of a satellite in orbit is such that its period of rotation is the same as that of the earth—and thus each satellite would "hover" over a spot on the earth just below it. A signal bounced off one such satellite would cover a large portion of the earth. And if the signal were bounced from one satellite to the others and thence back to earth, simultaneous round-the-world reception would be possible.

earth's surface under normal conditions. This is because HF signals are reflected back to the earth from a layer of electrons called the ionosphere, at an altitude of about sixty miles—rather as a stone can be made to skip great distances along the surface of a pond. On the other hand, VHF and UHF radio signals are not reflected by the ionosphere; they shoot out into space, and are lost forever.

The simplest type of communications-relay satellite is a large plastic balloon coated with aluminum paint so that it will reflect radio signals. The plastic balloon is not inflated until it has been carried by the rocket to an altitude of several hundred miles where the air density is very low.

When this type of satellite, called a passive relay, is in orbit, one ground radio station transmits a VHF or UHF signal, using an antenna aimed at the satellite. The signal bounces off and is reflected back to earth thousands of miles away. Here it is received by another ground station which has its antenna pointed at the satellite.

The maximum distance over the earth's surface at which the reflected signal can be received depends upon the altitude of the satellite. For example, if the satellite is at an altitude of 3,000 miles, it can relay messages between two earth stations that are 4,000 miles apart. Communication between two stations on the earth is possible only when the satellite is within view of both stations. Because the satellite is orbiting around the earth, it will remain in view of both stations for only a few minutes at a time.

If a number of such satellites are placed in orbit simultaneously, with suitable spacing between them (like horses on a merry-go-round), then at least one satellite will always be in view of any two ground stations.

Another type of communications satellite, known as an active relay, carries a miniature radio receiver and transmitter on board, together with batteries or other means of generating electric power. Any radio message transmitted up to the satellite from one earth station is immediately rebroadcast by the satellite. This enables the message to be received by another earth station thousands of miles away. The only requirement is that both stations be within view of the satellite at the same time.

If the two earth stations are many thousands of miles apart, a delayed relay, or "courier" type, satellite can be used. Here the message received from one earth station is stored on a tiny tape recorder in the satellite until it passes over the station for which the message is intended. At that time, the message stored on the recorder is broadcast to the second earth station.

It was such a satellite that in December 1958 transmitted a human voice from outer space for the very first time. The voice was President Eisenhower's, carrying a message of good will for the new year to the peoples of the world.

If a satellite is outfitted with a tiny radio transmitter, which continuously transmits a precise signal, the crews of aircraft, ships and submarines can determine the satellite's position relative to their own craft. This is the way navigators now use an optical sextant to sight on a distant star. Then, by means of special tables that show the satellite's position at every instant during the day, the position of the airplane, ship or submarine can be calculated.

By outfitting a satellite with tiny TV cameras and telescopes, it should be possible for it to perform military reconnaissance. One program under development is intended to produce satellites equipped with infrared sensors, which can detect the firing of ballistic missiles.

Within twenty years, earth satellites will be doing all kinds of jobs of great importance. The work they do promises to bring great changes to the world.

ALBERT EINSTEIN MEDAL

Dr. Willard F. Libby, nuclear scientist, resigned as member of Atomic Energy Commission to return to research and teaching at University of California. A gold medal and $5,000 in cash are given by the Strauss Memorial Fund for outstanding contributions to scientific knowledge.

Dr. Libby, best known for his work with radioactive elements, was first to find carbon-14 atoms in nature. He founded the technique of radiocarbon dating, thus providing a new way to establish the exact age of archaeological and historical discoveries that are often made.

AGASSIZ MEDAL

Dr. Martin W. Johnson, professor of marine biology, Scripps Institution of Oceanography, La Jolla, California. By the National Academy of Sciences for research in underwater acoustics during World War II, and contributions to a reference publication on oceanography, *The Oceans*, by Sverdrup, Johnson and Fleming.

Scientists in the NEWS

FRANKLIN MEDAL

Dr. Hans A. Bethe, theoretical physicist, Cornell University; and consultant to Atomic Energy Commission. The highest award of the Franklin Institute for his theory that the carbon-nitrogen cycle is instrumental in the sun's energy production, an aid to understanding of physical universe.

Dr. Charles H. Townes, physics professor, Columbia University. Award, by the Franklin Institute of Philadelphia, for developing a measuring device, called a maser, used to gather new information on planets and galaxies. It was instrumental in detecting radar echoes from Venus.

NOBEL PRIZES

NOBEL PRIZE
IN PHYSICS

Professors Emilio Segré (left) and Owen Chamberlain, both of the University of California Radiation Laboratory and members of the wartime atomic-bomb team. Share award of Swedish Academy of Science in recognition of their combined effort in discovering the antiproton, in 1955.

The university's bevatron was used in transformation of more than two billion electron-volts of pure energy into matter, opening the way for a demonstration of the existence of a subatomic particle, antiproton. It is a proton with a negative instead of a normal positive electric charge.

168

NOBEL PRIZE IN MEDICINE AND PHYSIOLOGY

Dr. Arthur Kornberg (left), Stanford University; Dr. Severo Ochoa, New York University. Shared Swedish Academy of Science award for pioneer research into the chemistry of life and heredity. They discovered enzymes, biological catalysts, with which they produced nucleic acids.

One, RNA, is known to have played a major role in the origin of life. It surrounds the nucleus of a cell and is believed to be essential to production of protein. The other, DNA, is found in chromosomes inside the nucleus of a cell and forms genes that transmit heredity, continuing life.

IN SCIENCE FOR 1959

ALL PHOTOS, UNLESS OTHERWISE SPECIFIED, WIDE WORLD

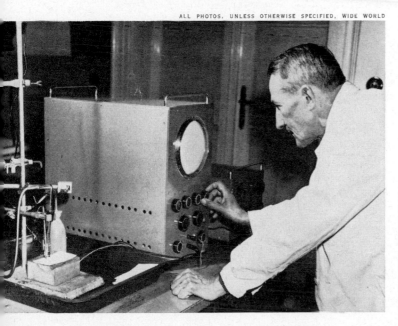

NOBEL PRIZE IN CHEMISTRY

Professor Jaroslav Heyrovsky, director, Polarographic Institute of the Czechoslovak Academy of Sciences, Prague. For his electrochemical method of analysis devised in 1922. Seen here in his laboratory, he is the first citizen of his country to be the recipient of a Nobel Prize.

169

THE EXPLORATION OF NEARBY SPACE

By WILLY LEY
*Engineer and
Rocket Expert*

M AN's first step into space, the first artificial satellites, resulted in a surprising discovery. After centuries of looking into space with telescopes, we were convinced that we knew about everything that could be seen in the space around us. We did not know that there was something invisible around our planet.

The radiation counters of the first American artificial satellite, Explorer I, did not work. It was not surprising that something would go wrong in such an experiment. There were two aspects alone that aroused scientists' interest. The Russians had already admitted that there had been an instrument failure in their Sputnik II. And why did the instruments in the American satellite fail above 600 miles distance and work perfectly below 600 miles? It occurred to Dr. James A. Van Allen that it might not be a failure but an overload. A laboratory experiment showed that an overloaded radiation counter of the type that was in orbit would simply stop reporting. That is how radiation shell, or Van Allen layer, was discovered. This layer surrounds the earth the way reefs surround some tropical islands. It is an area where electrons given off by our sun are trapped in the earth's magnetic field. When these electrons run into a solid body—or vice versa—X rays are produced. To find out whether the earth's magnetic field will actually trap electrons, the United States carried out Project Argus in which small atomic (uranium) bombs were carried high above the atmosphere and exploded there. Such an atomic explosion releases innumerable electrons, and the purpose of the experiment was to "inject" a massive dose of electrons into the earth's magnetic field to see what would happen to them. They were trapped.

An important first step in any space-research program is to find out everything we can about the Van Allen layer. This we already know about it: its lower limit lies at an altitude of about 600 miles above the tropics and areas bordering the tropics. The greatest intensity is roughly one earth radius (about 4,000 miles) from the surface. Then the radiation count goes down rapidly, and there is a zone in which it is quite low. But then a second layer surrounds the first, with a second area of maximum intensity which is about three earth radii from the surface. Some distance beyond that, space is clear of this radiation.

What we do not know is why there are two strata. We do not know why the thickness of the Van Allen layer fluctuates, although we know that it does. We do not know what conditions are like over the polar areas and the northern and southern portions of the two Temperate Zones. In these areas the Van Allen layer should be much closer to the ground. But how close? How many miles in thickness? How high is the radiation count? And is it still a double layer in, or rather, over the higher latitudes, or have the two strata merged there?

Many future decisions about space research depend on the answers to these questions. That is why the thorough exploration of the Van Allen layer is the first item on the agenda. Knowledge about the Van Allen layer will chiefly influence decisions about manned flights in space. Its existence can be almost ignored as far as unmanned research rockets, called probes, are concerned. It had been feared for a while that the Van Allen layer might interfere with radio transmission from research vehicles outside the layer, but this is fortunately not the case. Signals from the Russian moon rocket were received from beyond the orbit of the moon (240,000 miles), while the American Pioneer IV continued to broadcast from 400,000 miles away.

RADIATION BELTS—the Van Allen Layer and Project Argus

Outer Radiation Belt

Inner Radiation Belt

Argus Radiation Belt

A cutaway diagram of the radiation belts, looking like three doughnuts encircling the earth. This is just a scientist's guess; the belts do not have sharp boundaries. Their distances from the earth are still being studied.

171

Weightlessness: three astronauts undergo the strange experience of floating around in the cabin of a transport plane during their training for space flight. This state of weightlessness happens when the force throwing the vehicle outward exactly equals gravity's pull.

As far as fuel consumption is concerned, a rocket-propelled space probe can reach the vicinity of Venus and Mars almost as easily as it can reach the vicinity of the moon. However, shots to another planet present a timing problem that does not exist for artificial satellites or even for moon shots. An artificial satellite can be fired at any moment, and it will go into orbit provided it is fast enough. A shot to the moon can also be counted down any day, though there is a three-day period once a month when a moon shot is somewhat simpler than during the other days. This has nothing to do with distance: it is a question of the tilt of the moon's orbit. However, if you fired a shot to the planet Venus just because the rocket happened to be ready, the chances are that it would be a wasted effort. In this case your rocket, assuming that it worked perfectly, would reach the *orbit* of Venus, but the planet itself would be nowhere near.

There was a chance of reaching Venus during the first week of June 1959. The next chance won't come until early in 1961.

The problem of reaching another planet is so interesting that it deserves to be described in some detail.

The orbit of Venus is inside the orbit of the earth. Venus is, on the average, 67,200,000 miles from the sun and needs 224.7 days to go around the sun once. The earth is, on the average, 93,000,000 miles from the sun and needs one sidereal year, or about 365¼ days, to complete one orbit. Venus moves in its orbit with a mean velocity of 21.7 miles per second; the earth is a bit slower and moves with a mean velocity of 18½ miles per second.

Since each planet completes a full circle of 360° when going around the sun, the velocities of the two planets can also be expressed by saying how many degrees of arc they travel per day as seen from the sun. By dividing 360 by 224.7 we find that Venus travels daily 1.6° of arc, while the slower earth travels not quite one degree of arc, namely 0.98°, daily. This is important to know because the rocket fired to reach Venus must swing through 180° and will need 146 days for doing so. During these

146 days the earth will move through 143° of arc while Venus will move through 233½° of arc. The movement of Venus is, therefore, more than a half circle, which means that at the moment of firing Venus must be *behind* the earth in its orbit. (See diagram.) It must be behind by 233½ minus 180 or 53½°.

If the rocket is fired at the moment when Venus is that much behind the earth both Venus and the rocket will reach the same point in the orbit of Venus at the same time.

During those 146 days Venus has raced through 233½° and the rocket through 180°, but the slower-moving earth has gone through only 143°. This means that at the moment the rocket reaches Venus the earth is 180 minus 143 or 37° behind Venus (and the rocket). The distance between the rocket and earth at that time will be about 55,000,000 miles. In order for the planetary probe to report on conditions near Venus the radio transmitter carried by the rocket must be able to send signals strong

VENUS PROBE—Trajectory Sketch

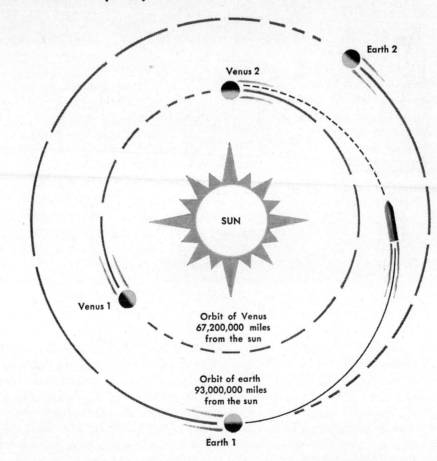

Venus 1   Position of Venus when rocket takes off.
Earth 1   Position of earth when rocket takes off.

Venus 2   Position of Venus when rocket arrives.
Earth 2   Position of earth when rocket arrives.

173

Control jets reverse capsule to face in opposite direction—the proper position for orbiting. Ship and shore stations track capsule as it swings around earth. For return, reverse rockets slow capsule below orbiting speed while gravity pulls it toward the earth.

Booster rockets fall away (below); escape rocket (above), used to free capsule in emergency, and capsule separate.

MAN IN SPACE— How it will happen

The vehicle is launched. It contains a two-ton titanium and stainless-steel capsule carrying instruments and pilot who lies on a form-fitting couch.

enough to be received on earth over this distance. One of the first things we would want to know is whether Venus has a Van Allen layer too.

If our rocket were to be shot to the planet Mars the problem would be similar to that of the shot to Venus. Mars moves around the sun in an orbit outside that of the earth. The rocket would need 258 days to swing through the 180° arc leading from the orbit

of earth to that of Mars. Because the earth is the faster moving of the two planets, Mars would have to be ahead of the earth on the day of firing. At the time the rocket reached Mars the earth would be ahead.

Since planetary probes can be fired only when the earth and the target planet have such a specific position to each other, the dates on which such shots can be made are comparatively rare. They happen at inter-

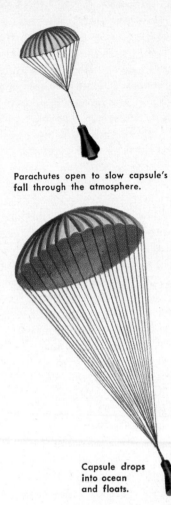

Parachutes open to slow capsule's fall through the atmosphere.

Capsule drops into ocean and floats.

Special task force picks up pilot and capsule. Man's first space trip is over.

vals between 1½ and 2 years. Because the Van Allen layer does not interfere with planetary probes, any useful date that comes along can be used. Manned space travel can be begun in the portion of safe space between the upper atmosphere and the lower portion of the Van Allen layer, in orbits that are mainly over the tropics.

The first manned flight into orbit will be in a so-called capsule. This term has been chosen to show that the first manned space vehicle is not a true space craft; it is not a ship that follows the captain's orders. It is merely a capsule that protects the man inside from the airlessness of space and provides him with some food and liquid for the duration of the ride.

The plan is to fire this capsule (from Cape Canaveral) into a rather low orbit, not more than 200 miles from the ground.

The main rocket to lift the capsule will be an Atlas or a Titan. On the way out of the atmosphere the astronaut will lie on his back (the position in which a man can best stand the acceleration). But the acceleration will last for less than 300 seconds. From then on until the capsule re-enters the atmosphere, the astronaut will feel weightless. With such an orbit, it will take almost precisely 1½ hours to go around the earth once. How many times the first astronaut will make a circuit around the earth is not yet known.

The decision hinges on the question whether a sleeping period should be included in the first trip. If there is to be no sleeping period the astronaut, after 4½ revolutions around the earth—not quite seven hours after take-off—will ignite a solid-fuel rocket charge that fires in the direction he is moving. This rocket will burn for only a few seconds, but it will slow down the capsule enough so that it will assume another orbit, one that leads it into the atmosphere at a very shallow angle. In the course of this descent into the atmosphere the capsule will go not quite halfway around the world, so that the actual re-entry will take place over the Atlantic Ocean.

In the thin upper atmosphere a metal-mesh drag chute will be thrown out to steady the capsule and to reduce its speed. At the same time "chaff" will be released. Chaff is the term for small pieces of aluminum foil which produce a good radar echo so that radars on the ground (or on shipboard) can pick up the capsule's trajectory easily. When the capsule's velocity is down to below the speed of sound the main parachute will be thrown out. This will land the capsule gently in the ocean. As it touches the water a radio signal will start automatically, lights will flash and dye bags will empty themselves into the water to produce a large colored spot.

In the capsule flight the astronaut inside is a rider rather than a pilot. He does not have much to do, and even the things he has to do can be done for him by remote control in case he loses consciousness. In the second project there will be a pilot, and the vehicle that comes after the capsule will be maneuverable. The project has been called "Mrs. V.," (*M*aneuverable and *R*ecoverable *S*pace *V*ehicle). The Mrs. V. ship will probably look like a delta-winged jet fighter. The third manned flight will be a manned artificial satellite.

Then will come the job of penetrating the Van Allen layer with a manned ship. How this can best be done is something that nobody knows right now. We first have to find out more about the Van Allen layer. The main idea is to go through it so fast that no harm will be done to the astronauts. But whether this can be done best over the equator or over the magnetic poles or over the middle latitudes is not yet known.

The first voyage for a ship that penetrates the Van Allen layer is going to be around the moon. Not *to* the moon, because landing on the earth's moon is a fairly difficult problem. This is because the moon has no atmosphere that could be used to slow the ship down and because it is a fairly large body (2,160 miles in diameter) with a strong gravitational pull. For a first attempt this rules out an actual landing. With the fuels we have today a ship could go into orbit around the earth, refuel there, and then make the long loop around the moon, returning into an orbit around the earth.

The actual landing on the moon is about ten or twelve years in the future. If you have power enough to go to the moon it takes only a small amount of extra power to go to one of the neighboring planets. The main reason why a moon landing will be tried first is not a question of fuel, but of the duration of the voyage. A manned ship would, of course, need 146 or 258 days to go to Venus or to Mars, whereas the moon trip would take only between 3 and 5 days.

The Atom Keeps House

By SENATOR CLINTON P. ANDERSON
*Chairman, Joint Congressional Committee
on Atomic Energy*

Dɪᴅ you know you were radioactive? Don't worry, because this is a characteristic shared by every other human being. Through atomic science, we have learned that there are 460,000 atoms "exploding" inside of us each minute of our lives.

Now, if you happen to own a Geiger-Müller counter and might be planning to check the radioactivity count of your neighbor, I must disappoint you. To count the bursts of energy from these exploding atoms within us, you will need some very special and highly sensitive instruments used by the Atomic Energy Commission.

The fact that we are able to trace these radioactive atoms inside our own bodies shows that we can also trace them in other places. This is made so by one of the most remarkable developments of the atomic age, the man-made radioisotope.

The radioisotope is to the modern scientist what grape jam is to the mother. Telltale purple stains . . . and mother knows immediately that her son has been into the jam and that he has handled in succession the kitchen chair, the light switch and her best towel. In the same way, it takes but an instant to find a radioactive needle in a haystack.

By making calcium slightly and harmlessly radioactive, a scientist can trace the movement of calcium atoms into the soil, into the grass, or into the cow, into the milk, through the dairy and into a small boy. Inside the boy the calcium atoms can be followed into the bones and teeth.

177

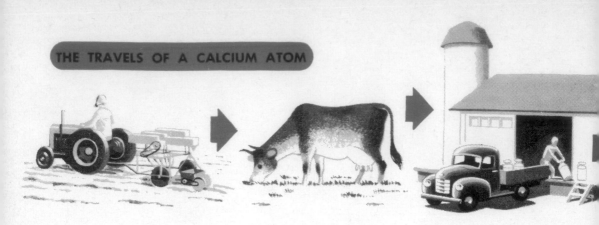

Some authorities have said that this is the greatest aid to scientific research since the microscope was invented back in the seventeenth century. But even the microscope cannot equal in importance this newest tool of the scientist. The radioisotope is giving us invaluable knowledge which can be used in countless ways to improve the life and health of human beings. It is revealing the inner workings of life itself.

Members of the Joint Committee on Atomic Energy live with the stories of isotope miracles day after day, and I would like to share with you some of the things I have heard and seen. Young people once learned in First Year Chemistry, as I did, that there was a total of 92 elements. Today, some scientists tell me there are 102, but the count keeps climbing. These elements are composed of atoms. Some elements have atoms of slightly different weights. The variations of the same element are called isotopes, from the Greek meaning "same place." Some isotopes try to get rid of their extra weight by radiating particles of energy. This makes them radioactive—radioisotopes. Radioactivity is easily detected with modern instruments.

Furthermore, by the use of atomic reactors, or "furnaces," we can manufacture dozens of radioactive elements and then trace them wherever they may go—into a tree or into the air, into a metal casting or into a human being. These man-made isotopes—some of them—are radioactive for only a few seconds, a few hours, a few days or months. We can choose and use our tracers just as we point a flashlight.

I cannot tell you about all the important results of the laboratory experiments that are being carried on with these new

USING RADIOACTIVE TRACERS

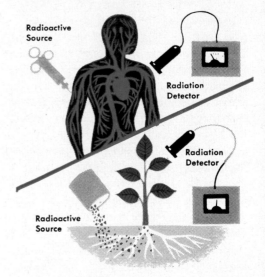

atomic tools. I wish I could, for each of them, somewhere, somehow, is having an impact on our lives, and will have an ever greater impact as time goes by and technology improves. But it has occurred to me that we might look at the atom as it helps us around the home.

Maybe we should begin our atomic

housekeeping by looking at the surroundings of your home. If you are a green-thumb gardener, you want your house looking well.

If you work in the garden, you should be extremely interested in the use of isotopes, particularly as their use relates to the uptake of fertilizer. For eight years the scientists have been working with radioactive phosphorus—phosphorus 32. They have found that trees respond more rapidly to foliar feeding than root feeding. The area of a tree exposed in its leaves is about ten times that covered by its shadow on the ground, and the scientist therefore checks food values by spraying a radioactive substance like phosphorus 32 on the underside of the leaf. Tracer studies have shown that certain plant nutrients, applied to leaves in soluble form, resulted in a 95 per cent uptake of fertilizer, but if applied to the soil, the uptake is not more than 10 per cent. Thrifty gardeners

who want to save on fertilizer bills will naturally use the foliar system with its 95 per cent efficiency.

The by-products of atomic energy have taught us something about the season to feed plants. People believe that you cannot fertilize a plant in winter, but work in California and Oregon showed that winter application of radio-zinc, even when applied at below-freezing temperatures, resulted in plant food moving into the tree. The Geiger counter could detect the radio-zinc moving 18 inches to 2 feet in the branches above the point of application in 24 to 48 hours.

Maybe your garden is for more than just beauty. Maybe it is for utility, and you want to have a few trees and a little vegetable patch. Here again, atomic energy comes into the picture. Peach trees for centuries have been bearing fruit at a certain season, with the result that all the peaches in a locality become ripe in about

FOLIAR FEEDING

As a tractor pulls it, a sprayer applies a radioactive solution to the foliage of plants being given a foliar feeding.

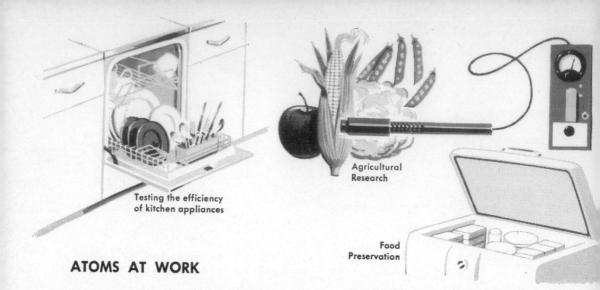

Testing the efficiency
of kitchen appliances

Agricultural
Research

Food
Preservation

ATOMS AT WORK

the same week. Now, through atomic energy, we are learning how to advance or hold back the dates of maturity so that all the fruit does not come on the market or into the kitchen at the same time. You could have five peach trees in your garden, and they could mature in rotation, each a week apart! Your family and your neighbors could either eat the fruit in small quantities or could can a little bit of it each week.

But let's assume that you green-thumb gardeners have used atomic isotopes to beautify the outside of your home and now you want to improve the inside. Let us go into the kitchen. Here the atom has really been put to work, particularly with the foods we eat.

For example, the flour we put into bread comes from one or more of the two-hundred-odd varieties of wheat, all of which, unfortunately, are more or less susceptible to a disease called black stem rust. The loss of wheat from such disease is estimated at about $20,000,000 annually. The housewife shares in this loss through a higher price for flour. It is most important that some way be found to eliminate or reduce this disease.

In the past, by crossing different strains of wheat over a 10- to 25-year period, scientists have produced some rust-resist-

ant varieties. Now they have learned that they can cause beneficial changes, or mutations, in living plant and animal cells by subjecting the cells to beta and gamma rays—and can do it in from one to three growing seasons. By means of artificial mutations, they have developed new and improved strains of wheat, rice and tobacco in relatively short time.

Atomic scientists have also learned that they can kill germs by atomic radiation. They are seeking to use this knowledge to preserve food uncooked and unfrozen for long periods. Meat is sterilized so that it can be kept at room temperatures for several weeks without spoiling. Potatoes can be kept from sprouting and bread from forming mold. There is a suspicion, however, that radiation may completely destroy the natural vitamins found in the food. Research continues and some day you may be able to buy a fine steak, put it on a plate or platter on a kitchen shelf, leave it for weeks without danger of deterioration and then bring it out to cook with no delay for thawing before it goes into the broiler.

The atomic peanut is on its way to your kitchen. A North Carolina scientist planted radioactive peanuts and developed a new variety, an improved strain, through atomic research. He put powerful X rays

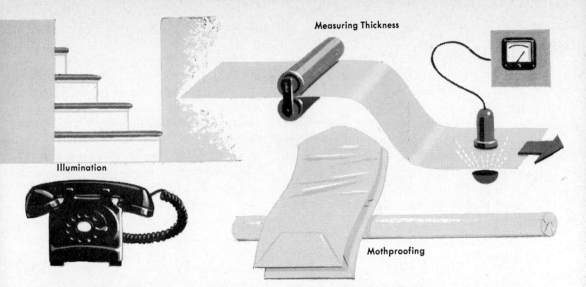

Measuring Thickness

Illumination

Mothproofing

through a bag of peanut seed, got dwarfs and giants, plants that stood up and others that lay flat, some that resisted disease and others that courted disaster. Out of some eleven thousand mutations one has been selected (NC4X) that will be available for your sandwiches soon.

In these days of increasing crop surpluses, it may seem strange that the Department of Agriculture is trying to increase crop yields. But when we consider the different crops, we realize that the problems are different for each of them. We have no national surplus, for instance, of fresh fruit or fresh vegetables. The main problem with fruit and vegetables has been to grow enough and to keep it fresh long enough to arrive in good condition in your kitchen. Through mutations by atomic energy, we will soon find ways to develop new and better vegetables, at much lower cost. We can foresee, for instance, a tomato that will grow quite ripe without the skin cracking. When these things happen, none of us will need to go without fresh vegetables and fruits.

Will the house itself have some new and interesting device for this space age?

Let's look at what the atom is doing for some appliances in the kitchen, the dishwasher, for instance. Four or five years ago, a certain manufacturer of automatic dishwashers studied the problem of washing dishes really clean, and after much research he found the hardest thing to wash off a breakfast plate is dried egg yolk. He set out to build a dishwasher that could wash off a dried egg yolk and leave not a trace. About that time he heard about atomic tracers. He decided he'd put his machine to the ultimate test. He decided to make an egg radioactive, let it dry on a plate and then wash it. Sulfur, as you know, is an ingredient of egg yolk. So the manufacturer had his laboratory tag some egg yolk with radioactive sulfur. He also fed a special kind of food to a hen. The hen did her duty and laid a radioactive egg. The manufacturer kept on improving and changing his dishwasher until he had perfected one that could really pass the radioactive-egg test. His machine is on the market now, and the housewife who buys it has an improved dishwasher.

Do you want softer light, a luminous glow? Radioisotopes, if mixed with certain materials, will cause them to emit a soft, glowing light, which will last for years. This unfailing light can be manufactured in a wide variety of sizes, shapes and intensities—and is usually made through the use of the radioisotope tritium. These lights have tremendous commercial potential and will undoubtedly be in wide use

181

as soon as the necessary materials become rapidly available. For instance, luminescent wall panels could be installed in closets, bathrooms and baby nurseries where low-level light, particularly at night, is desired. Night illumination of telephone dials, light switches, house numbers and walks and stairs would be possible.

Research has shown that there are great possibilities for extending the storage life of fruits and vegetables by exposing them to low levels of radiation. A home refrigerator hydrator tray has been designed that has a small amount of radioactivity incorporated in the enamel. Fruits and vegetables exposed to this small amount of radiation while stored in the home refrigerator remain fresh for several days longer than is now the case.

An atomic watchdog can silently guard your home by keeping an ever ready lookout for the smoke that means a fire. These devices, which may be placed on the walls or ceilings of the home, depend on the ability of smoke to stop or slow down soft radiation. The watchdog is made of a source of soft radiation set a small distance from a sensitive detector, very much like an electric eye. As the smoke comes between the two, the steady stream of radiation is decreased. The change in radiation activates an alarm system that warns of the presence of fire. Since the device is quite sensitive, early detection of a fire is possible. This means that in the future, young children can be left at home with less worry that they may be hurt by a sudden fire that even the most sensitive nose would never detect.

An atomic gauge can be built in the furnace fuel-oil tank to keep the tank from running out of fuel just when the weather is coldest or in the middle of the night. Such a gauge not only tells you how much oil remains but also activates a flashing light or bell that can ring out loudly when it is time to order more oil.

Thus the new atom-world gadgets go—on and on, endlessly. They can improve your kitchen as greatly as the new electric frying pans and ranges with push-button control improved the open hearth of George Washington's day.

We might go through every room in the house, letting the atom share our housekeeping duties. Radioisotopes are being used to create new and better dyes for draperies and carpets. They are being used for measuring minute thicknesses in fabrics, plastics and paper, for calculating the depth of ink on wallpaper and for monitoring the thickness of thread.

Let's take an example of the atom at work in the storage closets of the house. Atomic irradiation helps you to get rid of the moths that attack stored woolens. It is now possible to mothproof blankets, carpets, clothing and other woolens by passing them beneath atomic beams. Merely clean a suit, seal it in a paper container and then have it irradiated. In an instant and without objectionable odors, the suit is mothproofed as if by magic, and it stays that way until you remove it from the container. This type of irradiation destroys even the unhatched moth eggs that have survived the dry-cleaning process.

As wonderful as the atom is in the kitchen, the living room and the clothes closet, it's in the sick room that atomic radiation makes its most thrilling and heartening contribution. Body processes, both in sickness and in health, are fundamentally chemical. These processes are carried on in such a dynamic, complex and wonderful way and on such a microscopic scale that they often defy analysis. Through radioisotopes, however, the atomic physician has opened a whole world of medicine and surgery. He is acquiring new knowledge and he is coming upon surprising discoveries all the time. In general, the major discoveries have involved heart studies, and treatment of brain diseases, goiter and cancer. And we are gaining new insight into that very, very ancient puzzle—why do we grow old?

One application of atomic energy in medicine is not only dramatic but perhaps prophetic of the atomic benefits of the medicine chest of the future. This case involves a brain cancer. Now certain brain cancers can be removed by surgery, while others cannot. To remove the so-called spider-web type would require virtual removal of the entire brain.

Scientists at the Brookhaven National Laboratory discovered one day that an isotope of boron sends out minute beta rays upon exposure to a beam of neutrons. They also found that cancerous brain cells have a great hunger for boron. Normal brain cells absorb boron more slowly. They brought in a patient in an advanced stage of brain cancer, which could not be operated on, a man long immobile and unconscious because of his disease.

There was no need to give him an anesthetic because the use of atomic radiation does not cause pain. The doctors gave him an injection of boron and, after an interval, placed his head beneath the beam of neutrons. The neutrons, when they penetrated the cancerous brain cells, reacted with the boron in such a way as to produce beta rays three millionths of an inch in length. These tiny rays were not strong enough to pierce the walls of the healthy cells. But they could and did destroy the cancer cells.

After another interval the patient was removed to his hospital bed, and several hours later he awakened for the first time in weeks and sat up. He inquired where he was and in every way showed that his brain was back to normal. He left a few days later for Florida and a vacation. This experiment was repeated on thirty-six other terminal-stage patients and in each case destroyed cancerous cells.

I wish I could tell you that each of these patients lived happily ever afterward, but I cannot. I believe all of them are now

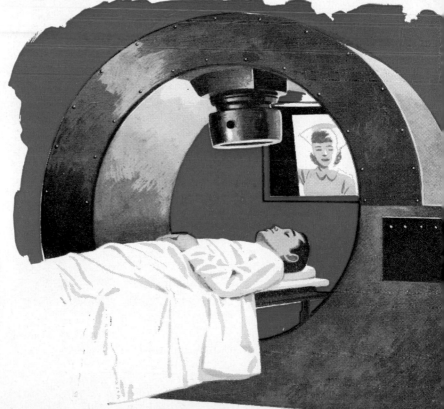

RADIATION THERAPY

In many hospitals today radioactive materials are being used to treat cancerous tissues. Often these new techniques are proving helpful and they offer much promise for the future treatment of cancer and other deadly diseases.

dead. Some died for reasons unassociated with their brain cancer. Others died for reasons not fully understood by the doctors at Brookhaven. We must wait and hope and continue the researches. We must remember that cures are frequently made in stages of two steps forward, one step backward.

Where the diseased tissue can be irradiated, the radioisotope cobalt 60 is being used in many cases. There are other radioactive materials which can be "seeded" within the cancer itself. This is an old use for radium, a natural radioisotope.

The AEC's medical research branch is concentrating its energies now on studies of bone-marrow transplants. These studies, they feel, hold the key to successful treatment of persons who have been subjected to massive doses of radiation. They may also some day lead to a key for curing leukemia. This research was brought into dramatic light recently when successful bone-marrow transplants were made in four Yugoslavs who were victims of a radiation accident. The study of marrow transplants began with the dawn of the atomic age and its attendant radiation dangers. Scientists found that when a person receives a massive "whole-body" dose of radiation, death is caused by the destruction of the cell-manufacturing bone marrow. Marrow transplants were the obvious solution, but the human body is very unreceptive to foreign matter. Its natural immunizers attack and kill the new cells and destroy the transplant. However, researchers found that the cells destroyed by radiation are the very same cells that produce the body's immune reaction. Therefore, the body of a radiation victim will accept a marrow transplant.

This is a fact not recognized until recently. And since radiation accidents are blessedly rare, there has been little opportunity to test the theory.

As exciting—as promising—as these

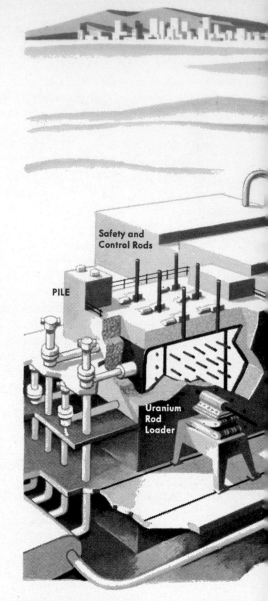

Safety and Control Rods

PILE

Uranium Rod Loader

atomic developments are, they are at least equaled by other, broader atomic developments, specifically, nuclear power and nuclear propulsion, both in industry and in the armed services.

What does this mean to your families and your homes? It means ample supplies of electric power to run the wonderful new appliances you've been reading about.

In Pittsburgh tonight many housewives will cook their dinners and light their homes with atomic power—with electricity flowing from the atomic power plant at

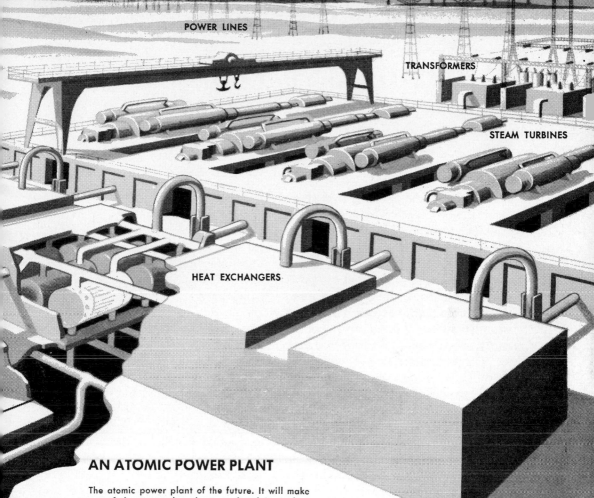

POWER LINES

TRANSFORMERS

STEAM TURBINES

HEAT EXCHANGERS

AN ATOMIC POWER PLANT

The atomic power plant of the future. It will make use of the tremendous heat produced in nuclear reactions to create steam to drive its generators.

Shippingport. In the near future, this will be happening in Chicago and in New England and then in more and more cities. For the American and Canadian people and industry have an insatiable demand for electric power—they have been doubling their use of it every ten years throughout this century. And as the demand becomes more massive, atomic power plants will certainly spring up throughout the land to help meet it.

But consider what unlimited amounts of low-cost power could and will mean in the larger picture of the future. We could air-condition whole central cities, summer and winter. We could keep aircraft aloft indefinitely. We can deice our highways. We could gather food from the deepest depths of oceans. We could change large volumes of sea water into fresh water and make the desert bloom.

The promise of atomic power and of atomic radiation is unlimited. Only our ability to use them is limited. Some day we will find ways to make full use of all that they offer us.

185

FISSION AND FUSION

By EDWARD HUMPHREY

Everything in the universe is made up of atoms, tiny particles of matter which the ancient Greeks called *atomos,* meaning "uncuttable things." They thought atoms were the smallest pieces of matter. Today, however, we know that atoms are cuttable or breakable and that within each of them are smaller particles of matter. Three of the most important of these tiny particles are protons, neutrons and electrons. The protons and neutrons are found in the core, or nucleus, of the atom. Electrons whirl about the nucleus, making a kind of protective nest of shells around it. Protons have a positive charge of electricity, and electrons have a negative charge. Neutrons have no charge at all. Within them, however, they have particles called mesons. As the neutron breaks down, electrons are created from the mesons.

The ancient Greeks believed that all atoms were alike, but again they were wrong. There are more than 100 different kinds of atoms. An atom of ordinary hydrogen has 1 proton in its nucleus and 1 electron speeding around the nucleus. This is the simplest atom. An atom of ordinary uranium, which is one of the most complex, has 92 electrons whirling around a nucleus in which there are 92 protons and 146 neutrons. We list atoms from 1 upward according to the number of their protons. We call the sum of the protons the atomic number of the element.

Besides their atomic number, atoms have what is called a mass number. We find the mass number of an atom by adding up the protons and neutrons in its nucleus. Ordinary hydrogen has only 1 proton, as we have seen, and no neutron. Therefore its atomic number and its mass number are the same—1. But ordinary uranium, which has 92 protons and 146 neutrons in its nucleus, has an atomic number of 92 and a mass number of 238 (92 plus 146).

Substances that are made up of only one kind of atoms are called chemical elements. All atoms of an element have the same number of protons, but they may have different numbers of neutrons. Such varieties of an atom are called isotopes. Every element known has at least two isotopes. Isotopes are either stable or unstable. A stable isotope does not change by itself into something else. But an unstable one— uranium 235, for instance—has a nucleus too heavy for its binding force. Sooner or later an unstable isotope decays—particles shoot out of its nuclei. When this happens, we say that the isotope is radioactive. All the atoms whose atomic numbers are bigger than 83 are naturally radioactive. Indeed, the atoms whose atomic numbers are higher than 92 are so unstable that they are not found in nature.

Radioactive isotopes send out rays which we call alpha, beta and gamma after the first three letters of the Greek alphabet. Alpha rays are really particles made up of two protons closely locked together with two neutrons. Beta rays are fast-moving electrons that have been created from me-

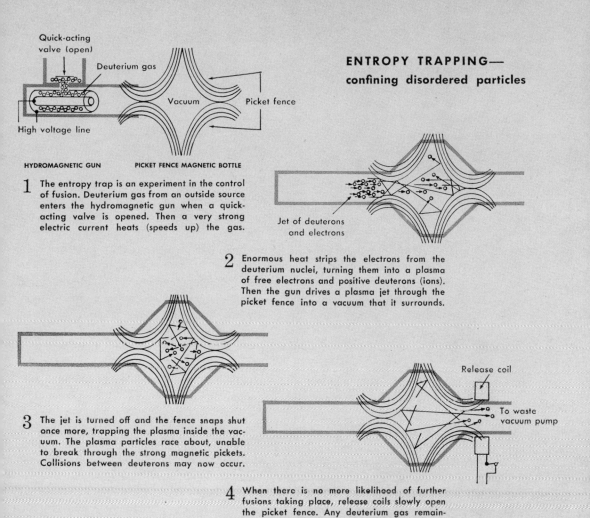

HYDROMAGNETIC GUN **PICKET FENCE MAGNETIC BOTTLE**

Quick-acting valve (open)

Deuterium gas

Vacuum Picket fence

High voltage line

1 The entropy trap is an experiment in the control of fusion. Deuterium gas from an outside source enters the hydromagnetic gun when a quick-acting valve is opened. Then a very strong electric current heats (speeds up) the gas.

Jet of deuterons and electrons

2 Enormous heat strips the electrons from the deuterium nuclei, turning them into a plasma of free electrons and positive deuterons (ions). Then the gun drives a plasma jet through the picket fence into a vacuum that it surrounds.

3 The jet is turned off and the fence snaps shut once more, trapping the plasma inside the vacuum. The plasma particles race about, unable to break through the strong magnetic pickets. Collisions between deuterons may now occur.

Release coil

To waste vacuum pump

4 When there is no more likelihood of further fusions taking place, release coils slowly open the picket fence. Any deuterium gas remaining inside the vacuum area escapes and is scavenged by a vacuum pump for later use.

sons. When they are separated from other nuclear particles, mesons disintegrate— break down—into electrons and neutrinos. Gamma rays are like X rays, only much more powerful and very dangerous.

All this nuclear energy—energy released from a nucleus—can be tremendously useful to mankind, and we are learning how to use it. Nuclear energy can be set free only if something breaks into the core of the atom and disturbs its particles. The breaking sometimes takes place in nature. When an atom of the isotope U-235 captures a neutron straying about inside rock that is rich in uranium ore,

the atom changes into an atom of U-236, another uranium isotope. This U-236 is extremely unstable. In a twinkling it splits into two lighter elements. The split, or fission, sets free great amounts of energy, as well as more neutrons that can stray about. Such neutrons can enter more atoms of U-235 and start new fissions. But it is more likely that they will just continue to wander aimlessly about.

When scientists had learned this much about atoms, they set about finding ways to make free neutrons meet and enter U-235 atoms in such a way that they would continue to set off fissions. The machines called atom smashers are designed to do just this work. They aim the neutrons shot out of atoms of U-235 at other atoms, which in turn split and set free more energy and more neutrons. That is what is called a chain reaction.

Enormous amounts of energy are set free by fission. Less than ten pounds of uranium fuel are enough to drive a ship 60,-000 miles. It would take thousands of tons of coal or diesel fuel to do the same.

But you have seen that besides giving us useful energy, atoms that split also release dangerous gamma rays. To keep them from injuring us, we must shield ourselves from them by thick lead walls. Because gamma rays will remain dangerous for hundreds of years, they are a very serious problem. Yet even if we could somehow make all rays harmless, fission would still not be the answer to the world's power problem. There would come a time when all the fissionable material was used up, and there would be no more power to run machines and do work.

These two reasons have caused scientists to look for energy in other atoms—atoms of a kind that we will not run out of—and to look for safer ways to release their energy. Instead of splitting atoms, physicists are now trying to force atoms to join together, or fuse. When atoms are fused they set nuclear energy free. This kind of fusion of atoms has been going on inside the sun for billions of years.

We cannot imagine the world's oceans ever running out of water, so there could be no better place to look for endless atoms to fuse than in sea water. As it happens, atoms of deuterium, an isotope of ordinary hydrogen and just the thing needed for fusion, are found in water. Each atom of deuterium has one proton and one neutron in its nucleus.

The deuterium atoms strongly repel each other. To get them together requires almost unbelievable force. First they must be stripped of the electrons that guard their nuclei. Then the nuclei must be made to move about at such high speed that they will no longer be able to repel each other but will collide. When two nuclei collide one grabs either a proton or a neutron out of the other. If it is the proton that is seized, the result will be an atom of helium 3. At the same time one of the neutrons will be set free and also 3,250,000 electron volts of energy. If it is the neutron that is captured, an atom of hydrogen 3, or tritium, is made; a proton is released; and we gain 4,000,000 electron volts of energy. At this rate you can see that there is enough energy in deuterium atoms to supply us with power for millions of years.

But the trick still to be learned is how to control these fusions so that they will produce not just bursts of energy but a steady supply. Several experimental machines have been built to try to do this. Among them are the torus, the stellarator, the magnetic bottle and the magnetic mirror machine.

The job of all of them is to speed up deuterium atoms so that the heat of their motion will break them down into what is called plasma. Plasma is a gas of electrons and ions. Ions are atoms that have an electrical charge. Among the ions in the plasma are many nuclei, stripped of their electrons. In the plasma state the atomic nuclei are moving at enormous speed, enough for fusion to take place. This means that the ions have extremely high kinetic (motion) temperature. How to handle this "hot" plasma is the problem. If it touches anything it will at once lose its speed and no fusions will be possible.

Some of the experiments designed to confine plasma and make it yield continuous energy are shown here.

Full-color pages
devised by RICHARD F. POST
and executed by DON GIBBINS

ENERGY

FROM

ATOMS

An atom that has very many particles in its nucleus cannot hold on to them all. Sooner or later some particles will shoot out. When they do, we say the atom is decaying. Atoms that decay are called radioactive. Radium is a naturally radioactive element that comes into being when atoms of uranium 238 lose some of their particles. We can make radioactivity far more powerful than any that takes place naturally in radioactive elements. One way is to smash large nuclei into smaller nuclei. This is fission. The other way is to force together two smaller nuclei so violently that they fuse in a larger nucleus. This is fusion. Both fission and fusion release the atom's enormous amounts of energy. The pages following show how the two processes come about.

The "life story" of radium begins when a nucleus of **uranium 238** loses one alpha particle (a combination of 2 protons and 2 neutrons). U-238 has a half life of several billion years. With one alpha particle gone, U-238 becomes

uranium-X₁. This form of uranium has a half life of three weeks; it quickly loses a beta particle (1 electron) and becomes

uranium-X₂. The half life of U-X₂ is no more than one minute, so the change it undergoes takes place at once. It loses a second beta particle and becomes a nucleus of

uranium 234, an isotope of uranium. U-234 has a half life of 300,000 years. Very slowly it loses an alpha particle, becoming

ionium 230 (half life of 83,000 years). When the ionium 230 loses an alpha particle we get

radium 226. This most-famous radioactive element will itself decay until all that is left is a stable form of lead.

STRAYING NEUTRON

U-235 ATOM

FISSION

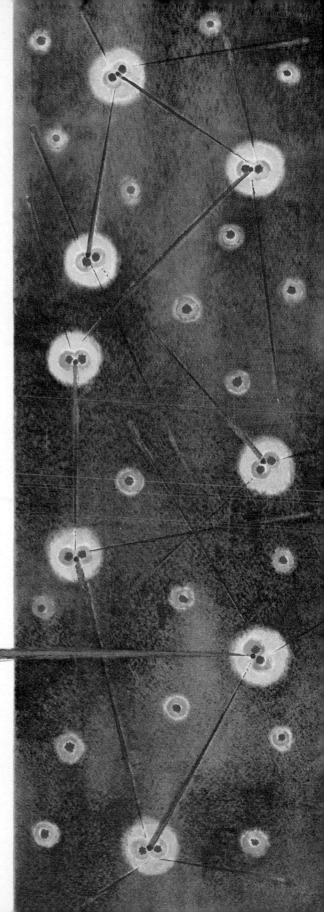

A straying neutron (top, left) moves toward the nucleus of an atom of the uranium isotope U-235.

The neutron is captured inside the U-235 nucleus, thereby changing it into a second uranium isotope, U-236. This isotope is extremely unstable. Instantaneously the U-236 nucleus starts to divide, or "neck-off" (center, left).

The nucleus flies apart. As it does, it sets free two or three neutrons. The neutrons and the two parts of the split atom together now weigh less than the whole atom did. The weight they have lost shows up (yellow) in the form of energy —200,000,000 electron volts of it.

In a dense mass of U-235 atoms (at right) one of the neutrons sent straying by a split nucleus may be captured by another nucleus that will then split in its turn, set free more neutrons and release more energy. When this happens, we have a chain reaction. The whole chain of splittings takes place in about one billionth of a second.

FUSION

Hydrogen has three isotopes—ordinary hydrogen, deuterium and tritium. Deuterium is found in water, about one part to every 5,000 parts of ordinary hydrogen. This means that there is an endless supply of deuterium for us to use as fuel in fusion reactions. Deuterium nuclei, called deuterons, can be stripped of their electrons. Stripped nuclei, called ions, have a positive charge. A gas of ions and electrons is called plasma. The drawing at the right represents plasma. Plasma is made by raising the temperature of the deuterium nuclei to something like 100,000,000 degrees. This is not heat as we think of the heat a fire makes (caloric temperature), but the heat that comes from motion (kinetic temperature). When the plasma is at 100,000,000 degrees, its electrons will be moving at a speed of 90,000 miles a second and the deuterons will be moving at 1,500 miles a second. At these tremendous speeds, collisions can occur. If they do, the deuterons can fuse. Deuterons can fuse in one of two ways. If the two protons fuse with one neutron (upper collision), they become a nucleus of helium 3. The second neutron is set free and 3,250,000 electron volts of energy are released. If the two neutrons and one proton fuse (lower collision), a nucleus of hydrogen 3, called tritium, is made. Then a proton is set free and 4,000,000 electron volts of energy are released. The two ways of fusing occur with about equal frequency.

ION

ORDINARY HYDROGEN
Nucleus: 1 proton

DEUTERIUM
Nucleus: 1 proton and 1 neutron

TRITIUM
Nucleus: 1 proton and 2 neutrons

NEUTRON

3,250,000 ELECTRON VOLTS

HELIUM 3

HYDROGEN 3 (TRITIUM)

PROTON

4,000,000 ELECTRON VOLTS

ELECTRON

PROBLEMS IN FUSION CONTROL

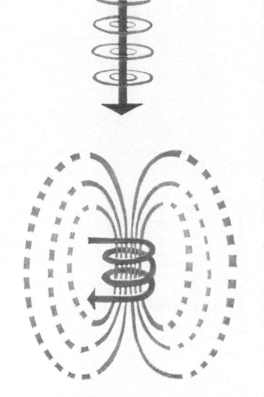

Physicists know what they want deuterium nuclei to do but not how to make them do it under human control. The problem is to find a way to hold the plasma at the right kinetic temperature so that fusion will take place continuously. If the hot plasma merely touches the walls of any container made of some solid material, it at once cools down — loses speed — and all hope of collisions between the nuclei vanishes. This has led experimenters to try magnetic fields as a way to bottle up the tricky plasma. Scientists have long known that a flowing electric current (blue) sets up lines of magnetic force (orange rings) around the axis of its flow. If the conductor of the current is coiled instead of being stretched out straight, the rings of magnetic force will form a kind of cylinder- or bottle-shaped magnetic field. This bottle-shaped field can be used to confine the plasma.

Strong electric currents sent through the plasma itself (yellow) pinch it away from the walls of the container. The lines of magnetic force act like rubber bands. Both the strong current and the pinching effect heat up the plasma. But even when it is pinched, the plasma does not remain stable for more than a few millionths of a second. Therefore it is likely to wobble out of the pinch, touch the container and at once cool down.

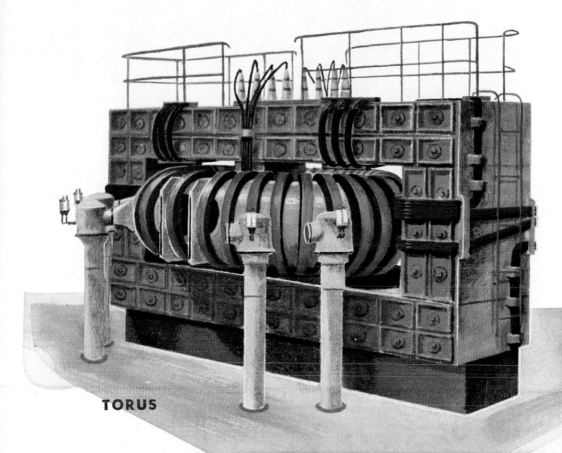

TORUS

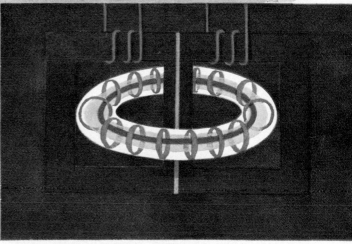

A torus (doughnut-shaped) tube makes use of the pinch effect to control plasma. The current in the square transformers sets up a strong current (blue) wthin the plasma (yellow). The current pinches the plasma, but it is very unstable and does not stay pinched. In a fraction of a second it can escape from the magnetic field (orange rings) and destroy itself. The "perhapsatron" is a torus.

STELLERATOR

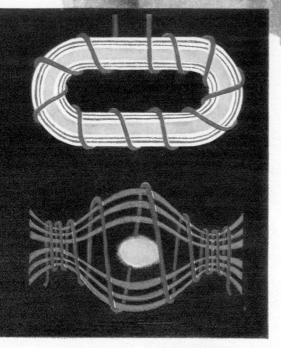

The stellerator is another form of magnetic bottle. Here external coils (blue) produce magnetic field lines (orange) running around the inside of a racetrack-shaped tube. These lines act as a furnace liner to keep the plasma from touching the walls of the glass tube.

The mirror-machine form of magnetic bottle holds the plasma within magnetic-field lines which are narrowed together at each end. The narrowed ends force the plasma particles to bounce back and forth between them much as two mirrors bounce light between their surfaces. For this reason the narrowed ends are called magnetic mirrors. Plasma is heated by increasing the strength of the bottle's magnetic field in such a way that the plasma is compressed toward the center of the machine.

MIRROR MACHINE

196

SCIENCE
HIGHLIGHTS

By BRYAN BUNCH

Two of the most important scientific announcements in 1959 were of events that occurred during 1958. The United States exploded three atomic bombs three hundred miles above the Atlantic Ocean to test whether the earth's magnetic field would trap electrons. It did, proving a theory of Nicholas C. Christofilos, formerly an elevator engineer in Greece. Mr. Christofilos is now working on a device at the University of California's Radiation Laboratory that will produce the same effect on a small scale. It is hoped that his invention, the Astron, will create controlled thermonuclear fusion.

The other event was the first bouncing of radar signals off Venus by a team from the Massachusetts Institute of Technology. It took five minutes for the signals to make the round trip from earth to Venus and back to earth. Two days later the experiment was repeated. This time it took 7½ minutes longer, because Venus and earth had moved 696,640 miles farther apart in the two days between the experiments. As techniques become perfected, radar will help us to determine the size of the solar system with an accuracy never before dreamed possible. This experiment could

not have been accomplished without a recent device called the solid-state maser. We will consider some aspects of the maser later.

Both of these important events happened a long time before the world at large knew about them. The Venus contact was made in February of 1958, and the atomic bombs were exploded over the Atlantic in late August and early September 1958. It was not until March 1959, however, that news of either event was released. Data about the explosions had been withheld for security reasons. The reason for the delay in giving out the Venus contact information was different. It took over a year for the scientists to make certain that they had actually reached earth's sister planet.

But these stories of data withheld pale beside the story of the discovery of an ancient Greek computer. Although this relic of two thousand years ago was discovered in 1900, it was not until early in 1959 that a published article told what it was. The computer, which was used to calculate the orbits of planets as long ago as 65 B.C., had become very much corroded. It was found in a sunken ship by Greek sponge divers. According to Dr. Derek J. Prince, who recognized what the computer's function was, the ancient Greeks "were not far behind where we are now."

The Greeks may have had a word for "computer," but it was the Russians who named the first artificial planet. They called it Mechta—"A Dream." It was launched at the moon in early January but failed to orbit it. Now it revolves about the sun and should for many years to come.

The United States also launched an artificial planet. The United States planet (also aimed at the moon, which it also failed to orbit) was called Pioneer IV and was launched March 3, 1959.

Scientists are not very fond of fanciful names. Although we speak of "Dreams" and "Pioneers," scientists call the two new wanderers Artificial Planet One and Artificial Planet Two.

Flinging chunks of metal out in space is a tremendous achievement, but man can best learn from these experiments if the chunks can report back what they find. To do this, they need radio. In both the American and the Russian artificial planets, the radio failed early on the trip.

Researchers at the Martin Company have built a new type of thermocouple—a device that produces electricity from heat—to combat this problem. This is called SNAP III (Systems for Nuclear Auxiliary Power), and it can produce as much as five watts of electricity. SNAP III is operated by radioactive polonium 210. The heat that this element produces is converted into electricity by fifty-four small thermocouples in an arrangement about the size of a grapefruit. SNAP III can be used to power radios in rockets, satellites and artificial planets. It could also have important uses here on earth—for example, as a power source for lights in buoys to mark shipping lanes.

At Los Alamos Scientific Laboratory another thermocouple was developed that converts nuclear energy directly to electricity. The Los Alamos device is called a

U. S. NAVAL RESEARCH LABORATORY

UNITED STATES NAVY'S MASER

A maser amplifier with associated apparatus is mounted at the focus of the Naval Research Laboratory's fifty-foot reflector. The solid-state maser, which uses a ruby to pick up a weak radio wave from outer space and amplify it to greater strength, helped bounce the first radar signals off the planet Venus.

FUTURE "BIG DISH"

Artist's conception of the world's largest radiotelescope being erected by the United States Navy at Sugar Grove, West Virginia. When completed, the telescope will give the United States a powerful "ear on the universe." Naval scientists will then be able to tune in on radio signals from stars or clouds of interstellar gas as far as 38,000,-000,000 light-years out in space. Instrument will be 600 feet in diameter.

199

plasma thermocouple. It makes use of the fourth state of matter—plasma. When inserted into a nuclear reactor, the plasma thermocouple can produce forty watts of electricity.

Not all scientists in 1959 were concerned with atoms and space. Medical researchers continued to discover important new treatments. A beam of protons was used in brain surgery for the first time; Dr. Jonas Salk recommended a fourth polio shot (later in the year, other doctors recommended a new shot every year); Dr. Warren Cole at the University of Illinois developed a chemical approach to preventing the spread of cancer cells throughout the body. All of these improvements will help to lengthen the life span of man.

To provide food for the multitudes of men, both old and young, scientists have turned to algae. A cook among them has even put out a recipe for algae cookies, to be eaten by men on extended space flights.

In England a scientist has made an artificial "cow." This wonderful machine can be fed grass and it will produce proteins. It has been found that pigs thrive on these protein products, but no man has yet tried to live on grass steak.

A biochemist in Pittsburgh, Dr. Klaus Hoffmann, has gone further than that. Starting from scratch he has built the proteinlike molecule a-MSH. Another important organic compound was synthesized by two scientists at the University of British Columbia. By making coenzyme A in the laboratory, Drs. John Moffatt and H. Gobind Khorans have opened the way to a much clearer understanding of the nature of life.

Scientists in 1959 showed that hot solutions of the eighteen common amino acids would cool into something very much like protein. It is believed that this is how life originated on earth. The amino acids are much simpler compounds than proteins and could have been formed chemically ages ago when the earth was hot. The protein molecule, so necessary for life but very complex, could have then formed as the earth cooled.

L. S. and Roger Penrose performed another interesting experiment that threw light on the origin of life. They built machines that could reproduce themselves. The Penrose machines are very simple devices that produce copies of themselves when they are shaken together with a number of prebuilt parts. Man is still required to do the shaking.

In 1959 a machine first gave orders to other machines. This machine is a computer, called APT (Automatically Programmed Tool), that translates simple English into mathematical equivalents. Most machines cannot read English, but they can read a kind of numbers called binary numbers. APT punches these numbers on tape. When the tape is fed to an automatic machine, the machine is programmed. That is, it knows what job it should do.

Although most machines cannot read, computers that translate languages are now being developed. One such device at Harvard translates Russian into English. The results still require shaping by a human editor, however.

There was some development of the maser over the past year. Maser stands for microwave amplification by stimulated emission of radiation. This means that the maser will receive a weak radio wave and put out a stronger wave of the same frequency. These have proved very useful in radiotelescopes, which pick up the weak signals that come from outer space. Scientists at Bell Telephone are now trying to produce a maser that will amplify light waves. Another new amplifier, called a tunnel-diode amplifier, is simpler than the maser and better than the vacuum tube or the transistor.

Using these new amplifiers in radiotelescopes has proved to be a great help to astronomers. They have been able to "see" farther into space than ever before, recording radio waves from galaxies so distant that the waves must have originated aeons before man walked the earth.

Other astronomers looked closer to home. According to recent theory Pluto, the ninth planet, was once a satellite of Neptune, the eighth. Beginning in 1979, for twenty years, Pluto will be inside Neptune's orbit, making Pluto the eighth planet. If scientists are correct, however, Pluto should not be counted as a true planet at all.

Astronomers have also re-estimated the age of the universe and revised the estimated size of our galaxy, the Milky Way. By measuring the light from a kind of star that pulsates—called a cepheid variable star—astronomers have decided that the universe is ten billion years old instead of two billion years old. The recalculations have shown that the size of the part of the

UNIVAC

A UNIVAC programed to translate Russian into English. This large-scale computer is installed in the Computation Laboratory at Harvard.

HARVARD UNIVERSITY NEWS OFFICE

TEMPERATURE-HUMIDITY INDEX

The curved lines on the graph represent T.H.I. values for different weather conditions. When the humidity is 81 per cent and the temperature is 83° F., for example, the T.H.I. is 80.

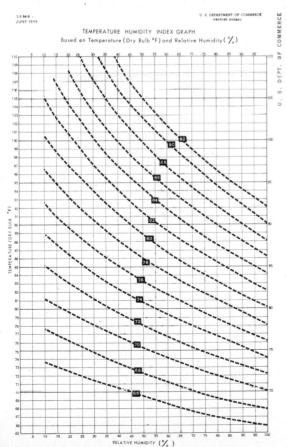

TEMPERATURE HUMIDITY INDEX GRAPH
Based on Temperature (Dry Bulb °F) and Relative Humidity (%)

U. S. DEPARTMENT OF COMMERCE
WEATHER BUREAU

U. S. DEPT. OF COMMERCE

ATOMIC SURGERY

Dr. The Svedberg, director of the Gustaf Werner Institute, gazes at the proton tube used in atomic surgery at the University of Uppsala, in Uppsala, Sweden.

LENNART NILSSON, PIX

201

MISSILE DETECTION SYSTEM

Under Project Tepee the Office of Naval Research has developed a method whereby it has been able to detect nuclear bomb explosions in the Soviet Union, as well as rocket firings. Shown here is the "breadboard equipment" used to make the missile detection.

universe that we can see is about double what we used to believe.

Man has not yet begun to explore the immensity of space personally. Able and Baker, two female monkeys, were the first primates to visit space. On May 28 the two astronauts were blasted three hundred miles above the earth in a Jupiter missile. They were successfully recovered in the nose cone in the Atlantic Ocean.

Able, the larger monkey, died as a result of the general anesthetic applied while removing an electrode from under her skin. A careful autopsy revealed no harmful effects from the trip.

The scientific events discussed so far are, although very important, not fundamental discoveries. Not every year do scientists create or destroy basic theories.

Dr. Edwin Land has accomplished one of the most interesting revisions of basic theory. In doing so, he managed to modify a theory of Newton's. Newton had stated that color is perceived through the eye's recognizing the frequencies of light. Thus, a spot of yellow emits a certain frequency that the eye can identify. Dr. Land has shown that the eye can determine all colors just from the interplay of long and short wave lengths. This has made it possible for Dr. Land to show color pictures on a screen when regular black-and-white negatives are used. Two negatives, taken through different-colored filters, are flashed on the screen simultaneously. One projector uses a light of one particular wave length—say red—and the other may use plain white light. All colors in the original scene will be reproduced.

Before this, Dr. Land was known as the

developer of the Polaroid Land Camera,
the camera that develops pictures sixty seconds after they are taken.

A chapter in physics was closed—for the
time being at any rate—when the neutral xi
particle was observed in 1959. It was the
last predicted subatomic particle of ordinary matter, making a list of thirty particles.

Professor P. A. M. Dirac, whose theories
have predicted some unusual particles in
the past, has developed the mathematics
that could be used to describe a gravity
particle. (A gravity particle transmits the
force that attracts one body to another.)
According to the usual method, a mathe-
matician should use Dirac's approach to
make the description. Following that, a
physicist could detect such a particle. In
science, important discoveries often start
with what seem to be baby steps.

Scientists continued to talk about the
weather in 1959. The weather bureau unveiled its Temperature-Humidity Index—
designed to tell you how uncomfortable
you are. Studies in Antarctica showed that
the world is getting warmer at a rate of
two or three degrees Fahrenheit per century. And the July issue of *Scientific American* included an article that pointed out that
carbon dioxide in the atmosphere holds
the heat of the sun. Man is releasing six
billion tons of carbon dioxide each year
just by burning coal and oil. Some scientists say this accounts for the warming
trend.

That a weather trend should be world
wide is not surprising, but a possible world-
wide layer of volcanic ash is. Early in 1959
J. L. Worzel published a report on his discovery of an extensive layer of ash on the

floor of the Pacific Ocean. Later in the year a study, supported in part by the United States Atomic Energy Commission, showed that the Worzel ash layer apparently originated either from one giant volcanic eruption or from several eruptions simultaneously. The volcanic dust released from an explosion of this size, cutting off the light and heat of the sun, would have lowered the earth's temperature for a time, possibly enough to begin an ice age.

The problem of air temperature seemed to crop up in every scientific field during 1959. Research on satellite data produced the startling fact that the air above the Arctic is much hotter than the air above the equator. The Arctic air is heated by particles from the sun drawn to the poles by the earth's magnetism. These solar particles produce a drag on satellites and also excite air molecules, or increase their speeds. This magnetic drag, or slowing, was quite noticeable. Scientists, trying to find an explanation for the slowing of satellites, found by luck a possible key to the origin of the aurora. Two of them, Robert Jastrow and Thomas Kelsall, believe that more of these particles are trapped in spring and fall, thus exciting the air and producing the northern and southern lights.

The most important scientific trend in 1959 made no headlines. Science was moving away from specialization toward unification. Chemists were learning to talk to physicists; oceanographers to astronomers. The trend had been developing since World War II, but only very recently has it become normal for the whole family of sciences to work together.

For example, doctors tackled the problems of health with tools of all kinds. An electronic brain was developed that could make diagnoses, electric currents were used to fight cancer in mice, and an educational theory was given a practical application in the study of brain structure.

The "brain," or digital computer, proc-

essed questionnaires filled out by patients in New York hospitals. Forty-four per cent of the time it made the same diagnoses as the doctors attending the patients had. When the doctors were given only the questionnaires and did not see the patients, the computer actually outscored the doctors. Don't expect a robot to prescribe your next aspirin, however—the computer's purpose is not individual diagnosis but evaluation of medical surveys.

The fact that electricity can kill some tumors without harming normal cells opens a new front in the battle against cancer. In carefully controlled tests on mice, 60 per cent of one type of cancer was shrunk and removed. On another cancer, however, the tests did not give very good results. The effects of electricity on still other types of cancer in other animals are not yet known.

Studies of brain waves of conditioned animals led to new knowledge about the function of various areas of the brain. The animals were conditioned by sounding musical tones as a warning against electric shocks that followed. After a while the tones would produce tension, even if no shock were given or the animal were asleep. Electrodes were implanted in various areas of the brain to see which areas reacted to the tones or in what order areas reacted. The results showed that the cortex, or gray matter of the brain, is less involved in many reactions than had previously been believed. To a large extent the studies confirmed the theories of the Russian physiologist Ivan Pavlov, famous as a pioneer in conditioning animal reflexes.

The work of another Russian, P. S. Chanturishvili, was confirmed in England. The Soviet scientist had replaced destroyed lenses in rabbit eyes with bits of lens tissue from embryonic rabbits. Tissues from embryonic rabbits were used because antibodies in the blood fight the proteins in tissues from adult rabbits. The bits of tissue grew in a short time to form new lenses. The scientists who duplicated this technique in England have begun working on ways to improve it. They are subjecting the adult rabbits' eyes to high radiation. This is expected to help overcome the reaction to foreign proteins.

In 1958 much attention was paid to the problem of thermonuclear fusion (the energy source of the sun and of the hydrogen bomb). When man learns to control it, he will have a virtually unlimited supply of power. British scientists thought that they were on the right track with their machine named ZETA, but they decided to abandon the project in 1959. Exploding nuclear bombs high in the atmosphere late in 1958 was done partly to test one theory that controlled nuclear fusion might be produced by a machine called the Astron.

In late summer of 1959 a small device without a name apparently achieved controlled fusion for about one hundred thousandth of a second. Dr. Alan C. Kolb,

THE BACK OF THE MOON

The moon's far side as revealed for the first time in photographs taken by the Russian space rocket. The broken line on the left separates the portion of the moon visible from the earth from the back side. The solid line is the lunar equator. Though there are apparently fewer craters on the moon's far side, Russian astronomers have given names to a number of them, such as Moscow Sea and Joliot-Curie Crater. The very large one they named Sea of Dreams, and a mountain range is called the Soviet Mountains.

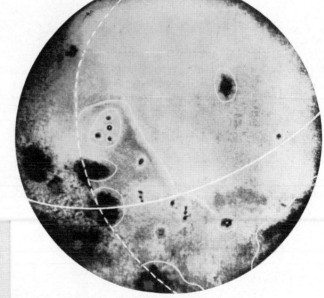

PHOTOS, SOVFOTO

LUNIK III

The Russian space rocket Lunik III before being launched on its journey behind the moon. Shaped something like a top, Lunik weighed 614 pounds and was covered with antennas and solar cells. Among its many instruments was a pair of cameras with powerful lenses. The cameras photographed the far side of the moon, developed the film and transmitted the pictures by radio back to earth.

who developed the device, was quite careful not to make extensive claims, but all the results of tests were positive. The apparatus uses "magnetic mirrors" to contain a very hot plasma of deuterium. Since deuterium is a form of hydrogen found in all sea water, the fuel can be produced fairly cheaply. The high-temperature physics program that led to Dr. Kolb's device cost the United States Government $1,500,-000 over three years.

The lack of a name for a new development is a rarity since nearly all government projects are assigned code names. When Dr. William J. Thaler was asked to name his project he was a little puzzled at first. No title seemed quite right. Since other workers in the Office of Naval Research called it Thaler's Project, he finally decided to use that name's initials—T.P.

Project Tepee turned out to be very important to the United States. It is a new form of radar that can detect missiles or nuclear explosions from thousands of miles away. The Tepee system uses radar waves that bounce back from the ionosphere in the same way that radio waves do. Conventional radar, like television or FM, is limited to line-of-sight wave lengths. Hot gases from bomb explosions or rocket exhausts are ionized and reflect the waves of Tepee radar.

Conventional radar was put to new uses in 1959 by the United States Weather Bureau. The first weather-radar station was installed in Miami to detect hurricanes as they form. It was expected that, by July 1960, thirty-one radar stations would be warning against hurricanes, tornadoes and flash floods. Flood detection is possible be-

TEST FLIGHT

Testing pilots who are preparing to go up to high altitudes is everyday work for the space scientists. Here a Soviet scientist gives last instructions to the pilot who is about to make a "flight" inside the high-altitude test chamber.

cause certain radar signals bounce off rain or snow, allowing the meteorologist to tell how much is falling and where it is falling.

The Soviet Union remained under the influence of Lysenko in genetics. This Russian scientist holds that the effects of environment can be transmitted by heredity. Soviet botanists claimed that wheat could be made drought-resistant by soaking the seeds in water, then drying them. This resistance to dry spells is reputedly inherited by future generations of wheat. Western biologists, who believe that environmental effects are not transmitted by heredity, were skeptical.

The Soviets were the first nation to land a man-made object on the moon. On September 14 (Moscow time), 1959, the Soviet moon rocket crashed near the seas of Tranquillity, Serenity and Vapors. The trip of 236,875 miles took about 35 hours. The payload weighed 858.4 pounds and carried scientific instruments, and pennants bearing the Soviet coat of arms. What did the rocket find on the moon? It is not known, for its radios stopped broadcasting at impact.

From 1952 to 1958 there was much speculation about the possibility of an atmosphere on the moon. This was contrary to what most laymen believed. But scientists pointed out that the moon is made of the same substances as the earth. Some of these substances are radioactive. In the decay process, radioactive potassium produces the inert gas argon. Gravity, holding this gas near the surface of the moon, should produce an atmosphere. Very recently astronomers have seen a lunar volcano erupting. This process would also

PHOTOS, SOVFOTO

SPACE DOGS

Scientific work is going on everywhere to protect pilots preparing to reach high altitudes not achieved before. Devices are being worked out to compensate for lowered air pressure and to protect pilots from the surges of acceleration needed to reach these new altitudes. Soviet scientists, for example, are using dogs in high-altitude test chambers. Shown here are test dogs Tsiganka and Mishka being dressed in their space suits for the "flight."

tend to allow the moon an atmosphere, for volcanic activity always produces gases.

In 1959 all these theories were blown to the solar winds. The solar wind is composed of protons thrown off by the sun. These protons, colliding with the gases around the moon, knock most atmospheric molecules off into space. The earth's atmosphere, however, is protected from the solar wind by earth's magnetic field—a sort of geophysical windbreaker. Data radioed from the Russian rocket before it hit the moon showed that the moon has no magnetic field.

It is therefore probable that the Soviet rocket hit nothing but rocks and dust on the surface of the moon.

On October 4 Lunik III was launched by the Soviet Union. Its elongated orbit carried it beyond the moon far enough so that its camera was able to take several photographs of the side of the moon never before seen by man. The photographs, released later in the year, showed the far side of the moon to be somewhat smoother than the familiar face of "the Man in the Moon." This bears out a theory that some of the huge craters facing earth were caused by the pull of gravity. When radio contact with Lunik III was lost in November, Soviet scientists said they thought the rocket might have hit a large meteor.

Meteors are, of course, only one of the hazards that the first man who travels to the moon must face. In preparation for his trip, American cartographers are preparing the first topographic map of the moon, to be ready sometime in 1960.

This article began with some significant 1959 scientific events that occurred in 1958. Actually all scientific progress has its roots in work done earlier. Even before 1959 was over, some of the important science news stories of the early 1960's were beginning to take shape.

One that quickly captured people's fancy was the Mohole. The Mohole will be a hole bored through the earth's crust and into the mantle beyond what is known as the Mohorovicic discontinuity. The actual depth of the shaft will be from 31,000 to 50,000 feet—at least 5,000 feet deeper than man has yet drilled. Because the earth's crust is thinner under the ocean floor, that is where the Mohole will be bored.

This bold idea was conceived by AMSOC—the American Miscellaneous Society—and is backed by the National Academy of Sciences and the National Science Foundation. It is believed that the Mohole will, by providing a continuous core sample, establish for the first time what the earth is really made of. Paleontologists are hoping that fossils will be uncovered that will throw light on the origins of life. It is expected that the Mohole will be completed in 1962.

While AMSOC is putting a drill bit into the earth, physicists hope to be raising a clock above it. Contracts were awarded by the National Aeronautics and Space Administration in 1959 for the development of an atomic clock to be placed in a satellite. Its purpose will be to test Einstein's general and special theories of relativity.

Other objects will visit space in the not-too-distant future. The United States intends to land a seismograph on the moon to measure movements in the lunar crust caused by seismic activity or by meteorite impacts. Private industry is considering launching satellites for communications purposes. The Soviet Union has agreed that a ban on nuclear tests could be policed by low-flying satellites.

But the greatest adventure of all will be putting a man into orbit. In the United States seven test pilots were chosen in 1959, one of whom will be the first American in space. It was believed that the Soviets were also planning to put a man in a recoverable space capsule before long. They have been working on the project.

AMAZING

HALF-CENTURY

By STERLING NORTH
Editor, Author and Critic

Many of us who were alive in 1910 can remember splitting wood for
the kitchen stove, hitching Old Nell to the buggy for a drive or watching
early melodramas on the nickelodeon's flickering screen. Now we casually
zip across the continent on superhighways, board a jet airliner for a transatlantic crossing and contemplate the probability of travel through outer
space. Standards of living have risen tremendously in fifty years. Modern
houses with a hundred laborsaving devices can be cooled, heated and
powered from a distant electric dynamo. We are doctored, not with evil-
tasting sulfur and molasses, but with antibiotics of surprising efficiency.
The news and entertainment of half the world come into the living room
on a TV wave length—a miracle undreamed-of fifty years ago.

It has been said that we have progressed further in this amazing half
century than in the previous four thousand years of recorded history.
But not all of the change has been progress. It has also brought us many
grave problems. Most terrifying of all are the atomic and hydrogen bombs
—needful, alas, to guard our democratic freedom.

A greater safeguard of our freedom, however, is education—knowledge
of the principles for which we stand, the sciences that support our high
standard of living and the arts that make living meaningful and gracious.
Unless we know what has happened in the past and what is now happening, we will be ill prepared to face the challenge of the future. Our greatest
single resource is the upcoming generation. These boys and girls must be
able to harness our splendid discoveries and inventions for the betterment
of mankind, not for its destruction.

I salute *The Book of Knowledge* on its fiftieth anniversary for helping
to awaken and enlighten hundreds of thousands of young people who
will soon have the fate of the world in their hands.

MEDICINE

AND

HEALTH

By PAUL DE KRUIF

Writer on Medical History

THIS is a personal reminiscence of fifty years of life among the chemists and the doctors. It is in no sense a history of the fight against death that has made our epoch so miraculous. It is only an impressionistic sketch of certain high moments of lifesaving which, in the past fifty years, has surpassed that of fifty previous centuries.

As I first observed it in the decade 1910 to 1920, the birth of modern medicine was uncertain and slow to crystallize into a mass saving of life. The era opened with a fanfare. Paul Ehrlich's magic bullet, salvarsan-606, was supposed to knock out syphilis in one shot. But the hoped-for miracle had to be prolonged to continuous treatment over eighteen months. It was so uncomfortable and even dangerous that many patients abandoned treatment. It took thirty-five years before the one-shot

miracle of penicillin came with a real hope of conquering syphilis.

The German Emil von Behring had introduced a toxin-antitoxin serum for diphtheria in 1894, which had reduced the diphtheria death rate. It was not until the 1920-30 decade that a diphtheria toxoid was developed that could really wipe out this terrible disease. Then for years cases of diphtheria became fewer and fewer until now it is virtually eliminated.

Fifty years ago many of the poorer people in the southern United States, Spain, Africa and India suffered from pellagra, a disease that affects both the gastrointestinal and the nervous systems. In the decade 1910-20 Joseph Goldberger of the United States Public Health Service discovered that pellagra was caused by a dietary deficiency, a hidden hunger of the human body. Though he did not know the exact vitamin involved in the deficiency, he treated pellagra in a simple way, by direct improvement of the diet, making sure it included lean meat, eggs and fresh milk. In this way Goldberger was able to prevent—and control—the disease. Twenty more years, however, went by before the cause was traced to lack of niacin. Since then, pellagra has been cured, quickly and cheaply, by including niacin, one of the B-complex vitamins, in the diet.

The identification of vitamins, of course, as vital substances essential for human health and well-being, took place in the first decades of this century. In 1912 Casimir Funk named these substances "vitamines." In the years following there was a great stir over vitamins—people bought them for every kind of ailment. More than one vitamin "huckster" took advantage of a health-seeking—but often gullible—public. Today we know much more about the various vitamins and their properties than did the pioneer investigators. We also know that not one vitamin but several, as well as minerals and proteins, are needed for a properly balanced diet and good health. In the early days, as each new

The horse-and-buggy doctor served his community faithfully and often with brilliance.

vitamin was isolated and identified, it was named after a letter of the alphabet— vitamin A, B, C and so forth. This system proved unsatisfactory. For example, vitamin B was later found to be not one but a group of several vitamins. Each of these had to be given a name of its own, but the group as a whole is called the vitamin B complex. Today's chemists give each new vitamin a name that corresponds to its chemical composition—riboflavin, thiamine, biotin, pantothenic acid and so on.

The second decade, 1920-30, was more brilliant than the ten years that preceded

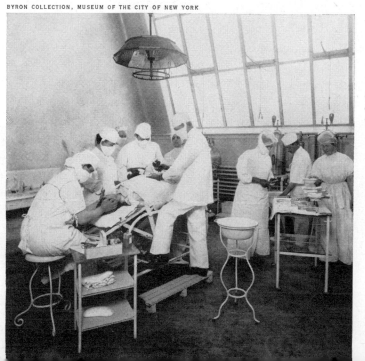

Operating room of a large city hospital in the first decade of the 1900's.

it. It marked the beginning of control of ills for which there had been no hope at all. In a laboratory cubbyhole in a hot attic at the University of Toronto, Frederick G. Banting and Charles H. Best brewed insulin, first saving doomed diabetic dogs, then youthful human victims who were brought to them, dying of diabetes.

For his discovery of insulin in the treatment of diabetes Dr. Banting (together with J. J. R. Macleod) received the 1923 Nobel Prize. Today the life span of many severe diabetics equals that of normally healthy human beings. One of the most widely known examples of triumph over this disease is William Talbert, the tennis star, who has been a diabetic since he was ten years old. Without insulin even his courage and determination could not have saved him.

In 1924 Providence intervened to help save victims of another disease that in those days was 100 per cent fatal. George Minot, a Boston pathologist who was thought to have a hopeless case of diabetes, was saved by Banting's insulin. He himself later rescued many sufferers from pernicious anemia. It had long been believed that there was no cure for this wasting disease. Minot, however, after years of research and experiment, succeeded in finding the cure. In his private office he fed dying pernicious-anemia patients whole liver, thus restoring their strength.

BROWN BROTHERS

Tuberculosis sanitarium. Years ago mountain air was considered the only hope for tubercular people.

In the middle 1930's it appeared that para-aminobenzenesulfonamide (sulfanilamide) might have some curative importance. It had been synthesized as a mere laboratory exercise in 1908 by a young chemist, P. Gelmo, of Vienna. It had then taken researchers twenty-four years to find out that this substance prepared by Gelmo was the safest and most powerful microbe destroyer so far discovered. Within four years, chemists concocted derivatives of this sulfanilamide, including sulfapyridine, sulfathiazole and sulfadiazine, thus preventing many deaths.

CONQUERORS OF DISEASE

Charles Best   Frederick Banting   George Minot   Thomas Spies

Clinic founded 1915 at Rochester, Minnesota, by Drs. Charles and William Mayo. In the foreground, new building (1955); rear, old building (1929).

In this third decade, 1930-40, the organic chemists had so revolutionized medicine that the death-fighting power of doctors was more than doubled. Though very nearly half of all our physicians were serving in World War II in the early 1940's, the civilian death rate did not rise.

At the same time, in this third decade, the chemists characterized and synthesized key compounds that are vital to the human body. In 1936 Dr. Robert R. Williams synthesized the B-1 vitamin, thiamine, which he had isolated earlier. No fish, no frog, no tree, no snake, no baby or

Casimir Funk

baboon could develop and grow without thiamine. Then came the vitamin riboflavin, to help thiamine carry on the oxidation process within human cells. Also discovered was the vitamin niacin, vital to the working of the central nervous system. These crystal-pure vitamins made their bow in the same period as the sulfas.

Measured doses of these chemicals, shot into people with nervous disorders, were calming in their effect. To some in deep dementia the chemicals restored sanity. To some who were going blind they restored sight.

There continues to be a great outcry against the routine use of large doses of multiple synthetic vitamins. Many people ask: How can we be suffering from chemical starvation when we eat three good meals a day? The physicians who began fighting "hidden famine" had an answer.

In matters of nutrition, nature has played a trick upon her children and has been miserly with the amount of the vital B-vitamin chemicals she has put into some foods. Even on our "three meals" a day many of us may be near chemical starva-

A typical drugstore in 1910. Besides filling prescriptions it sold patented tonics and remedies. Right, a modern pharmacy specializing in prescriptive drugs such as the antibiotics.

tion. Prophetic famine fighters, notable among them Dr. Tom D. Spies of Birmingham, Alabama, warned that many still mysterious ills might turn out to be vitamin deficiencies.

In recent decades, things have been made worse by refining necessary vitamins out of foods. The National Research Council tried to remedy this by recommending enrichment of bread and flour with the addition of B-complex vitamins.

During the 1930-40 and even the 1940-50 decades, some scientific and medical authorities regarded these hopeful possibilities with disbelief. The fourth decade, 1940-50, saw their doubts dispelled. Penicillin had no sooner arrived than it was followed by other antibiotics, the tetracyclines. Their discovery did not come from government research or from medical-college research laboratories but from the pharmaceutical industry.

The contribution of the ethical drug companies to society during the past twenty-five years has been great. If there were no modern industrial pharmaceutical research, there might well be no modern medicine, a fact that is often overlooked.

In 1948 Dr. Benjamin M. Duggar, a retired professor working at Lederle Laboratories, found a golden mold, a fungus that produced aureomycin. That was the first of the tetracyclines. The power of aureomycin, and of its derivative tetracyclines, over microbes is great. The tetracyclines are fatal not only to pneumococcus and streptococcus but also to a wide range of urinary-tract infections resistant to penicillin and the sulfas. They have cured diseases as widely different as Rocky

Iron lung (1935) helps polio patient to breathe.

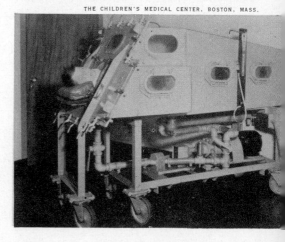

A 1909 laboratory (left) where smallpox vaccine was given its final processing and packaged. At right, a modern laboratory where scientists carry on basic research to develop new products.

Mountain spotted fever and psittacosis and have been useful against nearly a hundred maladies upon which penicillin and streptomycin had been tried in vain.

Aureomycin (chlortetracycline) given by mouth—not by injection—rapidly became a widely prescribed drug. Parke Davis and Company's researchers developed a wonder drug, chloromycetin, that cured hitherto incurable typhoid fever and also has often overcome the staphylococcus bacteria, which the tetracyclines can't kill.

In new iron lung, patient can see room in mirror.

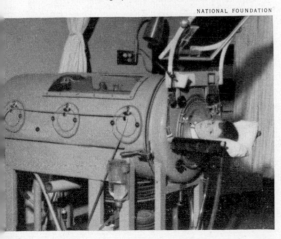

The Eli Lilly Company's microbiologists developed yet another antibiotic for use in cases where chloromycetin might fail. The company's vancomycin, injected into the veins of patients as a last resort, can destroy the resistant staphylococcus, the curse of our hospitals.

It has been calculated that, on the basis of lower death rates from pneumonia and other infections, the sulfa drugs and antibiotics alone saved the lives of at least 1,500,000 Americans between 1938 and 1958. This figure has now been far surpassed.

When we ask who is curing us so wonderfully, the credit, of course, goes to the doctors. But let us not forget the dedication and ingenuity of the researchers of the pharmaceutical industry.

There is a sad side to the great results that have been achieved by the marvelous sulfas and antibiotics. By saving aging people from pneumonia, for example, they are confronting millions with the grave problems of old age. Medical science has extended the human life span by effectively checking infectious diseases, such as pneumonia, influenza and tuberculosis,

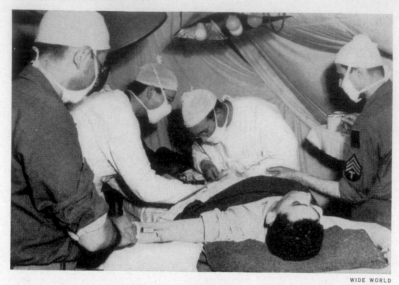

World War II: Army surgeons operate under fire.

but it has added little to the vigor and vitality of later years.

The geriatric wards of our hospitals, voluntary and public, are crowded with confused, bewildered and disoriented patients with little hope for tomorrow. This condition is modern medicine's bitterest challenge.

For the extension not of mere life span but of a longer *vital* life span there is now a glowing hope. In the 1940-50 decade Dr. Tom D. Spies and his associates at the Hillman Nutrition Clinic in Birmingham, Alabama, made a valuable discovery. They found that many of the ills of patients who were middle aged and older were not caused by the lack of just one vitamin. They were the result of deficiency in many vitamins of the B complex, as well as proteins and minerals.

In 1950, at the Hillman Nutrition Clinic in Birmingham, this reporter saw a group of patients just up out of the pain and paralysis of dangerous anemia. Their tissue integrity had seemed damaged to the point of no return.

I made another visit to the clinic some eight years later. Then, in 1958, this same group of patients were assembled for a reunion. They looked hale, they looked hearty, they looked actually younger than they had in 1950 when nutritional therapy first saved them. Some, who told me they were 75, looked no more than 60. One of them, Kenny Weldon, aged 53 in 1950, had then been a bag of bones.

Weldon's loathing for food had been such that he had refused to eat when he first came to the clinic. On the new nutrition treatment, he developed a tremendous appetite. In 1958 Weldon was 223 pounds of bone and muscle. He has been working steadily as a miner these past eight years.

Dr. Spies in such cases explains that the real heroes are the cells of his patients' bodies. He says that the signs and symptoms of their mid-life illnesses are alarms from damaged tissues. These signs do not mean the tissues are finished. Give the starved cells the nutriments they need, and they have a good chance to recover.

More and more physicians now treat older patients with a routine regimen of therapeutic vitamins, proteins and minerals. They realize that maximum nutrition is basic to the well-being of all their patients, no matter whether they are being treated in their homes or in the hospital.

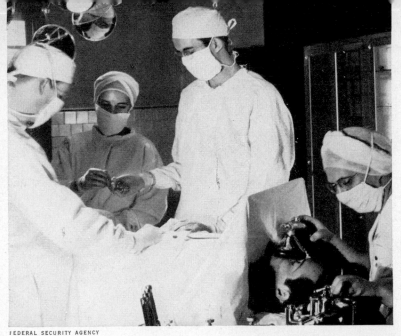

Giving anaesthetic at Public Health Service hospital.

Left, mobile units give free X rays in tuberculosis surveys. Right, broken leg in traction until bone knits.

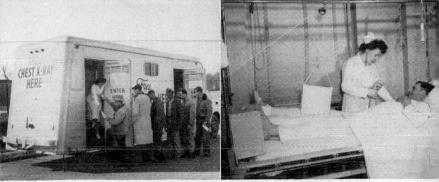

Left, Dr. Jonas Salk supervises making of his polio vaccine. Right, children receive protective shots.

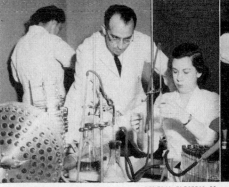

Electricity helps. Left, paralyzed muscles exercised by new device. Right, machine detects nerve injury.

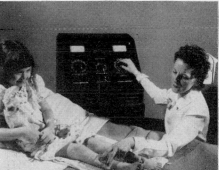

One of the saddest of all the sicknesses of old age is what is called senile dementia. Until recently this was thought to be due to arteriosclerosis, a hardening of the arteries. To many of these aged patients, more and more of whom are filling our mental hospitals, chemistry is now bringing hope. For certain mental diseases have been discovered to be caused by chemical changes in the body. Dr. John T. Ferguson, of Traverse City, Michigan, has notably reduced the mental confusion and dis-orientation of many of his psychoneurotic patients by treatment with behavior medicines—such as the tranquilizer Serpasil, for those who are disturbed, and the energizer Ritalin, for those in melancholia. Many of these patients have been returned, in good health, to their families.

The hope of this combined therapy against mental disease lies not so much in our asylums as with our family doctors. Skillfully using behavior medicines and preventive nutrition, they will be able to

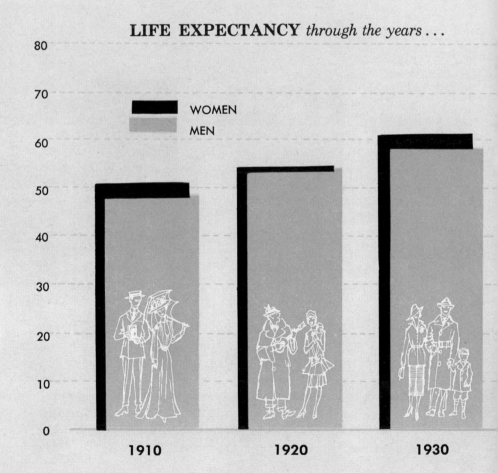

LIFE EXPECTANCY *through the years...*

WOMEN

MEN

1910   1920   1930

keep many probable senile mental cases from commitment and restore them to useful lives. A powerful new ally has arisen against mental disturbances—the amazing red vitamin—B_{12}.

One of the most spectacular discoveries of the past few years is the wonder drug Diuril, developed by the chemists and biologists of Merck Sharp and Dohme. By removing excessive sodium and its accompanying excess water from victims of congestive heart failure, Diuril brings hope to hundreds of thousands of sufferers from overloaded hearts. Many of them have already returned to health and full activity after daily doses of this remarkably safe and powerful medicine.

And this Diuril has a lifesaving dividend. Dr. R. W. Wilkins of Boston and Dr. E. D. Freis of Washington, D. C., have found that when Diuril is added to hypotensive drugs, it makes them much safer and more effective in the treatment of severe high blood pressure.

1940   1950   1959

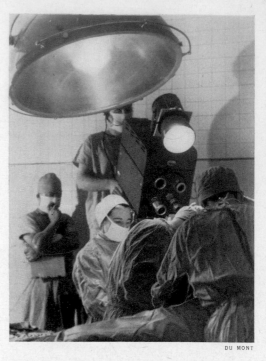

Color televising an operation for students in another room to view.

DU MONT

The 1950-60 decade has seen some spectacular advances in heart surgery. Hearts seriously damaged by rheumatic fever or otherwise defective are now operated on by surgeons with amazing success. More and more plastic parts for the heart are being used. And some surgeons think that it is only a matter of years before a whole new heart can replace a diseased one.

The near-conquest of polio, the scourge of children and young adults, is an example of modern medical teamwork at its best. In 1954-55, after careful field trials with the Salk vaccine, which contained the three known strains of poliomyelitis virus, results showed that the vaccine could be considered 60 to 100 per cent effective. Nationwide inoculation of school children was started by the National Foundation for Infantile Paralysis. Over 75,000,000 Americans have received some vaccine. The decline in polio cases is heartening, and everyone should get the necessary vaccine shots in order to wipe out this crippling disease once and for all. Scientists meanwhile are experimenting with a live vaccine to be taken by mouth.

This brings me to the end of my personal observation of fifty years of triumph by our doctors over diseases that have been considered "continuate and inexorable" through the ages. Many more victories are in the making, such as that of the corticosteroid hormones—cortisone and its more safe and powerful derivatives—in the relief and the control of severe arthritis, though not its cure. So great is progress in reducing the misery of these hundreds of thousands of afflicted, that a hopeful report on the *prevention* of arthritis may be possible in not too many years.

But what can I say of progress against the archenemy, cancer? Despite the present annual expenditure of hundreds of millions of dollars of government and other public funds on research, the big killers— lung and stomach cancer and the leukemias—remain deadly and tragic enigmas.

This does not mean that certain cancers will remain forever beyond cure. But it is my conviction that, in the cancer fight, one thing is needed—men like Banting, who conquered diabetes with his courage and his brains, and like George Minot, who learned to control pernicious anemia in his private office—both of them with very little research money. They would have plenty of skilled researchers in the pharmaceutical industry and the great university laboratories to help them. Perhaps such men will appear in the decade just ahead.

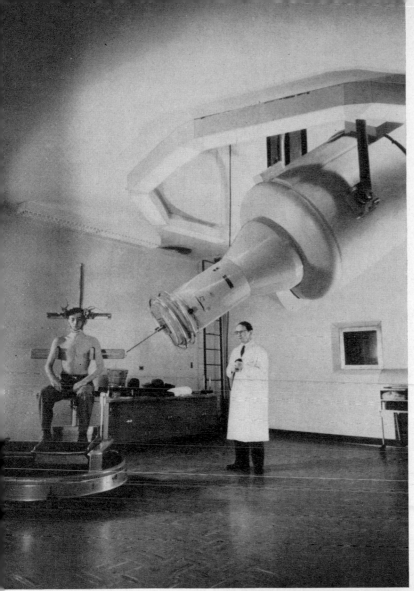

Two-million-volt X-ray machine for treatment of deep-seated cancer.

Plastic hearts and valves of various shapes and materials. Some of these may serve to replace damaged parts of the human heart.

TRAVEL AND TRANSPORT

By ROBERT G. ALBION
*Gardiner Professor of Oceanic History
and Affairs, Harvard University*

I F you could journey back through time to the year 1910, you would find many familiar sights and sounds, but some of those most familiar to us today would be missing. No giant airliners would cast swift shadows on field and town. Instead of the network of concrete highways, you would see winding dirt roads, with a few miles of gravel or macadam near the towns. Instead of today's ceaseless flow of automobiles and motor trucks, you would see all sizes and shapes of horse-drawn vehicles—with just an occasional motorcar, frightening the horses as it rattled past, leaving clouds of dust and gasoline fumes behind it. But the railroads would be there, in essentials very much as they are today, though they have improved in speed, safety and comfort.

In 1910 the railroads were almost at the peak of their long importance. They car-

ried nearly a billion passengers and more than a billion tons of freight, and their 240,000 miles of roadbed were close to the all-time high of 260,000 miles in the latter part of the 1920's.

Then as now, the railroads' chief profits lay in their freight, which accounted for three fourths of their revenues of $2,500,-000,000. At this time, by the way, the roads charged about two cents a mile for carrying either a passenger or a ton of freight.

The make-up of the trains was basically the same as it is today. There were the ordinary day coaches with two long rows of double seats—stiff, plush covered and not too comfortable—with an aisle between them. Some of these were designated for smokers. It was before the days of air conditioning, and the black soot and smoke from the coal-burning locomotive sifted through the usually closed windows to settle over everyone.

For those able and willing to pay a little more (60 cents on a hundred-mile, $2.00 trip), express trains had parlor cars furnished by the Pullman Company. They had reserved, rotating chairs for each person, and a porter to handle bags and brush off the cinders that penetrated even those select precincts. For overnight travel, there were Pullman sleeping cars where the seats could be opened up into berths. A heavy green curtain separated these from the center aisle. Both parlor and sleeping cars had a so-called drawing room at one end for families or other small groups traveling together. At the other end was the smoking room. The well-equipped train also had a dining car where, in cramped space, meals were served at small tables. Some passengers preferred to take advantage of the

gage cars were for the passengers' trunks and heavier bags. Because of the bulkier and more formal clothes of the time there was always a good deal of baggage. Up to a certain weight, these bags were carried free on one's railroad ticket. A car or two also usually belonged to one of the big express companies—American, Adams, Southern or Wells Fargo. These companies gave door-to-door service, carrying packages, perishables and valuables with greater speed and security than by ordinary freight. In 1913 the Government took over parcel post. That shifted part of the small freight burden to the third type of head-end cars—the railway mail cars. Here postal clerks sorted letters and gathered in mailbags (sometimes on the fly from stations where the train did not stop) and threw them off at their proper destination.

Such were the full-dress trains of 1910.

PHOTOS, NEW YORK CENTRAL RR

Old 999 held speed record for many years.   The Aerotrain—new, fast, diesel-engined.

"ten minutes for refreshments" at stations where the engines took on water. Some of the western trains carried no diners at all but utilized station restaurants. A few very special limited trains, with extra fare charged, had observation cars with broad windows and open rear platforms; a few even had barbershops.

Those main-line express trains also had several so-called head-end cars. The bag-

Most of the cars were still built of wood—a tremendous danger in case of accident. Passengers and crewmen were apt to be trapped in splintered wreckage that might catch fire from the lamps or stoves. In 1910, 9,682 persons, including 324 passengers, were killed; and 119,507, including 12,451 passengers, were injured. However, these terrible figures are mild compared with later automobile casualties.

Millions of people have passed through New York's Grand Central Terminal since 1913.

The local-accommodation trains were slower and simpler, but they brought the railroad's services to all the little communities along the line. Stations were fairly close together—the Central Massachusetts, for instance, had forty in the hundred miles between Boston and Northampton. The accommodation trains had no Pullmans or diners; their cars were often old open-platform affairs, with stoves for heat, and sometimes were half-smoker, half-baggage or mail car.

The role of the other locals, the commuting trains, was more specialized. Their passenger load was concentrated in the morning-and-evening rush hours as they carried workers to and from their city jobs, on runs averaging about fifteen miles. Such daily passengers used monthly commutation tickets at reduced rates (hence the word "commuters"). In New York City, Grand Central and Pennsylvania stations, both new at the time, were the busiest in the country, with about six hundred trains in and out each day. Stations in Philadelphia, Boston, Chicago, Louisville and other cities also accounted daily for thousands of commuters in vast morning and evening tides.

224

CANADIAN PACIFIC RAILWAY

Interior of a sleeping car, about 1905-10.

However, the American railroads gave their greatest service—and reaped their richest reward—in handling freight traffic. The red boxcars with their thirty-five-ton capacity were familiar sights on every spur and siding. The long, chuffing trains were made up of scores of such boxcars. They were loaded with grain or flour from the Midwest, refrigerated steaks from Chicago or Kansas City, out-of-season fruits or vegetables. They carried raw materials and other supplies of every sort to factories and distributed the finished products around the country. Along with the boxcars might be long strings of open cars with coal from the Appalachians, or flatcars with heavy steel products. The "Whoo-Whoo-Wh'-Whoo" of the steam locomotives at crossings was a familiar sound throughout the United States and Canada.

In 1910 the seacoasts and the Great Lakes region were not so dependent upon the railroads as were the inland cities and towns. They also had water transportation for freight and passengers; this was cheaper than rail and often much pleasanter for the latter. Such water-borne transportation costs less because, aside from the vessels, all that a steamship line needs are wharves where its vessels can stop. A railroad, in

addition to engines and cars, has the heavy extra expense of acquiring and maintaining its right of way. The particularly important night boats furnished passenger and freight service between ports as far as two hundred miles apart. The Hudson River Night Line plied that river between New York and Albany. The Fall River Line ran through Long Island Sound between New York and Fall River, Massachusetts, where trains connected with Boston. The Old Bay Line went nightly through Chesapeake Bay between Baltimore and Norfolk. The Eastern Steamship Company had a number of services radiating from Boston to New York, to Portland, to the Kennebec and Penobscot rivers, and to New Brunswick and Nova Scotia. There were similar runs on the West coast. On the Great Lakes, the chief overnight trip was between Detroit and Cleveland. Thousands of passengers preferred a night on the water to a railroad sleeper or coach; shippers could send their freight to the piers in the afternoon, knowing that it would be at its destination next day, at much less than the cost by rail. There were also longer coastal voyages from New England and New York in seagoing vessels down past stormy Cape Hatteras to Charleston, Savannah, New Orleans and Galveston. Hundreds of smaller steamers plied shorter coastal and lake

NEW HAVEN RAILROAD

Interior of a modern railroad dining car.

CUNARD LINE

Coal-burning sea queen, the old Mauritania.

HOLLAND-AMERICA LINE

Sleek, swift new Rotterdam, fueled by oil.

The river passenger steamboat Priscilla.

The nuclear-powered merchantship Savannah.

was iron ore taken by big lake steamers from Lake Superior to Cleveland and other lake ports.

All those domestic runs were barred to foreign shipping by law, but on the distant sea lanes it was another story. United States ships, which had once carried 90 per cent of American foreign trade, were now carrying less than 10 per cent. British, German, Scandinavian and other vessels carried the rest. The crack luxurious liners linking New York with Europe were always most conspicuous on the foreign runs. In 1910 and for years afterward the "blue ribbon" for speed went to the Cunard liner Mauretania. Two years later the White Star liner Titanic on her maiden trip from England sank with great loss of life after speeding into an iceberg. Such ships carried very little ordinary cargo; most of the world's commerce went in freighters, some of them serving regular routes on definite schedules while others, as tramps, picked up cargo wherever they could find it around the world.

In hundreds of cities and towns around the country this was the heyday of the trolley car for local transportation. Cars drawn by horses along rails in the street had been common since Civil War days or even earlier. In 1887-88, Frank J. Sprague put into operation in Richmond, Virginia, a successful substitute with electric power transmitted through a trolley pole from overhead wires extending the full length of the system of rails. The early cars were small; the passengers faced each other across the aisle. Later cars had double seats like railroad coaches. In the summer, there were open cars with rows of crosswise seats. For five cents, one could travel most of the main streets of a city, with paper transfers from one line to another. Some of these lines built up popular resorts several miles out of town, with restaurants, theaters and other attractions. A few places had variations from the overhead trolley: New York

routes. Moonlight rides and other such excursions were popular pastimes of the period, especially on great rivers like the Ohio and the Hudson.

The lower cost also caused much bulky cargo to be sent by water. Coal from Hampton Roads, Virginia, for New England moved almost entirely by water, much of it in five- and six-masted schooners, some of them the largest wooden vessels ever built. But they were beginning to feel the competition of steam colliers and of strings of barges towed by steam tugs. Some oil was shipped north from the Gulf of Mexico by tanker, but it was only a trickle compared with what it is today. Smaller sailing vessels carried large quantities of lumber and granite down the coast from Maine. One of the heaviest movements and Washington streetcars picked up their power from a slot between the rails, while moving cables were gripped to take cars up and down San Francisco's steep hills.

The larger cities needed something more effective than the trolleys, clanging through the crowded streets, to carry large numbers of people back and forth quickly, particularly at the rush hours. This was especially true in New York. As early as 1867, New York began to experiment with elevated trains, drawn by little locomotives, which ran up and down Manhattan Island mounted on high tracks far above the streets. In 1897, Frank J. Sprague, who had started trolley cars nine years before, introduced trains of electric-powered elevated cars in Chicago; New York soon adapted them to the elevated system. That same year, Boston experimented with putting its "rapid transit" in a subway beneath the street. By 1910, trains on a single route would sometimes be elevated part of the way and subway the rest. Trains of trolley cars would emerge from the subway to run on the surface.

Despite all such devices and the coming of motorcars the horse was still much in the picture in 1910. In the country the farmer still usually hauled his crops or milk by wagon to the nearest railroad station; in the cities, big drays, pulled by powerful horses, rumbled over the cobblestones, but those who were accustomed to having their own horses and carriages were turning to automobiles. The taxicab had arrived, especially in the larger cities, but the horse-drawn hack from the livery stables was still around.

In the half century since 1910 there has been a virtual revolution in our transportation system. By 1960 the various forms of motor transport loomed as large as the railroad had done in 1910. The airplane had already taken over much of the profitable long-distance passenger and mail service from the railroads and the ocean liners.

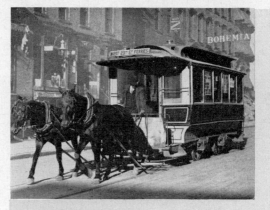

New York still had a few horsecars in 1910.

Streetcars with underground trolleys, 1916.

PHOTOS THIS PAGE, CULVER SERVICE

Double-decked "el" station, New York, 1929.

CULVER SERVICE

An early subway car, reserved for women only.

N. Y. TRANSIT AUTHORITY

The well-lit interior of a modern subway car.

The passenger automobile, the local and long-distance buses and the motor trucks had almost eliminated the trolley and the overnight coastal steamers. At the same time short-haul railroad services were fast diminishing. The amazing spread of the automobile had had a profound effect upon American life in general.

If any one person could be credited with bringing about all this, it would be Henry Ford. He announced in 1908: "I will build a motor car for the great multitude. It will be large enough for the family but small enough for the individual to run and care for . . . It will be so low in price that no man making a good salary will be unable to own one—and enjoy with his family the blessings of hours of pleasure in God's great open spaces." There had been automobiles of sorts for at least fifteen years, but they were still considered playthings for the well to do. A popular song of Irving Berlin referred to:

Dukes and lords and Russian Czars,
Men who own their motor cars. . . .*

In the horse-and-buggy era the average person with a good salary did not consider furnishing his own transportation. Even if the expense was not too great, the amount of work and time involved in keeping his own stable would have been.

* Copyright 1913, Irving Berlin. Copyright renewed.

Ford's Model T cars, turned out by assembly-line methods at Detroit, were bought by the millions. By the time Ford finally changed the model in 1927, fifteen million "tin lizzies" had been sold—as many as all the other makes combined. Car owners—194,000 in 1908—had jumped to 5,500,000 by 1918, 21,300,000 by 1928 and would continue on up to 66,000,000 in 1958.

Since the first one was built in 1904 the number of motor trucks had also been increasing rapidly. One of their first important uses was to help farmers bring their crops, livestock and dairy products to market more easily. Urban areas were able to get fresh vegetables, berries, fruit, milk and other foods from a much wider radius. Trucks also began to carry general freight of the sort that had previously gone by rail or by coastal steamer. They had the advantage of door-to-door service which steamers or freight trains could not furnish. More and more, particularly at night, processions of huge trucks thundered along the main highways.

The third big type of motor-transport activity was the bus, carrying numerous passengers for short local hauls at first and gradually working into long-distance operations. The bus came into general use gradually after World War I.

New York's Fifth Avenue bus, about 1914.

A lady steps into the popular Model T Ford.

Modern cars: the de luxe Cadillac, the sports Corvette and (lower right) the trailer truck. Left, the clover leaf, part of a superhighway network.

It was only natural that the transportation methods of 1910 would change under the impact of these new devices. Some were driven out completely, while others had to make difficult adjustments in order to survive at all.

In urban transit, the trolley was a victim of the car and motorbus. It gradually gave way to the motorbus with its greater flexibility and its cheaper operating costs. The desire to get the old trolley tracks out of the streets accelerated the process. In the quarter century between 1914 and 1939 the number of active streetcars dropped from 62,000 to less than 2,000, and their trackage from 40,000 to 4,000 miles. Only 15 cities out of the former several hundred still had streetcar service in 1959, and most of them were planning to get rid of them quickly. In addition to the motorbuses, part of the new competition came from trackless trolleys, which get their cheap power from overhead wires but do not need rails. Most of the rapid transit subway and elevated systems, on the other hand, still continued to operate. New York got rid of all but two of its completely elevated routes in the late 1950's. The combination of union demands for high wages, plus the competition of the automobile, has made it difficult for the transit systems to meet expenses. Both in New York and Boston the cities make up the heavy deficits out of general funds in order to keep fares from going still higher.

In the middle range of distances (from about 15 to 200 miles) the first victims of the new age were the coastal steamers on the overnight runs. The automobile cut into their flourishing passenger business, while the motor truck with its door-to-door pickup-and-delivery service had a more ruinous effect. The drastic increase of stevedoring costs by the wage demands of the longshoremen's unions completed the hopeless picture. It often cost more to lift a box or bale a few feet from a steamer's hold to the pier than to bring it 200 miles

Transferring mail from truck to plane, 1920.

up the coast. Virtually none of the overnight services, except the Old Bay Line on the Chesapeake, survived World War II. Many of the longer coastal services also succumbed. Some later lines offset high stevedoring costs by carrying already loaded freight cars or truck bodies. The opening of the Panama Canal during World War I led to active intercoastal freight service between Atlantic and Pacific ports. Lumber, steel and other heavy cargo could be carried much more cheaply than by rail, and the distance was too long for trucking. In 1940, however, domestic shipping rates came under the control of the railroad-minded Interstate Commerce Commission which soon cut out the natural advantage of cheap water transportation. That was almost the only victory for the railroads in their competition with other forms of transportation. In the later period the one flourishing branch of coastal shipping was the steady procession of oil tankers from the Gulf.

The planes' history is usually dated from the flight of the Wright brothers at Kitty Hawk, north of Cape Hatteras, in 1903. The airplane was still in a highly experimental state until World War I when military needs led to its rapid development. In

1918 the Government began regular airmail service. For a few cents extra postage, letters could travel much faster than by train. In the mid-twenties private companies were encouraged to take over the mail routes and carry passengers too. The Government gave financial assistance, while cities usually paid for the new airports. In 1926, when such scheduled service got under way, 5,700 passengers were carried, in addition to much airmail and a very small amount of express or freight. In ten years the passengers had jumped to 931,000; 24 companies with 280 planes

WIDE WORLD
A pioneer coast-to-coast air transport.

were serving nearly 30,000 miles of routes. That year, 1936, saw the first of the big DC-3 planes which would be the standard passenger carrier for years. The DC-3 could comfortably carry 22 passengers with two pilots and a stewardess at a cruising speed of around 200 miles an hour.

By that time overseas flights were also developing rapidly. Their possibility was dramatically demonstrated by the solitary flight of young Charles Lindbergh from New York to Paris in 33 hours in 1927. British and Dutch companies soon had service to India, the Far East, Australia and South Africa. Pan American World Airways started American service modestly in

1929 on the short Miami-Havana run and soon extended operations down through the Caribbean and South America. In 1937 its flying boats began transpacific service with stops at Hawaii, Midway, Wake, Guam and Manila. Regular transatlantic flights by British and American lines were just getting under way when World War II started in 1939. Such flights were commonplace by the end of World War II and several nations quickly started commercial service.

Planes with piston-driven engines and whirling propellers had made good speed records, but with the introduction in the late 1950's of planes propelled by a jet of escaping gas much faster flights became possible. In military use these jet planes had already exceeded the speed of sound. Now they could travel between New York and San Francisco in about four hours (trains needed nearly four days) and between New York and London in seven. The smooth action of the jets gave a much quieter ride than the vibration of the older planes.

The plane's competition has been most felt in the long-distance service of both ships and trains. Its speed has given it a

PORT OF NEW YORK AUTHORITY
A Pan American 707 jet plane in New York.

tremendous advantage against both. On the ocean runs to other continents the steamships cannot compete in speed against planes that can reach Europe in seven hours and Africa in a single day. People on business or those who have only a brief vacation period have been quick to take advantage of the plane's speed. One major steamship line tried to counter the airlines with the slogan "Getting there is half the fun," stressing the comforts and relaxation of shipboard life. By the late 1950's the number of passengers arriving from abroad by sea and by air was almost exactly equal, with air gaining constantly. Planes now carry much of the letter mail and a growing amount of air express or freight. For example, if mining machinery breaks down in South America, new parts can be flown in overnight; so, too, can drugs to combat an epidemic in Africa. For normal heavy cargo, however, the freighters are still holding on. One of the major shipping developments since 1910 has been the return of American ships to all the major sea routes, with government subsidies to offset cheaper foreign costs.

It is in the long-distance sleeping-car runs that the plane has been making its greatest headway against the railroads. With its tremendous speed advantage, it has captured much of the passenger, mail and the lighter express shipments. In freight, the railroads have held their own fairly well, particularly on the longer runs and with the bulkier commodities like coal, ore and lumber. In 1955 they were hauling 1,400,000,000 tons as compared with 1,000,000,000 in 1910.

The railroads themselves had begun soon after 1910 to make changes in various ways. For safety, steel cars gradually replaced the wooden ones, light stainless alloy steel being used in the newer ones. Diesels, cheaper and more convenient to operate, almost completely replaced the old steam locomotives after World War II.

Single self-powered cars were used on runs where it did not pay to run full trains. Among the improvements designed to offset automobile and plane passenger competition were adjustable seats, comfortable for sleeping, and roomettes which gave a privacy lacking in the old upper and lower berths. Trains were speeded up, with fast freights running at the rate of passenger trains. Some railroads operated trucks for pickup and delivery of freight; some even carried trucks or trailers in "piggy back" service on flatcars.

The railroad's competitive position has so far been least affected on the medium-length runs. The plane's superior speed is offset here in part by the need to get out to the airport at a cost more or less equal to the free meals on the plane. Train service is generally the more dependable; about a tenth of the plane flights are likely to be canceled for weather. In competition with the automobile on such runs, many people prefer the flexibility that their own vehicle provides. They like the easing of packing and baggage handling and the chance to take the whole family at no extra cost. However, the expense is about the same for the single motorist, especially if he uses the new toll roads. Others prefer the freedom from responsibility in a public conveyance, and, so far, a train is generally favored over a bus for comfort and relaxation. Finally, the railroads have the best safety record of all; for example, only 24 passengers were killed in 1955, as compared with 324 in 1910.

But the plane and the motor vehicle were not the railroad's only new competitors. Years before, the railroads had crowded out the colorful river steamers on the Mississippi and other rivers. Now, on those same waters, deepened by Army engineers, groups of barges pulled by powerful towboats were carrying large quantities of oil, minerals and other heavy cargo that once went by rail. Similar barges operated on

The new La Guardia Airport, near a highway, will include large parking areas.

the sheltered intracoastal waterways along the southern coasts between ports on the Atlantic and the Gulf of Mexico.

Another competitive device, operating underground and so escaping general attention, was the pipeline that carried crude petroleum, refined gasoline or natural gas. There had been some of these back in 1910, chiefly for the assembling of crude oil. However, the increasing demand for gasoline led to an expanding network of pipelines that carried what formerly went in railroad tank cars.

Whatever the railroads' future might be in freight, their passenger service was steadily going from bad to worse. The number of rail passengers had fallen from 971,-000,000 to 430,000,000 between 1910 and 1956, with 315,000,000 going by inter-city bus and 45,000,000 by plane in 1956, plus the huge numbers by automobile. Citing their heavy losses in passengers and revenue, the railroads sought with increasing success to persuade the state and federal authorities to relieve them of their charter obligations to furnish adequate service. They were allowed to cut heavily many schedules and to abandon passenger service completely on many unprofitable runs. Some roads were even accused of deliberately trying to discourage passenger traffic by giving poor service. Diners and parlor cars largely disappeared. The railroads complained that while other forms of transportation—highways, airlines and airports, local transit systems, steamship lines and inland navigation—received government financial aid, they had to keep up their expensive routes by themselves and pay heavy taxes at the same time.

By 1960 the motor vehicle had already changed the life of America. The hard-surfaced roads, demanded by the early motorists, had developed into broad divided superhighways. The automobile created a national wanderlust and provided the means to gratify it. The extra mobility made a new pattern of life for country and city dweller alike. The cities themselves were different; old municipal boundaries gradually lost their significance. As more families moved out into the surrounding country, in-town business faced competition from suburban shopping centers. Even the average daily routine of many people was affected by centralized schools and a myriad of other changes brought about by the transportation revolution.

MOTION PICTURES

By BOSLEY CROWTHER
Film Critic, the New York Times

FIFTY years ago, on the downtown streets of any city one was sure to come upon a curious and conspicuously gaudy sort of store. It would be a smallish building, rather like a shoe box, with an elaborate front. Large posters hung across its façade would show the merchandise available within.

One poster in lurid colors might picture a sinister fellow dashing off into the night pursued by a policeman. "The Baffled Burglar" would be the words beneath. Another might show a sturdy newsboy helping a doddering old gentleman across the street. "Poor but Honest" would be the pious title underneath this scene. "The Mill Girl" might be another, or "The Engineer's Sweetheart" or "The Passion Play, Episodes from the Bible"—all with appropriate scenes.

Such a store was a nickelodeon, a primitive motion-picture theater, and one of thousands where the movies (then called flickers) were first sold to a mass audience.

How different these little store shows were from the huge and elaborate picture palaces of a later day! How crude were the brief and clumsy pictures that showed on their bed-sheet screens in comparison with the three-hour productions (in brilliant color) that move across the giant screens of today!

Yet it has been but half a century—exactly the same length of time that *The Book of Knowledge* has been in publication—since the movies were being introduced in those little false-faced stores.

To be sure, the cameras and projectors had been invented before that. It was in

Movie night at a New York vaudeville theater in 1914.

the mid-1890's that they were first publicly displayed. Thomas A. Edison is credited with developing the mechanism, called the kinetoscope, with which moving pictures were first shown commercially in an American theater. But for a decade or more the earliest flickers (brief scenes without dramatic plots) were shown only as novelty bits on vaudeville programs, much as newsreels are shown today.

Picturemakers soon found that they could use the new medium of photographed action to tell little stories and dramatic plots. The first of these was *The Great Train Robbery,* performed in about eight minutes.

When a few enterprising showmen, mostly owners of penny arcades, put movie projectors in the back rooms of their little funshops or in vacant stores and admitted customers to see these films for a nickel, the movies were truly born.

Between 1905 and 1910, close to ten thousand nickelodeons sprang up in the United States. And in them millions of people laughed at the antics of such early comedians as John Bunny, Mack Sennett and the Keystone Cops, suffered from the nerve-tearing suspense of Western adventures with "Bronco Billy" Anderson and William S. Hart or cried over the poignant enactments of soulful playlets by "Little Mary" Pickford or the "Biograph Girl," Florence Lawrence.

The short films shown in the nickelodeon were silent, of course. Printed subtitles, flashed with the action, conveyed the essential dialogue. Music was provided by tireless pianists who had wide repertories of numbers to suit the various moods of the films. There was vitality in the nickelodeons, but had anyone predicted that the movies of today would grow from them, he would have been considered mad.

The emergence began a few years later when more imaginative picturemakers dared to try stories that ran longer than the usual twenty minutes. It soon became impossible for the tiny nickel theaters to handle the crowds wishing to see these pictures, and regular theaters were rented for the showings.

The first great advance of movies came in 1915 when David Wark Griffith produced a two-hour film, *The Birth of a Nation.* This was a drama of the American Civil War and of postwar Reconstruction. Not only did it deal with a highly inflammatory subject—racial tension in the South—but it told its story with fresh and inventive use of long shots and close-ups and cutting. These were the new techniques discovered by Griffith and others to create pictorial imagery. They held audiences spellbound and gave them an illusion of historical reality.

The Birth of a Nation was shown widely

235

A Sennett picture with Mabel Normand, c. 1913.

Mabel, Fatty Arbuckle and Keystone cops, 1913.

CULVER SERVICE
Lillian Gish in *The Birth of a Nation*, 1915.

Covered Wagon: J. W. Kerrigan, Lois Wilson.

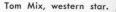
Tom Mix, western star.

in theaters, with full orchestras equipped with various noisemakers to play its specially written musical and sound-effects score. Statesmen and college presidents, drama critics and ministers praised and discussed it in public. The rich possibilities of the new medium were revealed and discovered in Griffith's picture, the first great epic of the American screen.

The year before, in April 1914 on Broadway in New York, the first large theater (three thousand capacity) built exclusively for the showing of films had been opened. The era of size and grandeur in motion pictures had arrived.

The trend was now toward longer films and larger theaters. Slowly the little nickelodeons were forced to give way although their lives were extended for a few years by the introduction of the serial. In the serial an adventure story was extended through a series of weekly episodes. Each episode, running for about twenty minutes, was deliberately arranged so that its hero (or heroine) was left in a perilous predicament at the end. This is why they were called "cliff-hangers." Most famous of the serials were *The Perils of Pauline*, with Pearl White, and *The Adventures of Kathlyn*, with Kathlyn Williams. Their vogue lasted only a few years.

Almost from the beginning of dramatic movies, the public was particularly interested in the leading actors and actresses

STARS OF SILENT FILMS

who appeared in one picture after another and were known as stars. The admirers of a star were called fans, and the success of a picture largely depended upon the popularity of its star or stars. This led to what was known as the star system, where the names of the leading performers were given more prominence and importance than the titles of the films they were in.

This cult of the movie star grew tremendously in the decade after the first World War. This was an era of great silent-film production and consolidation of companies within the industry. Before the war, most of the film makers were located around New York and operated in small, individual units. During and after the war there was a general movement of producers to California. Hollywood now became the center of production of American films and took on the gaudiness and glamour that have made it famous around the world.

It was in this period that the great stars came into their own. Such comedians as Charlie Chaplin, called "the Little Tramp" because he always appeared in baggy trousers and a battered derby hat; Buster Keaton, who always kept a straight face; Ben Turpin, who had crossed eyes; and Harold Lloyd, who wore horn-rimmed glasses, elevated the screen commodity of slapstick and pantomimic humor to the level of a penetrating art. Theda Bara, the actress who originated the vampire, or vamp, role, meaning a sleek, seductive woman, gave way to more ornate and high-class vamps such as Gloria Swanson, Pola Negri, Nita Naldi and eventually the "It" girl, Clara Bow.

GENE KORNMAN

William S. Hart

Theda Bara

Harold Lloyd

Douglas Fairbanks

Mary Pickford

Chaplin, Coogan

Rudolph Valentino

237

THE BIBLE IN FILMS

Ben Hur, with Ramon Novarro, May McAvoy and Francis X. Bushman; MGM silent movie, 1927.

Cecil B. DeMille's great Biblical story The King of Kings, a silent picture, about 1927.

ROMANCE ON THE SCREEN

Greta Garbo and John Gilbert

Clara Bow

Other great stars were Rudolph Valentino, a tango dancer who became the most popular symbol of masculine glamour in a famous desert picture, *The Sheik;* Lon Chaney, character actor who played a variety of cripples, monsters and grotesques, such as the Phantom of the Opera and the Hunchback of Notre Dame; the Gish sisters, Lillian and Dorothy, distinguished dramatic stars; and the leading cowboy actors William S. Hart and Tom Mix.

Above all, there were Mary Pickford, the "Little Mary" of earlier days, and Douglas Fairbanks, the most dashing, athletic and romantic of the men. Miss Pickford was called "America's Sweetheart." She typified an ideal of innocence, purity and sentiment that had wide mass appeal. Mr. Fairbanks played resplendent cos-

tumed heroes, as in *The Thief of Bagdad, Robin Hood, Don Q, The Son of Zorro* and *The Black Pirate,* which was, incidentally, the first notable film done in color photography.

Conspicuous in this era were the epic films that stemmed from Griffith's *The Birth of a Nation.* The famous director's own *Intolerance,* James Cruze's *The Covered Wagon,* a saga of the overland trail, and John Ford's *The Iron Horse,* which visualized the linking of our nation by rail, were memorable films in this category. Cecil B. de Mille came forward at this time as a spectacle director with a preference for Biblical themes such as *The Ten Commandments* and *The King of Kings.* Outstanding was a mammoth production of General Lew Wallace's

An average theater of the early 1920's. Buster Keaton on screen.

novel *Ben Hur, a Story of the Christ,* which cost over $4,000,000 and was the most expensive production in the era of silent films.

During the 1920's the early pattern of film making by small independent producers gave way to big consolidations of producers in a comparatively few companies, or studios, each of which would turn out as many as fifty pictures a year. Among these were Metro-Goldwyn-Mayer, Paramount, Warner Brothers and United Artists. All have continued to this day.

The ownership of theaters was concentrated in so-called chains, the largest of which embraced some several hundred theaters each. Many of these chains either controlled or were controlled by the large studios. The silent movies had become a big business in less than two decades.

In the mid-1920's their prosperity was gravely endangered by a new device of mechanical entertainment—radio. This marvel broadcast a variety of audible entertainment which included music of all sorts, dramatic dialogues (some of which continued from day to day in the manner of the old movie serials) and reports of news and sports events. These broadcasts could be picked up without charge on radio receiving sets placed in homes. The

Radio crystal set, 1921.

RADIO CHALLENGES FILMS

Jessica Dragonette

Announcer Graham MacNamee

Kate Smith

JAMES J. KRIEGSMANN

MOVIE PALACES
AND TALKING PICTURES

Al Jolson: *The Jazz Singer*, 1927.

The Roxy Theater, one of the elaborate theaters of the 1920's.

CULVER SERVICE

novelty and convenience of this new pastime made it extremely popular. Such early radio entertainers as singers Jessica Dragonette and Vaughn De Leath and sports announcers Grantland Rice and Graham McNamee became almost as familiar and popular as some of the top movie stars.

Because of radio competition, there was an alarming slump in attendance at motion pictures in 1927, and the industry was haunted by the fear that movies were doomed.

Then an amazing thing happened! Experiments, started in 1925 by Warner Brothers and scientists of Bell Telephone, to find a practical way to add sound to silent motion pictures had produced short films of concert performers and a couple of dramatic films fitted with "synchronized musical scores." These were interesting and impressive, but it wasn't until a film called *The Jazz Singer,* starring Al Jolson,

came along in October 1927 that the possibilities of sound were suddenly revealed. This was because two song numbers and a few lines of spoken dialogue were introduced in the continuity of the otherwise silent film. The effect of giving vocal dimensions to a character in an emotional scene was discovered to be more powerful than anyone dreamed it would be.

The public response was overwhelming. In a season when other films were doing indifferent business, *The Jazz Singer* packed them in. Customers flocked to see it, fascinated by the picture that talked. The talking films, or talkies, were what a kindly fate provided to meet the competition of radio.

The transition from silent films to sound was slow and fraught with difficulties. These included the mechanical problems of perfecting equipment for recording, of standardizing the mechanisms and of installing sound projectors in the theaters.

240

Bessie Love, Anita Page, in first musical, *Broadway Melody*, 1929.

There were also difficulties involved in writing, directing and acting pictures with dialogue.

Most of the old Hollywood screen writers were stumped. To meet the challenge, playwrights and top dramatic authors were hastily recruited to write dialogue. Stage directors were rushed out from New York to direct stars who, in most cases, did not know how to talk.

After the success of *The Jazz Singer* it took twelve to eighteen months for the transition from silent to all-talking films. And in this time—and for a while after—there were many important changes in the character and content of American films.

Pictures with music, in the nature of musical comedies, came into style. *Broadway Melody* was the first in a long succession of musical films about backstage life. *Rio Rita* was the initial example of a musical comedy transposed from the stage to the screen. King Vidor's *Hallelujah* was a remarkable early effort to break ground with a form of original musical drama, a story of Negro farmers in the South.

Ironically, sound pictures led to the decline of the great pantomimic comedians. Harold Lloyd faded fast. Buster Keaton did a few hilarious talkies and then discreetly "retired." Charlie Chaplin laid off entirely until 1936, then did *Modern Times,* his first sound picture in which he himself did not speak a word. He gave up "the Little Tramp" thereafter and did not make another film until 1940, when he did *The Great Dictator,* a bitter burlesque of Adolph Hitler.

During this period the transfer to the screen of the musical comedy *The Cocoanuts* introduced the four Marx Brothers to the movie audience in a new kind of noisy, gag-studded, knockabout farce. It was notable that their brand of comedy, like that of W. C. Fields, depended as much on the humor of dialogue as it did on the art of pantomime. But even these madcap comedians eventually faded. The mass audience became more literal-minded as it grew accustomed to sound.

To fill the vacuum caused by the decline of the Keatons and the Lloyds, a type of talking picture known as the sophisticated comedy was developed. Directors who were masters of this type were Ernst Lubitsch, Frank Capra and Gregory La Cava, and memorable performers of it were Carole Lombard, Irene Dunne, Claudette Colbert and William Powell.

Soon after the turn to sound came the gangster pictures. These violent melodramas were inspired by prohibition racketeering. There was a harsh realism about them enhanced by the addition of sound. They were full of the shock effect of underworld lingo and the noise of gunfire and screeching tires. The earliest gangster pictures, such as *Little Caesar* and *Public Enemy,* had a definite social value because they did much to alert the American people to the peril of organized crime. They also brought realism onto the screen, and introduced a new crop of masculine stars, including James Cagney, Edward G. Robinson, Clark Gable, Spencer Tracy.

Once the movie industry had made the transition to sound and once the dark years of the depression (the early 1930's)

241

THE GOLDEN AGE OF TALKING PICTURES

Little Caesar: 1931, a gangster picture; Edward G. Robinson, Douglas Fairbanks, Jr.

It Happened One Night; 1934, with Clark Gable and Claudette Colbert.

were passed, American motion pictures entered such a phase of production and commercial prosperity that there was justification for calling it the golden age of sound. The screen of the 1930's was crowded with so many fine screen dramas and musical diversions, sleek comedies and strong adventure films that to give a full list of them would require the remainder of this space.

Worthy of mention, however, were the live production *The Wizard of Oz* and Walt Disney's animated cartoon *Snow White and the Seven Dwarfs.*

The Wizard of Oz, in color, was a memorable enactment of the popular children's story, with a happy musical score. Its star was Judy Garland, then a seventeen-year-old girl and one of the top child actors in a period that offered Shirley Temple, Jackie Cooper, Deanna Durbin, Freddie Bartholomew, Cora Sue Collins and Mickey Rooney, to name but a few.

Mr. Disney's *Snow White* was the fulfillment of his dream to make a feature-length cartoon, after many years as the leading producer of cartoon shorts. He had taken up the business of making animated cartoons, a familiar but not too profitable form of movie entertainment,

before the transition to sound and had created the character of Mickey Mouse in three short silent films. Mr. Disney's efforts (and his mouse) began to soar when sound gave Mickey a voice and musical range. As he appeared in many short films, within a few years Mickey was as famous as any movie star.

Other cartoon characters were created by Mr. Disney in his *Silly Symphonies,* another series of shorts made in color. They included Pluto the Pup, Donald Duck and the Three Little Pigs. These latter characters, who defied the Big Bad Wolf, were born in 1933 in a famous short that did as much as any film of the time to help the morale of the American people during the depression.

With *Snow White* in 1938 Mr. Disney entered the field of feature-length cartoon production, which included such pleasures as *Fantasia, Pinocchio, Bambi* and *Dumbo.* In *The Reluctant Dragon* he combined live action with the cartoon.

The end of the 1930's and of the golden age of sound was appropriately marked with the production of one of the most popular and famous films of all time. This was the film made from Margaret Mitchell's best-selling novel *Gone with the*

Carole Lombard

GLAMOUR GIRLS

Rita Hayworth

MGM

Gone with the Wind: 1939; Vivien Leigh and Thomas Mitchell in the great Civil War epic.

Wind. In color and with a star cast headed by Clark Gable and Vivien Leigh, it told a dramatic story of a Southern family during and after the Civil War. It was comparable to *The Birth of a Nation* as a milestone in the making of American films.

For already the guns were firing in the first phase of the second World War. This period was a test of the capacity of the movies to serve the nation in time of war with information, as well as entertainment.

Significantly, the motion pictures that best met this test were not the ones produced in Hollywood to inspire and entertain, but those prepared by government agencies and the military services to in-

form. Hollywood's output of pictures during the second World War was not up to its previous standards of quality.

There were, however, a few distinguished pictures about the dramatic aspects of war—such pictures as *Mrs. Miniver, Air Force* and *The Story of G. I. Joe*—and a dozen or so good entertainers like *Woman of the Year, Meet Me in St. Louis, Yankee Doodle Dandy* and *Going My Way.* The record of the well-established studios during the four war years was memorable only for commercial success. The public was eager for entertainment and able to pay for it, and the American motion-picture industry had its greatest period of prosperity then.

CARTOONS GROW UP

Two landmarks in the development of the cartoon; *Steamboat Willie,* 1928, *Snow White and the Seven Dwarfs,* 1938.

Two kings of television comedy, Jackie Gleason and Milton Berle.

Even though they are not too well remembered today, many of the films turned out by the Government and the military services were extraordinarily good. These films, known as documentaries, were a type of factual film that had been developed in the 1930's, notably by the *March of Time*. They brought to the screen reports that ranged from mobilization on the home front to actual combat in the theaters of war.

The motion-picture industry, rich from its profits during the war, did not worry about another medium of motion-picture transmission that was just starting. This new medium was television, the sending of motion pictures through the air in the same way that sound is transmitted by radio.

The mechanics of television had been known for many years to electrical scientists, the military services and the radio-company engineers. However, facilities for broadcasting programs by television were not generally set up until after the war. At first the programs were mainly sports events and comedy acts, music and assorted short dramas, much as they had been in the early days of radio.

At this time it was a standard joke that, to see television, one had to go to a bar or saloon. That's where most of the existing four thousand receiving sets were to be found in 1946.

The picture had changed considerably by 1950 when there were some nine million sets spread around the country. Most of these sets were in homes, and the variety of programs and the number of broadcasting stations had increased tenfold. By now it was clear to the motion-picture industry that it was losing attendance in staggering numbers to a competitor even more formidable than radio.

The appeal of television to children was notable, and many programs, such as Kukla, Fran and Ollie, were directed exclusively at them. However, most television viewers were grownups, and they were the ones for whom the majority of musical spectaculars, quiz programs and even western dramas were and still are designed.

The movie industry, deeply worried by the steady loss of customers, began to look for a gimmick to save the business. Already they had invented and developed the drive-in theater. These attracted families who could come in and watch the show from their automobiles. Though seasonal in operation, there were more than three thousand of these outdoor theaters around the country in 1950, and they were drawing a sizable summer trade.

But what Hollywood hoped to find was a physical improvement in the projection of films that would show their superiority over television—something comparable to the addition of sound!

The technicians first came up with stereoscopic, or three-dimensional, films that, when viewed through special eyeglasses, conveyed an illusion of depth.

These experiments were forgotten, however, when, in 1952, they brought forth a new projection system called Cinerama, which filled a giant wall-to-wall curved screen. The image was thrown by three projectors, each covering one third of the screen, with the individual images joining neatly along the so-called match lines to give the appearance of one image.

The pictorial effect was powerful, especially when accompanied by stereophonic sound (several outlets around the theater). This system received considerable acclaim when the first Cinerama program of travel and thrill pictures opened in New York. Since the mechanism for Cinerama was bulky and difficult, something more practical was needed for use in all theaters. This was brought forth a few months later in the form of a wide-angle lens that could be fitted on a single standard projector to throw to a reasonably wide, faintly curved panel. This was known as Cinemascope.

The larger screen, along with the multiplication of sound and the use of color, led to larger and longer films—known as blockbusters. These did the trick of regaining lost audiences. Such a mammoth film as Cecil B. de Mille's new *The Ten Commandments,* offered in 1957, is likely to surpass in a few years the record money earnings of even *Gone with the Wind.*

Now, in 1960, a fair balance appears to have been reached in the relationship between theatrical motion pictures and television. Television is now reaching some 55,000,000 sets with a great variety of programs (including all the Hollywood movies turned out during the prosperous 1930's and 1940's). At the same time attendance at theaters is satisfactory once more.

Indeed, there is a tendency of the two media to cross-fertilize. Not only have the Hollywood studios sold their old movies to television, but several of them are now in the business of making short films directly for TV. Hollywood stars and directors have long been working in television shows. In turn, television is providing the studios with young actors, directors and story material for theatrical films. It is probable that the two will be more closely joined when the proposed systems of pay television (or "fee vee") are put into operation. The prospect is that these systems will bring new Hollywood movies—the biggest and best—right into the home. They will be paid for by the home viewers, probably through some device like a coin box on the set. What effect this will have on the theaters remains to be seen.

WIDE WORLD

The drive-in theater combines the silver screen and the great outdoors.

DIAMOND-GARDNER CO.

Homes and Homemaking

By JOHN PETER
Home Living Editor, Look

Houses are for people. Fifty years ago the people in the United States numbered 92,000,000. Today there are 179,000,000. In 1910 America had 20,000,000 families. In 1960 it has 49,000,000 families. In the hectic half century just past, the population has nearly doubled. From a predominantly agricultural country in the early 1900's, America has become a great industrial nation, with high per capita and high per family incomes. The increased population, the shift from an agrarian economy to an industrial one and the greatly increased personal income have all had a strong influence on the Americans of this century and the way they live.

Over the past fifty years, owner-occupied homes have increased from 36.5 per cent to about 60 per cent. The growth of home ownership is due to increased purchasing power and to easier home-mortgage credit given by government agencies like the Federal Housing Administra-

Houses in rows: two-story and basement, 1910.

246

tion. Besides making home buying easier, the FHA has established and promoted, through its mortgage-insurance requirements, sound minimum standards of construction, design and location for housing of families of moderate means. Completely new social and economic conditions have made contemporary housing very different from that of 1910.

From colonial days the persistent American dream has been the freestanding house on a plot of land. At the beginning of the twentieth century the lot was viewed in the great English lawn tradition, as a setting or decoration for the house itself. It was used, if at all, by the family in a formal way. Today the grounds around a house are considered a part of the house itself, and architects such as Garrett Eckbo advocate using "the entire lot at once as a co-ordinated series of rationally connected and related indoor and outdoor rooms."

This extension of the activities of the house into the yard was prompted by the Spanish patio tradition of the Far West and Southwest. It was further encouraged by the shrinking size of the average home and the growth of a more informal way of life that has made home barbecues and swimming pools centers of social activity.

This move to make greater use of the out-of-doors for everyday living is not restricted to the suburbs or country but can also be seen in and near our larger cities. Groups of garden apartment houses are a common sight in smaller towns and on the edges of our cities. Thanks to slum-clearance projects and city-planning boards in the heart of our densely populated metropolises, there are appearing groups of large, many-storied apartment buildings. They are separated but oriented to each other with free, open spaces used for gardens and recreation areas. The increasing number of apartment units being designed around pools and boat basins, with open-air restaurants and underground parking facilities, shows that the trend toward improved utilization of urban land is only at the beginning.

It is in the architectural design of the individual residence, however, that we can most easily see the great changes that have taken place in America's living in the past half century.

In the late nineteenth century many Americans had made money and their

Frame bungalow covered with creosoted shingles, 1923.
TWO PHOTOS, CULVER SERVICE

The modern equivalent: better planned, better looking.
RODNEY MCCAY, PHOTOLOG

Fordham Hill, an apartment-house development in New York. Such projects are being built in many cities to replace outdated housing.

homes made no secret of it. Showy adaptation of Gothic castles were very much the mode. Translating this new Gothic into homes for people not in the millionaire class, builders used less expensive materials than the original hand-carved stone and invented decorations that have since been dubbed everything from Carpenter Gothic to Jigsaw Gothic, to Steamboat Gothic. Underneath these fanciful decorations important changes in building construction began to take place.

Toward the end of the nineteenth century, Chicago saw the introduction of what has come to be known as the balloon-frame construction, so called because of its lightness. It consisted of a frame and "skin" made of standardized lumber, cut on the site and assembled with machine-made nails. Despite its lightness, it was remarkably strong and very easy to build. With improvements in materials and refinements of technique this is the standard system of building today. After the turn of the century, America started turning its back on the bewildering ornateness of Victorian architecture and began looking for means of simplifying design. As early as 1870 Henry Hobson Richardson built a series of houses on the east coast that were marked with an unornamented vigor

that set the stage in America for modern styles of design. These houses were praised by Chicago's Louis Sullivan, the father of the modern skyscraper, as "direct, large and simple." Sullivan's most gifted protégé was Frank Lloyd Wright. To him we are very largely indebted for today's popular open-plan houses. The open plan was a recognition of the improved mechanical facilities, such as heating and plumbing, and the opportunities provided by new building materials. Here the boxlike rooms of the eighteenth century were broken up. Space flowed from one room to another, the outside flowing in through glassed walls. As one architectural critic has said, "Wright's realization of flexible treatment of the inner space of a building is probably his greatest service to architecture. It brought life, movement, freedom into the whole rigid body of modern architecture."

At this same time, on the west coast the growing Japanese influence was reflected in the work of the skilled brothers Greene and Greene. These talented architects turned out houses that seemed perfectly suited to their sites. Primarily wooden houses, their distinctive, long low roof is seen again and again in today's houses.

Architectural styles always have to wait

a while before they are popularly accepted. We find in the America of the first decade of this century that the "Gothic" was followed by a choice of architectural styles that were erratic and eclectic (a combination of many different styles). Perhaps it was best summed up in the bungalow, the forerunner of today's ranch-style house, which was a combination of Oriental and Spanish Colonial. This freewheeling, residential-architectural style has now been broken down to Colonial, French Provincial, Western Ranch and Modern.

"Modern" is a word so loosely used in describing housing today that it seems almost meaningless. However, from the standpoint of design it can be narrowed down to two related but different approaches to residential architecture. They are related because all modern is based on a rejection of the styles of the past and an acceptance of the machine. They are also different. One style is described as "organic" by its chief exponent, Frank Lloyd Wright. It emphasizes a close relationship between the house and the land around it, and a wide use of natural materials. It respects the native and regional styles developed by local craftsmen. Finally it draws inspiration from the ancient traditions of the Far East and the possibilities of modern materials.

In contrast to this natural modern is what might be called machinelike modern or, more specifically, the International style. This was sponsored by such Europeans as the Swiss Le Corbusier (pseudonym of Charles Édouard Jeanneret) and the German founders of the Bauhaus movement. (The Bauhaus was an art and craft school started in Weimar, Germany, in 1919 and headed by Walter Gropius.)

They combined a liking for modern abstract art with an admiration for the products of industry. In Le Corbusier's words: "Everywhere can be seen machines which serve to produce something and produce it admirably, in a clean sort of way. There is no real link between our daily activities at the factory, office or bank, which are healthy and useful and productive, and our activities in . . . the family which are handicapped at every turn."

In the 1930's many leaders of the modern movement such as Mies van der Rohe, Walter Gropius, Marcel Breuer and Richard Neutra came to the United States. They designed a series of houses that inspired a generation of young American architects.

It is safe to say that a modern house in the mind of the average homeowner is something that looks either like the dramatic Falling Water house of Frank Lloyd Wright, the steel and glass pavilions of Mies van der Rohe or anything that approaches these extraordinary works.

PHOTOS, NATIONAL HOMES CORP.

Two stages in the erection of a prefabricated house. All the parts—walls, roof sections, windows—are made in a factory, shipped to the home site and put together.

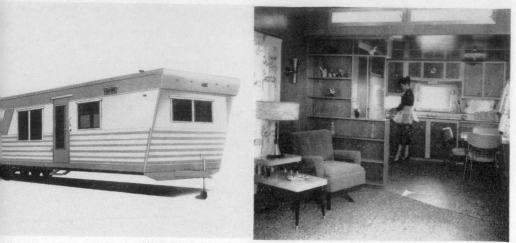

NASSAU TRAILER & MOTOR SALES   BAYONNE TRAILER SALES CO.

Trailer life is a development of the past fifty years. Right, inside a big trailer.

Whether today's house is modern or traditional in style, it is certain to be built with new construction methods and new building materials—most of them products of the twentieth century. Light enclosing walls are used instead of heavy walls that bear the weight of the house. Isolated points of support combined with cantilevered floors and roofs make possible larger areas of windows and doors. Lightweight metal alloys, durable plastics, and plywoods replace traditional building materials. Increased fabrication in the factory has replaced hand labor on the site of the building.

Prefabrication of complete homes and the use of larger and larger components is converting the "handicrafted" house into a product of the factory. Probably the most mass-produced form of housing today is one scarcely recognized as such because of its origins. The development of the automobile, combined with the Americans' love of travel, produced the automobile trailer. Trailers grew in size and convenience until, with the sudden housing demands of World War II, they became a form of permanent housing. Today it is estimated that one out of ten American families lives in a trailer. Their complete facilities, which include kitchen

MINNEAPOLIS-HONEYWELL REGULATOR CO.

Thermostats make it easy to regulate house temperature.

equipment, built-in furniture and decoration, as well as their factory construction and low cost point the way in some minds to housing of the future.

The period between the two world wars (1918-39) has been called the time of mechanization. There was mechanization before and after, but during this time the development of machinery that could perform human tasks reached a peak never known before. Mechanization, which began in industry, moved into the home, and it has had a profound and lasting effect on the way we all live.

The automobile, the machine that has

changed the landscape with highways and parkways and our activities outside the home, has even changed our homes and their location. With the advent of the low-priced motorcar, America was made mobile. Where a person lived was no longer completely controlled by its nearness to employment or public transportation. This is a basic reason for the phenomenal rise of the suburb in the twentieth century. The auto has come to be part of the house. Housing the automobile in an attached garage has even changed the façade of our houses. Finally, the auto has become the one possession an American is least willing to do without.

Mechanization of the home, which began in the nineteenth century, is the single, greatest homemaking development of the twentieth century. However, even before mechanization there was a move toward scientific housekeeping. In 1841 Catherine Beecher wrote her *Treatise on Domestic Economy*. She believed there was no reason why housework should be drudgery, since it all depended on organization of the work processes. Her work has been amplified and expanded in this century by such household engineers as Christine Frederich and Dr. Lillian Gilbreth, who have used time-motion studies to lighten the housewife's burden.

Man's house has always been a shelter against the elements. Heating the home in the nineteenth century was largely a matter of burning wood or coal in an open fireplace or stove. With the advent of the small electric motor, great advances have taken place in home heating. Today the three principal methods of heating are: warm air, including the small space heater, the gravity furnace and the forced-air furnace; steam heating; and hot water, using radiators in rooms or through radi-

AIRTEMP DIVISION, CHRYSLER CORP.

Air conditioning gives comfort both winter and summer.

BOTH PHOTOS, WESTINGHOUSE

Today's kitchen is bright, colorful and compact, with plenty of storage space.

ant or panel heating. Then there is air conditioning, which is more than a method of cooling the house in the hot months of the year. It is exactly what its name implies—a way of conditioning, or treating, air. A complete air-conditioning system heats, cools, humidifies, cleans and circulates the air. It may also extract excess moisture from the air—the dehumidifying process. It is easy to predict that total air conditioning will someday be as essential to every home as central heating is today.

In lighting as in air conditioning, electricity was another basis for modernization. Edison perfected the incandescent

the home—living, working, resting—in such a manner as to give over-all, area and spot lighting. Today, lighting is considered a help in combating fatigue and promoting a feeling of well-being.

Such lighting is no longer confined to the interior of the house. Treating the house and its grounds as indoor-outdoor rooms raised the problem of lighting the "outdoor rooms." Many lighting fixtures are available now for gardens, terraces and patios. Designed to fit in with the landscaping, they are unobtrusive by day, yet provide illumination by night. Spotlights are often used to create a night view to be seen from the interior of the house.

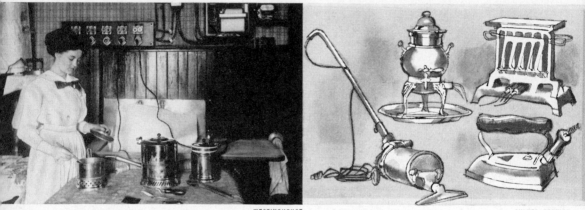

WESTINGHOUSE

CULVER SERVICE

Many electric appliances, including irons and washers, were used before World War I.

lamp in 1879. When electricity was first used for lighting homes, it was used in much the same manner as gas. In many cases it was simply incorporated into existing gas fixtures. Since then, special fixtures and installations have made the most of its unique possibilities. New lighting units have been introduced, such as fluorescent tubing, making it possible to give uniform light to large areas. Such refinements as the light dimmer help to control lighting. Today lighting engineers work closely with architects in planning houses. Built-in lighting is keyed to the areas of

While such home appliances as the electric iron and coffee maker were introduced as early as 1893, it was not until about fifty years ago that American housewives took them seriously. Faced with the problem of fewer domestic servants, householders began looking for ways to cut down heavy housework. To help them, inventors and manufacturers began to apply to the home the production equipment and techniques learned in the factories. The first electric stove was developed by A. L. Marsh of Detroit for laboratory use. The first refrigerator was invented by a

French monk and patented in this country as an industrial unit. The domestic refrigerator was introduced in 1912. Dishwashers, garbage disposers, freezers and mixers followed, one after another. Today, electronic ranges that cook food in seconds, and automatic clothes washers and dryers that do laundry in minutes, are among more than a hundred different labor-timesaving devices for the housewife.

As the kitchen became the center of this mechanization and as the scientific housekeeping advocated by Miss Beecher and the later household engineers took root, the work-planned kitchen came to day designed and manufactured specifically to fit in, under or above continuous work-counter space. Kitchens may be L-shaped, U-shaped, corridor type or peninsula type, but whatever their design, they save time and space.

In 1960 family life has gained renewed importance, and informal home entertainment has become an important part of the American way of life. The benefits of modern electronic equipment extend to the living areas of the home, too, and supply home entertainment in the form of television and sound reproduction.

At first glance the average menus of 1910 and 1960 do not seem very differ-

FRIGIDAIRE

CULVER SERVICE

Today there are complete electric kitchens, besides many individual appliances.

the fore. Originating in Europe in the 1920's, the new kitchen was a product of the architect rather than the female household engineer. The Dutch architect J. J. P. Oud introduced an L-shaped kitchen with continuous working surfaces. It was organized to suit different work processes and had continuous storage, cleaning-preparing and cooking centers. For the first time the kitchen was an integrated unit. Later, American designers took the lead and refined these kitchen-planning ideas. Appliances such as the range, refrigerator, automatic dishwasher and so forth are to-ent. But there is a difference and it lies in the greater availability of foodstuffs and in their preparation. Now modern transportation with refrigerated railroad cars and trucks makes it possible for everyone, no matter where he lives, to have fresh vegetables, fruits and meats all year round. Today seasonal foodstuffs know no season. Frozen foods, packaged mixes, instant foods, prewashed and packaged vegetables (all new since 1910) are in the supermarket.

Not only are foodstuffs easier to obtain, they have also become more varied, and vegetables, such as zucchini, which formerly would have been recognized only by a person of European origin, are commonplace today. America is becoming gourmet-food conscious. It is not uncommon to find "gourmet corners" in supermarkets next to the frozen-dinner display. The housewife turns to prepared foods to save time on regular meals and to Escoffier to spend it in creative effort for her guests.

The American bath of today had its origins outside the home. In 1908 the Statler Hotel in Buffalo, New York, was opened with the slogan—"A bed and a bath for a dollar and a half." Designing the bathrooms for hotels posed the problem of economy of plumbing and produced the compact bathroom with all the fixtures on one wall. Around 1920 the bathroom achieved a form that has made American plumbing, along with central heating, a standard for the world.

The bathroom seems to be headed in the direction of prefabrication. This means that the bathroom would be factory-made, then shipped to the house site in sections where it would be assembled. R. Buckminster Fuller designed just such a bathroom in 1938. The House of the Future designed by the Massachusetts Institute of Technology has a prefabricated bathroom made entirely of molded plastic materials.

Another aspect of the home that has been receiving much consideration is the mechanical core. The mechanical core is a section of the house, centrally located, or perhaps on the perimeter of its walls, that would house all the machinery needed to run the house—heating, air-conditioning plants and plumbing outlets for bath and kitchen. To reduce costs some designers feel that the whole mechanical core should be prefabricated as a completely integrated structural unit and manufactured on an assembly-line basis, like automobiles.

More recently, chemical science has joined with mechanical science to help the homemaker. Detergents and latex paints have improved maintenance. Lightweight and easy-to-clean plastic and synthetic materials are being used in everything from dinnerware to floor coverings. Plastics themselves have come of age in less than one hundred years and have risen to compete with such ancient materials as metal, wood and glass in finishing and furnishing homes. The first plastic, Celluloid, was invented in 1869 and was used for billiard balls and wipe-clean collars for

A 1910 design: floor, wainscot, tub enclosure of wood.   Modern: bath and dressing table in windowed alcove.

BOTH PHOTOS, AMERICAN-STANDARD

men. But it wasn't until the accelerated development of plastics during World War II that people became aware of the abundance of these new synthetic materials. The popularity of plastics is based on their light weight, wide range of color, good physical properties, adaptability to mass-production methods and, often, lower cost. Although many items in the modern house, such as telephones and phonograph records, may be quickly recognized as plastic, there is a growing number of synthetics that are used in curtain materials, upholstery fabrics and rugs.

In 1910 the prevailing popular style of furniture was mission. Heavy-looking and usually made of fumed oak, it was an outgrowth of William Morris's furniture of the 1860's. It was in some ways the forerunner of today's functional furniture. It represented a direct and simple use of material and with its movable parts made an effort to adjust to the user's needs.

In 1925 two different exhibitions were held that started the style of American furniture off in two directions. The opening of the American wing of the New York Metropolitan Museum reintroduced the charm of early American furniture and Federal styles. This furniture showed that functional and honest use of material is not the exclusive property of the moderns. In May 1925 the Exposition des Arts Décoratifs opened in Paris, and the world was introduced to Art Moderne. This new furniture style made lavish use of highly figured veneers, was extremely angular and had shining metal trim. Its popularity didn't last long, but furniture in this style can still be seen in some of the older ocean liners and movie palaces.

The late 1920's found machine-made furniture coming into its own. During the nineteenth century it imitated handcrafted furniture in clumsy and shoddy ways until designers discovered ways to combine the usefulness of machinery with new aesthetic standards. When this happened in the late 1920's it was possible to buy reasonably priced contemporary furniture of simple construction and line, decorated for the most part by only the natural beauty of color and graining of the wood. Furniture designs have since been extended to include a wide range of new materials—metals, plywood and laminated wood, plastic and glass. It was also in the late 1920's that the architect began to take the place of the decorative artist as the author of new furniture. Typical of this new furniture was the tubular steel chair. The original was introduced by the

Mission furniture contrasts with ornate wallpaper, 1912.

Glass-walled living-dining room of modern design, 1957.

architect Marcel Breuer in 1925. It has proved so popular that thousands of households boast a tubular metal dinette set. More recently, bent plywood chairs designed by architect Charles Eames have found a popular place in American homes. Influenced by contemporary living conditions, this furniture complements the open planning of modern homes. It is also characteristic of our times that there is less furniture in each home. Increasing amounts of furniture and storage space are being built into the house itself. Clutter in decoration is also kept at a minimum with more emphasis on simple patterns, color and texture in drapery, upholstery fabrics and floor coverings.

The growing concern with "taste" led to the development of a profession that had been more in the realm of arts than in business—the professional interior decorator. In the nineteenth century, decorating, when it didn't mean merely someone who could paint and wallpaper the house, was in the hands of artists and architects and was looked on as a side line. One of the first people in the United States to decorate professionally was Elsie de Wolfe, who began in the first decade of this century. She made her mark so

strongly that many of her ideas—such as the use of chintz as a drapery and upholstery fabric—are still with us. Today, the work of the professional interior decorator is big business, department stores retain decorators on their staffs to advise their customers, and the term "decorator styled" is commonly seen in advertisements for home furnishing. The job of the decorator or designer is not only to give professional advice on the decoration of a home but also to assemble all the elements needed to finish and furnish a house. He must also hire carpenters, plasterers, painters and others needed to complete the job.

Writer Russell Lynes has observed, "It was not until almost everybody could afford to be concerned with taste that the taste makers as we know them today had any real function." But concern over taste no longer lies only with artists, architects, designers, writers and intellectual leaders; it is now the concern of the average homeowner. Writer Gilbert Burck reports that "Price is important and always will be, but in a society looking forward to an average family income approaching $7,500 a year after taxes, price becomes relatively less important. American consumers

A recreation room that can be used as a guest room. Reddish brown quarry tiles and natural-finished woodwork blend in warm yet restful color tones.

Prairie house built in 1909 by Frank Lloyd Wright started new trend in home design.

as a group today tend more and more to let their senses make up their minds. In these days when even professional consumer-testing services are hard pressed to find important technical differences between brands of similar products, what counts more and more is the aesthetic quality of the products."

If taste can be described as the capacity to discern fitness, beauty, order or excellence, it can be said that American taste at home has improved markedly over the past fifty years. While today's home has become in near reality what the architect Le Corbusier referred to as "a machine for living," this has been accomplished without losing the human values

that are the essence of man's traditional dwelling place. In fact, these human and social values will receive even more attention in the next fifty years. Perhaps we may even live up to the estimate of the great residential architect Frank Lloyd Wright, who said, "In building homes, we have the key to, and the cornerstone of, whatever culture our nation is capable of."

Plastic "House of the Future" in Disneyland Park has four curved wings cantilevered from central utility core. Massachusetts Institute of Technology, Monsanto and twelve other companies did research for it. Architects were R. W. Hamilton and M. E. Goody.

Fashion

I<small>N</small> 1910 a woman was kept pretty well in her place by the sheer weight of her clothing. A flat-front, back-bumper corset thrust her majestically forward with its steel bones. She also wore a corset cover, drawers and ruffled petticoats; silk stockings if she were rich or lucky, and high button shoes.

Her outer wear was heavy enough to keep her happy at the North Pole. A fur coat was apt to weigh as much as thirteen pounds. Nowadays she complains if more than four pounds of precious mink is laid across her shoulders. One of the latest dress hits is one that weighs four ounces and can be folded into a handbag.

Besides the weight of her clothes the perfect lady in those days carried a mound of hair on her head. To top it all, she wore a hat that might have been designed by the Wright brothers.

High style originated in Paris, though America had already produced its own first great home-grown fashion. This was the shirtwaist, skirt and straw sailor of the Gibson girl, the first of the wholesome, outdoor fashion heroines America was to create.

In 1910, clothes were copied, mostly from fashion-magazine illustrations, by hundreds of little dressmakers. Fashion was completely personal. Women looked quite different from each other and the quality of a fabric was often the criterion for the well-dressed.

American ready-to-wear began with cloaks and suits (the name "cloak-and-suiter" still lingers) in 1898. As late as 1910, though, wiseacres were predicting that the business of fitting each individual wasp waist would go on forever.

On the eve of World War I, in Paris, women were draped, hobbled, veiled and hidden under huge peach-basket hats. Their clothes were based on the assumption of women's mysterious and almost supernatural deadliness to man. The vamp didn't mean well and it showed in her clothes.

Three women—a swimmer, an actress and a dancer—cleared the air. They were Annette Kellerman, Mary Pickford and Irene Castle. In 1910, Annette Kellerman startled the world with the first one-piece bathing suit. Before that, women had been going to the beach in sailor dresses made of ten yards of fabric. It took them ten more years to shed their cotton stockings and beach shoes and almost forty more to peel down to the bikini.

Mary Pickford may have been disliked by sophisticates but her blond curls and baby face did in the vamp and launched the youth trend in American fashion. Never since Mary danced and pouted across the screen in little-girl ginghams have women felt happy in completely adult clothes.

Irene Castle outdated the plump girl and supplanted her hourglass figure with the new ideal of a long, slim boyish build. A girl with the courage to be comfortable, she loosened corsets, waists and hobble skirts. Up to then elegance had been synonymous with stiff, formal fabrics. Irene Castle switched to soft fabrics, and her Euro-

By EUGENIA SHEPPARD

Women's Feature Editor

New York Herald Tribune

pean dressmaker, Lucille (Lady Duff Gordon), cut her clothes on free, flowing lines. Her chiffon dress with the torn hem cut in deep points became a great fashion rage and was still being copied ten years later. Irene Castle, herself, became a fashion idol.

The famous Castle bob, in 1914, came about through sheer chance. On her way to a hospital for an appendectomy, Irene Castle stopped in front of a mirror just long enough to whack off her long hair with her own shears. Because her hair was slow to grow out, she tied a seed-pearl band round her forehead and wore the new hairdo to a dinner party in a Manhattan hotel. The first week after her picture was published, 250 women cut their hair. The second week, more than 2,500 stormed men's barbershops!

The age of individuality in fashion was soon over. In 1920, America's rapidly growing ready-to-wear industry in New York City moved uptown to its present quarters on Seventh Avenue. In this decade the fashion industry, rid of the wasp waist at last and able to think in standard sizes, rose spectacularly to its present place as one of the great industries in the United States.

The end of World War I touched off the biggest fashion rebellion in history. Women cast off all the old-fashioned taboos. They slouched backward instead of leaning forward. They caricatured the boyish build. Skirts shot knee high. (Actually they have come down only twice since then, once in the thirties and, again, for Dior's New Look in 1947.)

Short hair did away with the honest-to-goodness hat that had been built on a wire frame and brought in the hat as we know it today, bent and manipulated from a soft piece of felt or fabric. The old-time dress, as full of complications as a road map, vanished in favor of the tube with no waist or just a belt around the hips. The new slide fastener still further speeded up the process of dressing.

Short skirts called for pumps instead of high shoes; and with legs out of hiding, silk stockings became more and more sheer. The career woman and the slimming diet were born and the lipstick became a must.

The thirties opened a reaction against the boyish girl in the form of a rehash from fashion history, the Empress Eugénie hat. This piece of nonsense was a felt derby trimmed with an ostrich plume.

The thirties were one of the most charming periods in fashion history. Of the thirties, *Vogue* magazine said, "Never have so many women looked so beautiful."

Skirts dropped and hair grew longer until it reached the shoulders and became the great glamour bob. The era of spectator sportswear dawned. Women for the first time appeared in slacks, culottes, pedal pushers and shorts. The sweater became indispensable. Costume jewelry arrived in all its glory. Up until then a "lady" wore the real thing, or else!

Although fashion leadership still came from Paris, as early as 1931 there was talk of American designers and of an American look. American designers took cotton out of the house-dress category and gave it proper social standing in high-style clothes. They introduced rayon and later all of the wonderful synthetics.

Film stars like Carole Lombard and Joan Crawford were watched eagerly and copied down to the last detail of collar and cuffs. The power and glory of American ready-

259

to-wear was demonstrated when, in 1937, versions of the Duchess of Windsor's wedding gown, which had been designed by Mainbocher, were selling six weeks later priced as low as $14.95.

On the west coast, Adrian created a thirties successor to the Gibson girl. Her wide-shouldered suit-jacket, padded out like a football player's, and her skinny, trousers-like skirt showed she could take life like a man, while the long hairdo waving over one eye proved that she was still as feminine as ever.

World War II froze fashion in the broad-shouldered attitude. Because of restrictions on fabrics, skirts were as short and scant as possible. There was also an embargo on silk. In spite of these restrictions, American designers showed great ingenuity and talent.

Many felt that the war had finished Paris as a fashion center, but in 1947 Paris came back with Christian Dior's New Look. The New Look was even more spectacularly successful than the Eugénie hat, for it reversed the trends of the last forty years of fashion. It replaced wide, padded shoulders with meek, sloping shoulders, and short, skinny skirts with long, full ones. It even restored the tiny waist, the waist-pincher corset and many of the paddings and under-pinnings that women had discarded such a short time before. The New Look brought Paris back to the top and made Dior, who was a genuinely creative designer, the hero of the fashion world.

After the war came the great American fashion boom. Nylon stockings became available in unlimited quantities and, together with the increasing number of new miracle fabrics, made American women the envy of the world. For the first time teen-agers were recognized as a separate fashion entity, probably because, during the war, they had invented the sloppy look of blue jeans and daddy's shirt, worn with the tails hanging out.

Beginning with the fifties, fashion became big business. The number of great Paris designers dwindled, and their styles and ideas became more alike. Paris felt the influence of American fashion, especially the pursuit of youth.

The fifties actually saw the gradual loosening of the silhouette in reaction to the waist pincher of the New Look. But the ill-fated chemise, its ultimate expression, was laughed out of existence.

If the twenties are characterized by the flapper, the thirties by the film siren, the forties by broad shoulders and the New Look, the fifties can be tagged as the decade of fashion confusion. Skirt lengths went up and down. Waistlines went up and down and out altogether. The American fashion industry ran through whole families of colors with frightening speed.

Actually the decade's freshest inspiration was neither French nor American. Credit goes, not to Italian fashion, but to the Italian woman.

The Italian woman is responsible for the shift from traditional make-up to the so-called natural look of pale mouth and black-rimmed eyes. She started the messy, bedroom hairdo, the glorification of the bosomy build and the fashion of wearing no hat. She also launched the bikini bathing suit, the pull-over shirt, the tight pants and the fashion for wearing them everywhere.

As the sixties start, fashion is international, ageless and seasonless. The ideal of style is the same everywhere, and few clothes show any indication of their national origin. Matrons to teen-agers choose essentially the same clothes. Fashion has broken down the seasonal barrier, too, and done away with winter and summer labels once attached to specific fabrics and colors.

The sixties may bring a return to originality. More likely, women's clothes will continue on the road they have traveled for the past fifty years.

1910

Big hats covered with plumes or flowers, and narrow draped skirts were in style almost up to the eve of World War I. Men wore high starched collars, and small boys quickly wore out the knees of their serge knickerbockers in strenuous play. Motorists covered their clothes with linen dustcoats—women wearing veils, men caps and goggles.

261

1915

A wartime debutante could happily
brave the winter winds in a belted,
high-collared coat lined and bordered
with fur. Pumps and high-buttoned
spats kept her ankles warm.

1918

The end of World War I brought
in higher waistlines, and skirts
began to grow shorter. Girls wore
Mary Jane pumps, and boys wore
belted Norfolk jackets with shorts
that ended above the knee.

On the beach in 1922. Bathing suits were more streamlined, but one still could not get a complete suntan.

1924

Haircuts were shorter, with the back often shingled. Evening dresses hung slim and straight from the shoulder and sparkled with sequins or pearl embroidery.

263

1927

The height of the jazz age is symbolized by the sheik and the flapper, the ukelele and the Charleston. Hemlines rose to the knees, and waistlines disappeared entirely. On the golf links, men wore plus fours and visored caps.

264

Glamour Girl of 1939

1933

The depression followed the jazz age. Clothes became more practical, with natural shoulders and straight skirts. The zipper began its long reign.

1943

World War II brought rationing of cloth. Skirts became short again, shoulders broad. War-plant workers established slacks for street wear. The wide skirt persisted only in the cotton dirndl, an adaptation of a colorful peasant costume.

A wealth of new synthetic fabrics added glamour to the styles of 1953.

1947

Fashion excitement reached a high pitch with the postwar designs of Christian Dior — the New Look. Materials were no longer restricted. Long, billowing skirts and pinched-in waists were the extremes.

1958

Families seemed to spend more and more time out of doors, and clothes followed the trend. Shorts and slacks were designed—and worn—for many occasions by young and old, even on city streets.

Chemise Balloon Trapeze Empire

1960

The end of the half century saw men's suits cut on slim, narrow lines. Women's skirts were generally short — one famous designer had them above the kneecap, but this was too short for most women.

The Redwood Groves

By DONALD CULROSS PEATTIE
Author and Naturalist

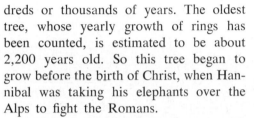

THE tallest trees in the world are the redwoods of the coastal region of northern California. Greater heights have been claimed for some of the Australian gum trees. But they were measured long ago and not accurately. To know the height of a tree in a dense grove is a very difficult thing. It usually takes a trained surveyor and some higher mathematics to measure such a tree.

And by these standards the redwoods along U. S. Highway 101 are certainly the tallest trees now living. The tallest of all is the Founders' Tree, 364 feet high, named for the founders of the Save-the-Redwoods League. These were three men who, on a camping trip, discovered that the redwoods were being logged at a fearsome rate.

They saw that something must be done, and quickly. They were scientists, not rich men; they couldn't buy the whole redwood forest. They had to ask the public for money. And the money came in— from the rich and the poor alike. It came from many people who had never seen the redwoods and probably never expected to, for they lived in Wisconsin or New Hampshire or Alabama or New York. And in those days travel to California was expensive. Exploring the redwoods was difficult.

And yet one beautiful grove of trees after another was saved in this way, to live on for no one knows how many hundreds or thousands of years. The oldest tree, whose yearly growth of rings has been counted, is estimated to be about 2,200 years old. So this tree began to grow before the birth of Christ, when Hannibal was taking his elephants over the Alps to fight the Romans.

The redwood is a cone-bearing tree with evergreen needles like a pine or, still more, like a hemlock, for the needles are short and flat and lie all in one plane in a spray. The cones are surprisingly small. But the most remarkable feature of an adult redwood is the straightness of the trunk, with no taper sometimes for 150 feet. That's what makes the redwood groves look like a temple or church filled with mighty pillars.

It is surprisingly dark even in daytime in a big redwood grove—so dense is the crown of foliage at the top of the tree. And, too, there is almost always a sea fog, high or low, rolling in. The redwood will hardly grow where there is no fog. So everything seems subdued and mysterious. And deeply quiet! Even the automobiles move slowly, honk seldom; and when people enter the groves they feel as if they were going to church. They are hushed by such age, such quietness.

The stillness under the trees seems to hold down your pulse beats and still your voice to a whisper. The chief sounds come from the bickering of some little stream disputing with its pebbly bed. Or the soft,

twirling song of the black-throated gray
warbler, so high up that you cannot see
the little bird. Or the sound of the wind
passing like a great sigh in the forest tops.
Or the rackety call of a Steller's jay deep
in the grove.

Your footsteps make no sound, for the
forest floor is covered with a dense car-
pet of sorrel (boys and girls often call
it sour grass). Every fallen log has a deep
clothing of moss—the most beautiful you
have ever seen; you might compare it to
those fernlike frost crystals you see on the
windowpane. There is always deer fern
or sword fern perched upon the log. When
they are caught in a long slanting shaft
of sunlight, they look like an offering on
some green altar.

The wild flowers are most of them little,
as if the colossal trees had used up all the
bigness allowed by nature. There is the in-
side-out flower, with its fleck of tiny blossoms like a dash of spray, and leaves like a
maidenhair fern's. There are the deerfoot
and sugarscoop, which are named for the
shapes of their leaves. The white flowers
are mere sprites dancing away under the
somber trees. Other flowers you can
scarcely believe in when you see them—
the wild ginger, with its little jug-shaped
flowers half hidden in the earth, and the
phantom orchid. If you come in the right
season you may see rosebay (a purple rho-
dodendron), a fragrant azalea, and the
sweet shrub with its dark red petals and
strawberry odor. And a starry white dog-
wood.

If you are quiet in your movements, if
you are sharp-eyed—and lucky—you
may see some of the animal folk who call
the redwoods their home. The raccoon always looks as though he had on a mask—
if you can catch a glimpse of him. You
wash your hands before you eat; brother
coon washes his food. He doesn't care so
much about his paws. Sometimes you will
see a skunk's tracks. They look like the

footprints of a baby with crooked feet. My advice to you is to make tracks in some other direction. The Douglas squirrel spends his time high up where the cones grow, stripping the cones of their scales and eating the seeds. He is clever about keeping on the other side of the tree from you. But if there are enough youngsters to watch a tree from all sides, one of you is bound to see him, with his dark brown back and gray or reddish underparts.

Chipmunks are favorites with everybody because they soon learn that human beings are likely to bring them peanuts. Many chipmunks are so tame that they will come right to children's hands and take the peanuts, stuffing them in their cheek pockets till their mouths are simply bulging. Just tap with a peanut on a piece of wood, sit perfectly quiet and hold the peanut out on your hand—and you will soon have a chipmunk friend.

Best of all, people love the black-tailed deer, which feed on huckleberry bushes, acorns, the buds of trees and shrubs. Or they may browse the meadow grass and mountain iris, like cows in a meadow. The best time for seeing them is at sunset when they come down to the stream to drink. If you stand still and if nobody slams the car door, the deer will look in a friendly way at you from their great liquid brown eyes. The pretty spotted fawns, the deer children, are especially winning. But don't try to pick them up or even caress them. Their mothers are always near and may not understand your friendliest gestures. With their sharp hoofs they can attack you fiercely. Just look and enjoy yourself, or take pictures—deer are as used to being photographed as movie actors. They don't object, as long as you keep away from their children.

Some people are horrified to hear that much lumbering of the redwoods still goes on. For the redwood is one of the most valuable trees in the world, with its resistance to termites, its lightness in proportion to its strength, the ease with which it can be planed or sawed for every sort of work, and the great length of its boards. The first pioneer babies of California were rocked in redwood cradles, and the children were taught from redwood "blackboards"—a plank three to five feet wide and any length the schoolroom would ask for. As you read this, redwoods are being used for railway ties in Nicaragua, because this wood does not rot in contact with the soil.

So we have to have a redwood lumbering industry. And at the same time we have to have a Save-the-Redwoods League, which is slowly buying up the most ancient and lofty trees along U. S. Highway 101. The lumber companies themselves are planting redwoods, and they don't have to wait a thousand years or so to get results. The fastest growth occurs in the redwood's youth, and a growth of second generation trees all about the same height and thickness is more useful, perhaps, than the primeval forest. For the never-before-cut forest contains a large number of trees that are past their best for practical use.

But it is these very trees in their noble old age that you and I love most. And it is right then that they should be preserved. Sometimes rich people will buy a whole grove and dedicate it to the memory of some member of their family or of some friend. The Garden Clubs of America have done much through the years to save these mighty trees. There is even a Children's Forest, which loving parents have bought, tree by tree. But there are still plenty to be saved by contributions large or small. Only a few of the groves you will see on the Redwood Highway are owned by the State Parks system of California, the United States Forest Service, or private individuals with big hearts. The rest might be cut down at any time.

Tiger Cubs

By WILLIAM BRIDGES
Curator of Publications
New York Zoological Society

THIRTY-ONE baby tigers have been born in New York's great Bronx Zoo in the past ten years, all to the same mother and father. Just as it would be in a big human family, these tiger brothers and sisters have all been different in many important ways. Some have been slow and lazy. Some have been energetic and full of high spirits. A few have been suspicious and bad-tempered and quick to snarl and scratch. But several have been unusually gentle and trusting with their human friends, and of all these the zoo's favorite is the sweet and playful little female that was one of two cubs born on November 8, 1958.

Her name is Dacca the Second. Her mother, Dacca the First, is the mother of all the thirty-one cubs, and the Bronx Zoo considers her one of the finest tiger mothers in the world today. "Mother Dacca," as the zoo people sometimes call her, has a perfect disposition for tiger motherhood in a zoo. She was hand-reared from birth, so she is friendly with her keeper. Nothing ever seems to worry her or make her short-tempered. She is affectionate and tolerant and playful with her cubs.

The only thing wrong with Mother Dacca is that she is getting old and may never have any more babies. But now that Dacca the Second has come along, the zoo is no longer worried about having cubs in the future. Three or four years from now Dacca the Second will be old enough to have cubs of her own; and to make sure that she will be as friendly and gentle as her mother, she is getting a very special upbringing in the zoo.

The story of the Bronx Zoo's experience with baby tigers really started in the winter of 1944. One February morning the keeper of the Lion House heard faint squalling sounds coming from the small room, called the sleeping den, that opens off the big indoor tiger compartment. All he could see with his flashlight were the

UPI

greenish yellow eyes of old Jenny, the tigress, but from the squalling sounds he knew that some babies had been born and that Jenny was standing guard over them.

Jenny had had babies before, but she was not a good mother and they all died. This time the zoo decided to take the babies away from her and give them to Mrs. Helen Martini, the wife of the Lion House keeper, to rear in her own home. It was easy enough to lock Jenny out of the sleeping den and for the keeper to crawl through a side door and pick up the cubs. There were three of them and they were cold and hungry. One was a female, which Mrs. Martini named Dacca. The other two were males and she named them Rajpur and Raniganj. All are named after cities in India and Pakistan.

Just as the zoo expected, Jenny did not mind having her babies taken away. She did not even seem to notice.

Mrs. Martini kept Dacca, Rajpur and Raniganj in her home across the street from the zoo. For the first few weeks she had to give them a bottle every three hours, night and day. Their eyes were closed when they were born, and their eyelids had to be bathed with an antiseptic solution until they opened about ten days later. All three babies had to be weighed

and measured every week, for the zoo keeps accurate records of the growth of its most important babies. While they were in her home, Mrs. Martini played with them for hours every day. Naturally, with so much love and affection, they became gentle and affectionate toward human beings.

Even as tiny cubs it was easy to tell what they would be like as adult tigers. Raniganj was a fat and lazy baby—and he is fat and lazy today. Rajpur was bold and strong. Little Dacca was a sweet and trusting cub, and she has stayed that way all her life.

By 1948 Dacca was old enough to have her own first babies. There were four of them, healthy and perfect. Having been brought up by her keeper and his wife, Dacca trusted them to take the babies away from her each week long enough to weigh and measure them. Some tigresses might have refused to take care of their babies if human beings had touched or handled them, but Dacca seemed to understand that it was all right. She *knows* from her own experience that human beings are friendly—and that is the kind of feeling the Bronx Zoo wants little Dacca the Second to have.

Starting in 1948 and every year there-

UPI

WIDE WORLD

after up to 1958, Dacca has had a family of cubs except once, in 1955. The Bronx Zoo did not have room to keep so many tigers, and so all the cubs except the last two were disposed of to other zoos in the United States, in Europe and Australia, as soon as they were old enough to leave their mother.

Then, in 1958, the zoo suddenly realized that Dacca was getting old and that she might not have any more babies. Unless she had one more family—and there was a female in the litter—the Bronx Zoo was going to have to go out of the tiger-cub business!

However, on November 8, Dacca did have one more litter—perhaps her last—and one of the two cubs was a female.

Everything had been planned in advance, on the chance that there would be a female. Mrs. Martini carried the squalling, orange-and-black baby home with her, just as she had carried Dacca the First home with her back in 1944. She

Helen Martini has had plenty of experience in coaxing baby tigers to eat, even timid ones.

275

named the baby Dacca the Second. The baby brother was left with old Dacca. Mrs. Martini named him Rajpur the Second, after his father.

Both babies were fine little tigers. Dacca the Second weighed 2 pounds 14 ounces at birth, Rajpur the Second 3 pounds—just about normal for baby tigers.

Dacca the Second thrived under Mrs. Martini's care and showed every sign of being as gentle and trusting as her mother. Both she and her brother grew rapidly, and when they were three months old and it was time to wean them, they weighed about 30 pounds each.

The next step was to separate baby Rajpur and Mother Dacca, and to introduce the brother and sister to each other. One late winter morning, Mother Dacca was moved to another compartment in the Lion House and Rajpur was left alone.

He seemed quite contented. The only time he was uneasy was when the keeper approached the front of his cage. Having been brought up by his own mother and not knowing very much about people, he was not friendly toward them. The sudden appearance of the keeper always made him crouch and slink off to the dark sleeping den, snarling.

He took refuge in the den when Mr. and Mrs. Martini brought Dacca the Second back to the Lion House, and there he stayed while little Dacca was put in the cage. She too was unhappy—but for a different reason. She didn't like being separated from her human friends, and she started running along the bars at the front of the cage and crying to be held in their arms.

Mr. Martini finally decided that perhaps she would be happier if she saw her brother, so he crawled into the sleeping den and made Rajpur come out. He came out crying and squalling.

All the time that Dacca the Second had been crying, Mother Dacca paid absolutely no attention. Stretched out on the floor of a cage a few yards away, she seemed half asleep.

But when Rajpur the Second started to cry, Mother Dacca woke up in a hurry. She cried back at him, a high, wild *scriouw* sound that tigers make when they fear something is happening to their cubs.

The babies raced up and down, bumping into each other and tumbling head over heels but paying no attention to each other—Rajpur crying for Mother Dacca, Dacca the Second crying for Mrs. Martini.

At last it seemed that the only thing to do was for Mr. and Mrs. Martini to go away, out of sight, and let the babies discover each other.

It worked. Gradually the realization seemed to come to them that even though they couldn't have Mrs. Martini or Mother Dacca, they had each other.

At first they merely stopped pacing and crying long enough to look at each other. Finally Rajpur put out a paw and touched sister Dacca's twitching tail. Their pacing grew slower and finally stopped, and so did their crying. Mother Dacca stopped pacing too and went back to sleep.

Within two days anyone would have thought that they had always lived together. They ran and they leaped on each other, they pounced and tumbled and chewed each other's ears and tails.

They no longer cry or give any sign of being lonesome for the tiger mother or the human foster mother who took care of them as babies. Rajpur is still a little standoffish toward human beings, but that is gradually fading away and will probably eventually disappear altogether. Dacca the Second is still sweet and friendly and trusting.

The Bronx Zoo is sure, now, that when the time comes for Dacca the Second to have babies of her own, she will be just as good a mother as her own mother was—old, but still sweet, Mother Dacca.

Grizzly Bears

By MARIUS BARBEAU

Folklorist for the Government of Canada

"GRIZZLY bears [*Ursus horribilis*] are living dynamite, espccially the she-bears with their twin cubs. Whoever stands in the way of a grizzly—whether a white man or an Indian—should climb up a tree and wait there until the storm is past, unless he can shoot the bear through the eye, the ear, the heart or the small of the back, to break the spine.

"A grizzly with three legs, his two hind legs intact, is as good as with four. He will fight you standing on his hind legs. As to the skull, it is a hard nut to crack. You can do it only with a high-powered rifle, and I would not try it. You are a good shot if you manage to get a bullet straight into the eye or into the ear. Half an inch aside is enough to make it glance off the skull, and there you are, worse off than at the start. When you miss the target with your first shot, you get excited and shoot wide of the mark. It's not healthy!"

That is what Angus Beaton, a big-game hunter and guide, had to say on a subject that he knew about from long experience. I met him at Hazelton, northern British

Columbia, many years ago, and he was my guide in an expedition up to the headwaters of the Skeena River. The Cassiar District in the northern Rockies and the high plateaus of the interior nearby are the best districts for big game—moose, caribou, mountain sheep, mountain goat—and the grizzly. A grizzly may stretch out ten feet long from snout to tail.

While on our way up the river, at the end of August, one night we camped on a high plateau in the midst of a huckleberry patch, where bears might happen to be feeding on the luscious wild fruit. But cowbells hung from the necks of our saddle horses, and the sound was enough to warn the bears off the trail. A bear does not attack unless taken by surprise or with cubs. But the atmosphere was favorable to bear stories—for there is a grizzly-bear folklore in the country, and whole evenings may be spent just telling tall tales of woodland adventure. Another night, we camped close to the Kshwan (upper Skeena) at the mouth of a creek where the salmon were running upstream to spawn. Wild celery covered the flat. We saw fresh tracks there, the slender plants being trampled, as the bears fed on them.

As we sat there under a tent flap, with a smudge fire to drive away the mosquitoes and the nosee-ums (Indian-English word for black flies), we began to talk bears. My party consisted of Beaton, the guide; Kamanoot, the Indian interpreter; Gervais, the cook; and myself. I was engaged on field work for the National Museum of Canada. My escorts were full of stories, mostly from firsthand experience. And I was all ears, with a notebook for shorthand on my knee.

The first question was, "Are grizzlies man-eaters?" "Man-eaters, no!" answered Angus Beaton, who had hunted in the Cassiar for over thirty years, part of the time as a guide to American big-game hunters. Beaton was the keenest observer of wildlife I had ever met. Kamanoot (once a famous outlaw, who had shot two white men one morning at Hazelton) shook his head and argued, "I have seen human hair caught between the teeth of a grizzly, after it was killed. The Stikine Indians had punished it: it was a man-eater. Our people are much afraid of grizzlies, and for good cause."

"There are bears and bears," declared old Gustave Gervais, who, in spite of his present low status as a cook, had seen and shot many bears during his long life in the Klondike. "What do you mean?" I wondered, "bears and bears?" "Never be too sure of what a grizzly will do," he answered. "It usually runs away from you before you have seen it. But when it starts the other way, the trick is up to you."

"In the first place," I inquired, "where

do you find grizzlies?" He answered, "You meet them with their food. And this varies according to the district, all up and down the Rockies, as far north as the Yukon and as far south as the States. Also at the foothills east of the big ranges, in Alberta and the Territories, but not on the seacoast. As soon as you move into new districts you find things a bit different— the bears, like the rest. Before you discover your quarry, you have to catch on to the ways of the country. Up here in the north the grizzlies, from the spring on, feed on the grass of the mountainsides. Then you get them in the hills, wherever wild fruits ripen or a bit before they get ripe. The grizzlies thrive in the berry country and burnt timber until the early fall. Then they go down to the rivers and grow fat on salmon spawning at the mouths of the creeks. Grizzlies also dig out ground hogs and devour them. No, they are not, as I have heard some people say, strictly vegetarians. Far from it. They like fish and hunt for meat too."

"The best hunting ground for grizzlies is east of Groundhog Mountains," added Kamanoot, who knew those parts like his pocket, having hidden there for many years as an outlaw. "This place is called Larh-weeyip, Place-of-Grass; there the bears are quite fierce."

"They are, wherever you surprise them," added Gervais, "in the Klondike too. They will charge, unless *you talk to them.*" And his index finger bent forth as if to pull the trigger.

Kamanoot resumed his story: "A man, named Ahkwedzah, once was killed in the grassy hills of the Stikine. He shot twice at the grizzly but failed to bring it down, good hunter though he was. The bear chased him back and forth, up and down, until he became exhausted. Then it took hold of him and killed him, while his brother Larhay, helpless on a cliff above, watched the fight. Aroused, the people started on the warpath against the grizzly, to avenge the death of their relative. For this retaliation they would not use guns but only spears and long, sharp knives. They did not travel very far before they found a grizzly. Infuriated, they piled on the brute and killed it with their spears. Looking into its mouth, they found human hair in its teeth. So this was the bear they were looking for—the killer. They skinned it, dried its skin and stuffed it. It looked as if it were alive. The Stikine hunters did this for the sake of revenge, while I lived with them. And the stuffed bear is still in Larhay's house."

I have seen such trophies, with arrows imbedded in the brown fur, in the cabins of Gitksan Indians of the upper Skeena. From trophy to totem is only a step. For the grizzly, to the natives, embodies a divine spirit on the high mountains, the highest of all spirits known in the far north as far as Siberia. The epic tale of Bear Mother is known and rehearsed everywhere, even among the Haida of the Queen Charlotte Islands, where the grizzly itself is unknown. And Bear Mother with her twin cubs, sometimes shown in human form, figures prominently on the totem poles of three or four native nations. So the grizzly is a true totem, a guardian spirit also carved out as a totem on tall poles in front of ancient lodges.

The respect that the Indians show for their totems—the Thunderbird, the Grizzly, the Killer Whale, the Wolf, etc.— did not keep my guide Kamanoot from telling a yarn at the expense of one of his fellow tribesmen. Here it is as a tailpiece.

Gervais had said, "You cannot always choose to run away. If you can, take my advice: climb a tree quick, the right one, big enough. For a grizzly cannot climb." Kamanoot laughed at the idea: "A brave hunter climb a tree! It sounds foolish." It reminded him of something, someone he had known. He said, "The bear waits there at the foot of the tree until you fall into its mouth. That nearly happened once, when I was still young, to my uncle, Kail. He hunted the grizzlies with a muzzle-loader and it was quite a job. One day, on the trail, he shot a grizzly but did not quite kill it. He dropped his gun, ran, climbed a tree and stayed there. The grizzly stood up maybe ten feet high, put his great arms round the tree and tried to shake my uncle down, tried and tried. But the tree was too big and my uncle held fast.

"Kail stayed there in the tree a whole day. The bear, at the foot, kept him good company. Most of the time they looked at each other. Then they parted, the bear getting tired of it first.

"When Kail arrived at his village and told of his adventure, his people asked him, 'When you were up there, why did you not shoot the bear right in the eye? Had you not plenty of time to take your aim?'

"Kail answered, 'A bird's nest stood right in my way. Because of the nest, I could not see the bear.'

"He was too proud to confess that in his haste he had dropped his gun to the ground. A shameful thing to do! The people after that could not forget about the bird's nest. They found it too funny for words and nicknamed him Bird's-Nest!"

Prehistoric trees. Millions of years ago forests covered large areas of the world.

Our Wandering Trees

By RUTHERFORD PLATT

Author and Lecturer

IN 1869, at the village of Gilboa in the Catskill Mountains of New York State, Schoharie Creek went on a rampage. It washed out roads, carried away bridges, roared down ravines. It would have been long forgotten as a local incident except for one thing. When the flash flood subsided a fine collection of solid-rock tree stumps was exposed in the creek banks. Fossils had no wide appeal in those days. Both the tree stumps and the obscure old report of them were forgotten for fifty years. In 1920, construction of the Gilboa Dam for the New York City water-supply system broke deeply into the mountainsides of the area. This time, forests of stumps were exposed at different levels of rock strata, showing that these forests must have been there for millions of years.

With today's skill in interpretation we know that the trees were forty to fifty feet tall and that sprays of large fern fronds sprang from the tops of the trunks. These, unlike ordinary tree branches, elongated by uncoiling, as do the spiral crosiers of our ferns today.

The stumps, which measure as much as four feet across, stand upright in the mud (which has also turned to stone) in the same positions in which they were growing in the Devonian period, 300,000,000 years ago. The stumps are the oldest record of a forest on earth. The trees have been given a good Greek name, *Eospermatopteris,* which is three short words combined (*Eo, dawn; sperm,* seed; *pteris,* fern).

This is like finding the life of a faraway planet right under our feet. When those fern trees were living, all the kinds of forest life that we would recognize were millions of years in the future. The dawn-fern trees glimpsed through the mists of time seem weirdly lonely. Their fronds cast quivering flecks of shadows on dead gray surface of mud. A silence like that of outer space is broken only by the rustle of fronds in the wind and the roar of cloudbursts. There were no songs of birds, calls of animals or buzzing of insects.

The earth whirled through 65,000,000 years after the appearance of the dawn-fern trees, and we find another kind of forest—the jungles of the fabulous coal age. Hot, wet weather had prevailed around the earth for thousands of years. Perpetual hot rains eroded the steaming, bare rock of the mountainsides, filling continental depressions deep with sediment. The spores of

Tulip trees

ferns and mosses of earlier ages fell into the wet mud, and life sprang up rapidly far and wide. The mineral sands of granite are rich nourishment for plant life. After that, as the warm, wet weather continued, all sorts and sizes of plants flourished and died, building the rich muck ever deeper. Jungles of big trees now grew in the swamps. Among them were salamanders 10 feet long, dragonflies with 30-inch wingspreads, and cockroaches 4 inches long.

The trees were destined to return to the sunlight in our time. When they toppled, their bodies sank deep into the mud. There, sealed off from air and under great pressure, they turned to coal. Much of our heating and electricity comes from the sunlight power stored up in those trees 200,000,000 years ago.

Two kinds of trees were dominant in the coal age. One of these had a beautiful hollow trunk, unlike any tree trunk today. It was straight, with almost parallel sides, and fluted like the column of a Greek temple. Its bark was covered with grains of silica from the mineral mud—glass bark. Under the glass it was green with chlorophyll, so that the whole trunk served for food making, in place of leaves. These were reduced to slender whorls. The descendants of this tree are the slender little horsetails and scouring rushes of our world.

The other outstanding tree had more branches than the horsetail trees. Still it bore no leaves, except tiny overlapping leaves that served in place of bark. The center of the trunk was pithy, but as the trees were crowded together they held up each other. (This is the way the trees of tropical rain forests today, with their shal-

Shagbark hickory

Sycamore

low and unstable roots, stand upright against the beating of rain and wind.) The descendants of these trees are the club mosses and ground pines on the floor of our woodlands.

One other tree, comparatively inconspicuous among the horsetail and club moss trees, was an exciting innovation. It reproduced by seeds, formed in cones, instead of by the age-old spore method of ferns and mosses. What is more, its trunk was wood. We call the tree *Cordaites*.

When at long last the earth grew drier and cooler and the great swamps began to shrink, the horsetail and club moss trees disappeared. Then *Cordaites* survived and prospered. It had seeds. Its strong wood trunk could stand erect without help and could store up water sap which would not evaporate in a dry wind. It was the ancestor of the pine family.

Between the end of the coal age and the rise of flowering plants, the geological calendar has a period of about 70,000,000 years, labeled the Age of Reptiles. Plants

and animals were uniform, in a world-wide mild, dry climate. The feature of the time was the rise of life that could live out of water. Plants and animals spread inland. There was plenty of room, there was no pressure of competition, and huge individuals developed. There were no grasses and herbs to graze on, no small animals for prey. The monster reptiles ate each other and browsed on the branches of trees that grew higher and higher.

Two trees are prominent in the book of fossils from that time. One is the cycad. It seems to have defended itself against browsing monsters by developing one big cone bearing hundreds of flowers on the top of its trunk. This did not rise above the armament of surrounding leaves. Instead, the leaves, as tough and sharp-edged as cactus, sprayed above the cone like the crown of a palm tree. Cycad is a compound tree with features of ferns, palms and the agave of our southwestern desert. Its cone and seeds are pinelike. It was wonderfully successful and grew all over the world in

Sycamore and elm, leaf-dropping hardwoods

the Age of Reptiles. Cycads still grow today as humble plants of tropical regions and as a feature of botanical gardens.

Ginkgo accompanied cycad on its globe-trotting in the Age of Reptiles. It is not a fern tree though it has leaves like those of the maidenhair fern. It reproduces with seeds—but these are formed like blueberries. Instead of fertilizing seeds as do the pines, with pollen, ginkgo uses swimming sperms in the way that ferns and mosses fertilize their spores.

We see ginkgo today, not in our wild landscape, but planted in parks and along big city streets. This tree wonder, which can withstand the desert dryness of pavements and smog-laden air, is exactly like its ancestors. It is as though it had been delivered to us by parcel post from the Age of Reptiles. It may be regarded with the same interest as a crocodile in the city.

We have just seen two interesting tree artifices in the Age of Reptiles. Cycad and ginkgo look as though they had been assembled with parts from various kinds of trees. This mixing of characteristics brought new powers of survival. For the first time, trees were able to step out across the continents away from a constant water supply. Yet plant life still had little variety. There were only a few kinds of ancient trees, growing along wadies where floods from an occasional cloudburst coursed. There was no ground cover. Hillsides and plains were glaring rock and sand. Something else was needed to produce our world of flowering plants with their colorful communities of insects, birds and animals.

The flowering plants seem to have burst on the world in a period called the *Cretaceous* from the Latin word *creta,* chalk. This refers to a peculiar kind of rock deposited at the beginning of the period. Chalk is a kind of limestone, mostly from shells, that forms at the bottom of shallow seas. In the early Cretaceous the polar caps melted, raising sea levels while land subsided. Half of North America was under water. What is now the Gulf of Mexico extended north to Illinois. A big arm of the Pacific filled a trough in the interior of Oregon and California, where there are high mountains today. The Sahara desert was submerged.

Just before this time of change, the world had swung from ancient spore plants to seed plants, with cycad and ginkgo—and with a wonderful development of pines. But all these seeds were naked. They were born exposed on the scales of cones.

The most important basic patent of the development of plant life was the *incased* seed. It is a miniature plant prepared to endure and travel. The tiny plant has a weatherproof case, and it is surrounded by a portion of moisture and food on which it can exist for a long time. The disturbances of the Cretaceous—the spread and retreat of seas, the alterations of ice caps, the uprising of mountains, the winds that blew hot and cold, moist and dry—stimulated the production of incased seeds and with them all sorts of new plants. Thus life became varied, mobile, versatile, through coping with changing conditions.

We know no time and place when the oaks, maples, walnuts, sycamores and so on, with bushes, grass, wild flowers, birds and animals, made their entrance on the stage. They must have had mysterious, faint beginnings in the coal age and the Age of Reptiles. Cretaceous events brought them to a swift climax.

We first discover the hardwood forest with modern features after millions of years of travel and evolution. It was growing near Disko island—off the west coast of Greenland, about 200 miles north of the Arctic Circle—about 75,000,000 years ago. At that time ginkgoes were growing in New Jersey, sequoias in Virginia, cycads in Kansas. The forest in the far north held sycamore, magnolia, breadfruit. Toward the end of the Cretaceous, walnut, poplar, elm, maple, oak, sassafras, birch and most of the other trees and bushes of a New England woods were added.

The Disko forest was a fragment of a great circumpolar forest, growing at a time when the climate around the Arctic Ocean was like that of New England today. Discoveries have been made in Spitsbergen, Iceland, northern Siberia, northern Canada around the mouth of the Mackenzie River, and polar Grinnell Land of fossils of "modern" hardwood forest from the epoch after Disko.

The ice age that began about 2,000,000 years ago—geologically speaking, in our time—did not destroy the hardwood forest. It could travel with its incased seeds. The forest retreated southward, spreading out into all the continents. When the face of the Big Ice was farthest south in our continent, it stood along a wavy line from New York to Cincinnati and westward. Then the refuge of the retreating forest centered in the southern Appalachians, around Chattanooga. As the ice has melted back dur-

ing the last 25,000 years, the trees have marched northward again to the places where we see them.

Seeds are the footsteps of the forest. They always turn in the right direction. Even adverse winds and gravity do not stop them. Associations of plants move against the wind and up mountains, wherever lies more hospitable ground and climate. Seeds seem to be scattered in a haphazard fashion, but nature loves to use the law of averages. When cold is increasing, more seeds will sprout on the warmer side of the tree. When aridity is spreading, more will sprout on the moister side. In this way the forest was brought to us intact across thousands of miles.

We first discover our forest when it was circumpolar, but where was it before? There is an interesting theory that may answer this question.

Northeast Asia has many counterparts of our plant life. Our tulip tree, hickory and sassafras are found elsewhere only in central China. Skunk cabbage is native only in our northeast and in China and Japan. Trailing arbutus is peculiar to the Appalachians and Japan. The only other species of May apple in the world is in the Himalayas. And there are many other pairs. A traveler near Darjeeling, about seven thousand feet up in the Himalayas, would think he was in a New England forest!

Was eastern Asia, particularly the Himalayas, the cradle of our woodland? The theory is that there, hot and cold climates, summer and winter conditions, created leaf dropping and developed our familiar species. In later periods they radiated north and became a polar forest at a time when today's continents were joined. For instance, there was a land bridge across the Bering Strait or at the Aleutian Islands.

Uncounted ages have rolled over, turning the pages of the story written in rocks. Creation needs no timekeeper. The wonder is what happened, not how long it took.

OWLS

By LEWIS WAYNE WALKER
Author and Naturalist

Biggs

Most living creatures sleep at night and carry on their activities in the daytime. There are some birds and animals, however, who do the exact opposite, and among these are the owls. When all the world is dark these birds drift over field and woodland on strong, silent wings, looking for food. When an owl's keen night-seeing eyes spy some luckless rodent, it dives down and scoops up its prey.

Rats, field mice and house mice, shrews, weasels and other destructive animals of the sort are the owl's favorite food. But because it hunts at night when human beings are not around to observe its ways, the owl has often been misunderstood and unjustly condemned.

Late in the nineteenth century, owls were accused of being killers of practically everything that man wanted to protect. Bounties for dead owls were paid across the country. At this time, Pennsylvania, which today has practical fish-and-game laws, passed the "scalp act." Over several years $120,000 was paid for the heads of hawks and owls. In the next few years, however, rodents increased to so great an extent, because their natural enemies, owls and hawks, were being killed off, that the state was forced to spend $80,000 in an effort to keep rats and mice under control. Lessons like this went unheeded, and to the present day many people still do not realize the dire consequences that result from disturbing the balance of nature.

Owls, to be sure, are just a single link

HORNED
OWL

SNOWY
OWL

SCREECH OWL

in the long chain of predatory animals that keep our world in economic balance. As an example of their beneficial qualities let's go back to a study I made on barn owls that nested in a church belfry at Flushing, Long Island. The nest that I observed for a period of 4 hours each evening for 96 nights had been in existence since its discovery in 1880 by Daniel Carter Beard of Boy Scout fame. During that 46-year occupancy there had been a constant change of mates, but in each instance of bereavement the remaining one lured in another to share the dwelling.

During my watch the first of 11 eggs to be laid appeared in February, and 96 nights later the last of the fledglings took flight and deserted the belfry. Each evening during this period, however, they were watched from 8 o'clock until midnight. The incubation of the eggs was definitely established at 32 days. Yet due to the barn owls' peculiar habit of beginning another setting before a full clutch is completed, there was a 2-week difference in the size of the young.

All owls devour their prey whole. After it is swallowed, strong digestive juices go to work utilizing every bit of the food. So only a few bones and the fur are left. After about 8 hours the fur is coughed up in the form of pellets. Examination of these is a sure check on the kind of foods eaten by the birds that frequent a nest or roost. One hundred pellets picked up at the Flushing nest disclosed the following: 122 field mice, 86 Norway rats, 19 house mice, 1 shrew, 1 weasel and 1 bird.

Other studies of barn owls around the world have shown them to be universally beneficial. However, this research is often ignored. A few years ago some chicken farmers of Lord Howe Island, a small bit of land off the coast of Australia, decided that their barn owls should be eliminated. The bounties that were offered brought about the complete extermination

288

of the native owls. In a very short time, rats started to increase. The result was that a main industry of the island, the raising of sapling trees for export, was brought to a standstill when the hungry rodents began to strip the bark of the seedlings. Finally the islanders appealed to England for help. The request was relayed to the United States and the San Diego Zoo collected and shipped several dozen live owls to replace those that had been foolishly killed.

Barn owls, because of their size and prowess and because they prefer human dwellings, are primarily rodent eaters. Other species that exist in certain parts of the country are especially adapted for the catching of different foods. A few take birds. Some catch an occasional fish, and many live almost exclusively on insects and arachnids, such as spiders and scorpions. The elf owl, smallest owl in the world, belongs in this latter class. A bird of sparrow size, it lives in the saguaro cactus in holes originally drilled by woodpeckers from 10 to 30 feet above the ground. These small owls are extremely secretive, more often heard than seen, but in spite of their tendency to hide, those watched around a nest soon become tame.

A pair near Tucson's Desert Museum permitted the construction of a platform within four feet of their nest. On the evening of its completion the birds began to use it as a perch to view the surrounding desert. Observations made from the platform supplied much new information about elf owls.

Most owls have extremely soft feathers with the forward edges of the quills furred with tiny barbules. They make the birds' flight almost noiseless and, in theory at least, allow the birds to approach their prey undetected. Elf owls, however, seem to have lost this family trait. Those observed near Tucson would often hover in front of the nesting hole, and their

289

NATURE

SHORT-EARED OWL

ELF OWL

BURROWING OWL

BARN OWL

beating wings were clearly audible for a distance of 10 or 15 feet.

These smallest of owls are just the right size to fit the holes drilled in saguaro cactus by Gila woodpeckers. If the hole entrances are enlarged the least bit, then screech owls move in and the elf owls are forced to go elsewhere.

Although the eared owls are only slightly larger than the elf owls, they are wonderful hunters. Insects make up about half of their diet, and most of the rest consists of injurious rodents, some as big as full-grown house rats. Some eared owls show great bravery in the protection of their nests. They drive enemies away by raking them with their sharp talons. They have used the same technique on the author, drawing blood with every drive.

The common name "screech owl" is a misnomer. The calls of these birds have a whistled dovelike quality. The call starts high and then quavers down in pitch as the syllables are uttered faster. Screech owls with slight variation are to be found throughout North America. Those in the eastern states occur in two distinctive color phases, red and gray. Sometimes a brood of young will have both colors no matter whether the parents are mixed or both gray or both red. Color differences are definitely not due to either age, sex or season.

Every five or ten years the northern states and southern Canada are invaded by tremendous migrations of snowy owls: large white birds flecked with tiny spots of black. In the Arctic, their normal home, this feather pattern blends with the snow, concealing them from both enemies and prey alike. On our brown fields it is a disastrous advertisement to trigger-happy gunners. In the memorable migration of 1927 over five thousand of these beautiful birds were slaughtered.

The popular saying "blind as an owl" is completely incorrect. All owls seem well able to see in the daytime but they prefer to hunt during darkness because most of their chosen prey are nocturnal. Some species, such as the snowy, great gray and hawk owls, live in the northern lands of the midnight sun where, in summer, the light, in varying intensities, gleams twenty-four hours a day. The eye pupils of the entire owl family are very adaptable. They enlarge in darkness to let in more light, and in sunlight contract to mere pinpoints to cut out glare. This remarkable control can be worked independently by either eye. When an owl is perched sideways to bright sunlight, the pupil of the eye on the sunny side will contract, while the pupil of the eye on the shady side will enlarge.

There are many myths about owls. One false story, widely believed, credits rattlesnakes, prairie dogs and burrowing owls with harmonious association. The burrowing owl nests underground and can dig its own burrow but prefers to remodel and use a burrow deserted by some small mammal. The homes of prairie dogs are well suited for the purpose. The prairie rattlesnake, a venomous reptile, is incapable of digging, but a number of them will hibernate through the winter in a deserted prairie-dog hole. Bird and reptile simply make use of the prairie dogs' hard work.

If you observe a prairie-dog colony carefully over a long period of time, you will see that certain burrows are used only by owls, others by prairie dogs, and still others by hibernating rattlesnakes. Only when there is a sudden alarm will one species trespass on the territory of another. When all is serene the real ownership of the burrows cannot be mistaken. Another reason for the persistence of this myth is the rattling call of fledgling owls. If a burrow is being excavated every scrape of the shovel brings a rattling noise from the nesting chamber. This sound is so like the buzz of angry rattlers that many excavators consider the yarn proved, and dig no deeper.

Baseball Golf Basketball Hockey Track and Field Boxing Tennis Football
Swimming Horse Racing Chess Auto Racing Rowing Baseball Golf Basketba
ll Hockey Track and Field Boxing Tennis Football Swimming Horse Racing
Chess Auto Racing Rowing Baseball Golf Basketball Hockey Track and Field
Boxing Tennis Football Swimming Horse Racing Chess Auto Racing Rowing
Baseball Golf Basketball Hockey Track and Field Boxing Tennis Football
Swimming Horse Racing Chess Auto Racing Rowing Baseball Golf Basketba
ll Hockey Track and Field Boxing Tennis Football Swimming Horse Racing
Chess Auto Racing Rowing Baseball Golf Basketball Hockey Track and Field
Boxing Tennis Football Swimming Horse Racing Chess Auto Racing Rowing
Baseball Golf Basketball Hockey Track and Field Boxing Tennis Football
Swimming Horse Racing Chess Auto Racing Rowing Baseball Golf Basketba
ll Hockey Track and Field Boxing Tennis Football Swimming Horse Racing

SPORTS REVIEW

By PAUL GARDNER

Writer on Sports

BASEBALL

Baseball achieved a spectacular climax in 1959 as the Los Angeles Dodgers, transplanted from Brooklyn, won the National League pennant, then the World Series.

Los Angeles, a wobbly seventh in 1958, caught the pace-setting San Francisco Giants and the defending champions, the Milwaukee Braves, in a strong onrush at the end of the season. The Dodgers and Braves were tied, necessitating a play-off. The Los Angeles club won the first two games of the best-of-three play-off.

In the American League, the Chicago White Sox had a hard-hitting ball club which won Chicago its first pennant in forty years. Luis Aparicio and Nellie Fox, a talented shortstop–second base combination, spearheaded a drive that toppled the mighty Yankees, 1958's world champions. Cleveland placed second in a fairly tight race, which was settled late in the campaign when the White Sox thrashed the Indians four times running in a vital series.

When the White Sox and the Los Angeles Dodgers squared off in the grand finale the result was figured as a tossup. Instead it went six games and drew 420,784 spectators, an all-time record surpassing the previous seven-game total of 394,712. The remarkable relief pitching of Larry Sherry plus the fierce hitting of Charley Neal and veteran Gil Hodges swung the series toward the Dodgers.

The first game was a surprise. The

291

1959 WORLD SERIES RESULTS

	Game	R.	H.	E.	Batteries
1.	Los Angeles	0	8	3	CRAIG, Churn (3), Labine (4), Koufax (5), Klippstein (7) and Roseboro
	Chicago	11	11	0	WYNN, Staley (8) and Lollar
2.	Los Angeles	4	9	1	PODRES, Sherry (7) and Roseboro
	Chicago	3	8	0	SHAW, Lown (7) and Lollar
3.	Chicago	1	12	0	DONOVAN, Staley (7) and Lollar
	Los Angeles	3	5	0	DRYSDALE, Sherry (8) and Roseboro
4.	Chicago	4	10	3	WYNN, Lown (3), Pierce (4), Staley (7) and Lollar
	Los Angeles	5	9	0	CRAIG, Sherry (8) and Roseboro
5.	Chicago	1	5	0	SHAW, Pierce (8), Donovan (8) and Lollar
	Los Angeles	0	9	0	KOUFAX, Williams (8) and Roseboro, Pignatano (9)
6.	Los Angeles	9	13	0	PODRES, Sherry (4) and Roseboro
	Chicago	3	6	1	WYNN, Donovan (4), Lown (4), Staley (5), Pierce (8), Moore (9) and Lollar

MAJOR LEAGUE STANDINGS

AMERICAN LEAGUE

	WON	LOST	PCT.	GAMES BEHIND
CHICAGO............94	60	.610	
CLEVELAND..........89	65	.578	5
NEW YORK...........79	75	.513	15
DETROIT..............76	78	.494	18
BOSTON...............75	79	.487	19
BALTIMORE...........74	80	.481	20
KANSAS CITY........66	88	.429	28
WASHINGTON........63	91	.409	31

NATIONAL LEAGUE

	WON	LOST	PCT.	GAMES BEHIND
* LOS ANGELES.........88	68	.564	
MILWAUKEE..........86	70	.551	2
SAN FRANCISCO......83	71	.539	4
PITTSBURGH.........78	76	.506	9
CHICAGO.............74	80	.481	13
CINCINNATI..........74	80	.481	13
ST. LOUIS...........71	83	.461	16
PHILADELPHIA........64	90	.416	23

* Los Angeles defeated Milwaukee in best-of-three play-off after season ended in tie. First game, Los Angeles, 3; Milwaukee, 2. Second game, Los Angeles, 6; Milwaukee, 5 (twelve innings).

MAJOR LEAGUE LEADERS

AMERICAN LEAGUE

BATTERS	A.B.	R.	H.	PCT.
Kuenn, Detroit	561	99	198	.353
Kaline, Detroit	511	86	167	.327
Runnels, Boston	560	95	176	.314
Fox, Chicago	624	84	191	.306
Minoso, Cleveland	570	92	172	.302

RUNS BATTED IN		HOME RUN HITTERS	
Jensen, Boston	112	Colavito, Cleveland	42
Colavito, Cleveland	111	Killebrew, Washington	42
Killebrew, Washington	105	Lemon, Washington	33
Lemon, Washington	100	Mantle, New York	31
Maxwell, Detroit	95	Maxwell, Detroit	31

NATIONAL LEAGUE

BATTERS	A.B.	R.	H.	PCT.
Aaron, Milwaukee	629	116	223	.355
Cunningham, St. Louis	458	65	158	.345
Cepeda, San Francisco	605	92	192	.317
Pinson, Cincinnati	648	131	205	.316
Mays, San Francisco	575	125	180	.313

RUNS BATTED IN		HOME RUN HITTERS	
Banks, Chicago	143	Mathews, Milwaukee	46
Robinson, Cincinnati	125	Banks, Chicago	45
Aaron, Milwaukee	125	Aaron, Milwaukee	39
Bell, Cincinnati	115	Robinson, Cincinnati	36
Mathews, Milwaukee	114	Mays, San Francisco	34

White Sox had been pulling one-run victories out of their caps all season but this time behind Early Wynn they pommeled the Dodger pitchers for an 11-to-0 triumph at Chicago's Comiskey Park. (Wynn won 22 games during the season.)

It was different in the second game, when 156-pound Charley Neal, the Dodger second baseman, excelled with two home runs to help win the 4-to-3 victory. According to some experts, base running by Sherman Lollar in the eighth inning, as a White Sox rally was checked at the plate, might have been a decisive factor.

In the third game, at Los Angeles (viewed by 92,294 people), relief pitcher Larry Sherry was called on again when he relieved Don Drysdale. Carl Furillo's pinch single in the seventh drove in two runs at the last moment as the Dodgers won, 3 to 1.

The fourth game, with another capacity crowd in the stands, saw the Dodgers take a 4-to-0 lead in the third inning and the White Sox charge back to 4 to 4 in the eighth. But Gil Hodges homered for Los Angeles with the clincher in the home half of the inning for a 5-to-4 verdict. Sherry relieved as usual, this time following starter Roger Craig.

With their backs to the wall the White Sox managed to win the fifth game, in Los Angeles, by the narrow margin of 1 to 0. Although Bob Shaw outpitched Sandy Koufax in this tingling duel, Dick Donovan had to come in to save the White Sox ace by stopping the Dodgers with the bases full in the eighth. Chicago scored the lone run of the ball game on a double play in the fourth inning.

In the sixth game, home runs by Duke Snider, Wally Moon and Chuck Essegian enabled the Dodgers to conquer by 9 to 3 and thus to succeed the Yankees as world champions. In this final game the husky 24-year-old Sherry relieved once more, this time saving Podres, and picked up two hits in the bargain.

292

Rocco Colavito, infielder, the Cleveland Indians: the home-run champ of the American League.

Gil Hodges of the Los Angeles Dodgers strikes at a pitch in the first inning of the sixth game of the World Series. Sherm Lollar of the Chicago White Sox is catcher.

Harvey Haddix, pitcher for the Pittsburgh Pirates, pitched twelve perfect innings against Milwaukee's Braves, only to lose the game finally in the thirteenth inning.

There was an important new development in American baseball in 1959. Inspired by William A. Shea, a New York lawyer, a group of millionaires in various cities announced that it planned to form a third major league, the Continental League. Branch Rickey, one of baseball's immortals, was named as president of the Continental League which hoped to start operations by 1961. The Continental League would include a team in New York, once the home of the Dodgers and the Giants.

Two All-Star baseball games were played in the majors in 1959. In the first, at Pittsburgh, the National League won by 5 to 4. The tables were reversed in the second meeting, at Los Angeles, when the American League triumphed, 5 to 3.

In the Junior World Series, Havana beat Minneapolis 4 games to 3.

GOLF

Stout, easygoing Bill Casper, Jr., bespectacled Bob Rosburg and solemn-faced Art Wall, Jr., cornered golf's three major championships in 1959.

Casper shot a 282 to take the United States Open at the Winged Foot Golf Club in Mamaroneck, New York. The open was postponed for one day for the first time in its history, owing to rain, but the weather conditions did not bother the relaxed Casper, one of America's great putters.

Rosburg, six strokes off the lead entering the final round, closed with a 277 total to gain the PGA championship. The early leader, little Jerry Barber, who faltered with bogies on the final two holes, tied with Doug Sanders for second.

Wall, leading money winner of the year, triumphed in the Masters at Augusta with a 284 score. The national men's amateur went to Jack Nicklaus, a 19-year-old junior from Ohio State, who defeated Charles Coe in the final to become the youngest man in fifty years to take the men's amateur. In the women's national amateur final 24-year-old Barbara McIntire of Lake Park, Florida, won over Joanne Goodwin.

Betsy Rawls overshadowed the women's professional golf field, winning the women's PGA, the Triangle round robin at

293

Canoe Brook Country Club and most of the other top events. Although Mickey Wright, Louise Suggs and Beverly Hanson were also in the limelight, on the 1959 record Betsy Rawls stood as the legitimate successor to the late Babe Didrikson Zaharias in women's golf.

Mickey Wright excelled as she achieved the United States Women's Open for the second year in succession. Her total of 287 was the lowest since the event came under United States Golf Association auspices in 1953. At Denver, Bill Wright, 23-year-old Western Washington College senior, became the first Negro ever to win a USGA golf title when he triumphed in the 36-hole United States Public Links final, 3 and 2, topping Frank Campbell of Jacksonville, Florida.

In the national amateur mixed-foursomes final, Mrs. Marlene Stewart Streit of Toronto and Jack Penrose of Miami defeated Rosemary Neundorf of Toronto and Howard Everitt of Northfield, New Jersey, 10 and 9.

In the Walker Cup matches, America's experienced team easily subdued Britain 9 to 3, at Muirfield, Scotland. Series score: United States 16, Britain 1.

Betsy Rawls blasts from trap at 10th hole in second round: Round Robin tournament, Summit, N. J.

Victory smile: Bill Wright of Seattle wins National Public Links golf crown in Denver.

Jack Nicklaus, 19-year-old junior from Ohio State, youngest man in fifty years to win the Amateur.

BASKETBALL

California won the National Collegiate Athletic Association Championship at Louisville, Kentucky, defeating West Virginia, 71 to 70, in a thrilling final. The decision was settled with only 18 seconds left in the game. The winning points were made by 6-feet, 10-inch Darrall Imhoff from Alhambra, California.

St. John's triumphed in the twenty-second annual National Invitation Tournament at Madison Square Garden in New York. It won over Bradley, 76 to 71, in an overtime final contest.

League winners were as follows: Dartmouth in the Ivy League; Connecticut in

Split-second action in first half of National Invitation final at Garden: Bradley vs. St. John's.

the Yankee; St. Joseph's in the Mid-Atlantic; Mississippi State in the Southeastern; North Carolina State in the Atlantic Coast; West Virginia in the Southern Conference.

Eastern Kentucky won in the Ohio Valley; Michigan State in the Big Ten; Kansas State in the Big Eight; Bowling Green, on a play-off over Miami, in the Mid-American; Texas Christian in the Southwest; Texas Western, New Mexico State and Arizona State tied in the Border Conference; California in the Pacific Coast;

St. Mary's in the West Coast; Utah in the Skyline Conference and Idaho State in the Rocky Mountain.

Sparked by Bob Cousy, the Boston Celtics displayed some of the finest basketball of all time in crushing the Minneapolis Lakers in four straight games in the National Basketball Association final. Score, 173 to 139, was Pro history's highest.

Wichita conquered Bartlesville (Oklahoma), 105 to 83, in the national A.A.U. championship final at Denver.

HOCKEY

The Montreal Canadiens raced off with the National Hockey League championship for the eleventh consecutive year. The Canadiens won the Stanley Cup play-offs for the fourth straight season when they handily defeated the Toronto Maple Leafs, 4 games to 1.

The Belleville McFarlands of Canada triumphed in the world amateur championship at Prague, Czechoslovakia. They won the final round robin in which the United States was fourth.

Toronto's Bower slides to push puck from Henri Richard in first game of series, won by Montreal.

TRACK AND FIELD

At Philadelphia's Franklin Field in July the American men defeated the Russian men, 127 to 108, while the Russian women outscored the American women, 67 to 40, in one of the most tremendous dual meets ever staged.

Among the American men, the standouts were: Parry O'Brien, the shot-putter; fleet sprinter Ray Norton; 1,500-meter man Dyrol Burleson, a 19-year old; 800-meter man Tom Murphy; broad jumper Greg Bell and discus thrower Al Oerter.

Vasily Kuznetsov starred for the Soviet

Triple gold medallsi, Ray Norton of San Jose won the 100- and 200-meter dashes and anchored 400-meter relay team at Philadelphia.

Union, coming within seven points of his own world decathlon mark.

The Pan-American games, held in Chicago, were largely dominated by the United States although a sprinkling of victories did go to the Latin-American contingent, who were outmanned, but nevertheless played with courage and brilliance.

Outdoors, the Southern California Striders dominated all rivals in the national AAU championships with 144 points to 76½ for second place New York Athletic Club. The New York A. C. triumphed indoors with 21½ points. In track and field the Tennessee A. & I. State team won both the indoor and the outdoor women's championships.

John Thomas, the phenomenal 18-year old from Boston University, created an indoor world record of 7 feet, 1¼ inches in the running high jump. Experts considered

Vasily Kuznetsov, Russian world decathlon champion, rolls over a high-jump bar during a workout at Franklin Field where he competed in the track meet.

this feat at the national AAU indoor-title meet one of the greatest performances of track and field history.

BOXING

One of sport's earthquakes struck in 1959. Ingemar Johansson, a Swedish heavyweight who had failed dismally in the 1952 Olympics, vindicated himself by knocking out Floyd Patterson in the third round of a scheduled 15-round bout at the Yankee Stadium to win the world championship.

The 182-pound Patterson was highly favored over his Swedish opponent who was fourteen pounds heavier. There were two rounds of careful sparring, with Johansson boxing very cautiously and defensively. Early in the third round, Johansson's short straight right crashed through Patterson's so-called peekaboo defense.

Two other bouts caught public fancy in

Ingemar Johansson, heavyweight boxing champion, waves his famous right hand at fans—and floors Floyd Patterson with it.

296

1959. One was the return match between Archie Moore, the light heavyweight title-holder, and Yvon Durelle of Canada. In their first fight Durelle had had Moore down and Archie had been forced to pull a miracle to put away his man. However the second fight was never really a contest. Moore set his rival up beautifully and stopped him with a variety of punches in the third round. The other was the middle-weight combat between Carmen Basilio and Gene Fullmer for the honors left un-defended by Sugar Ray Robinson.

In the contest between Fullmer and Basilio in San Francisco, Fullmer's counter-punching was too strong for Basilio. Fullmer wore Basilio down, ending the fight in the 14th.

Joe Brown successfully defended his world lightweight title as he outpointed Johnny Busso in fifteen rounds at Houston.

Jose Becerra, 117½-pound Mexican, stopped Alphonse Halimi in the eighth round to gain the world bantamweight title.

TENNIS

Australia regained the Davis Cup by 3 to 2 from the United States in the challenge round at Forest Hills and Neale Fraser of Australia and Maria Bueno of Brazil won the United States men's and women's singles respectively at the West Side Stadium.

Alex Olmedo slipped from his number one position of the previous year when he lost to Fraser in both the Davis Cup play and in the final of the national singles. A sore arm contributed to his defeat in the finals as Fraser won by 6-3, 5-7, 6-2, 6-4. Olmedo, a native of Peru who plays for the United States, was more fortunate at Wimbledon, in England, where he triumphed earlier in the season as did the peppery

Maria Bueno of Brazil charges the net in her semifinal match at Wimbledon, England. She won the match and later the title.

Neale Fraser of Australia reaches for the ball in a match at Forest Hills. He won the match and later the United States singles prize.

297

Miss Bueno in the women's singles series.

Bernard Bartzen of Dallas defeated Whitney Reed of Alameda, California, in straight sets, 6-0, 8-6, 7-5 in the national clay court men's singles final. Sally Moore of Bakersfield, California, conquered Sandra Reynolds of South Africa in the women's final.

For the seventh straight year Pancho

Gonzales took the professional championship indoor honors at Cleveland. He was also the leading money winner on the tour of top pros, although Lew Hoad of Australia outscored him in their individual matches.

Fraser and Roy Emerson won the United States doubles, downing Olmedo and Earl Bucholz, 3-6, 6-3, 5-7, 6-4, 7-5.

FOOTBALL

Syracuse University, with a powerful and versatile team, ran up tremendous scores and was superb on defense. Syracuse gained recognition as the strongest team in the country according to both the Associated Press and United Press polls.

Navy, defeated by Syracuse 32 to 6, came back with one of the most inspired of all its service victories when it stampeded Army, 43 to 12, before 100,000 fans at

Philadelphia. This Navy score was the highest ever registered by a winning team in the historic service sports rivalry. Army tied with the Air Force Academy, 13 to 13, in their interservice competition.

Wisconsin won the Big Ten championship to qualify for the oldest of the Bowl tests—the Rose Bowl—against the University of Washington, coholder with Southern California and the University of California

Syracuse back Robert Hart (19) reaches for a pass but West Virginia's Dick Herrig (25) bats it away.

Carrying the ball, Notre Dame end Monty Stickles is tripped by Angelo Coia of Southern California.

PHOTOS, WIDE WORLD

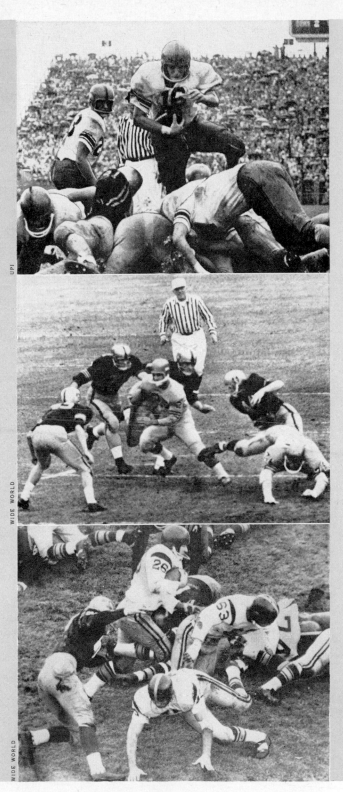

Syracuse-Navy: here Gerhard Schwedes plunges over line for Syracuse touchdown. Syracuse won 32-6.

Army-Navy: Joe Bellino breaks through Army for a twelve-yard gain. Navy won game 43-12.

Notre Dame—Southern California: Jerry Traynham (26) fights through Notre Dame's line.

at Los Angeles of the Big Five title on the Pacific Coast.

In the East, Pennsylvania replaced Dartmouth as Ivy League champion and Harvard was tops in the Big Three. Oklahoma triumphed in the Big Eight for the twelfth consecutive year; Clemson in the Atlantic Coast Conference; Connecticut in the Yankee Conference; Virginia Military Institute in the Southern; and Georgia in the Southeastern.

Texas Christian, Texas and Arkansas tied for leading honors in the Southwestern Conference; North Texas State and Houston in the Missouri Valley; Wyoming conquered in the Skyline; Arizona State College in the Border; Tennessee Tech in the Ohio Valley; Bowling Green in the Mid-American; and Idaho State in the Rocky Mountain. In Middle Atlantic contests, Delaware proved best in the university division, Albright in the northern college division, and Johns Hopkins in the southern college division.

OTHER SPORTS

The Indianapolis Athletic Club gained the men's outdoor swimming title with 102 points as compared to 71 for the Los Angeles Athletic Club in second place. It was touch and go in the women's outdoor swimming as the Berkeley YWCA outscored runner-up Santa Clara Swimming Club, 76 to 75.

Indoors, the University of Southern California gained the men's honors with 62 points while Berkeley YWCA tallied 78 to lead the women's competition.

The 1959 Kentucky Derby, a $163,750 race, went to Tomy Lee over Sword Dancer by a nose, as Willie Shoemaker rode the winner brilliantly. In the 83rd running of the Preakness, though, it was Royal Orbit by a four-length margin over Sword Dancer. In the last of the famous trio of American horse races, Sword Dancer, piloted by Shoemaker, placed first in the Belmont Stakes.

Parthia, ridden by Harry Carr, took the 180th Epsom Derby and a $101,018 first prize in the English racing classic.

Before a crowd of 48,000, Jamin, the French champion, won the first International Championship Trot at Roosevelt Raceway in Long Island. Eight trotters— one each from France, Norway, Germany, Sweden, Canada and the United States and two from Italy—competed.

Wisconsin outraced Syracuse for a surprising victory in the International Racing Association Regatta.

For the second straight year, 16-year-old Bobby Fischer of Brooklyn won the United States chess championship.

Thirty-eight-year-old Roger Ward of Los Angeles raced the Indianapolis 500-mile automobile route in the record speed of 135.857 miles per hour, but barely led home Jim Rathmann by a matter of 23 seconds. The crowd at the race approximated 200,000.

Best-in-show at the Westminster show at Madison Square Garden was a black miniature poodle, Ch. Fontclair Festoon.

A thrilling finish at the Kentucky Derby: Tomy Lee, on the rail, beats out Sword Dancer. First Landing is third.

ALL PHOTOS, WIDE WORLD

Aquaplaners and water skiers skim placid waters of mountain lake and seaside lagoon.

WATER SKIING

By DICK POPE, JR.
Champion Water Skier

TODAY, water skiing is probably the most rapidly growing sport in the world. On lakes, bays, rivers and even oceans, from Hong Kong to Florida, water-sports enthusiasts from six to sixty can be seen skimming over the water on skis. The first skis were invented in 1924 by the late Fred Waller, inventor of Cinerama. Waller was first seen riding around on skis of his own design on Long Island Sound. Shortly thereafter, the talented inventor applied for patents on his water skis, and it is certainly he who earned the title of the "Father of Water Skiing."

Waller's Akwa Skis resembled the aquaplane in principle. Each ski was attached to a rope connected to a bridle, which in turn was pulled by the boat. In 1928, Dick Pope, Sr., made skiing history by riding a pair of skis over a low wooden ramp, thus becoming the first man to jump water skis. Not long after, in 1929, water skiing was begun on the Riviera. Count Pulaski and a girl companion were aquaplaning when the girl fell into the water. To keep the riderless aquaplane from causing an accident, the Count placed one foot on each board. A few days later the Count had constructed two narrow aquaplanes 6 feet long and 12 inches wide with rubber bands for foot binders and became the first man to ski on the Mediterranean. This same year in

301

the Alps, a group of officers from the famous Chasseurs Alpins were attempting to ski on the water with snow skis. Finding them too narrow, they constructed a shorter, wider ski with boots for a foot binder.

In the United States, the pioneers of water skiing were busy improving equipment and attempting new and harder stunts on skis. Bruce Parker was to evolve as the first actual instructor of water skiing and later the national champion when he won the First American National Water Ski Tourney, at Jones Beach in 1939.

In 1939 the American Water Ski Association was organized to stimulate interest in the sport, disseminate information and sanction and govern competition. The AWSA today has numerous purposes: promoting water skiing, authorizing tournaments or exhibitions and setting up rules and governing contests. The AWSA approves and certifies records of performances in the sport.

In 1946 the World Water Ski Union was formed, uniting the American and European associations and co-ordinating skiing efforts between the continents.

Skiing for everyone, not just professionals, has become ever more popular with the introduction of bigger and more powerful outboard engines and boats. Now it is possible for anyone to own his own boat

PESKIN, FPG

Skimming over the water gives a sense of freedom and power that even snow skiing cannot surpass. An occasional spill is part of the fun. However, no one who cannot swim should take up the sport.
MILLER, FPG

Water skiing is fascinating to watch as well as to do. Skilled performers skiing in intricate formations make living pictures, swift and graceful as ballet.

and skis. The retiring champions are going into ski-manufacturing businesses, safety equipment and boat-motor companies. Experts are planning and testing the equipment you buy in sports stores.

Before World War II, boats were almost solely in the yacht and launch class. Immediately after the war, however, boating began to boom. First, smaller inboards began to show themselves; then outboard-motor manufacturers began producing, in record volume, newer and more powerful motors. Boating began to grow into America's largest participating sport, and along with it water skiing.

When Fred Waller patented his original Akwa Skis in 1925, a new business was born. At present, there are numerous ski factories around the world, where new models are being tested and designed on a year-round basis. There are many types of skis. Trick skis average 54 inches long and 8 inches wide in the center and in most cases taper to rounded edges at front and back. These skis are used in the performing of tricks in competition. The slalom ski varies in length with an average of about 68 inches. It is used in competition for the slalom course, and you will see many noncompetitive skiers using the slalom for sheer enjoyment. It has a full binder and a half binder mounted right behind it to enable the skier to keep both feet on its narrow surface, about 7 inches wide; also a deep, metal fin is used instead of the usual shallow, wooden one. Jumping skis are heavier and more sturdy. Their sole purpose is to take the terrific punishment that a water skier gives them when he lands sharply on the water after a long flight through the air. They are 72 inches by 6½ inches; they will weigh approximately 19 pounds. The standard ski, for everyone from beginners to pros, is 68 inches long and 6¾ inches wide and weighs about 15 pounds. The evolution of water-skiing equipment has kept pace with the rapid growth of the sport and will continue to do so.

A frogman explores the depths of the Mediterranean on a new one-man submarine, the Pegasus.

UNDERWATER SWIMMING

By JAMES DUGAN
Secretary, United States Liaison
Committee for Oceanographic Research

AMERICA'S fastest-growing sport today is free diving and underwater swimming. Since 1951, when the original aqualung was introduced into the United States, automatic compressed-air breathing devices have freed the undersea explorer from helmets and lines to the surface.

Although free diving is as old as man's quest for underwater food, pearls, sponges, coral and pearl shell, the modern free-diving sport was inspired by the humorous writer Guy Gilpatric. He began diving with goggles in the Mediterranean Sea in 1928 and wrote the first book on the sport, *The Compleat Goggler,* in 1938.

World War II frogmen wore masks and flippers, and oxygen-breathing "lungs," which do not allow safe submersion below thirty-five feet. The compressed-air aqualung, invented in 1943 by the underwater explorer Captain Jacques-Yves Cousteau and the engineer Emile Gagnan, allows free divers to go safely into greater depths. Cousteau was coauthor of a best-selling

book, *The Silent World,* 1953, and made a film of the same name in 1956.

Beginners are usually attracted by hunting fish with spear guns. As they become sportsmen, divers abandon fish-sticking. The happiest free divers today are those who observe nature under water, photograph it and explore sunken wrecks.

Divers started the science of underwater archaeology. Off Marseilles, France, they have salvaged a third-century B.C. Greek ship buried in the floor 130 feet down. In Sweden they are bringing up warships sunk in the seventeenth century. A young American diver, Peter Throckmorton, has surveyed more than thirty ancient wrecks in the eastern Mediterranean, dated from the first century B.C. to the eighth century A.D. In the Florida Keys, Arthur McKee is taking gold and silver from a Spanish ship sunk in 1733. Free divers have penetrated deep in sacred wells of the Incas, Maya and Aztec to bring up treasures. In Florida springs they have found masto-

L. WILLINGER, SHOSTAL

Combining sport with business, a Laguna Beach couple test underwater equipment of their own design and manufacture. Later they will put it on the market.

Midwest also has thousands of enthusiasts who dive in the Great Lakes, rivers and dams and even sometimes under the ice in winter.

Among the more than five hundred diving clubs in the country, there are all-girl clubs, junior clubs, mixed clubs and some that keep their membership low by requiring very high standards of proficiency under water. In February 1959, United States clubs and councils united in the Underwater Society of America, which stresses sport, science and safety. The "USA" is a member of the World Underwater Confederation, to which thirty nations belong. It conducts international diving and flipper-swimming competitions and promotes scientific exploration beneath the surface.

When they dive, divers place a special flag on a buoy above them so that boats will not run them down as they enter and leave the water. (The diver's flag is a red square with a diagonal white stripe.) Experienced divers never go down alone. The essence of underwater safety and enjoyment is the "buddy system" followed by United States Navy free divers. The pro-

don bones; in the St. Lawrence River and Lake Champlain, wrecks of the War of 1812. They are searching for the second ironclad, the USS Monitor, off Cape Hatteras, and for sunken relics of the vikings in Cape Cod. When you visit the United Nations headquarters in New York, take a good look in the main lobby at the magnificent statue of the Greek sea-god Poseidon. The original was found under the sea by free divers. In order to benefit from each other's skills, divers and archaeologists have recently formed the Council for Underwater Archaeology.

The best diving in the Western Hemisphere is around the Florida Keys, Bermuda and the West Indies, where the water is usually warm and clear and filled with glorious corals and tropical fish. As you go farther north the water becomes colder and visibility lessens. Despite that, the busiest diving area is off the North Atlantic states, which have passed Southern California in the number of divers. The

Law and order do not stop at the water's edge: two New York State troopers equipped with rubber diving suits begin an underwater search at Peck's Quarry for spear guns used illegally by some amateur divers.

RICHARD MCWAIN, SHOSTAL

St. Andrews State Park, Panama City, Florida: a skin diver prepares for some underwater fishing, chiefly mangrove snappers, groupers and cravelle.

ROBERT LEAHY, SHOSTAL

cedure for breathing compressed air in varying water pressures is governed by strict laws known as diving tables. The deeper down the less time the diver may spend without risk of the bends, a crippling, sometimes fatal, disease. The greatest hazard for beginners, however, is air embolism, caused by retaining compressed air in the lungs while swimming up into lighter water pressure. As the diver rises, the air inside him expands, rupturing the lungs and causing other internal injuries. To avoid air embolism, divers must breathe naturally and regularly at all times. Compressed-air devices are safe for the beginner to about 90 feet; for experienced divers to 150 feet; but even the most experienced person is in danger below that.

Conditions that affect divers in relation to pressure are not due to pressure itself but to the effects of breathing compressed air under pressure. Thirty-three feet beneath the surface the pressure of the at-

mosphere is doubled. It is tripled at 66 feet, and so on down. The aqualung automatically feeds air at the exact compression needed to withstand the water pressure at any depth. The bends are avoided very easily by observing the time and depth tables, just as air embolism may be avoided by breathing evenly during all levels of compressed-air diving.

Most kinds of accidents can be prevented by always going under with one or more friends as an underwater-exploring team. If the basic laws are observed, free diving is a safe sport. Fractures and muscular injuries are almost unknown, and negligence kills only the negligent diver himself.

Free diving is sometimes incorrectly called "skindiving," a term originally used to describe Polynesians who dive nearly naked, without breathing apparatus. Free divers employ compressed-air lungs and wear rubber suits against the cold. The free diver's skin is not seen.

The longest time an active swimmer

SOCONY MOBIL OIL CO.

Forty feet down in the Gulf of Mexico, geologists study the sediments of the continental shelf for clues in the search for ancient oil deposits.

The Mediterranean is a rich field for the underwater explorer for it is strewn with the wreckage of three thousand years. Here a diver nears the weed-covered bones of a sunken ship.

can stay under water on one breath of air is not much more than two minutes. With a compressed-air lung the time you can spend "downstairs" in one dive is not determined so much by the amount of air in your bottles as by the diving tables. However, you should make absolutely certain before a dive that your bottles hold enough compressed air for the dive you have planned. If you have a junior air bottle, holding 38 cubic feet of compressed air, you can safely stay down at not more than 10 feet for 30 minutes and at 50 feet for 15 minutes.

Rubber foot fins add 40 per cent more power to the diver's kick and are very useful to topside swimmers as well. The airtight face mask brings underwater scenes in focus and is a great help to the surface swimmer since it keeps water out of the eyes and nose.

Free divers regard themselves as the only true "space men," since they swim "weightlessly" in three dimensions in the watery depths. The best divers pride themselves on lazy, almost effortless movement, using the feet only.

Today public-spirited diving clubs aid the police in recovering bodies, submerged cars and stolen goods; serve as instructors in public-bathing places; and make up volunteer rescue squads for Civil Defense.

Scientists, particularly oceanographers —those who study the oceans—have added diving lungs to their working tools.

A new field of skilled work is opening up for free divers in underwater engineering. Submerged pipelines are being laid in many parts of the world, supervised by divers. They also work in harbors, dams and shipyards. Diving geologists are employed by oil companies at offshore wells. Diving clubs often assist fish-and-wildlife boards in surveying oyster beds, taking fish censuses and conducting scientific observations under water. As mankind harvests more food from the sea and gathers more natural resources hidden in the depths, the free diver will become an explorer, the roamer of a new frontier.

The best free-diving tables are in *The Complete Manual of Free Diving*, compiled by the French Navy Undersea Research Group. A monthly organ of diving is *The Skin Diver*, Lynwood, California.

JOSEPH COSTA, KING FEATURES SYNDICATE

SPORTS

Below, sky diver leaving plane and assuming basic stable position: arms and legs spread, face down, body parallel to earth.

CHARLES JACKSON, ATLANTA "JOURNAL"

SPORT PARACHUTING

By JACQUES ANDRÉ ISTEL
President, Parachutes, Incorporated

Sky diving is the popular name for sport parachuting. As an international competitive sport it has had a tremendous growth in Europe since the end of World War II and more recently in the United States and Canada. Competitions include a world championship held every two years.

In a parachute meet the object is to land directly on target, with points awarded for form and style in the air. It is very much like a high-diving competition. Accuracy in landing is the distance measured in meters or yards from the center of a target, usually in the shape of a cross, to the first point of impact of the parachutist. New steerable parachutes, accurate methods of wind measurement and increased skill of partici-

Left, the parachutist is in free fall after he has cleared the plane.
Right, successive steps in the opening of the parachute.

pants in the sport have led to spectacular world records.

World records are based upon average distance on two successive jumps. In 1957 two world's records were made: 12.4 feet with parachute open at 1,000 meters (3,280 feet) and 3.4 feet with parachute open at 1,500 meters (4,920 feet). The record with parachute open at 600 meters (1,968 feet) is 8.6 feet from the center of the target. It was made in 1958. These records will no doubt soon be broken.

Style is judged while the contestant is in free fall (the interval after leaving the aircraft and before opening the parachute). In competition this interval varies from 20 seconds in some events to 40 seconds in others. Since parachutes, for reasons of safety, should be opened at 2,000 feet above the ground, the jump altitude for a 20-second delay is 5,000 feet and for a 40-second delay it is 8,500 feet. Contestants are required to assume the basic stable position. In this position the arms and legs are spread, the face is down and the body is approximately parallel to the ground. In certain events the contestant is required to keep his body on a given heading during the 20-second free fall. He is penalized for buffeting (rocking of the body). He is also penalized for fishtailing (a horizontal swaying motion). If the contestant falls on the side he loses 30 per cent of his style points. A back to earth position (except in controlled loops) or a disordered fall results in his disqualification.

In longer free-fall pure-style events the contestant is required to make precise maneuvers within certain time limits. These have included 360° horizontal turns to the left and right and backward loops. During competition the actual sequence of turns to be performed is given by visual signal from the ground while the contestant is in free fall. This requires the parachutist to think and make decisions during his descent. This event is judged solely on style during free fall and ends when the parachutist opens his parachute at 2,000 feet.

Interesting sky-diving exercises include relative work, that is, controlled free fall by two or more parachutists. An experienced parachutist knows how to vary his rate of descent while maintaining stability. The combination of controlled forward speed, controlled turns and a variable rate of descent has made it possible for a baton to be passed back and forth from one parachutist to another during free fall. This feat was first accomplished in France in 1957 and, as skill and techniques have improved, it has become almost commonplace.

Another example of relative work is the crossover, in which two parachutists crisscross over each other's path in the sky during a delayed fall lasting from 40 to 60 or more seconds. This is far easier to accomplish than passing the baton.

Hitting the target from a high altitude

Other high altitude exercises are judged solely upon precision in landing. In the air under light wind conditions a parachutist can track, or drift, approximately half a mile in any direction during a 50-second free fall. Failure to point properly (direct his body during free fall) to the opening point indicated by a wind drift indicator may cause the parachutist to miss the target by a wide margin. Accurate landings

from high altitudes not only require good style in free fall but also the ability to sail an open parachute.

Equipment used in sky diving includes two parachutes on a single harness, the main chute worn on the back and the reserve on the chest. Boots, a helmet and coveralls are also necessary. Special, highly maneuverable sport parachutes with a reduced opening and landing shock are normally used. Free fall parachutists also use a stop watch and an altimeter mounted on an instrument board which fits on the reserve parachute. Non-fogging plastic goggles and gloves complete the basic equipment for sky diving.

The sport has a remarkable safety record

The outstanding safety record of sport parachuting may seem strange, but no fatalities have occurred in sport parachuting conducted in accordance with the basic safety regulations of the Parachute Club of America.

In the United States the sport of parachuting is controlled by the Parachute Club of America, a nonprofit affiliate of the National Aeronautic Association and official representative of the Fédération Aéronautique Internationale for parachuting matters. Lieutenant General James M. Gavin, who commanded the 82d Airborne Division in World War II, heads the board of directors of the P.C.A.

In May 1959 the P.C.A. opened the first sport parachuting center in America at Orange, Massachusetts. The parachute instructor examination of the Parachute Club of American is very stiff. It covers theoretical knowledge; practical parachute rigging; demonstration of complete control during free fall in the horizontal, vertical and longitudinal axes of the body; ability to vary forward glide and rate of descent; and ability to follow safely and judge a student during free fall.

Yankee Bat Boy

By PAT FERRY
as told to Harold Rosenthal

THERE will be other jobs, other interests in my life when I finish college and enter what I hope will be some field in communications, but I know that my years as bat boy with the New York Yankees will always loom large in my memory. It isn't because the Yankees were the best in baseball during the years when I was with them, but because being a bat boy for any major-league club is a rare privilege that comes only to a handful of boys. Luck has to play a big part in getting the job.

Many people think there are only sixteen bat boys in the big leagues. Actually there are three times that number. Each club has a bat boy: for the home team; to look after the visiting club; and a ball boy.

311

This job may not seem important until you remember how annoyed the people in the stands get when a game is held up for even a few seconds waiting for balls. As a new recruit you usually start out as ball boy, then you become bat boy for visiting teams. Finally you reach the home team's dugout and on-deck circle, where you kneel alongside some of the greatest sluggers of the game as they await their chance to knock one out of the park.

After that you may go to college and then on to something else, although there have been bat boys who stayed with the job for ten or twelve years. One was Charley DiGiovanna, of the Dodgers. He was married and the father of several children when he suffered a fatal heart attack last year. DiGiovanna was a bat boy who had broken in at Ebbets Field and had moved to the West Coast with the Dodgers.

My most important move came last year (1959) when I graduated from Archbishop Molloy High School, in New York, and entered Fordham University—I'm getting a little ahead of the story.

Like most American boys I played sandlot ball. Little League baseball was not organized in my section of New York in those days, although my younger brothers have since played in the Little Leagues.

My father was always a baseball fan. He would take me to both Yankee Stadium and the Polo Grounds, formerly the home of the Giants. I remember my first baseball autograph was that of Wes Westrum, the Giant catcher. I stuck a program through the screen behind home plate, and he obligingly put his signature on it.

Westrum signed the program in pencil, and during the game the perspiration from my hands rubbed out the signature. I was shattered at the end of the game to discover it had disappeared. One day a big East-West sand-lot game was put on at the Polo Grounds by a national newspaper chain. One of the men connected with it lived in my neighborhood. One day in the summer of 1955 he asked me whether I would like to work as the visiting-team bat boy at the Yankee Stadium—the regular boy had gone on vacation. Would I!

The next year, I was the regular visiting-team bat boy, and the following year I moved up to the role of Yankee bat boy which I have held for three seasons.

The pay hasn't been too much, but there have been several World Series shares voted me by the generous ballplayers which will help send me through college. More important even than this are the friendships I have made with such men as Bob Turley, Tony Kubek, Bobby Richardson and Hank Bauer, to name only a few. There just isn't enough money in the United States Mint to buy that kind of relationship.

High points of my career with the Yankees have been the western trips the club has given me each year. As I said, each club in the majors is supposed to supply a visiting-club bat boy; but there's a gift of a trip of approximately two weeks when you visit cities like Detroit, Cleveland, Chicago and Kansas City.

Like a lot of New Yorkers I had never been farther west than just across the Hudson River. It was a revelation. With the team I lived at the best hotels. There were the big games in ball parks I had never seen before, and there was swimming in the daytime (most of the road games are at night) with such fine men as Bobby Shantz, Bob Richardson and Bob Turley.

It isn't all play though. There is work to

be done and it must be done promptly, without fuss or getting rattled. You must have the bats in their proper places in the bat rack in the dugout at the right time; you have to be there with the bats when the players go up to the plate, and you have to learn the mannerisms of each.

For instance, there's the weighted bat. This is a regular bat made extra heavy with lead, which the batter swings before he goes up to the plate. His regular bat is supposed to feel a lot lighter after he's swung this along with two or three other bats. The bat boy has to be right there as the batter gets rid of it, and every batter does this in a different way. Some players hand it to you, others let it swing out from their wrist, and you must be there to catch it. Others roll it toward you.

You must have the right batting helmet ready for each player. When hitters go up to the plate in a tight situation they don't want to have to scramble around first trying to match up their bat and their helmet. There have been stories about one player using another's bat by mistake and starting on a hitting streak, but mostly the players want their own bats—and in the right slot in the bat rack.

It's the same with the ball boy. A major-league game will start with fifty-six balls, all rubbed with that special mud the umpires use to take the factory gloss off. When the plate umpire motions for more balls he wants them right away; he doesn't want to wait while you rummage through a box for them. And when the supply dwindles in the late innings, because of losses

through fouls and so forth, he doesn't want to have to hold up the game while you race back into the clubhouse to get a new supply. You must anticipate.

While a player's job is over when the game ends, the bat boy's task is far from done. He has to make sure that all the bats, helmets, resin bags, pitchers' jackets and so forth are returned to the clubhouse. He must run a quick eye along the bench for stray gloves or caps that are fair game for any souvenir hunters. And he has to be on the alert for souvenir hunters in the strangest places. Like groundskeepers for rival clubs.

I wore a Yankee uniform just like all the players except it had no number. I warmed up on the field every day, usually catching with either Mickey Mantle or Enos Slaughter. Well before the game my working day opened with an errand or two for the players. I handled the fan mail for several players who got swamped with it, and after the game I still had to make myself available before I took off for home.

During the season a bat boy's life is a lot like a player's. He will have to eat at odd hours and work until the job is done. Unlike a player he won't sleep late after a night game, either early in the season or in the last month—not when he has an 8:30 class next morning.

But bat boys are younger than players and sleep doesn't mean so much. I've read about a star infielder of the Giants—the Giants of John McGraw's championship days—who once exclaimed in a burst of enthusiasm, "It's great to be young, and a Giant." In my case it could be changed just a little. "It's great to be young, and the Yankee bat boy."

Young People's Books of the Year

By CLAUDIA LEWIS

Specialist in Children's Literature,
Bank Street College of Education

IT is a difficult thing indeed to write a review of the outstanding young people's books of the year. In the first place, many good books will certainly be overlooked, since no one reviewer could possibly read them all; and secondly, in the selection he makes, the reviewer cannot avoid reflecting his own personal tastes. The best books for you are the ones that excite you and touch your own feelings, regardless of what anyone else has to say.

The reviewer is bound to make mistakes, too, when he tries to indicate whether a book is for a younger or an older child. Some of the best books are hard to classify, especially the so-called picture books, which I am going to discuss first. Take, for example, *The Moon Jumpers* by Janice May Udry, illustrated by Maurice Sendak. This striking book is one many of you may want to return to year after year. It will remind you of the magical summer evenings when you ran barefoot in the grass around the house before you were called in to bed; it will help you to remember when you are older what it was like being a child. Barbara Cooney's *Chanticleer and the Fox* (winner of the Caldecott Medal for the most distinguished picture book of the year) is another to delight almost anyone, young or old. The bright blue and orange colors in many of the illustrations are so beautiful that one turns again and again to look at them.

The story is an adaptation of Chaucer's old fable of the cock and the fox, and it makes very good reading. In Antonio Frasconi's sophisticated picture book, *The House That Jack Built: A Picture Book in Two Languages,* boys and girls of any age who are interested in French will enjoy the old familiar rhyme in both French and English. In *The Pointed Brush* by Patricia Miles Martin, illustrator Roger Duvoisin has created authentic Chinese atmosphere. He has also given us as lovely a page of Chinese writing as one could find in any storybook. The pointed brush, of course, is the equivalent of a pen in China. What little Sixth Son accomplishes through his ability to write a letter in an emergency makes a story that will satisfy readers of many ages and tastes. *Houses from the Sea* by Alice E. Goudey, illustrated with color drawings by Adrienne Adams, is an exceptionally beautiful book about the shells that can be found on the beach in the summertime, a picture book for all members of the family.

Lovers of fairy stories will want to read Mary Norton's *The Borrowers Afloat,* her third book about those miniature, imaginary people who must make a living in secret in the human world. Perhaps the best way to suggest the special appeal of this book is to ask you to imagine that you are only six inches high and have to construct a stove for yourself out of an old

ADAPTED AND ILLUSTRATED BY BARBARA COONEY; PUBLISHED BY THOMAS Y. CROWELL

ILLUSTRATED BY ANTONIO FRASCONI; PUBLISHED BY HARCOURT, BRACE AND COMPANY

WRITTEN BY PATRICIA MILES MARTIN, ILLUS. BY ROGER DUVOISIN; PUB., LOTHROP, LEE & SHEPARD CO.

At the left in each row above is the picture on the jacket of
the book; at the right is a double page from the same book.

315

door lock and find a way to sleep comfortably in an abandoned teakettle. The Borrowers manage very well in spite of many narrow escapes. *The Long-nosed Princess* by Priscilla Hallowell is patterned after the old fairy tales but written with modern accents, and its princess—a particularly charming young lady in spite of her long nose—is one to remember for a long time. Harold W. Felton's *New Tall Tales of Pecos Bill* tells the story of that fabulous Texas cowpuncher who could shave himself with the shadow of his bowie knife. This book gets my vote for the best young people's storybook of the year. No one of you should miss the tale about Bill and his horse saving themselves from falling with a crash into the Grand Canyon, when they make an unsuccessful attempt to leap across. An exciting adventure story for those of you who are about eight to twelve is *The Treasure of the High Country* by Jonreed Lauritzen. This is a fast-moving, weird story of danger, bandits and the daring of two young boys when they go to search for their little sister, lost in the fantastic cliff country of northern Arizona. *The Perilous Road* by William O. Steele is just as exciting. A dramatic, swiftly moving story, full of Tennessee mountain flavor, it tells of an eleven-year-old boy who tries to take part in the Civil War, when the soldiers are stationed near his home. After many harrowing experiences he makes the discovery that all soldiers—no matter what side they fight on—are human beings.

A number of superior short novels for older boys and girls appeared this year. *The Witch of Blackbird Pond* by Elizabeth George Speare (winner of the John Newbery Medal for "the most distinguished contribution to American literature for children") is outstanding for its lively picture of life in Puritan New England and for its very appealing sixteen-year-old heroine. Kit Tyler has that

Two fine books on nature study.

courage to follow her own "different" path which is the mark of strength in any young person. When you read about her you will feel some of her inner fire. *Southtown* by Lorenz Graham presents an intimate picture of the life of a Negro family in the rural South today. Sixteen-year-old David lived in a quiet home, where "the warm kitchen smelled of vanilla," until a series of shocking and terrifying events shattered its peace. This book has the highest respect for the reader: it assumes a mature interest in current social problems and an ability to see the point of view of both sides, while offering him a dramatic and powerful story. In *Land of Foam* by Ivan Yefremov, a book of epic scope and sweep, the reader is carried from ancient Greece and Crete to the Egypt of the Pharaohs, and the jungles of Africa as he follows the perilous adventures of a young Greek sculptor struggling to escape from captivity.

Two books with African settings deserve special mention—*The Lion's Whiskers* by Russell Davis and Brent Ashabranner, a collection of Ethiopian folk tales, and Elizabeth Marshall Thomas' *The Harmless People,* a best seller on adult book lists this year. Mrs. Thomas, when she was a young woman in her twenties, went with her anthropologist parents to live for two years among the African Bushmen of the Kalahari Desert. Her book is not so much anthropology as it is a work of art—a beautiful and exciting picture of the daily lives of these most primitive people, for whom survival is sometimes a matter of digging pits to lie in to escape the burning desert heat. Also dealing with the customs and lives of people who differ radically from ourselves is Ruth Underhill's *First Came the Family.* The reader learns why in China, for instance, young people have been content to let their parents decide whom they shall marry and why adolescence in many parts of the world is lacking in the frictions so well known here. *Indians* by Edwin Tunis, another fine book that might be called anthropology for beginners, is notable for the beautiful detail of its more than 230 accurate drawings. Mr. Tunis is interested in Indian ingenuity—he tells us how they carried fire in shells and how they managed to avoid walking in circles when they were lost—but he also presents them as human beings basically like ourselves.

Of the many excellent books in the broad field of science I am going to mention three. *The Wonderful World of the Air* by James Fisher is a history of flight, from the earliest flying fish to the gliding snakes of Borneo, from the early kites to the latest rockets and jets. Illustrated with a lavish variety of colorful charts, photographs and paintings, it presents a panorama you will pore over for hours. *The Clock We Live On* by Isaac Asimov provides an exhilarating introduction to the tricky world of time and the complications accounting for some puzzling phenomena —such as the strange fact that George

Washington's birthday was once correctly celebrated on February 11, though now, as we all know, the date is February 22. *Science in Your Own Backyard* by Elizabeth K. Cooper suggests a whole summer of exploration and activity, with clear instructions for such projects as setting up worm farms, collecting and preserving spider webs and studying the eating habits of birds.

Many of the new biographies deserve wide reading. Among them is Rachel Baker's *America's First Trained Nurse: Linda Richards,* which presents a fascinating picture of life inside hospitals seventy-five years ago and the struggles of one woman to improve conditions. Another, *Pioneer Surgeon: Dr. Ephraim McDowell* by Josephine Rich, is the stirring life story of the doctor who was the first to operate on the human abdomen.

In closing, I want to mention two books of poetry which may give some of you as much pleasure as any of the books reviewed here. *Blackbird in the Lilac* by James Reeves has something for everyone. As for me, I am delighted with a poet who seems to know what cows would talk about if they could talk to each other as they graze! *A Way of Knowing: A Collection of Poems for Boys* compiled by Gerald D. McDonald brings together poems that are not usually included in anthologies, and they are witty, funny, tough and tender, just as Mr. McDonald suggests in his foreword.

The first book (left) is for younger readers; the other three are for older readers.

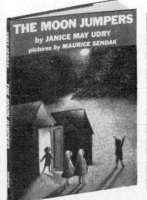

JANICE MAY UDRY
HARPER & BROTHERS

MARY NORTON
HARCOURT, BRACE & CO.

HAROLD W. FELTON
PRENTICE-HALL, INC.

ELIZABETH GEORGE SPEARE
HOUGHTON MIFFLIN COMPANY

YOUTH GROUPS

Three Girl Scouts demonstrate their skill in making pottery before the television cameras in a new series "Adventuring in the Hand Arts."

Girl Scouts' Adventure in Television

By SONDRA GORNEY
Girl Scouts of the U.S.A.

WHEN Girl Scouts of the United States ventured into nationwide educational television, they enlisted the aid of TV star Shari Lewis, a former Girl Scout. With Shari as hostess, they put on a ten-week series of half-hour programs called "Adventuring in the Hand Arts."

"Adventuring in the Hand Arts" revealed through films and discussion how people in many parts of the world still make things with their hands. The programs demonstrated skills in pottery, weaving, basketry, making toys and jewelry, masks, musical instruments, dolls and puppets, wood carving, and leathercraft.

Three different Girl Scouts appeared with Shari Lewis on each of the ten programs. They were Brownies (age 7-9), Intermediates (age 10-13) and Senior Scouts (age 14-17). With the guidance of a guest art expert, each girl created something beautiful and useful with her hands. One girl made an unusual wood carving, another a shoe-box mask, a third built a stringed instrument.

The guest experts told why people who live in remote corners of the world still use their hands to satisfy needs for food, shelter, adornment, religion, beauty and entertainment. Their materials, tools and techniques were seen on the film and demonstrated by the experts and the Scouts.

To ensure that the TV series was authentic, three nationally known authorities supervised the program for the Girl Scouts. The American Museum of Natural History lent valuable materials from their collection, for use on the programs.

In conjunction with "Adventuring in the Hand Arts," the Girl Scouts prepared a Leader's Guide and a Reading List. Girl Scout troops watched the television shows at their meetings, and leaders used the programs as a springboard to creative craft activities. Both the Guide and List were used in libraries, museums, churches, synagogues, schools and department stores. Many exhibits that featured the Girl Scout ETV series were shown throughout the country. Schools encouraged boys and girls to watch the series and relate it to their courses in art, history or contemporary civilization. "Golden Age" Clubs and hobby groups picked up valuable ideas from the show.

When the Girl Scout movement started almost a half century ago, it was a face-to-face program. Juliette Low, its founder, met with 12 girls in a room. Today, through the use of television, it is possible to reach as many as 12 million girls at one time. This series, which stressed a fresh approach to arts and crafts, was launched during the year when the Girl Scout theme was "You Can Count on Her to Be Creative."

4-H
Good Citizens

By FRANCES F. CLINGERMAN
U. S. Department of Agriculture

Boys and girls of the 4-H Clubs carry on many projects that help others as well as themselves. Most of the 2,250,000 young 4-H'ers serve their communities—besides improving their knowledge and skills—through a large variety of farming, home-making and other activities.

Nearly 800,000 members are now enrolled in citizenship projects, and about 874,000 share in farm, home and neighborhood safety programs of one kind or another. Those interested in accident and fire prevention work to remove hazards on the farm, in the home and around the neighborhood.

For example, 4-H boys in an Iowa county made red tags and signs to identify farm hazards in the area. At a special meeting, each member received fifty signs to attach to hazards on his own farm and those of co-operating farms: these tags to stay put until the hazards were corrected. A few weeks later, members invited their fathers and others to a safety meeting. Afterward they all took a tour to see how many red signs were left and to correct the remaining hazards on the spot. When the work was all done a picnic was held to honor those who took part.

In a North Carolina county, a 4-H group tore down ramshackle old farm buildings, put screens on porches and mended or made new porch steps for their neighbors. Kansas club members arranged safety window displays in business houses and put "No Smoking" signs on containers of gasoline and other combustibles. They also wrote short newspaper articles on safety, cut weeds on roadside corners to clear motorists' view of the highway and made first-aid kits for buildings on the State Fair grounds.

In a Colorado county, club boys and girls made and put up big road signs—enlarged route maps, diagrams and directional arrows—at all the main crossroads to save motorists' time and nerves.

In Utah where forty-seven members of eight clubs went on a painting spree, they got sixteen gallons of paint and painted the weather-beaten bleachers in the city ball park.

Some Vermont 4-H'ers built a neighborhood "swimming hole." In Missouri, 4-H'ers wired an old one-room schoolhouse for a community center, so that young people and grownups, who used the center, no longer had to use oil lamps every time a night meeting was held.

A favorite activity of most 4-H'ers is working for good causes—such as polio and other health funds. Many collect old eyeglasses and send them to "Eyes for the Needy," and provide baskets of food or gifts for the needy sick or aged at holiday time.

America's 4-H'ers truly believe that "Happiness adds and multiplies if you divide it with others."

Smokey Bear, symbol of fire prevention and forest conservation, greets two 4-H'ers visiting Washington, D. C.

Girl Guides at Home and Abroad

By DOROTHY C. HAMILTON
Girl Guides Association

CANADIAN Guides began their international visiting early in 1959. In the first week of January, eight Guides and two Guiders took flight from Vancouver and stopped in Honolulu long enough to enjoy meeting Girl Scouts there who showed them around. They then went on to Fiji. Continuing their flight they landed in Australia to attend an International Camp held near Melbourne. Despite an unprecedented heat wave, they enjoyed camping in the desert and had a wonderful time. After a visit in Australian homes, following the Camp, they flew back home.

As a result of a plan made at the 14th World Conference in Brazil in 1957, several Gatherings for Young Adults were held during 1959. Canada sent four young Guiders to Finland. The planning and staffing of the Gathering at Our Cabana in Mexico early in September were shared by Canada, the Girl Scouts of the United States, and Mexico. Canada sent one staff member and four delegates.

Early in July, sixty-four Canadian Guides, living in all parts of the country, journeyed by train and bus to Colorado where they encamped, "A mile high, a mile wide," with ten thousand Girl Scouts of the United States and Guides from other countries.

Visitor-Observer Exchanges with the United States were successfully completed. Two Girl Scout Leaders from the United States visited Canada for two months, one traveling in the eastern and one in the western provinces. Two Canadian Guiders enjoyed the same sort of arrangement in the United States, one traveling in the southeastern and the other in the southwestern states.

An important branch of International Guiding is the Canadian Guides on Foreign Soil. These are Rangers, Guides and Brownies whose fathers are serving with the Canadian armed forces abroad, stationed in France and Germany. A Camp was held in Germany for the Guides of these groups, organized by the German Girl Guides. Several times girls from these groups have been able to join up with Guides traveling from Canada and have attended Camps in Europe with their sisters from across the sea.

Whenever a Canadian Guide travels she brings back fresh ideas to her own Company and neighborhood. She sends to Headquarters any suggestions that may help other Canadian Guides. Travel is expensive, but there are Girl Guide centers throughout Europe where inexpensive accommodation can be secured. In our own hemisphere, Our Cabana in Mexico is ready to welcome visitors.

Four Greek Girl Guides show off their colorful national costumes while traveling in Canada during the summer.

In 1960, whether they be at home or abroad, the Girl Guides say "Thank you" to all who have shown kindness to Guiding throughout these fifty years of growth.

Boys' Club Amateur Cooks

By IRIS VINTON
Boys' Clubs of America

Appearing very professional in their tall chef's hats, three amateur cooks look over a winning sardine dish.

ONE of the unique characteristics of a Boys' Club is its diversified program. There is such a wide variety of activities that any boy can find something to interest him. He can be on a basketball team or take up tumbling in the gym. Or he can join a group of stamp collectors, catch up on his reading in the library or learn to play chess. There are arts and crafts, musical and dramatic groups—any number of activities that give boys who enjoy using their free time for self-improvement the opportunity to develop vocational skills and hobbies. They can even learn to cook—and not just the usual chuckwagon cookery that most boys learn on hikes and at camp. Boys' Club boys acquire real culinary skill.

In fact, cooking is so popular with boys that almost every Boys' Club has an enthusiastic group of young cooks. In some clubs the boys prepare and serve a dinner to the members of the board of directors of the Boys' Club. Many clubs conduct their own annual cooking contests and come out with winning dishes and recipes. Boys consider cooking fun and often a start toward a career. Several of these amateur cooks have gone on to become chefs in some of the most famous hotels in the nation.

Among the most recent explorers of this boys' interest in cooking food, as well as in eating it, has been the Maine Sardine Council. The council held, in co-operation with Boys' Clubs of America, a "Sardine Seacook" program involving Boys' Clubs in Maine, Connecticut, New York and Massachusetts. The project was focused on the nutritional aspects of a balanced diet, proper preparation of food and the furtherance of a healthy interest in helping to prepare family meals. Youngsters taking part in the project were asked to create their own sardine recipes, to prepare the dish and to take part in a competitive "cook-off."

The program won a reception that surprised even the most optimistic. Hundreds of boys in the four states enrolled, and a flood of sardine recipes was soon pouring in. There were burgers, croquettes, stuffed tomatoes, curries, spreads and many other creations using the sardine, as the Boys' Club members demonstrated their skill at cooking this particular fish.

The "cook-offs" proved to be of great interest to contestants and spectators alike and produced many examples of good cooking. The governors of various states met with the winners in their states to congratulate them. These states' winners, who ranged in age from nine to sixteen, met in a final grand "cook-off" on the famous rock-bound coast of Maine in the summer of 1959.

Three Horizon Club members (senior Camp Fire Girls) get together to fix some fancy outdoor cooking.

Camp Fire Jubilee

By ELIZABETH W. LESLIE
Camp Fire Girls, Inc.

GOLDEN Jubilee! That's something to sing about! Ever since its founding in 1910, Camp Fire Girls have been sharing fun and friendship, across the nation.

More than fifty years ago several brothers and sisters camped every summer on the shores of Lake Sebago in Maine with their parents, Dr. and Mrs. Luther Halsey Gulick. They swam, sailed, hiked, made pottery from local clay, wove native reeds and grasses, did metalwork and staged their own pageants and plays.

When fall came no one wanted to stop! Everyone had had such a good time and had enjoyed learning new skills and making beautiful things so much that they wanted to go right on through the winter. The boys could if they were Boy Scouts, but there were few such opportunities available to the girls. So Dr. and Mrs. Gulick and a group of interested educators developed a program that included many of the activities the girls had enjoyed so much during the summer, yet was adaptable to their lives at home. They called the new program Camp Fire Girls.

Fifty years is a long time and there have been many changes in our way of living. But there has never been a change in the desire of Camp Fire Girls to give service.

Camp Fire Girls have been giving a long, close look at their communities to see what they can do to preserve their natural assets. They have assisted in taking a census of trees; they have sown acres of seeds for new trees and shrubs; they have set out hundreds of saplings of various species to replace those destroyed by blight. Many a hungry bird has found seeds and suet awaiting him in the winter feeding stations made and placed by thoughtful Camp Fire Girls.

Horizon Club is the program for high-school girls. Here they find many opportunities for service to their communities. Some work as aides in hospitals or in homes for older citizens. Others work as trained attendants at baby-care stations or as assistants in the offices of community agencies during their annual campaigns. These jobs give a girl experience and help her decide her own future vocation.

The Blue Birds are the junior members of the program—girls from seven to ten years old, or in the second, third or fourth grades. When she is ten, or enters the fifth grade, a Blue Bird graduates into the Camp Fire program and starts to work in the Seven Crafts: Home; Creative Arts; Outdoors; Frontiers of Science; Business; Sports and Games; Citizenship.

Just as "Grandma was a Camp Fire Girl," the girls of today look forward to the time when they will be sharing the fun with their own granddaughters. And celebrating another Jubilee!

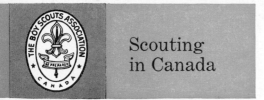

Scouting in Canada

By B. H. MORTLOCK
Boy Scouts of Canada

SINCE the close of World War II, in 1945, membership in the Boy Scouts of Canada has increased by 260 per cent, a much greater rate of increase than that of the population of the country. At the close of the war, there were 98,000 Wolf Cubs and Boy Scouts in Canada. Today there are well over 250,000, and numbers are rising rapidly.

To take care of this expansion, a new national headquarters for the Boy Scouts Association is being built in Ottawa. The new building will consist of a two-story section, housing the administrative offices, and a huge warehouse from which the uniforms, books and other equipment required for the operation of the program will be distributed.

The first national headquarters was located in the Banque canadienne nationale building in Ottawa. Later it moved to a site near the Parliament Buildings where the Confederation Building now stands. On the Confederation Building, erected in 1927 to commemorate the sixtieth anniversary of Confederation, are two Boy Scout figures, carved into the stone. They are placed there to commemorate the fact that this government building stands on the site of the second national headquarters, and also the fact that Canadian Scouts sought out the graves of all the Fathers of Confederation and decorated them during the year.

The third national headquarters was on the same street, immediately opposite the west block of the Parliament Buildings, and this site was occupied until the property on Metcalfe Street was purchased in 1931. This property has served as the national headquarters ever since. It was originally a private residence, built with castlelike battlements. Two additions were made to the building, as the organization grew, but it has now become quite inadequate. For a short time the building housed the Embassy of the Government of Japan and was also once the head office of the Canadian Forestry Association.

The new building is expected to serve the Boy Scouts of Canada for at least the next twenty years, but provision has been made in the plans for additional space.

An interesting feature of the new headquarters will be the museum. It will display many books, records and souvenirs of the early days of Scouting in this country, including many original Baden-Powell letters; Jamboree souvenirs; wartime badges; and an original Baden-Powell water color of the founder's last home, in Kenya. There will also be pictorial records of Baden-Powell's visits to Canada, in 1910, 1919, 1923 and 1935.

Old and new: present Scout headquarters, right, and the future building now being completed in Ottawa, below.

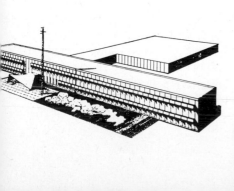

Boy Scouts' Safety Good Turn

By HERBERT W. LUNN
Boy Scouts of America

WHEN President Dwight D. Eisenhower requested the Boy Scouts of America to adopt "Safety" as a national service project, the entire movement was alerted for action. More than four million boys and adult leaders joined in this nationwide Safety Good Turn.

In developing their program of action the National Council of the Boy Scouts of America had four main aims.

1. To interest the youth of America in safety and, by doing so, reduce the tragic toll of accidental deaths and injuries.
2. To arouse public concern about accident prevention.
3. To co-operate with public officials, safety organizations and all those supporting the safety movement, by having members of the Boy Scouts plan and carry out safety projects.

4. To intensify the safety part of the Boy Scout program.

Everywhere during Boy Scout Week, citizens saw Scout safety work in the making. In Washington, D. C., twelve Explorers, representing Scouting's regions, told the President about their safety plans.

Mayors in communities from coast to coast proclaimed Scout Safety Days and Safety Weeks. In Detroit and Dallas, in Baltimore, and Butte, Montana—even in Hawaii, Alaska, Puerto Rico—boys put on huge shows, parades and pageants.

The safety-project book *Live for Tomorrow* was distributed to all units. It tells how to plan and carry out projects that teach safety.

During the program every Cub Scout pack, Boy Scout troop and Explorer post —enrolled as members of Scouting's safety team—went into action. They demonstrated traffic safety, outdoor and home safety. They worked on safety with sponsoring organizations, community groups, parents and neighboring units.

The whole safety program was divided into three general phases—traffic, outdoor and home safety projects. The traffic-safety phase included bicycle-safety checks, bike-riding road-e-o's, driver-safety literature distributions, window displays, traffic-safety surveys, pedestrian-safety leaflet distribution and driver-reaction testing projects.

The outdoor-safety program involved work on over 20,000 projects which included boating and canoeing demonstrations, swimming and water safety, forest-fire prevention, axmanship demonstrations and the clearance of hazards from vacant lots.

The home-safety phase of the program involved over 48,000 projects. These included home-safety demonstrations, window displays and the delivery of 36,000,-000 Civil Defense booklets to the homes of America.

Boy Scouts join with local police and firemen to learn how to combat a brush fire—an outdoor-safety project.

"THE HERALD-NEWS," PASSAIC-CLIFTON, N. J.

Not only fireproof but also heatproof; the suit's aluminum surface reflects 90 per cent of the heat from the blazing chair. The rest of the heat is absorbed by the quilted inner lining.

BERNARD NEWMAN

FIRE

The Great Destroyer

By L. A. VINCENT, *General Manager, National Board of Fire Underwriters*

THE cry of "Fire!"; the siren's wail; the fire engine's roar; all mean that somewhere flames are raging uncontrolled.

Only in comparatively recent times have measures been taken to prevent fires that destroy life and property. In spite of the progress made, property loss from fire still amounts to well over a billion dollars a year in the United States alone. In 1958 fire losses totaled $1,056,266,000. In addition, 11,500 persons died as a result of fire. Of these, about 1,800 were children.

Much of this loss of life and property was caused by fire in the home.

Reports from city fire chiefs show that there were 847,396 fires in 1957. Nearly half, or 400,858 of those fires, were building fires, and nearly three fourths of those building fires, or 288,704, were in residences.

Those figures are estimates of fires in cities of 2,500 population or more. They do not include all the fires that occurred in small communities or on farms.

325

Much of this destruction and loss of life—not just a portion of it—could most likely have been prevented.

What caused those fires that resulted in damage of over a billion dollars—money that could have been spent on schools or other useful things? The chief causes were the lighted match and smoking—careless use of matches, carelessly discarded cigarettes.

The National Board of Fire Underwriters has estimated from fire-insurance claims that matches and smoking accounted for 26 per cent of reported fire losses. The next major cause of fire is misuse of electricity. You often see examples

326

Forest-fire fighting. Helicopters are used to scout fires, to carry men and supplies from base depots to the fire line, to lay hose across rough areas and to take injured men to the nearest aid station.

of this: the octopus plug, frayed wiring, extension cords strung loosely or in places where they are hazards. Other causes are lightning and defective or overheated stoves, furnaces and boilers or their pipes.

Still other ways in which fires start are ignition of hot greases, overheated or defective chimneys or flues, hot ashes or coals, rubbish and litter. Once a blaze has begun, it may spread from room to room and from house to house, often far beyond its starting point. Of course, the farther it spreads the more difficult it becomes to get it under control.

It is said we learn from the past. So before beginning to learn how fire can be prevented and our homes and lives protected, let's go back more than 350 years to the first permanent English settlement in Virginia.

A year after the first three ships reached the marshy peninsula on the James River, the first recorded fire in North America burned down every house in the settle-

A fire lookout station in Gifford Pinchot National Forest. The lookout lives in the cabin, which has outward slanted windows of yellow-green glass to cut the glare of light.

After a forest fire is under control, fire tankers with pumps are used to cool down hot spots. This fire is in Bichota Canyon, in the Los Angeles National Forest, California.

ment. Captain John Smith wrote that it "destroyed most of our apparel, lodging and private provision." Thus, because of fire, fever and the attacks of unfriendly Indians, the colony almost had to be abandoned by the surviving settlers.

At Plymouth the Pilgrims didn't fare much better. There in 1623 Governor William Bradford recorded a fire that came very close to wiping out that little colony.

You can probably guess why the colonists were plagued by fire. Their homes were made of timber and thatched with

Battling a three-alarm tenement fire in a crowded section of Brooklyn, New York. Children playing in a nearby yard set fire to some rubbish and the fire got out of control.

ED HEAVEY

In November 1647, after Peter Stuyvesant became governor of the colony, he appointed fire wardens to enforce laws forbidding wooden chimneys and other fire hazards. Offending householders were subject to a fine of 25 florins—about $42. For every house a tax of one beaver, or 8 florins, was levied to provide for leather water buckets to use in fighting fires.

Peter Stuyvesant also appointed firemen. These men were called the Rattle Watch because of the noisemakers they used to sound the alarm. Eight of them, equipped with buckets and ladders, patrolled the streets of the little town. For the Massachusetts Bay Colony a fire regulation was enacted almost as soon as the colony was established. Lieutenant Governor Thomas Dudley wrote (in 1630), "We have ordered that no man shall build his chimney of wood, nor cover his house with thatch."

Many other cities developed fire-safety rules. Today, fire-prevention laws are in effect in nearly all communities. Before the adoption of these modern codes and before highly efficient methods of fire fighting were developed, great fires brought death and destruction to many cities.

In 1776, during the American Revolution, a fire broke out in New York, destroying nearly one quarter of the buildings in the semideserted city. Another destructive fire occurred in New York in 1835.

In St. Louis in 1849 a fire broke out in the steamboat White Cloud which was tied up at a wharf. When the blaze was finally put out it had destroyed twenty-three steamboats and burned fifteen city blocks to the ground. Portland, Maine, will never forget the Fourth of July in 1866. On that day a firecracker started a conflagration that destroyed 1,500 buildings.

straw—two very combustible substances.

In New Amsterdam, for instance, the first fire of record occurred when, in 1628, a thatched house caught fire from an overheated chimney and burned down. (Even today, overheated or defective chimneys or flues cause over 4 per cent of all fires.)

A smoke jumper for the Forest Service is parachuted down to an isolated spot in a burning forest area that cannot be reached except from the air.

Fire in Chicago. Rampaging flames driven by high winds swept through the town of Peshtigo, Wisconsin, and the area around it. The death toll of this disaster came to 1,152. The more famous fire in Chicago claimed 250 lives.

**Fires can occur
anywhere, at any time**

Such a disaster could easily happen today, and that is why Fire Prevention Week is held early in October every year: to gain public support in combating the loss of life and property by fire.

What can we do to help prevent fires? We can do two things: We can make our homes fire safe, and we can make our families fire-safety conscious. To do less is to gamble with lives and homes.

We can start by looking for fire hazards in our homes, by attempting to locate and eliminate the danger spots there. Making the "hazard hunt" a family project gets the whole family interested and, therefore, more safety conscious.

The Great Fire of Chicago, which has become an American legend, took place in October 1871, from the eighth through the tenth of the month. Whatever its real cause, this memorable fire brought about the destruction of more than 17,000 buildings, with a total property damage estimated at $175,000,000. In 1872, fire destroyed over 700 buildings and caused damage amounting to $75,000,000 in Boston.

On April 18, 1906, San Francisco was rocked by an earthquake and fire that wrecked most of the city and caused losses in property that amounted to the enormous sum of $350,000,000.

The greatest number of lives lost in a single fire occurred in 1871. This happened on October 8 of that year, on the very same day as the beginning of the Great

Because matches and smoking cause one fourth of all fires—in the home and elsewhere—you can urge your parents to be particularly careful. You can point out to them that smoking or lighting matches in dangerous places is a hazard. Careless disposal of cigarettes and matches is a hazard. Smoking in bed is a hazard. Allowing younger brothers and sisters to play with matches is a hazard.

Here are some other precautions dealing with matches and smoking that all can follow:

Ashtrays are designed for cigarettes, cigars and matches. Keep plenty of them handy—large fireproof ones that won't tip over.

Next, make sure every cigarette, cigar or match is out before emptying an ashtray into a trash can. Remember, also, never strike matches or carry lighted matches or candles in closets, attics or other confined places where clothing or combustible materials are kept.

The second most common cause of fire is misuse of electricity. Let's take a look at this common hazard, which causes about 15 per cent of all fires.

Today people are using electricity in their homes in record quantity. More than 45,000,000 homes now have a refrigerator, 41,000,000 an electric washer, 40,000,000 a television set and 32,000,000 a vacuum cleaner.

In addition, 8,600,000 homes are equipped with freezers, 5,600,000 with clothes dryers and 3,600,000 with air conditioners. Add to these such stand-bys as electric lights, radios, toasters, irons, mixers and the like, and you'll see the average family has gone electric in a big way.

The question is: Are our homes properly wired to carry this new big load? Too often they are not, because inadequate and faulty wiring is a key factor in the occurrence of fires due to misuse of electricity.

Therefore, when heavy-duty appliances are installed, people should have a qualified electrician find out whether additional circuits are needed. Appliances listed by Underwriters' Laboratories, Inc., a nonprofit testing organization, have been checked for safety.

Fires often occur because improper fuses are used. A proper fuse acts as a safety valve. The blowing of a fuse is a warning that the circuit is overloaded or defective. Only fuses of the right amperage

Fireboats are an essential part of the harbor life of a great seaport. The John Purroy Mitchel is a veteran of many years service fighting fires on wharfs and ships in New York Harbor.

ED HEAVEY

—usually 15 amperes—should be used. Using larger ones means you won't have the protective warning a blown-out fuse provides.

It would also be well to make sure that extension and lamp cords are out in the open in your house—and not run under rugs, over hooks or through partitions or door openings where they may wear and cause a short circuit. It's dangerous, too, to string wiring under rugs, over hooks, or in any exposed place where it may be subject to wear or mechanical damage.

Most other fires—particularly those in the home—can generally be attributed to bad housekeeping. For example, is your attic, like so many others, littered with stacks of old magazines or accumulated newspapers, broken furniture, rags and other combustible rubbish? These are some of the fuels that fire feeds on.

Still other examples of housekeeping hazards are dirty furnaces and chimneys, greasy stoves and carelessly stored rags, paints and flammable liquids.

Clearly, if we are to prevent fires, we can't wait until spring cleaning to do away with these common fire hazards. Clean up now—and stay cleaned up the year around. That is practical fire prevention!

Fire destroys, injures and kills. Yet fire is an enemy that we can stop. We can halt

332

Fighting fire in a steel-mill area. A converted tender holding 15,000 gallons of water, it can be drawn over the tracks by a diesel engine to put out almost any blaze in or around a plant.

"STEELWAYS," PUBLISHED BY THE AMERICAN IRON AND STEEL INSTITUTE

fire losses through alert, practical fire prevention.

Finally, be most careful of forest-fire hazards. An average * of nearly 120,000 forest fires every year burn over 7,380,000 acres of woodland in this country.

For instance in 1957, there were 83,-391 fires compared with 143,485 in 1956. The area burned in 1957 totaled 3,409,-038 acres, compared with 6,605,894 acres burned in 1956.

On federally owned lands—national parks—an average of nearly 2,465 forest fires every year burn over 1,230,000 acres of woodland in the United States.

You can help
to keep our forests safe

Therefore, when you go camping, pick a spot with good solid earth for your fire. Don't build fires on spongy porous earth or peaty soil, and keep the fire away from tree trunks, fallen trees and overhanging branches. Scrape the ground so you have bare soil five or six feet from the fire in every direction. Other campfire precautions you should observe are these:

Make sure matches are out before throwing them away, never leave a campfire without someone to watch it, keep water nearby, stack firewood ten or more feet from the fire, and keep all fires confined to properly built fireplaces.

When breaking camp, put fire completely out. Sprinkle it with water, spread sticks and coals, sprinkle again. If you are without water, spread sticks and coals, scrape out embers and cover with dirt.

It takes three things to make a fire. First is oxygen—which is in the air around us. Second is heat—a spark, or flame or just high enough temperature. Third is fuel—that's anything that will burn. If oxygen, heat and fuel get together, we'll have a fire. So you want to be sure they don't get together—unless, of course, they're under control in a stove or furnace.

Let's take a few examples to show you where to look for fire hazards. We'll start with the things that cause most fires of all: lighted matches and cigarettes. Actually, these are little fires themselves; but as a cause of big fires, they provide the heat. The air provides oxygen. So all we need to have a fire is fuel. Naturally, if we put those matches and cigarettes in ashtrays, there won't be any fuel. They'll just burn themselves out. But suppose we throw one into a wastebasket with paper in it—or out a car window into some dry leaves or grass? Or someone smokes in bed and the cigarette drops on the bedding? Or a child plays with matches and a lighted match falls on the rug? Paper, grass, leaves, sheets and rugs will burn—so now we have fuel, and we'll have a fire.

There's plenty of fuel around the house. Everything made of wood or paper or both will burn. Some liquids will burn, too. Paint, benzine, gasoline, kerosene, for instance. In fact, fumes from gasoline and heated kerosene won't only burn, they will also explode! So will benzine and many paints. That's why they should be kept in tightly covered metal cans and stored outside the house. Piles of rubbish are fuel too. They should be thrown away.

What to do if
your clothes catch fire

Suppose, in spite of your being just as careful as you can be, some unavoidable accident happens and your clothing does catch fire. Here's what to do:

Fold your arms—high, to protect your face—drop to the floor or ground and roll over and over. If you can roll up in a thick blanket or rug, so much the better. That will smother the flames. If you see someone else's clothing catch fire, try to roll them in a blanket or rug, or throw a heavy coat around them. Start at the shoulders and work down to keep the flames away from the face and eyes.

* Source: Cooperative Forest Fire Control of United States Forest Service.

The Soviet Union's Tu-114.

AVIATION

By ERWIN J. BULBAN
Southwest Editor

Aviation Week

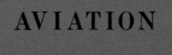

As the first of the Boeing 707 jet-airliner passengers stepped onto New York's International Airport after streaking across the United States from Los Angeles in four hours and three minutes, transport designers and executives were already studying plans for new planes that would slash this time to one fourth or one third.

The Tu-114 has four turboprop engines and is the largest and heaviest airliner yet flown. It can carry 220 passengers and fly 9,000 miles nonstop.

An interior view of the Tu-114.

The United States' Douglas DC-8.

This planning in the drafting rooms and conference halls of airline manufacturers and operators is being duplicated in nearly every phase of our great military- and civilian-aviation industry today as it moves forward at the fastest pace in its history. Planning in some cases is obsolete even before it is completed.

Airlines today are working on three major problems: 1. How to bring the new 600-mph jets into their fleets smoothly without disrupting schedules while they train pilots, mechanics and other specialized personnel to operate these unfamiliar aircraft; 2. How to dispose of their large fleets of piston-engine transports at favor-

The DC-8 has four jet engines and a swept-wing design. It has a speed of 590 mph and it can carry 189 passengers. Airlines have 143 on order.

PHOTOS THIS PAGE, DOUGLAS AIRCRAFT

An interior view of the DC-8.

335

able prices to help pay for the jets and related equipment (estimated cost $4,000,-000,000); and 3. Studying the next generation of transports, which will cruise at 2,000 mph at about 70,000 feet (twice the altitude of today's jet airliners) and cost $25,000,000 to $30,000,000 each— five to six times as much as the present new planes.

How soon will airliners with twice the speed of sound be ready? The first deliveries could be made in 1965, and even faster transports, flying at three times the speed of sound, could be available in 1972-75. These would probably look like giant darts, with their triangle-shaped wings. They would weigh over 500,000 pounds, carry more than 160 passengers and be powered by at least 6 jet engines. Cabin insulation might have to be a foot thick to protect the passengers from the tremendous heat generated by the friction of the air streaking over the outside skin surfaces.

During the year the Russians sent one of their latest turbine-powered transports to the United States. Powered by 4 jet engines driving propellers, the Tu-114 is the world's largest airliner and seats 220 passengers. It has a dining room seating 48 people; food is sent to this area from a galley on the deck beneath via a dumbwaiter.

The Tu-114's Moscow to New York nonstop flight in 11 hours and 6 minutes (it returned in 9 hours and 48 minutes) showed that the Russians have developed an airliner capable of nonstop service between their major cities and ours. They claim that they are ready to begin service over the Atlantic Ocean whenever permission is granted by the United States. The two governments are now negotiating the details of such a service. On this service the Americans would use long-range versions of the 707, like the one that carried Vice-President Nixon and his party to Moscow

last summer. The 707 can make the flight nonstop from New York in 8 hours and 45 minutes.

The Soviet airline, Aeroflot, has grown very rapidly in the past few years. In 1956 this government-controlled airline operated only a half-dozen jet transports. Today it flies more than 200 jet- and turboprop-powered airliners within the Soviet Union and to satellite countries, Europe and the Far East. Early in 1959 it started jet service to London from Moscow. The Soviets are determined to make Aeroflot a major competitor in international air transport and also to use it to improve the internal communications of their vast country. For example, the 100-passenger Tu-104 jets can fly from Moscow to Leningrad in 55 minutes compared to 12 hours by the best train.

What do the Russians think of our new jet transports? One of their top designers, Andrei Tupolev, responsible for the Tu-104 and the Tu-114, toured the major transport-manufacturing plants on the West Coast this past summer. He and a number of Soviet aircraft engineers and pilots flew in several of the latest American airliners and thought that they were first class in appearance and performance. Tupolev was also surprised at the size of our jet-transport production lines and said that he had not known that we were so far along in manufacturing these new airliners in quantity.

American pilots who have flown Russian jet transports say that they are built well and perform well, but that they are not as economical to operate as United States planes. This is probably because the first Russian jets are powered with engines originally designed for military planes without thought to economy of operation. Later models probably will be improved as the Russians get more experience.

Although the Russians appear to be formidable rivals in future air transportation,

336

there is little doubt that the United States still leads the world in civil as well as military aviation, with the best internal air-service network and international services.

When Russian pilots visited the United States they were impressed by the airports they saw. At New York International Airport they commented on its size, the number of runways and the way a number of planes could be dispatched or landed simultaneously on several runways. They also considered ground equipment, such as tractors for towing planes to the passenger ramp, superior to anything that they had seen previously.

The current growth of the United States airline industry is well illustrated by comparing its spending for new equipment with other top-ranking industries. The airlines industry estimates that it spent approximately $800,000,000 for new equipment in 1959. By comparison, the railroads expect to spend some $753,000,000, and the motor-vehicle manufacturers approximately $688,000,000.

United States airlines employ about 150,000 people and are currently paying approximately $950,000,000 annually in wages. In 1958 they had a total operating income of more than $2,200,000,000; this probably was slightly higher in 1959.

As of early 1959 the United States scheduled airlines owned 1,902 airplanes, with 179 more planes scheduled for delivery during the year. Some of these deliveries will replace airplanes now in service. Compared to the 347 airliners flying in 1939 this giant fleet shows how the air-transport industry has grown in the United States. Production programs for military-manned aircraft are small today compared to a few short years ago when approximately 2,000 B-47 Stratojet bombers and 7,000 Sabrejet fighters were built. The next generation of bombers and fighters will be small compared to earlier ones— for several reasons: the tremendous cost of

the newer airplanes; their greater destructive power; the extra money needed for missiles and space vehicles.

To get an idea of the cost of space programs, approximately $500,000,000 will be spent by the United States for space programs this year; within the next few years spending will skyrocket to approximately $2,000,000,000 annually.

Within the next year the United States plans to send thirty or more vehicles of many kinds into space.

Until missiles and space craft become sufficiently reliable, the main weapon of United States defense remains the manned airplane. There are many programs for increasing the effectiveness of the airplanes now in service. One of the ways is to design missiles that can be fitted to planes, enabling them to destroy the enemy at longer distances.

Latest production version of the Stratofortress, the B-52G, carries a pair of missiles, called the Hound Dog, which it can launch at ground targets several hundreds of miles away, while the airplane and its crew stay out of range of enemy missiles. Should the enemy have missiles capable of reaching our planes, we could use so-called decoy missiles, fired from the bomber to lure the oncoming enemy missile from its original target. Other missiles, used by fighters, are being improved to have longer reach and greater speed. United States airplanes are equipped with missiles having atomic warheads whose destructive power covers a much larger area than earlier explosives. One such missile is called Genie.

The most important airplanes now being planned for future American bomber and fighter fleets are similar to the canceled B-70 and F-108. They will fly at approximately three times the speed of sound and have triangular, or delta, wings. Stainless-steel covering will be used to provide the strength necessary to fly at such speeds and resist the heat caused by friction of the air passing over their outer surfaces.

Panels of this special material measuring ten feet by twenty feet are expected to be used in building these planes. The panels will not be single, thin sheets, but rather a "sandwich" type of construction (two sheets of metal having a honeycomblike center). The sandwich will be welded together using a material containing sterling silver. Extra care must be taken to make sure that these panels are perfectly made. The materials used are bathed several times in acid to remove all traces of the grease and oil that might prevent perfect bonding and are then kept in dust-free rooms to avoid further contamination. Workers must wear spotless white gloves while they are putting the sandwich together, since even human oils can spoil the finish. The actual welding of the sandwich is done in a special sealed chamber from which the air is pumped. It takes nearly twelve hours to finish joining the sandwich into a one-piece panel. When it is completed, the panel is so smooth that it looks as if it had been made from plastic.

One of the newest military planes is the United States Army's AO-1 Mohawk. It is designed to fly at low speeds and low altitudes above an enemy's lines and locate his missiles, tanks, trucks and soldiers. The Mohawk carries a crew of two and is equipped with radar, cameras and other special devices for locating the enemy and recording information.

This airplane is designed to take off and land in approximately 700 feet and to fly in and out of rough fields near friendly troops. It has a top speed of approximately 300 miles per hour. To escape faster enemy aircraft, the Mohawk has special air brakes it can use to slow down quickly.

There is a growing family of aircraft designed to operate at low altitudes and low speeds. These new aircraft are called ground effect vehicles. They get their name from the fact that they are supported by a cushion of air trapped under the vehicles. This cushion is supplied either by a downward jet stream or air from short helicopterlike rotor blades. Most of the air is guided by vanes or curved surfaces on the vehicles to prevent it from completely blowing outward.

Some of the experimental models of

Necessary in the delta wings of supersonic planes: a stainless steel covering made of two sheets of

metal with honeycomb center layer. A magnified view of the core (left); some of its many shapes (right).

NORTH AMERICAN AVIATION, INC.

The British SR-N1 Hovercraft is 30 feet long and 24 feet wide and weighs 3½ tons. A larger version is planned for use as a communication and supply vehicle in remote areas.

ground effect vehicles now being tested for the Army and Navy fly from a few inches to a few feet from the surface of the earth. One, called the Air-Car, has a flexible rubber skirt around the bottom of the vehicle, curved to trap the air under it. Since the Air-Car flies only inches from the ground, the flexible rubber skirt enables it to pass over small rocks without tripping.

The manufacturer of this novel vehicle believes that it has a great future in replacing wheeled vehicles, particularly where the ground is soft or swampy or where water must be crossed. It is equipped with a system of vanes on its sides so that some of the downward-rushing air can be channeled sideward to turn the Air-Car in its own length and even to make it scoot over the ground sideward or backward.

The British are testing a similar vehicle which they call the Hovercraft, for land and sea. The designers say improved larger versions of the Hovercraft could replace ocean vessels because they could move much faster than a conventional ship.

Since it does not require as much power to ride on a cushion of air as it does to fly through the air above it, Army and Navy personnel feel that the ground effect vehicle could replace the helicopter for some tasks and be less expensive.

An amazing development being studied by the United States Air Force is the use of the energy from radio waves to spin the rotor blades of helicopters. The helicopter's rotors would be driven by jet engines at their tips. Hot air, providing the thrust, would be obtained by converting radio energy beamed from the ground. The helicopter would take off burning conventional fuel in these tip jets. When it got to a certain altitude, the heat provided by converting energy of radio waves would take over to supply propulsion. This idea is being considered as a possible means of keeping an unmanned radar-warning set or radio-relay station aloft for weeks.

United States Army's AO-1 Mohawk, a turboprop observation plane intended for rough field operation.

Terminals
for the Jet Age

PORT OF NEW YORK AUTHORITY

By GLENN GARRISON
Aviation Week

MAJOR airports throughout the world are struggling to keep pace with the new jet age of commercial aviation. The problems as well as the promises of the airlines' new era are drawn to a scale hardly imagined a few years ago.

The swift and glamorous jet transports themselves have special operating problems, and these have intensified the difficulties brought about by the explosive growth of air transportation. Many airports have become outgrown and outmoded as fast as they were built. Airplanes are constantly increasing in size and weight and require greater lengths of expensive concrete runway. Passenger terminal buildings, fuel-storage tanks and truck fleets, traffic-control systems and electronic navigation aids, hangars and many other airport elements have been stretched to their limits, expanded and stretched again. The cycle seems endless.

Today huge jets, weighing up to 150 tons and capable of carrying as many as

189 passengers on a single trip, land and take off every day, and the airports of the world are straining to keep up with them. Expansion programs costing many millions of dollars are under way in New York, London, Montreal, Paris, Rome, Tokyo and other great crossroads of the air.

No single airport is exactly suited to the jet age, because the jet age is just beginning. Lessons now being learned will shape the designs of the future. But New York International Airport, at Idlewild, on Long Island, is a good example of the new terminals.

Idlewild, as it is generally called, has been open for business twelve years. During the first year, about 233,000 passengers were handled at the field. For 1958 alone the total number of passengers was almost 6,000,000, carried by 22 foreign and 12 United States airlines. More than half these passengers were traveling to and from overseas cities around the world.

From a passenger's viewpoint the heart

340

of Idlewild is Terminal City. It takes in a circle of 655 acres in the center of the airport. This development, now largely complete, cost $150,000,000. Although it occupies only about one seventh of the entire airport, it is bigger than all of busy La Guardia Airport, which also serves New York.

Terminal City is Idlewild's answer to the many problems posed by the ever larger terminal building. Instead of one immense structure to cope with all the airline planes and passengers, Idlewild's planners decided on a cluster of terminals. One of these terminals, itself eleven city blocks long, handles arriving international flights and foreign-flag airline departures. The foreign carriers rent space here for ticket counters and passenger lounges. United States Customs, Immigration and Public Health services also are situated in this center.

United States airlines, both domestic and overseas, are building their own individual terminals. These will make up the rest of the "city." The total cost of these buildings will run to about $97,000,000. Each airline is free to design its own building to suit itself, and to handle its jets on its own ramp as it sees fit.

Pan American's terminal is a circular building with an overhanging, umbrella-like roof under which the jets will roll to discharge or load passengers, free of weather worries. American Airlines' terminal provides a swinging, telescoping corridor to connect with the rear door of its jets, while a short fixed corridor accommodates the front-door passengers.

Idlewild's Terminal City also contains a control tower eleven stories high. It is topped by a dome housing special radar which scans the entire surface of the airport. All airplanes and even tiny airport vehicles show up on the scope of this radar in detail so that tower operators can direct traffic on the ground as well as in the air. The rest of Terminal City is made up of parking lots for 6,000 cars, 7½ miles of taxiways, 10 miles of roads, a landscaped park and the Central Heating and Refrigeration Plant.

Ringed around this central area of the airport are gigantic new hangars and vast fuel-storage tanks. There are also many additional miles of roadways, taxiways and runways, and various other buildings including the International Hotel, an animal hotel and a chapel. There is a large cargo center of five buildings which cost about $1,000,000 each.

Idlewild shows the size and complexity and the tremendous investment of money that the bigger jet-age airports involve. Since air traffic is expected to double again within the next few years the new airports will have to keep up with this fast rate of growth. At London, for example, some $48,000,000 has been set aside for further development of London Airport, where 3,500,000 passengers were handled in 1958 and where 9,000,000 are expected in 1965. Los Angeles has begun a program to rebuild its airport into a radically dif-

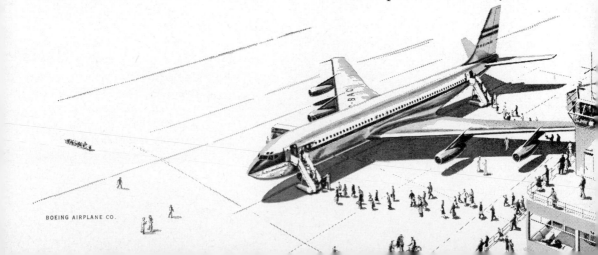

BOEING AIRPLANE CO.

A NEW CONCEPT IN AIRPORT PLANNING

Terminal City is the heart of New York International Airport. Covering 655 acres of the 4,900-acre field, it will not be entirely finished until some time in 1964. Its main landmarks are the International Arrival Building, which houses all non-American airlines, and the seven terminals built by the major United States lines for their own passengers.

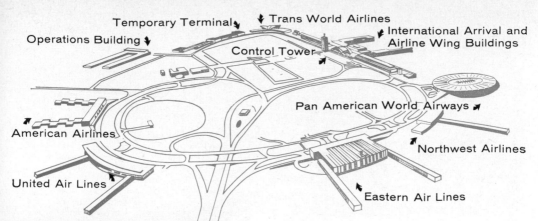

Temporary Terminal
Operations Building
Trans World Airlines
International Arrival and Airline Wing Buildings
Control Tower
Pan American World Airways
American Airlines
Northwest Airlines
United Air Lines
Eastern Air Lines

ferent new jet-age terminal. Dorval Airport at Montreal, already served by transatlantic jet aircraft, is undergoing expansion. And so it is at major terminals around the world.

Many experts believe that the wonderful new jets actually arrived on the scene a little ahead of time as far as the airports' readiness to handle them was concerned.

The biggest commercial jet in operation during late 1958 and the first half of 1959 was the Boeing 707-120, which weighs about 247,000 pounds when fully fueled and loaded. Generally speaking, for a long hop with a full load, the 707-120 needs a runway two miles long! Hot weather and height above sea level, which reduce the efficiency of a jet engine, can stretch this runway requirement further.

Very few airports now have runways of this length. In some cases they will be difficult to provide. At Idlewild, for example, the preferred jet runway has been extended to 10,000 feet. But to lengthen it will mean going out into Jamaica Bay for the simple reason that no other real estate is available. The rule of thumb for runway cost is something like $1,000 per foot. Filling part of the bay will bring the cost much higher than that.

Three smaller jet transports were in service by the middle of 1959: the Russian TU-104, the British De Havilland Comet 4 and the French Sud-Aviation Caravelle.

343

The airport of the future? This design is an attempt to solve the problem of handling both aircraft and passengers.

UNIVERSAL ATLAS CEMENT

The TU-104 and Caravelle are two-engined planes, which fly relatively short routes. The four-engined Comet is a medium-range aircraft weighing 152,500 pounds at the maximum. This is not a great deal more than the biggest piston-engined planes and less than the biggest turboprop transports. Because they weigh much less these three jets do not need as much runway as the bigger and heavier Boeings.

The biggest jets so far are the Douglas DC-8 Intercontinental and the Boeing 707-320 Intercontinental. They range from 250,000 to 310,000 pounds. Their runway requirements are even greater than the Boeing 707-120! However, this runway problem is critical only when the big jets are flown over very long distances near the maximum range and with full pay loads.

Another airport problem the jets have intensified is noise. Airport authorities at Idlewild banned all jets from the airport until the summer of 1958 because they felt the noise of the powerful aircraft would bring outcries from nearby communities. Jet service was allowed to begin on schedule there only under special rules. With the idea of keeping them as far from the communities as possible, these rules assign jets to certain runways and subject them to certain procedures. In effect, they make the airport's runway problem worse, and the airlines are not entirely happy about the situation. New York's noise problem is not unique; it has also been much in evidence in Paris and London.

To handle their new jet transports on the ground, United States airlines alone are investing a quarter of a billion dollars in all kinds of equipment, including hangars, maintenance bases and a variety of new airport machinery. This equipment includes huge, self-propelled vacuum sweepers. They keep taxiways and runways free of all debris that could be sucked into a jet engine. There are also big, powerful tugs to tow the planes; compressed-air trucks to start the jet engines; and fences to protect terminal areas from the blast of taxiing jets. Many other new items are appearing at airports where the jets have started to operate.

No one can safely predict the look of airports a few years from now. Technical changes in the planes themselves will be of the greatest importance in airport design. For example the vertical-lift devices to permit very short take-offs may cut runways to a fraction of their current lengths. Supersonic transports, flying several times the speed of sound, may some day bring new problems of their own. An answer must be found to the problem of transporting passengers between the airport and the city. Although this problem grows worse as actual flying times grow shorter, it may be solved by helicopter services.

In any case, the jet age is here—and the airports of the world are adapting to it.

PAN AMERICAN WORLD AIRWAYS

Pan American's terminal roof covers four acres.

TWA

TWA's home will be this boldly planned building.

EASTERN AIR LINES; CHESTER L. CHURCHILL, ARCHITECT-ENGINEER

Eastern's structure will be the airport's largest.

UNITED AIR LINES

United Air Lines' building has a length of 691 feet.

Ocean-going Oil Tankers

By LOREN F. KAHLE

Transportation Coordinator, Standard Oil Company (N. J.)

PETROLEUM is one of the most valuable products known to man—when it is where he can use it. Unfortunately, it is generally found hundreds, often thousands, of miles from the consumer.

Sometimes it can be carried to him by pipeline or railroad, as it often is in North America. About 6 or 7 barrels out of every 10 consumed in the United States take an overland route from well to consumer. In the industry a barrel equals 42 gallons.

Outside the United States and Canada, however, about 8 barrels out of 10—in some cases even more—must move along an ocean trade route. Western Europe, for example, is one of the world's chief oil-consuming areas but has only a small amount of oil of its own and, therefore, has to import. More than 9 out of 10 barrels used in Western Europe travel by sea. These facts make ocean-going oil tankers important to millions of people.

CUTAWAY VIEW OF AN OCEAN TANKER

1 Galley
2 Quarters for crew
3 Propeller shaft
4 Engineer's office
5 Senior 2d engineer's office

6 Officers' mess (pantry on left)
7 Fuel-oil settling tank
8 Cargo-pump turbines
9 Cargo pumps in after pump room
10 Center oil-cargo tank

The tankers follow well-defined ocean routes. One of the foremost, in length and in volume of oil carried, links the Middle East with Western Europe by way of the Suez Canal. Every day nearly 2,000,000 barrels are shipped through the Suez Canal from Bahrein, Iran, Iraq, Kuwait, Qatar and Saudi Arabia to Europe and other points westward. Most of this is crude oil but there is a small quantity of refined products, such as kerosene, gasoline and diesel oil. Other westbound tankers load about 950,000 barrels daily at pipeline terminals in the eastern Mediterranean. In recent years nearly half of the world tanker fleet has been employed in moving crude oil and products from the Middle East.

Tankers also carry large amounts of oil from the Caribbean area to distant markets. A portion of Caribbean petroleum goes to the United States. Tanker cargoes of this oil to all markets totaled about 2,700,000 barrels a day in 1959.

Although, as mentioned before, more of the oil consumed in the United States moves overland than by water, ocean tankers carry about 780,000,000 barrels a year. Much of it comes from southern and southwestern states. Either as crude oil or after it has been processed into refined products, it travels from ports on the Gulf of Mexico around Florida and thence northward. Some goes to refineries on the United States east coast or to terminals where gasoline, heating oil and other finished products are stored while awaiting delivery to consumers.

Indonesia is another large petroleum producer. Practically all of this petroleum goes for an ocean ride, for Indonesia does

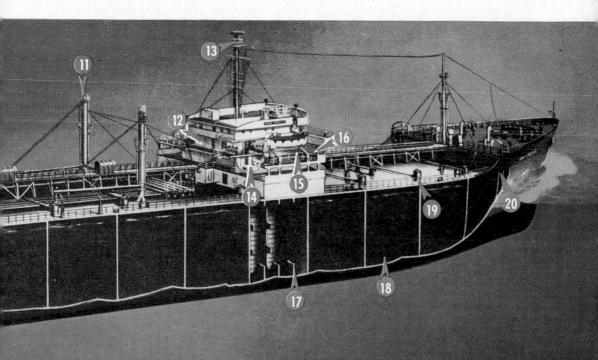

11 Hose-handling derrick	16 Navigating bridge
12 Ship's office	17 Water-ballast tank
13 Radar scanner	18 Wing oil-cargo tanks
14 Hospital	19 Cargo hatch
15 Captain and navigating officer	20 Dry-cargo space

not have enough industry to become a larger oil consumer itself. It does, however, profit from the sale of the oil abroad.

The modern oil industry rounded out its first hundred years in 1959. Throughout most of that time, oil was transported in ships of some kind. It was not until 1886, however, that the first direct ancestor of the modern oil tanker was launched. This was the Gluckauf, built in England and constructed on a new theory. Untested until then, this theory held that liquid cargo could be carried within the shell of a vessel, instead of in containers stowed aboard, as long as lengthwise and thwartship bulkheads divided the cargo space into smaller compartments to reduce the sloshing back and forth of the liquid. When the Gluckauf proved the theory sound, larger vessels followed. As years passed they acquired the tanker silhouette that is familiar the world over today: low in the water, decks practically awash when loaded, bridge midships, and engines and stack aft.

By World War I the world tanker fleet had grown to more than 2,000,000 deadweight tons. (By "dead weight" is meant the total weight of cargo, fuel oil, water and supplies the vessel can carry.) The war set the oil age years ahead as fighting fleets converted from coal to petroleum, and gasoline engines displaced horses. Afterward the tanker fleet grew to more than three times its prewar size to meet the new peacetime demands.

Then as the clouds of World War II gathered, new tanker designs appeared in American shipyards. During the war some of these ships operated as fleet oilers. Others were converted to small aircraft carriers, called "baby flat tops." Most of the wartime construction in the United States was of a 16,600 dead-weight tonner familiarly known as the T2. More than 500 were built. Even though smaller, slower and less economical than the modern ships, many still are hard at work.

Vessels smaller than 30,000 dead-weight tons make up about three fourths of today's world tanker fleet. The average size now on order or under construction is 35,000 tons. The tanker of more than 50,000 tons still is a rarity, but many about this size range or larger are planned or being built. It will probably not be long before a large share of the world's crude oil is carried by these very large vessels. One giant of 104,500 tons is already in service.

The reason for increasing the size of tankers is simply that as vessel size goes up operating costs go down, per barrel of oil carried. For example, with a 30,000 dead-weight-ton vessel, the cost per barrel carried would be only about two thirds of the cost with the smaller T2. Increasing the size to 50,000 tons or over should cut the cost by one half or even more.

However, large size brings problems too. Harbors have to be improved, terminals have to be enlarged, all at great expense. Luckily, some of these problems are being solved.

Since very large tankers cannot pass fully loaded through the Suez Canal at present, it is being widened and deepened so as to allow a loaded draft of 37 feet instead of the present 35 feet. The deeper the draft, the more oil a tanker can carry. International law prohibits the overloading of ships.

Only a few ports can accommodate the largest tankers because most of them have relatively shallow channels and approaches. Therefore engineers are talking of platforms or buoys in deep water possibly several miles offshore. Undersea pipelines would connect these to storage tanks ashore, and the tankers would not have to use docks. Mooring systems of this type are already in operation, but they are not yet able to take care of the largest tankers afloat today.

Increasing the size of tankers has brought many changes aboard the vessels

Hydraulic valves of the Trans-Arabian pipeline terminal at Sidon, Lebanon.

Operators watch the dials in the shore control room as tankers load offshore.

Oil is pumped from storage tanks on shore to a tanker's cargo space.

themselves. Speed and power are greater, and ability to maneuver and pumping capacity are improving. Oil is pumped, like water, from shore tanks through pipelines to the dock and then through flexible hoses into the ship. In discharging the process is reversed, with powerful ship's pumps pushing the cargo ashore from the ship's tanks. Top loading rates used to be about 30,000 barrels per hour, but today 40,000 barrels per hour and more are common in some ports.

Radical basic changes are also taking place or soon will be. For example, tanker designers are deeply interested in the idea of a nuclear-powered tanker. With a nuclear plant, space now needed for fuel storage could be used for cargo. On very long voyages, this would be a great advantage.

Another development is a tanker for liquefied petroleum gas, or LPG. This is sometimes called "bottled gas" and is used in many gas stoves. One recent project of this type is a tanker for LPG, fuel and crude oil; the LPG would be carried under the pressure at which it remains a liquid and stored in cylinders installed in the wing and center tanks. Another project is an LPG, fuel and crude-oil tanker to carry gas in liquid state under refrigeration; the liquid would be carried at 45 degrees below zero in special tanks placed inside cargo tanks loaded with fuel oil. New tankers are also being designed especially for other petroleum products, such as asphalt.

About fifty men can handle a tanker of 40,000 to 45,000 tons, only a few more than are needed for the smaller ships. Improvements in engine rooms and loading systems, more efficient gauges, and mechanically operated valves have all cut down the need for man power.

The crews themselves are at least as happy about the many new devices for their own comfort as they are about the engine-room improvements. Better equipment has reduced the time lost while a ship loads and unloads in port, and it has also shortened the crew's time ashore. Vessels often load and discharge at places far from any form of recreation. Some tankers, therefore, now have swimming pools and air conditioning to help keep the men contented.

On some supertankers, motion-picture projectors in recreation rooms give the crews a change from card games, checkers and the radio. Television sets supply entertainment on coastwise runs the first day and night out, until the ships are too far offshore for good reception.

Since good food is important to a sailor, refrigerators are stocked with a variety of meats, milk and eggs and green vegetables. The steward and his cooks and messmen serve up roast beef, veal, steak, chicken, fish and so on. Bread and pies are baked in the tanker's own galley. Coffee is drunk by the gallon; in fact "coffee breaks" are the custom. No liquor is permitted aboard most United States vessels, however, and smoking is restricted to specified areas. On the new Esso tankers each man has his own air-conditioned room with bunk, combination desk and chest of drawers, sofa

and sink. He shares a bath with his next-door neighbor.

The crew's quarters are in the stern, while the captain and deck officers are quartered in the center section, or midships. In this section is the bridge, the radio and chart room and such navigating and safety aids as radar. The engines are in the stern with the quarters for the engineering officers and the crew. Anchors, paint, tools, rope and other equipment are stored in the bow. The catwalks that run between the after house, midship house and the bow allow crew members to move safely about the ship in rough weather. The cargo of oil is carried in the body of the ship, which is divided into separate compartments. There are more than thirty of these in the large tankers, each connected with the other compartments by a system of pipes. On the decks are other valves and pipes through which oil is distributed among the compartments or pumped ashore.

Riding low in the sea when fully loaded, the large new tankers have a sustained sea speed of about 18 knots. Because they ride low in the water, they pitch and roll much less than do most vessels and are among the smoothest riding ships afloat.

The more than 300 vessels of the ocean tanker fleet sailing under the American flag have a combined cargo capacity of about 6,300,000 tons. The free world's total tanker capacity is about 53,400,000 tons. As individual vessels continue to grow in size, so the fleet itself continues to expand.

At this very moment many hundreds of these vessels are delivering oil to power automobiles, ships and diesel trains. The oil they carry will fuel electric generating plants, heat homes and perform countless other useful tasks that require energy or lubrication. A big job today, but the tankers will have a still bigger one in the future as the world continues to require more and more petroleum.

Making the Titan

By D. P. HERRON
The Martin Company

On February 6, 1959, the Titan intercontinental ballistic missile soared into the sky from its launching pad at Cape Canaveral, Florida. It was the largest missile the United States had launched up to that time. Even more important was the fact that it had taken only three years to develop the Titan from drawing board to successful test firing. This was an exceptional record in missile development and most heartening news to a nation that urgently felt the need of an intercontinental ballistic weapon system.

Such rapid progress was possible because of a special plant built by the Martin Company in Denver, Colorado, for the sole purpose of developing the Titan in the shortest time possible. In this plant were co-ordinated missile planning, assembly, testing and servicing along with quality control of each Titan part, component and system. Thus a novel pattern of development and a giant two-stage missile were born at the same time.

Fully assembled, the giant Titan is about 90 feet long and has a maximum diameter of 10 feet. Fully loaded it weighs over 220,000 pounds. Most of this weight is contributed by the missile's propellants. The Titan vehicle itself is amazingly light. By keeping the weight of the vehicle to a minimum, the high mass ratios required for intercontinental range were attained.

(The mass ratio is the ratio of the total propellant weight to the gross rocket weight.) A high mass ratio greatly increases the range of the missile.

One technique that reduced weight considerably was designing the airframe structure so that it also provided the walls of the propellant tanks. Special extrusion and chemical-milling processes remove further unnecessary weight. In the extrusion process, a metal (usually softened) is shaped by being forced through a shaped opening, the way toothpaste is squeezed from a tube.

The Titan's skin consists of integrally stiffened sections that are welded together. The integral stiffening is achieved by extruding the skin-forming stringers, or ribs, that run the length of the skin. A thin skin reinforced by ribs is much lighter than a skin thick enough to achieve the same strength by itself.

Workers give the Titan a careful check before it goes to Cape Canaveral for its first test flight.

The weight of this integrally stiffened extruded Titan skin is even further reduced by chemical-milling. Chemical-milling allows a chemical solution to dissolve excess metal from the less critical stress areas at a controlled rate. The critical stress areas are masked during the chemical bath of the skin and keep their original thicknesses. The skin, or airframe, of the Titan is formed of high-strength aluminum and magnesium alloys.

Although missile weight is kept down, the Titan's airframe is sufficiently rigid to support itself without internal pressurization. The missile is strong enough to withstand the huge engine thrust, as well as aerodynamic and structural loads.

The engine of the Titan has enormous power. The first stage of the engine has two thrust chambers which produce 300,000 pounds of thrust. This is equal to the combined horsepower of 15,000 average-size American automobiles.

Each stage of the Titan has its own engine, fuel tanks and complete propulsion system. Each propulsion system uses liquid oxygen and a kerosene-type liquid fuel called RP-1.

Interference such as a gust of wind may change the heading of the vehicle from the desired direction. A very slight deviation could actually cause the missile to miss its target by hundreds of miles. Therefore a flight-control system is used to keep the Titan on its course. When the Titan begins to roll, shift, or drift off course, it is immediately righted. This is done by the autopilot which moves, or gimbals, the engines and adjusts the direction of four vernier nozzles.

The autopilot receives its steering commands from the guidance system carried in the second stage of the missile. Correc-

Standing as tall as a thirteen-story building, the Titan dwarfs the men giving it a final series of tests.

RE-ENTRY VEHICLE

SECOND STAGE

FUEL

LIQUID OXYGEN

SEPARATION ROCKET

VERNIER NOZZLE

SECOND STAGE ENGINE

CONDUIT

LIQUID OXYGEN

FIRST STAGE

FUEL

FIRST STAGE ENGINE

The Titan is poised on a static test stand. These stands make possible the firing of both stages of the two-stage Martin missile.

tions are signaled to the autopilot when the guidance system senses an error as it compares the actual flight path with the predetermined route from launching site to destination.

Early operational Titans will be equipped with the radio-inertial guidance system, while later models will use the all-inertial system.

The computer portion of the radio-inertial system is based on the ground. It transmits new control orders to the missile as it is tracked in flight. The all-inertial system is contained entirely within the missile.

The flight of the Titan is divided into two general phases: powered flight and ballistic trajectory. Powered flight begins with the launching of the missile and continues through the operation of both the first and second stages.

The Titan's record for successful launchings is exceptional. Much of the credit for these successes goes to the Master Operations Controller, or MOC. This huge and complex electronic monitor was one of the remarkable developments at Martin-Denver. By using the MOC, checks of vital functions necessary to a successful test can be programed far in advance of the actual test flight. More important, proper function of all missile subsystems is verified automatically, instead of being dependent on human memory and snap judgments. The MOC also monitors performance of the missile subsystems during the countdown and launching. Should anything go wrong, the MOC signals a "hold fire" or shuts down the engine. The MOC even acts as a trouble shooter by giving a clue to the location of the malfunction.

The Titan soars into the sky on a successful test flight from Cape Canaveral, Florida.

When a Titan is successfully launched it climbs straight up for twenty seconds. Then it swerves from its vertical path and enters its curving trajectory.

At a planned altitude, in effect beyond the earth's atmosphere, the first-stage fuel is exhausted, and that stage separates from the rest of the vehicle.

Free of the weight of the first stage, the second-stage rocket engine fires and continues pushing the payload. Its purpose is to lift and accelerate the missile to the velocity, position and altitude necessary to deliver the re-entry vehicle to its destination. At one point the missile reaches a velocity of more than fifteen thousand miles per hour.

When the second stage has finished its job, it too separates from the re-entry vehicle by means of explosive bolts. The re-entry vehicle then coasts the rest of the way. The Titan is now on the second phase of its flight, the ballistic trajectory.

Though this phase of flight is by far the longer phase, no propulsion is necessary. Momentum carries the vehicle on its curved path toward the target. The highest point of this ballistic trajectory is above five hundred miles.

Of equal importance and interest is the Titan's ground support equipment (GSE). This is the equipment necessary to test, transport, handle and service the weapon system. Nearly every ounce of it had to be specially designed for work with the Titan.

The Master Operations Controller previously mentioned is part of this ground support equipment. So are the transporter containers, or transtainers. These are the curious trailers that carefully carry Stage I or Stage II from factory to test stand or to airport.

The huge test stands, where captive test firings are conducted, are of special interest. During a captive test firing, the missile is secured to the stand and prevented from taking off. Since the missile is in the vertical position, the stand must stretch many feet in the air to accommodate it.

Each stand has two motor-driven erectors: one to raise and service a complete missile, and the other to raise and service Stage II and the re-entry vehicle. The complete missile erector is 35 feet wide, 18 feet deep and 104 feet high. Each erector is made of steel beams and has many platforms that pivot to fold and unfold. This allows crewmen either to assemble stages and re-entry vehicle into a complete missile or to remove and replace missile components. The work platforms are enclosed by guardrails that fold and unfold with the platforms. An electric elevator carries men and equipment to all levels of the erector. Wherever you find a launch or test stand you will also find these tall steel skeletons.

Each test stand has "umbilicals." These are essential service lines that remain attached to the missile stages after the erector is lowered. These service lines are supported by a tower with platforms and booms, called the umbilical tower. The service lines include nitrogen, hydraulic, liquid oxygen topping, helium, conditioned air, instrumentation, and ground support electrical control lines.

For each two test stands there is a control building. This building houses all the Titan's instrumentation and control equipment. Underground tunnels connect the control building with the stands. The building is very strongly built, designed in fact to resist explosions of 200,000 pounds of TNT at the test stand. For the safety of the men it is shielded during test firings. Instruments used in this building record all the data required for test evaluation. Camera pads for television and motion-picture cameras are placed throughout the test-stand areas. The cameras are remotely controlled from the control building and televise and record test-stand activities. In addition to testing, transporting and servicing equipment, GSE also includes the equipment necessary to operate the Titan.

The operational Titan weapon system is organized into Strategic Missile Squadrons located within the United States. Each Strategic Missile Squadron operates several launch sites, arranged in launch complexes at an Operational Base. These launch complexes are constructed underground and are designed to withstand one hundred pounds per square inch of overpressure, as well as the shock and radiation from a thermonuclear blast. Each complex contains missiles, launching equipment, and accommodations for the men.

In addition, at each Operational Base there is a "soft" (relatively vulnerable) Support Base built above the ground. This base provides troop support and logistic requirements that are beyond the capabilities of the underground constructions.

One hundred and ten tons gross weight that lifts itself from its huge steel and concrete launching pad, the Titan is a powerhouse of boosting potential. Powerful, reliable, it is hoped that the Titan will be much more than a weapon system.

Possible future developments such as noncryogenic fuels, all-inertial guidance and increased propellant utilization will make possible the delivery of greater payloads over longer ranges with higher reliability. With these improvements the Titan will be able to provide an ideal orbital and deep-space payload carrier. Already a vehicle of tremendous booster strength, it may well be the foremost vehicle for future space missions such as circumlunar navigation, lunar landings and manned planetary reconnaissance.

Local Radio
a satisfying career

By STEVEN M. MERA

Radio Station WFDS-FM, Baltimore, Maryland

COMING from hundreds of small, local radio stations are the sounds of music, news, weather, shopping information and the chatter of a disc jockey. As you listen to one of these stations, you may wonder what the requirements are for a career in local radio.

In local radio, people are needed to work on the air as announcers, newsmen and disc jockeys. Others are needed to sell radio time, operate and maintain complex electronic equipment and write commercial announcements.

How do you get into radio? The most direct way, and the best, is to apply for a job at your local, small radio station. You probably won't get a job the first time you appear. However, since employees constantly leave small stations for bigger ones, there may be an opening for you in time.

It is important that would-be radio people get to know the local announcers and engineers. They will know when any jobs are open and will tell you about them. Moves from one station to another are often made through contacts with friends in the business.

Many young people who want to become radio announcers or disc jockeys attend radio schools. Most of these institutions offer valuable training. Yet in today's radio the school trainee is often no better equipped than the untrained newcomer —because each station operates in a different and special way of its own.

If you are thinking of going to a school, check first with the manager of your local radio station. Ask him for his opinion of the school you are interested in attending.

Many radio stations are reluctant to hire radio-school graduates. This is due to the fact that it takes too long for school habits and a school-inspired radio personality to wear off. School-trained men are often very critical of station operations. And, finally, most school graduates demand more money than local radio stations are willing to pay beginners.

The qualifications for jobs in announcing or disc-jockey work are very different from those of a few years ago. The only requirements now are that announcers be able to read English well and speak convincingly. The primary asset of a good radio man is versatility. A good grounding in high-school English, history, civics and current events will be a great help in learning the announcer's trade.

While announcing is the job most people aspire to, the engineering field draws many who are interested in electronics. The requirements for engineers are more stringent than for announcers. An engineer may not repair or adjust a broadcast radio transmitter unless he holds a first-class radiotelephone operator's license issued by the Federal Communications Commission. This license is given only to people who pass a stiff examination administered in one of the many FCC offices around the

Inside a Local Radio Station

Station manager, program director and star discuss the content of the show.

Engineering supervisor (left) and his assistant in the master control room.

country. Many good schools offer courses to prepare people for these FCC examinations.

To operate a transmitter, a skill needed by most radio announcers, requires a restricted license, which is issued to anyone meeting the requirements of age, citizenship, knowledge of English and knowledge of a few important laws concerning broadcasting.

For information about the requirements for various classes of FCC operators' licenses, write to the Federal Communications Commission, Washington 25, D. C.

People who hold a first-class license and who can announce or sell as well have the best opportunity for radio work. These "combo" men are in great demand and command high salaries. Every radio station would like to have a complete staff of announcer-engineers. Today the local radio stations' main need is for a few versatile employees who are willing and able to work at any station job.

Suppose that you have just been hired by your local radio station as an announcer. Your first job will probably be a

part-time evening shift, playing records and reading commercial announcements. If your station has adopted the top-forty records musical format, you will be limited in the selection of music you may use on the air. At the end of the evening you will probably have to throw a few switches to turn off the transmitter and studio equipment. Throughout your shift you will keep two logs—one for the programs and the other for the transmitter.

Your basic job in your first radio announcing position will be to learn the skills of clear speech, smooth reading, equipment operation and the care and handling of records. You will be constantly advised by other station personnel on the best way to improve these basic skills. Their criticism will be valuable, and you should listen carefully and try to develop the best radio habits. You will probably be encouraged to use the station's tape recorder to help you analyze your own speech.

When there is a full-time opening at the station, you will be asked if you wish to take the position. If your evening job has lasted long enough, you will also be of-

The news department supervisor monitors police, fire and coast-guard wave lengths.

In the newsroom the writer checks the ticker while rewriter prepares copy.

PHOTOS THESE PAGES BY DON MARKS, TAKEN AT STUDIOS OF THE NATION'S LEADING INDEPENDENT RADIO STATION, WNEW, NEW YORK, A DIVISION OF THE METROPOLITAN BROADCASTING CORP.

In the record library the librarian and the program producer choose a record.

The engineer operates the volume level on the control board as a record begins.

fered a raise in salary. At this point your radio career has begun. The full-time jobs are usually daytime work, often with split shifts. Some of your evenings will be spent at high-school record hops and other important local social events.

The new local-radio announcer often has very long working hours. He some-times works four hours in the early morning and four more in the late afternoon. The pay at the start is generally quite low and it takes many months to make a "radio personality." However, the rewards are many and satisfying for most people in local radio. They have a tremendous personal involvement in the business—read-

359

ing every trade magazine, studying the rating charts and finding new ways to improve a show. It is worthwhile to note again that one of the early rewards is not large quantities of money.

Local radio opens many doors. A person who is successful at selling radio time is on the way to becoming a sales manager or station manager. A good announcer or newscaster will keep moving until he arrives in one of the networks—where the hours and the pay are excellent. A person interested in sports and good at describing sports action may become a play-by-play sportscaster (a field, incidentally, that badly needs qualified announcers). The man who makes a hit on the early-morning record show is likely to keep at it for life.

A few examples show how people can advance in local radio—by going from station to station. Take WGPA in Bethlehem, Pennsylvania, for instance. In the past five years only one staff announcer has been over twenty-five years old. Only one had any previous experience. The current program director is twenty-three. Five announcers in this period have moved to local stations in Baltimore, Wilmington, and Allentown and Punxsutawney, Pennsylvania. In addition, one other announcer moved from his first radio job at WGPA to a Washington, D. C., network station within two years.

Four of the six men are still doing general announcing. One has become program director of a three-station operation, and another is now chief announcer of a prosperous local station.

WGPA usually hires announcers the year they graduate from high school. In a year or two these men usually move on to other stations. (Except for the chief engineer, all WGPA engineers are part-time employees who attend a nearby university.) None of these men had any special qualifications for radio except an interest in the field. They developed their skills through constant practice, and they will all be successful in the field because they have learned almost every job a radio station has available.

In the past few years all radio has undergone a revolution because of TV. The change has brought a streamlining of station operations, a new era of programing, and a reduction in the number of people employed by local radio stations. Local radio also changed in order to compete with TV. Many stations now broadcast a musical background for the day—a kind of programing that is always present but seldom really listened to. Radio rarely produces drama or lengthy newscasts nowadays—the programs consist largely of popular music, short, frequent announcements, and short headline news broadcasts.

With streamlined programing has come streamlined operation. Many stations now operate their transmitters by electronic remote control, eliminating the need for engineering operators on duty at all times. Some stations even run their programs automatically, using tape recorders and automatic jukebox-type record players. This type of station needs only four or five employees and a one-room studio.

The new era of broadcasting has also brought an unprecedented increase in the number of radio stations. More people are now employed in radio than ever before. The Federal Communications Commission is severely taxed to find room for more stations in the broadcast radio wave lengths.

This "new" radio has changed job requirements. At one time only college graduates could hope to get a job. Today the job seeker needs spirit, versatility, a reasonable knowledge of English and a consuming interest in the business. If you have these, you can have a satisfactory career in local radio, and there are few other fields where you can find such a combination of business and pleasure.

New York's Mounted Police

By ELIZABETH RUBIN

MOST of us are likely to think of the modern policeman as riding a motorcycle rather than a horse. However, several cities in the United States find a mounted-police unit indispensable—Dallas, Cleveland, Detroit, New York City, Philadelphia and Jersey City among them. New York City has the largest detachment of police horses in the United States.

Today 247 geldings patrol New York City from Westchester to Coney Island. The mounted squadrons are given duty in all areas of the city likely to be problem spots—the garment district, water front, business areas, food markets, and the bridle paths in the parks. There is no sign that the number of mounted men will be diminished—horses' hoofs will probably echo down the streets of New York for many years to come. In fact, police of that city estimate that one mounted man is equal to twenty foot patrolmen. People seem instinctively to respect the size of the horse and the unpredictability of his teeth and heels. And they respect the man who rides the horse. It is as if they sensed that while nearly anyone can learn to control a motor vehicle, it still takes a very special skill for a man to control an animal so many times larger and more powerful than himself. Whatever the reason, however, the mounted patrolman finds it easy to control crowds in situations where foot police would be nearly helpless. The horse police are especially efficient in keeping strikes orderly and in controlling riots and demonstrations. It is pointed out by police officials that while a rowdy crowd may overturn a police car, they have yet to overturn a horse.

The man on horseback is the best thing for smoothing dense traffic too. Because he has a better view, he can spot a jam from a considerable distance. He can also move through traffic snarls that would stop a man in a motor vehicle.

Many dignitaries, national and international, are brought into the city by a cavalry escort. A group of horse police leads all parades in the city. They make an agreeable sight, a brilliant sight—the gleaming brass, polished leather and perfectly turned out uniforms of the men; the glistening coats of the spanking bay horses, all a-prance in the excitement of the bands' blaring, some of them noising a muffled whinny of delight to their comrades. Beyond the viewers' pleasure, however, there are very practical reasons for the horsemen's leading the parades—a wedge of mounted men can prevent an excitable crowd from surging out among the marchers.

It is all in a day's work for the mounted police to control crowds at an unusual store sale, to stop a runaway horse on one

361

of the city's bridle paths or to catch a rid-erless horse abandoned by someone who doesn't go back to the stable to pay for his ride. A mounted man might also be as-signed to handle traffic in the theater dis-trict during the winter season—several well-groomed man-and-horse teams are al-ways part of the glittering scene at the opening of the Metropolitan Opera each fall, for example. It is not unknown for a horse patrolman to chase and catch a thief by the scruff of the neck, so to speak —or to pursue and corner holdup men.

All men and horses must pass exacting tests for admission to the mounted divi-sion. Since about twenty-five of the horses are retired each year (retirement age is twenty years), the same number are bought at auctions to replace them. The horses are usually purchased in Okla-homa at an average cost of $300 each. Most of them are tough Western cross-breds of the type known as Western chunks. Some carry Thoroughbred or quarter-horse blood, and this accounts for the many handsome and well-bred-look-ing animals on the force. Before being bought, new horses are examined and must be approved by the inspector of the mounted division, a veterinarian and sev-eral others. They must fit very rigid stand-ards. Their color must be bay (varying shades of brown with black points—that is, mane, tail and legs). A horse must be between 3 and 7 years old when pur-chased, weigh from 1,050 to 1,250 pounds and stand between 15 to 16 hands high (a hand is four inches). He may be green —relatively untrained—but he must have a good disposition and show intelligence. Each horse on the force is a gelding—no mares are purchased.

When the new horses are shipped to New York, they are brought to the re-mount depot in the New York National Guard armory at Madison Avenue and Ninety-fourth Street. Here in a huge in-door riding hall—the second largest in the world—the animals are given careful, pa-tient training by United States Cavalry methods. The horses are on probation for thirty days, and those who pass the trial period are given two or three months' training before they are assigned to regu-lar duty. The amount of training varies with the individual horse's disposition— a timid, rather high-strung animal, for ex-ample, will be trained more slowly over a long period of time.

After elementary training under saddle —many of the horses may have been rid-den only a few times before coming to the police force—the animals are trained not to shy at any sudden movements and noise. This important work is begun in-doors. Trainers surround the horse with noisemakers, yell, wave papers at him and so on. When the new mounts are bored by this procedure, they are consid-ered ready for outdoor work. Since the training depot is near Central Park, the horses' first experience outside the riding ring takes place there. Nearly any morn-ing, police, specially assigned to training duty, will be seen on the park's bridle paths giving the rookie mounts advanced training under saddle. Usually several of the new horses will be worked together, in company with an older, experienced vet-eran. After they are considered depend-able in the relatively quiet park area, the horses are assigned to various spots in the city for further training under actual traf-fic and crowd conditions.

The training for new patrolmen is as in-tensive as that given the horses. Many men who join the mounted division have never ridden before, but this is difficult to believe when one watches the riding style of the police at work on the streets. The new patrolmen are recruited from precincts all over the city and must have at least six months' satisfactory service on regular duty before they can apply for

Training is important. Horses are led through a maze of cars to accustom them to street traffic.

Ready for work, patrolmen receive instructions and, with their horses, line up for inspection.

Starting off for the day's routine. This may include patrolling the park or untangling traffic.

admission to the mounted division. All recruits must be under thirty years of age, weigh no more than 165 pounds and be fond of animals.

When he is transferred to the mounted division, the patrolman is given thirty days of intensive training. He spends up to five hours a day on horseback during this period. The rest of the day he learns to care for the horses. The mounted policeman is expected to consider his animal's comfort first. He must also understand how his horse's mind works and what he can and cannot expect, before working successfully with the animal. At the end of the training period, each man is given a bareback-riding exam. In it he must be able to keep a secure seat at a walk, and trot and canter with no saddle or stirrup. The men who pass the exam then go on patrol with some other more experienced riders.

Mounted patrolmen belong to a division known for its spit-and-polish policy. They must be devoted to their duty, for they work hard for the privilege of being mounted. The men arrive at the stable well ahead of turnout time and leave well after their tour of duty is over. Although grooms are employed, the patrolmen usually put the finishing touches on their animals' coats and flowing manes and tails before going out. Each man is responsible for the care of his saddle, bridle and other gear. His uniforms are more expensive than those of the foot patrolman. He may wear out two or three pairs of breeches in a year, each of which costs about $30. He has to buy regulation puttees, spurs and belts. The mounted man's duty can be hazardous. Accidents do occur—even the best-trained horse may suddenly shy and throw his rider; he may slip on icy pavements despite carefully calked shoes; he may be hurt in traffic. Often working shifts compare unfavorably with those of the foot police. And there are other problems in working with a horse in the city. When a policeman on duty wants to eat, he has to find a spot where he can safely tie his horse. On his "off days" he must arrange for his horse to be exercised.

Horses accepted for police duty work a forty-two-hour week. They have a veterinarian on call at all hours. They get vacations if they get stale on the job or are ill. When they are too old for duty they are retired to the country. Each stable has its own blacksmith shop, and horses get custom-made shoes as often as they need them, because the heads of the mounted division are convinced that the "hoof makes the horse." Hoofs are also carefully oiled to prevent cracking and other foot ailments, and pads are used under the steel shoes to absorb the shock of walking and trotting on hard pavements. A harness maker adjusts all harness to each horse's measure to prevent such troubles as sore backs and galled spots. Horses have smart blue-and-gold blankets to wear under their saddles in cold weather, "raincoats" to wear in rain and snow, and both dress and work "clothes." The most careful attention is given the animals' diet. However, police duty can be dangerous for the horses. Unruly crowds have been known to throw firecrackers or marbles under their feet or to stab them with hatpins. If ever a horse is injured on duty, an SPCA ambulance picks him up.

A careful evaluation is made of both the man's and the horse's personality before they are assigned to work together. A beginning patrolman is usually given an experienced horse with a steady, even temperament while the new horses are assigned to the experienced men, and assignments are for long periods. Man and horse learn to work together as a unit and often grow quite fond of one another. After a while the horse may learn to anticipate his rider's commands, especially in controlling crowds. He recognizes his master and welcomes him with a whinny or by nuzzling the man's arm or shoulder with his nose. Sometimes when a policeman is transferred or retires or dies after a long period of riding the same horse, the animal will refuse to eat or will grieve himself ill.

Occasionally, when a patrolman and his horse reach retirement age at about the same time, the man will ask to be given his horse. If the two have worked together for a number of years, this request is often granted. The mounted division also receives letters from hundreds of children each year asking to be given a retiring horse, but the horses are rarely given to civilians. At retiring age most of the horses are sent to a farm kept by the New York City Department of Health, at Otisville, New York. Here they receive the best of care and a well-deserved rest.

A secluded corner of the Alcazar gardens in Seville, Spain. This ancient fortress-palace recalls the days when the Moors ruled over southern Spain.

Gardens

OF THE WORLD

By LOUISE I. McDOWELL

GARDENS come in many styles and sizes. There is the old-fashioned, or cottage, type, which is simply a blaze of brilliant flowers, sweet-scented and beloved of the bees and hummingbirds. On the other hand there is the Japanese garden, which often has no flowers at all—just rocks, pebbles and sand arranged in exquisite harmony. The stiff, formal designs of the Renaissance and the romantic landscaping of eighteenth-century England differ from each other and from all the other types, but all are gardens and all are beautiful and interesting in their various ways.

Gardens sometimes reflect the way of life of the people who create them. This is especially true of those left behind when Ferdinand and Isabella drove the Moors out of Spain. The Alcazar in Seville and the Alhambra in Granada still have the tranquil patio gardens, set with cypresses, myrtles or lemon trees reflected in cool

365

KEN RICHTER, EUROPEAN

design is of the first importance. Balance and symmetry must always be observed. In the France of Louis XIV the formal garden reached its extreme point of development at Versailles. It was perfectly suited to the rigid pattern of etiquette that governed the daily lives of the King and his entire court.

The most charming Italian gardens to the modern visitor are those of the country houses, or villas. The men who designed most of them planned house and garden together, relating both to the countryside around them. Italy is a hot, dry country with plenty of marble for building material and many rushing mountain streams. Thus many Italian gardens appear to consist of marble, greenery and water, with no flowers at all. This is chiefly the case in the long, narrow part of the peninsula, where it is difficult to have an abundance of flowers except in the very early spring.

One of the most famous of the water gardens is that of the Villa d'Este at Tivoli near Rome. It was begun a little over four hundred years ago by Ippolito II, Cardinal d'Este, son of the Duke of Ferrara. Like many Italian villas it is built on a hillside. The turbulent waters of the Aniene, pumped up the hill, rush in a series of cascades down marble terraces to pools studded with fountains and shaded by cypresses.

Quite different is Isola Bella, an island in Lake Maggiore, up in Lombardy. On this tiny island, or rock, a villa, the Borromeo Palace, crowns a graduated series of marble terraces filled with flowers. The supporting wall of each terrace has orange and lemon trees trained against it like vines. The foundation of all this consists of massive vaulted arches but from a distance the flowery terraces look as if they were floating on the surface of the water.

streams with sparkling fountains. The Moors, who were Muslims, loved privacy. To them a garden was not a show place but a part of the home, so they built their houses around their gardens.

What we called the formal Renaissance garden originated in Italy and was a revival of the elaborate landscape architecture of imperial Rome. In the sixteenth, seventeenth and eighteenth centuries this formal style spread all over Europe and eventually crossed the Atlantic. In this kind of garden,

In the heart of Paris the gardens of the Tuileries gladden the eye with their formal beauty. The palace to which they belonged was built by Catherine de Medici and destroyed more than 200 years later during the Commune of 1871.

ACE WILLIAMS, SHOSTAL

So far we have mentioned only outdoor gardens, but there are many that bloom all the year round under glass. Most of the large ones are in the great botanic gardens such as Kew in London and those in Paris and New York. Perhaps the largest privately owned indoor garden in the United States is at Longwood, the Du Pont estate near Kennett Square in Pennsylvania. There the greenhouses cover a total area of three and one half acres with the immense display rooms in the center of the group. These glass-roofed gardens are so spacious that unless you look up at the roof it is easy to imagine yourself in an outdoor pleasance in a tropical country.

The growing-houses that supply plants for the Longwood Gardens grow orchids and camellias in addition to such familiar flowers as primroses, phlox, delphiniums and peonies, besides many bulbs. The gardens were opened to the public in 1921, and since that time millions of visitors to Longwood have enjoyed their beauty and fragrance at a time of the year when other northern gardens were brown and sere or

JOE BARNELL, SHOSTAL

A garden in the grounds of the Imperial Palace in Kyoto, the former capital of Japan. Stones and turf and foliage are used with charming effect, and the whole is reflected in the tranquil surface of the lake.

367

covered with a protective blanket of snow.

On this side of the Atlantic the most celebrated naturalistic gardens are those of the South Carolina low country near Charleston. Azalea time—March and April —is the season when thousands of tourists visit Middleton, Magnolia, Runnymede and Cypress, among others. Most of them were laid out by wealthy rice and indigo planters of the eighteenth century. Although no two of them are exactly alike, they all follow a basic pattern suited to the character of the land. The original owners were transplanted Englishmen, influenced by the landscaping styles of the great estates in the old country where formal design was blended with naturalism. In adapting these styles to the Carolina lowlands they produced something new.

The heart of the plan was usually a formal garden centered on the plantation house. This followed the pattern that pre-

Examples of topiary art in a garden at Pacific Grove, California: Monterey cypresses are trained and clipped in curious shapes.

Against a tree-hung curtain of Spanish moss, pink and flame-colored azaleas are mirrored in dark, still streams at Cypress plantation near Charleston, in South Carolina.

The fern room in the immense indoor gardens of Longwood, the Du Pont estate at Kennett Square, Pennsylvania. Tall ferns like feather dusters border the ivy-fringed pool.

vailed in the England of Queen Anne and the Georges: straight lines, clipped shrubbery, parterres of flowers, ornamental pools and fountains. The outer edges of this garden were gradually blended into the surrounding woodland, which was thinned out for a certain distance and then permitted to merge with the forest.

It is the woodland garden that enchants the visitor. At Magnolia, for example, there are approximately eleven acres of huge magnolias and live oaks, hung with lavender-gray Spanish moss, against which the brilliant colors of the azaleas and camellias burn like fire. All of this, mirrored in the dark, winding lagoons, makes you feel you are in a dreamland.

Near Georgetown, South Carolina, on

369

Generations of English children have played along the flower-bordered walks of London's Kensington Gardens and sailed their boats on the Round Pond. Barrie's stories of Peter Pan add to their fame.

the Waccamaw River is Brookgreen, the unique sculpture garden created and endowed by the late Archer M. Huntington and his wife, the sculptress Anna Hyatt. Here the spreading live oaks festooned with moss form a setting for a remarkable collection of marble and bronze statuary by famous sculptors. In addition to its beauty as a naturalistic garden, Brookgreen has the distinction of being an outdoor museum of art created by an artist.

Not all of the Carolina gardens date from the eighteenth century. Cypress, which is a part of Dean Hall plantation, near Charleston, was opened to the public in 1930. Once a marshy rice plantation, it was abandoned for more than a hundred years. The owner had the junglelike undergrowth of a century cleared out of the sluggish streams, creating islands which were connected with paths and bridges, and planted thousands of azaleas and flowering bulbs. The soil and climate then took over and no one today would dream

that the garden was comparatively new.

It is always exciting and rewarding to make the waste spaces blossom and this was successfully done in Victoria, British Columbia. Half a century ago a wonderful garden was begun by Mr. and Mrs. Robert Butchart in an abandoned stone quarry on their estate. The soft Pacific climate and the devotion of the family, who still own it, have made the Butchart Garden so famous that it is visited by more than 150,-000 people a year. The garden is illuminated at night and visitors often go to see it then as well as in the daytime.

If you turn back to page 369 you will see the Monterey cypresses that have been trained and cut in unusual shapes. The trees are over twenty years old. When they were very young their limbs were weighted and kept carefully pruned so that they would grow in the desired pattern. Once a month the trees are clipped with an electric clipper and brushed with a whisk broom. This is called the art of topiary and it is

370

at least two thousand years old. The Roman writer Pliny the Younger, who lived in the first century A.D., left a description of the many fantastic forms in which the boxwood in his garden had been cut. The art was popular during the Renaissance and has never entirely died out. There are several famous topiary gardens in England. One of them, at Levens Hall in the county of Westmoreland, was started 250 years ago. Another way of training ornamental trees is pleaching them to make arches or covered alleys. This consists of bending, pruning and interlacing the branches of two trees—or two lines of trees—so that they will make a perfect arch or tunnel as they grow. The foliage both inside and out is clipped smooth like a hedge. The Villa Gori, near Siena, Italy, had a long covered passage of pleached ilex trees leading from the front door of the house to the garden.

The greatest number and variety of gardens are to be found in Britain. There are several reasons for this, one being the climate, which is moist and rarely too hot or too cold, so that a very wide range of plants will not only grow but flourish there. The British people have always taken full advantage of their good fortune in this respect, and the result has been that one might say the whole island is a garden. According to the latest statistics there are approximately ten million home owners who cultivate gardens and some six thousand clubs and societies that hold regular flower shows.

There are, of course, the great public gardens, such as Regent's Park and Kensington Gardens, which were originally designed for or by royalty. Also, gardens that

JOE BARNELL, SHOSTAL

The steep hillside gardens of the Villa d'Este at Tivoli are a perfect example of the Italian Renaissance use of architecture, water and greenery.

MALAK, COURTESY THE BULB GROWERS OF HOLLAND

The Keukenhof at Lisse, Holland: ninety acres of forest and sand dune, carpeted with hundreds of thousands of flowering bulbs, from crocuses to tulips.

Sun-drenched lawns, rose-red stone terraces and brilliant flowers: the Mogul Gardens in the grounds of the stately presidential residence in New Delhi, capital of India.

everyone should see are those at Hampton Court Palace, with its Elizabethan "knot garden" planted with sweet-smelling herbs, its lovely velvet lawns bordered with wide mixed flower beds and the maze in which the wanderer gets completely lost.

The famous ducal estates, such as Chatsworth, home of the Duke of Devonshire in Derbyshire, and Blenheim Palace, in Oxfordshire, home of the Duke of Marlborough, can be seen by visitors on certain days. Indeed, there are few of the famous estates that cannot be seen for a small fee, usually for the benefit of charity.

Such places are magnificent, with vast water gardens, cascades, fountains and statuary and acres of rolling green lawns and stately trees. But they do not, somehow, seem quite as cozy as a garden should be. For this quality some of the old walled gardens such as the one at Arbury Hall, in Warwickshire, are best; or the Shakespeare gardens, at Stratford-on-Avon; or the eighteenth-century gardens at Crathes Castle, in Kincardineshire. Wherever you go you are sure to find flowers and lawns —all of them lovingly tended by their owners. One of the nicest things about people who have gardens is their delight in sharing their treasure with others.

Going to the Theater

By STEPHEN RUDDY

GOING to the theater is always fun and during the past season the theaters on Broadway and off Broadway presented a wide variety of interesting and enjoyable shows. On Broadway fifty-nine productions (dramas, comedies, musicals) were offered during the season. At the same time the little off-Broadway theaters offered a new record of eighty plays and musicals. There is one main reason for the greater number of off-Broadway shows; the relative cheapness of producing them. This is due to the lower wages paid the actors and the smaller number of backstage personnel.

On Broadway the chances of producing a hit are estimated at one in four. This year there were eighteen, about average. Off Broadway where the stakes are lower the risks are considerably higher. This season only ten or eleven of the eighty shows produced made the grade financially.

On Broadway one of the best dramas of the season was the work of a new young playwright. *A Raisin in the Sun,* written by Lorraine Hansberry, tells the story of a Negro family in Chicago and their hard struggle to improve their lot. It was beautifully acted by Claudia McNeil and Sidney Poitier as the stalwart old mother and her rebellious son. This fine play won the New York Drama Critics Circle award.

There were other good dramas. *A Touch of the Poet,* by Eugene O'Neill, tells the story of a New England innkeeper who lives in a dream of a past he never really had and of his rude and sad awakening to reality. The play had moments of vigor and power that are typical of O'Neill's best work. The four stars, Helen Hayes, Eric Portman, Kim Stanley and Betty Field, despite differing styles of acting, gave the play a spirited performance.

J. B. by Archibald MacLeish won the Pulitzer Prize as the best American play of the year. A retelling of the Book of Job, it is set in modern times and is written in verse. While often obscure in meaning and a bit pretentious, the exciting direction of Elia Kazan and the acting of a good cast made it worthwhile.

Sweet Bird of Youth by Tennessee Williams is a violent tale of corruption and

FRIEDMAN-ABELES

Claudia McNeil and Sidney Poitier play the mother and son in Lorraine Hansberry's prize-winning drama *A Raisin in the Sun.*

Redhead—Gwen Verdon gives a big hug to her co-star, Richard Kiley.

lost youth and innocence. It showed again Mr. Williams' wonderful way with dialogue, and Geraldine Page in the role of a faded movie star gave a shattering performance.

The best comedy of the season was *The Pleasure of His Company,* a light drawing-room comedy done with style by an expert cast. The story is about an international playboy who arrives on the eve of his daughter's wedding to complicate her life and that of her mother, his ex-wife. The part was winningly played by Cyril Ritchard who also directed the play and by Cornelia Otis Skinner, the coauthor with Samuel Taylor.

The best musical was undoubtedly *Gypsy.* Starring the great Ethel Merman it told the funny and touching story of a stage mama and her efforts to make vaudeville stars of her two daughters. It gave a vivid picture of backstage life in vaudeville's last days and brought to life two

The Miracle Worker with Anne Bancroft and Patty Duke is the big dramatic hit of the new season.

Madame Rose (Ethel Merman) has words with her babies, June and Louise, in the tough and touching Gypsy.

Cornelia Otis Skinner and Cyril Ritchard, the stars of The Pleasure of His Company.

wonderful characters, Madame Rose Hovak and her daughter Louise (Gypsy). Gypsy was written by Arthur Laurents with a score by Jule Styne and lyrics by Stephen Sondheim. The fine supporting cast was headed by Sandra Church as Gypsy and Jack Klugman as the agent. Ethel Merman was right in the middle of everything and every inch the star. Whether belting out a song or acting, she made you sit on the edge of your seat. Gypsy was a model of what a musical should be.

Two other musicals were worth seeing. Redhead had the wonderfully talented and gay Gwen Verdon in an old-fashioned musical set in Edwardian London. The plot was silly but Miss Verdon supplied her own special magic to make the evening enjoyable. Flower Drum Song was not up to the great Rodgers and Hammerstein hits of the past (Oklahoma, South Pacific) but entertaining nevertheless. Set in San Francisco's Chinatown it told the story of the conflict between younger and older generations of Chinese Americans. The high spots of the evening were provided by the charm of Miyoshi Umeki and the verve of Pat Suzuki, two very talented young women.

There was one unusual feature of the past season: the number and quality of one-man shows. Three of them were out-

Two scenes from *Flower Drum Song:* Pat Suzuki tells Ed Kenney "I Enjoy Being a Girl"; Miyoshi Umeki is carried in a traditional Chinese wedding parade.

standing entertainment. Leading the list was the memorable Shakespeare's *Ages of Man* given by John Gielgud. Utilizing his magnificent voice and stage technique the fine English actor read a wide variety of selections from Shakespeare's sonnets, histories, comedies and tragedies. The bare stage came alive under his spell and a dazzling pageant of exciting, tender and tragic scenes passed before the audience. Quite different in mood and style was *Mark Twain Tonight.* A young actor, Hal Holbrook, dressed as Mark Twain, read and acted out a wide variety of Twain's best work. It provided a stimulating and enjoyable evening with the great American humorist. The third show, *A Party with Betty Comden and Adolph Green,* was just that. It had two bright and attractive performers who sang and joked their way through the hit shows of their own bright musical-comedy careers, including *On the Town, Peter Pan, Wonderful Town.*

The off-Broadway contribution to the American theater is too often ignored by critics and playgoers alike. However, dur-

ing the past few seasons the energetic and enthusiastic young people working in the Greenwich Village area and around the fringes of Broadway have been encouraged by more and more public interest in their productions. As a result they are trying their wings and those of their backers more and more. Today there are more theaters available for this type of production than ever before. It is estimated that over seventy theaters of all sorts have been used in the past two seasons for off-Broadway productions.

Outstanding in the good 1958-59 off-Broadway season was *Our Town,* presented in the Circle in the Square. This was a good revival of Thornton Wilder's play about life in a small New England town. Beautifully staged by José Quintero, the play had a fine cast headed by Jane McArthur and Clinton Kimbrough as the young lovers.

Other noteworthy productions were the Arthur Miller adaptation of the Henrik Ibsen classic *An Enemy of the People,* and *Leave It to Jane,* a bright revival of the 1917 musical with music by Jerome Kern. And one cannot overlook the continuing success of *The Threepenny Opera,* the first really successful off-Broadway show, now in its fifth year.

Adolph Green and Betty Comden in a bright moment from their little revue *A Party*.

An Off-Broadway success; Clinton Kimbrough and Aina Niemela in a scene from *Our Town*.

FRED FEHL

John Gielgud and Margaret Leighton played comic lovers in *Much Ado about Nothing*.

In *Mark Twain Tonight!* young Hal Holbrook, left, impersonated the great American author at age of seventy, lower left.

Mary Martin, star of the new musical play *The Sound of Music*.

New Forms
in Architecture

Design for new city hall, Toronto, by a Finnish architect, Viljo Rewell.

VILJO REWELL—JOHN B. PARKIN ASSOCIATES, ASSOCIATED AR-CHITECTS AND ENGINEERS; HAVAS OF HELSINKI, FINLAND

The Guggenheim Museum in New York, designed by Frank Lloyd Wright. Pictures are hung on outside wall of spiral ramp.

Starlike windows light the interior.

Prefabricated Church of the Good Shepherd was designed and built by contractor Neal Rayburn at a cost of $24,000. The church is in Clay County near Kansas City, Missouri.

PHOTOS ON THIS PAGE, WIDE WORLD

The Seagram Building on Park
Avenue, New York, a bronze
skyscraper designed by Mies
van der Rohe, Philip Johnson.

A concrete shell forms the
roof of the new sports
arena in Rome. Pier Luigi
Nervi is the architect.

BOTH PHOTOS, WIDE WORLD

Stamford, Connecticut, church shaped like a fish (an early Christian symbol) uses colored glass with concrete ribs. Architect, W. K. Harrison; engineer, F. J. Samuely.

Modern art gallery being built in New York. Architect, Edward D. Stone.

ROBERT STAHMAN

EDWARD DJRELL STONE

The Mutual Fire Insurance Building, Hartford County, Connecticut. Architects, Sherwood, Mills & Smith; sculptor, C. Nivola.

Producing a TV Special

By GEORGE H. McMURRAY
Television Consultant

NIGHT after night during the 1959-60 season millions of television fans seated themselves in front of their sets. As they switched on their dials, they may have been looking for a play, such as *Little Moon of Alban* or *The Green Pastures,* that would provide them with a great emotional experience. Or perhaps they wanted to see a musical comedy or revue with dancing and music that they could whistle, a sparkling Mary Martin–Ethel Merman act or an evening with Fred Astaire or Gene Kelly.

All these programs are included in the television-programing concept known as the special (called the spectacular, originally). At the beginning of the 1959-60 season 325 of these super TV shows had been placed on network schedules, 250 on NBC, 60 on CBS and 15 on ABC.

What is a television special? It is a costly, grandly conceived, one-hour, ninety-minute or two-hour production that promises something extraordinary and more often than not delivers it. Many specials are one-shots—that is, scheduled for one showing only—but most of them are in a specific series, like the Hallmark Hall of Fame, Omnibus, Du Pont Show of the Month, and Playhouse 90. The idea of the spectacular is generally credited to Sylvester L. (Pat) Weaver, Jr., former president and board chairman of the National Broadcasting Company and now an executive with a major advertising agency. Weaver borrowed—with full credit—the application of the word "spectacular" from Douglas Leigh, the man who conceived and built a majority of the huge spectacular signs that glow so brightly in the Times Square area.

NBC-TV launched the first series of spectaculars on September 12, 1954. The first show was *Satins and Spurs,* starring Betty Hutton and produced in color by Max Liebman.

Even before this telecast and before the words "spectacular" and "special" came into use, two ambitious TV projects on the Hallmark Hall of Fame, Gian-Carlo Menotti's opera *Amahl and the Night Visitors,* and *Hamlet,* starring Maurice Evans, pioneered the era of the big show.

Because Hallmark presented the first big shows on television and has continued to offer a series of six each season and because I have had the opportunity to study the Hall of Fame, my observations of specials will be based on this series. These shows are produced and directed by George Schaefer, who heads his own producing firm, Compass Productions.

The viewing public has little knowledge of the tremendous amount of hard labor, creativity, teamwork and money that go into a special.

Even before a show is selected, scheduled and placed into production, there are scores of details to be worked out. Ideas for a special may come from many sources. The sponsor, the advertising agency, the network, the producer, all may suggest properties (plays and musicals).

One important consideration is setting the budget. Specials are expensive. Their cost ranges from $100,000 to $500,000,

The producer-director and staff look at designs for the play's sets.

FIRST REHEARSALS

As rehearsals begin: Helen Hayes takes her place in an empty ballroom; director Bob Mulligan goes over a scene with members of the cast; Burgess Meredith and Lloyd Nolan pose for a camera angle.

SETTING THE STAGE

A technician listens to instructions on his headset; the director supervises all the preparations in the studio from the control booth; an artist puts a final touch of paint on one of the stage props.

depending upon the length of the program, cost of the property, salaries of stars, type of sets and costumes, the rehearsal time required and the number of stations that will carry the show.

The first step is acquiring a property. For a dramatic show the producer may work in two areas. He may decide upon an adaptation of a stage play or a book, which can be altered to fit TV, or he may buy an original story. In the case of an original, a writer may be commissioned by the producer to prepare a play. James Costigan, who wrote the award-winning *Little Moon of Alban*, which starred Julie Harris, did it on a special commission. More often the playwright has a completed work that he tries to sell.

Television producers always hope that ambitious writers will concentrate on writing the great ninety-minute or two-hour television show instead of the great American novel. But the fact remains that acquiring a desirable property is problem number one for the producer. If the sponsor, the advertising agency and the network agree with the producer on the play—adaptation or original—he has selected, his next move is to sit down with the writer and work out the best way to adapt it to television. Almost all of these shows are ninety minutes long. This includes the time allocated for opening and closing and for the credits and commercials.

With the problems of timing in mind, the writer goes home, completes his first rough draft and has a second session with the producer. There are likely to be two or three rewrites before the first working draft is ready and sent to the sponsor and to the advertising agency for approval. When the play finally goes into rehearsal, invariably the script is found to be too long, and the writer and producer confer and keep cutting and revising it.

Meanwhile, casting has been going on. Selecting the stars and actors for featured roles, supporting and small parts is the responsibility of the producer and his staff. Names of stars are submitted to the sponsor and to the advertising agency for approval. If the show originates in New York, it has available a great pool of legitimate theater talent; if it comes from Hollywood, it depends primarily upon film actors.

Availability of talent and the show's budget are two important considerations in casting. The producer may visualize a dream cast but sometimes his budget will force him to go to second choice, particularly if there are numerous leading parts to be filled.

All the while casting is going on, many other important details are being settled. Costumes and sets are being designed, orders for the required number of cameras are placed, the technical director, lighting director and all other technicians are busy planning their parts. The producer-director must work closely with his designers, the cameramen and all of the others concerned because, once the show is in the studio, he is going to be limited to what has been agreed upon in these days of planning.

Presenting shows in color places added burdens on the shoulders of the director. The cameras are twice as large as those used for black and white, and due to their weight and bulk the director does not have the mobility and flexibility that he has with ordinary cameras. Knowing the type of cameras and booms with which he has to work and the studio space available to him, the director generally plots on paper as much of the action as he can. He must know which cameras he will have for which scene, where he can hide them, where he can use them and what the scene changes will be.

After the sets have been approved from drawings and models submitted by the designer, and the costumes selected from sketches and assigned to one of the costume houses, the director is finally ready to sit down and work out his rehearsal schedule in detail.

The Hallmark Hall of Fame devotes a full three weeks, including Saturdays and Sundays, to rehearsals. This is an unusually long rehearsal period, but the producer feels that length of time is needed to achieve a production of high quality. A one-hour special usually requires two weeks or less of rehearsal time.

Timing of the different elements on the television rehearsal schedule is something that a top director learns through experience over the years. He takes the play and breaks it down into short scenes in much the same way as a movie is made.

Four days before show day many of the big shows put on in New York rehearse at Central Plaza, a five-story building on lower Second Avenue, which is normally used for dances, weddings and banquets.

DRESS REHEARSAL

In the complete run-through of *Ah, Wilderness!* the cameras follow O'Neill's young hero as he meets his sweetheart on a dock, stops in a saloon and returns to his family's front porch.

The building has five spacious ballrooms and there are usually four or five shows in rehearsal there at the same time.

Just before going into rehearsal the assistant director and a production assistant block out the various scenes. They mark the placing of props and scenery and the movements of the actors with masking tape on the floor of the rehearsal hall.

The first day of rehearsal is devoted to a reading of the play by the cast, with the director and his associates paying close attention. After the reading the director talks to the cast, gives them his conception of the play and how it should be played and tells the cast what he expects of each of them. He has, of course, read the script over many times and has it virtually memorized.

After the initial rehearsal day two weeks may pass before the whole cast is together again. This is because director George Schaefer works with each individual scene separately, and only the actors appearing in a particular scene may be on hand at the same time. This spares the actors tedious sitting and waiting.

Another factor in the scene-by-scene rehearsal pattern is the financial saving. Under union rules the show has a minimum call of three hours a day. Any overtime is paid by the hour. This is not important in the case of the stars, whose salaries are far over scale, but they like Schaefer's rigid schedule because it allows them free time for costume fittings and for some of their own personal and professional business.

During the last week in the rehearsal hall there are run-throughs of the play without any stops exactly as it will be seen on the home screens, with the necessary time allowed for the commercials and station breaks. Without interruption for ninety minutes the director is able to observe the performances of his cast and correct faulty interpretations.

When the show goes into the studio, an entirely new set of problems confronts the actors and the director. In the rehearsal hall the actor is all important. His performance has been carefully worked on and protected by the director. Suddenly, in the studio on camera, he is moved around as if he were one of the props.

But if his director has planned with great care and timing, the actor will know where he is going at all times during the action, since it has been carefully explained to him before he faces the cameras. In the few days he has before air time there are more run-throughs, and he has ample opportunity to get used to the sets, the position of the cameras and all of the transitions and costume changes required of him.

On show day a final dress rehearsal is held. Let us assume that the show goes on the air at 9:30 to 11:00 that night. On Hall of Fame shows the dress rehearsal is usually scheduled for 4:30 to 6:30. It can't be closer to air time because the technicians need an hour for dinner and the color cameras need two hours for test patterns and balance to assure perfect pictures.

At the end of the dress rehearsal the actors usually go out to dinner and upon their return they spend 45 minutes with the director to hear his notes and his final instructions. Then 45 minutes for final retouching of make-up and adjustment of costumes. Their union contract provides a half-hour for relaxation or doing what they please.

When the actors finally bring their play to the home screens, they have to go on the air and really give. There is no stopping. There is no turning back. They have to be able to think, to act with validity. Tricks that might slip by on the stage will be glaringly exposed under the merciless eye of the camera.

The same degree of perfection must be attained by the cameramen and others in the technical crew. The picture that goes on the air must be carefully composed and

A complex network of lights, cameras and sound equipment is used by the technicians as they shoot a scene of the play.

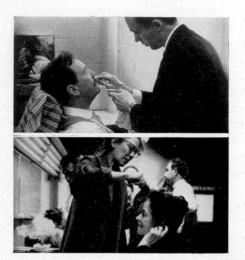

Final makeup: artists give mustache to Burgess Meredith and 1900 hairdo to Helen Hayes.

A cameraman takes notes as the play moves on to another set.

THE SHOW IS ON

lighted. The cameras have to move on a specific mark at a certain height and employ certain lenses, with each camera set up for a particular pattern and movement previously outlined for it.

Many, many people are involved in the production of a live—or video taped—television special (more than 300 on an average Hall of Fame show). Of this number 180 work behind the scenes on the technical end of the production. The cast varies from 25 on some dramas to 80 on a show like *The Green Pastures,* and even more on a *Kiss Me, Kate* with an orchestra of 30. There are assistant directors, a unit manager and his assistants, production assistants, agency and network publicity and promotion people, photographers and many others never seen by the viewing public.

In addition to the people who work on the show itself, another group of more than fifty are concerned with the commercials. Commercials on many shows are filmed or they may be partly filmed and partly live.

Commercials are created by the advertising agencies. Usually an executive in charge of television and radio, the account supervisor, the copy supervisor and the director are the principals responsible for production of the commercials.

When the written commercial has been completed, the TV and radio man meets with his basic crew, including the director and the costume and set designers. Layouts and designs are created for agency and sponsor approval. Final revisions are made if needed, and two days before the show goes on the air the commercials go into rehearsal. Hallmark commercials are done live from an NBC studio in Rockefeller Center. Each one is different and, because the same greeting cards are never featured twice, is never repeated.

Few people at home realize just how much talent, work and time is necessary to bring them the ninety minutes or two hours of fine entertainment that is theirs at the flick of a dial. The sum of all this equals the magic that sometimes makes a special something very special indeed.

The crew laughs at a funny bit of action.

Curtain up! The director watches final result.

THE quality of television during the 1958-59 season was a poor comment on the industry's position as a leading source of entertainment. "A national disenchantment with television has set in," wrote Abel Green in *Variety,* the bible of show business. "Just as it was once fashionable to say 'I haven't seen a movie in years,' many people are now saying 'I can't remember when I turned the set on last.'"

It was apparent during the year that the high cost of TV had reached a point where even an increased budget could not be depended upon to improve the quality of the product (program mediocrity reduced the audience, the reduced audience weakened the medium's economics, weakened economics brought on more mediocrity). Television made its greatest impact during the year with such relatively inexpensive programs as public affairs, educational TV and conversation shows.

The conversation show flourished on Edward R. Murrow's Small World, on the Jack Paar Show, on Arthur Godfrey's morning show, on David Susskind's Open End show and NBC's The Open Mind. Talk flamed about everything, even topics that were explosive and controversial—the hotter the better. People who once blamed television for discouraging parlor conversation now said how nice it was on TV. It was, if only because the "talk" shows recaptured the qualities that characterized early TV—spontaneity and unexpectedness.

During the year the money quiz shows blew up in their owners' faces. A disgruntled contestant on Dotto took his complaint to the New York district attorney's office. This eventually led to a Congressional investigation. "Anyone want ten unconnected dots?" chortled the comedians. NBC tried to run an honest quiz, Brains and Brawn, only to discover that very often a real "brain" made a poor

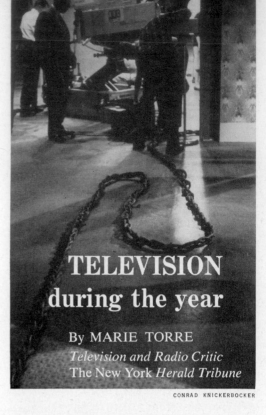

TELEVISION during the year

By MARIE TORRE
Television and Radio Critic
The New York *Herald Tribune*

CONRAD KNICKERBOCKER

quiz contestant, as when music expert Deems Taylor couldn't recognize Enrico Caruso's voice singing *La Donna è Mobile.*

The big-name comedians came back with a fanfare in 1958—and took large pratfalls. Jackie Gleason returned with a weekly Friday night show which went off before his thirteen weeks were up. A subdued Milton Berle, Mr. Television himself, set only a small blaze on his return. George Gobel's hour-long show was canceled, and his outlook for the following season was a half-hour show every other week. Outside of a few comedians of the angry-young-man school, the only big impression was made by a pair of Canadians, Wayne and Shuster, whose literate humor won wide acclaim when they appeared on the Ed Sullivan shows.

Generally it was a bad year for live drama. In place of Studio One, once a leader in the drama field, viewers had the Westinghouse Desilu Playhouse, which unfortunately had none of the originality

388

of its predecessor. Du Pont continued with live shows and some of them were excellent. These shows included *Wuthering Heights, The Winslow Boy, Count of Monte Cristo, Hamlet* and *The Browning Version,* but the suspicion grew that the Du Pont Show of the Month was playing it safe in the story department. The highly respected Hallmark Hall of Fame also remained true to proven favorites like *Green Pastures, Ah, Wilderness!, Kiss Me, Kate* and *Johnny Belinda.* Only one time during the season did Hallmark depart from the policy of adaptations. At Christmas time it presented an original work by Hollywood's inventive Helen Deutsch titled *Christmas Tree.* It was a warm and tender play which drew praise from critics and viewers alike.

Most of the live original drama was found on Playhouse 90. Among the best of its dramas were J. P. Miller's *The Days of Wine and Roses, The Time of Your Life* (starring Jackie Gleason) and *Judgment at Nuremberg* (starring Claude Rains). Despite these successes it was announced that Playhouse 90 would be curtailed to an alternate-week schedule in the 1959-60 season. This meant still a further blow to live drama.

The dance, both popular and classic, was given a full showing during the 1958-59 season. The first company to literally dance up a storm was the Soviet Union's Moiseyev dancers who appeared on Ed Sullivan's show. Fred Astaire's debut performance on NBC was one of the great TV shows of the year. The show was repeated four months later before a larger audience than the first one. Gene Kelly provided another interesting dance show on Omnibus. The New York City Ballet company presented Tchaikovsky's *The Nutcracker* on Playhouse 90, with George Balanchine's choreography.

Fine music on TV was sparse, but what there was of it was generally good, particularly on Voice of Firestone (canceled in May of 1959). The Bell Telephone Hour brought music lovers such fine singers as Renata Tebaldi, the great Italian opera star, and Harry Belafonte, leading folk and calypso singer. Leonard Bernstein did a once-a-month series for CBS inspired by the New York Philharmonic's novel Thursday evening preview concerts in Carnegie Hall. He also did a Young People's Concert series which was well received. The NBC Opera Company marked its tenth season by presenting once more its appealing Christmas colorcast of Gian-Carlo Menotti's *Amahl and the Night Visitors* and also his new *Maria Golovin.*

During the year the networks stood out more than ever before as powerful agencies for bringing news, public affairs and education to the attention of a far flung audience. An attempt to use television as a giant country-wide classroom turned out to be the biggest single achievement of the 1958-59 season.

NBC's Continental Classroom, with more than 300,000 viewers five days weekly, became the world's largest class and the first nationwide TV course for college credit. The two-semester course in atomic-age physics was offered in partnership with leading American educational and industrial organizations. It was designed to ease the shortage of qualified science teachers and was offered for credit in more than 270 colleges and universities in the United States. Its compelling teacher was the eminent physicist Harvey E. White; its guest lecturers included seven Nobel Prize winners.

Equally impressive were the strides made in spot reporting and detailed coverage of national and world news, some of it in the best nighttime viewing hours. NBC stepped up its coverage of world events by 20 per cent during the year through its more than 300 correspondents at home and abroad. At the same time, CBS presented a record number of scheduled and special reports. There was a stream of news specials on the top issues of the year, such as the desegregation struggle, satellites and space travel and United States–Soviet relations.

The experimental Kaleidoscope series on NBC was new in pictorial journalism, probing such activities as wire tapping and electronic eavesdropping. Another outstanding newcomer was The Great Challenge, a series of symposia, or group discussions, on subjects of current importance.

The Project 20 production of *Meet Mr. Lincoln* was novel and exciting. Camera animation of a kind new to television was used to give movement and flow to century-old still pictures, so that the viewer felt that he was seeing Lincoln as the people of his time saw him.

Ironically, TV increased its coverage of news and public affairs without the expert services of Edward R. Murrow, who confined his activities to radio, Small World and Person to Person when CBS canceled his excellent news series, See It Now. Murrow publicly expressed his resentment when, some months later, he acted upon a clause in his contract which permitted him to take a year-long rest. However, the famous news analyst patched up his differences with CBS before he left for a year of "traveling, reading and listening."

A strongly established type of TV program, the "special," continued to be spotted here and there on the season's schedule. Three specials received critical praise. They were the two-hour *Wonderful Town,* starring Rosalind Russell, *Art Carney Meets Peter and the Wolf* and Mary Martin's matineé and evening song shows on Easter Sunday.

Regular schedules of comedy, variety, audience participation, adventure and

DANCE

An Evening with
Fred Astaire
and Barrie Chase.

Moiseyev dancers
appeared on the
Ed Sullivan show.

NBC-TV

CBS-TV

CONVERSATION

David Susskind and
his panel on
Open End.

drama revolved around Steve Allen, Loretta Young, Perry Como, Dinah Shore, Groucho Marx and Arthur Godfrey (until illness forced him to withdraw). Other headliners were Jack Benny, Danny Thomas, Walter Brennan, Red Skelton, Pat Boone and the durable Ed Sullivan, who completed his tenth consecutive year on TV.

Among the new weekly shows that came on the scene were Peter Gunn, Bat Masterson and The Ann Sothern Show. The best of these was Peter Gunn, which had an old cops 'n' robbers setting but a new musical background. This combination of music and action was much imitated in later shows. Another new member of the weekly television ranks was Garry Moore. After eight years on the daytime schedule at CBS, he introduced his own

OF SPECIAL INTEREST

MUSIC

Maria Golovin.

Renata Tebaldi: songs from Madama Butterfly.

Harry Belafonte: songs from many lands.

CHILDREN'S CLASSICS

Art Carney Meets Peter and the Wolf delighted audiences of all ages.

DRAMA

Playhouse 90's Judgment at Nuremberg.

EDUCATION

Dr. Harvey White: Continental Classroom.

full-hour nighttime variety show. Although the Moore show had a sluggish beginning it gradually won itself a sizable audience.

Westerns continued to be the most popular fare, with Wagon Train, Gunsmoke and Maverick staying among the top-rated shows. The early-morning Today, leaning heavily on news features, and the refreshingly informal late-night Jack Paar Show enjoyed increasing popularity as the season progressed.

By season's end, color television had yet to get off the ground. This was despite NBC's telecasting a record high of 664 hours in color during 1958 (averaging three color programs a day). Its progress lagged behind that of video tape which came into wide use during the 1958-59 season. Video tape gave new flexibility to programing and particularly to news reporting. This new tape enabled reporters to record on-the-spot happenings with greater ease and efficiency.

There was one other electronic miracle during the season. In June of 1959 the British Broadcasting Company in conjunction with NBC made an experiment that was a major step toward live transatlantic television. About two and a half hours after Queen Elizabeth flew from London Airport to visit Canada, America's viewers saw a one-minute scene of the royal departure! This scene was transmitted by telephone cable. Although engineers say the transmission of longer than one-minute films would be impractical under the system, it is generally agreed that the experiment was a great advance in communications.

MUSIC

By JOHN TASKER HOWARD

Author, Composer and Critic

After a concert in Moscow, conductor Bernstein has a talk with Boris Pasternak.

The New York Philharmonic, led by Leonard Bernstein, plays in Istanbul, Turkey, on its good-will tour.

PHOTOS, COLUMBIA RECORDS

An unusual number of music anniversaries occurred in 1959. The most widely observed was the bicentennial of the death of George Frederick Handel, in London, on April 14, 1759. In New York a committee was appointed by the Mayor to provide for a series of events that were given over a two-and-a-half-month period—March 1 to May 20. Works of Handel that are seldom heard today were featured at the concerts. The ode *Alexander's Feast* was performed at the opening, and a week later an oratorio was featured—*Samson*. The New York Philharmonic devoted two programs to Handel's works, one offering the *St. John Passion* and the other the *Ode for St. Cecilia's Day*. Other oratorios heard were *Judas Maccabaeus* and *Israel in Egypt*. Two of Handel's operas were produced—*Ezio*

and *Xerxes*. Handel composed over forty operas altogether, but they are known today only for an occasional excerpt. *Xerxes* is distinguished for its aria *Ombra mai fu,* better known today as an instrumental piece—the famous *Largo*. The New York festival ended with a performance by the Little Orchestra Society of Handel's *Water Music* and *Royal Fireworks Music* at the Bethesda Fountain in Central Park. The *Water Music* was first played in 1717 on the royal barge on the Thames River; and the *Royal Fireworks Music,* in London's Green Park in 1749.

Only a few observances marked the three hundredth anniversary of the birth of Henry Purcell, one of the greatest of English composers. Nor did the anniversary of Felix Mendelssohn's birth (February 3,

1809) receive attention equal to that given to Handel. The centennial of Victor Herbert's birth (in Ireland, February 1, 1859) was marked by numerous radio and television programs and by a banquet in Washington, D. C., given by the society he helped to found, the American Society of Composers, Authors and Publishers.

A little more than thirty-three years after its first performance in Berlin (December 14, 1925) the opera *Wozzeck,* by the late Alban Berg, was put on by the Metropolitan Opera Company (March 5, 1959). The earliest American performance had been given twenty-eight years before by the Philadelphia Grand Opera Company under Leopold Stokowski. In 1951 *Wozzeck* was played in concert form by the New York Philharmonic, and in the following year it was given a stage production by the New York City Opera Company.

The Metropolitan's long delay in offering *Wozzeck* is perhaps understandable in view of the forbidding nature of both its subject and its music. The libretto tells of a downtrodden, psychopathic soldier who stabs his unfaithful sweetheart and then commits suicide by drowning. The score is

Eleanor Steber and Kurt Baum in Metropolitan performance of the German opera Wozzeck.

LOUIS MÉLANÇON

composed partly in the twelve-tone, atonal idiom of Berg's teacher, Arnold Schönberg. There is not much regular singing, and a great deal of vocal declamation. Rudolf Bing, general manager of the Metropolitan, must have felt that by now the conservative audiences of his opera house were ready to accept a work that was so far ahead of its time when it was written.

Bing's optimism was justified. The critics hailed *Wozzeck* as a masterpiece, and the performances drew sold out houses. The opera was presented in English, the principal parts were sung by Herbert Uhde and Eleanor Steber, Karl Boehm conducted, and the production was staged by Herbert Graf.

Continuance of New York's place as the nation's music and theatrical center seemed assured when President Eisenhower broke ground for the first building of the Lincoln Center for the Performing Arts. Financed principally by corporate and private gifts, this center will house the new auditorium of the New York Philharmonic (the first building to be erected), the Metropolitan Opera House, a repertory theater, a library and museum, the Julliard School of Music, and the downtown campus of Fordham University.

Music was provided by the New York Philharmonic under its director, Leonard Bernstein. The soloists were Risë Stevens, soprano, and Leonard Warren, baritone. Commenting on the music of the Philharmonic and the soloists, the President remarked that if they could do so well in a tent, he wondered why they needed a hall.

In the spring of 1958 the Ford Foundation made a grant of $105,000 to the New York City Opera Company for the production of operas by ten contemporary American composers. (See *1959 Annual,* article on music.) The purpose of the grant was to find out whether an extensive repertoire of American operas existed and how interested the public might be in supporting it.

The results were gratifying. The audiences were as large as those that attended the so-called classical operas. It was felt, however, that the demonstration was incomplete; that the experiment was only local, and the audiences may have been attracted by the novelty of the first season. The Foundation made a second grant, this time of $310,000, for a second season in New York and for an extensive tour of the country in 1960.

In the second New York season (spring of 1959) three operas performed in 1959 were repeated (*Susannah* by Carlisle Floyd, *The Ballad of Baby Doe* by Douglas Moore, and *Regina* by Marc Blitzstein). Nine operas new to the City Center were added: *Wuthering Heights* by Carlisle Floyd, *The Triumph of St. Joan* by Norman Dello Joio, *Street Scene* by Kurt Weill, *The Devil and Daniel Webster* by Douglas Moore, *He Who Gets Slapped* by Robert Ward, *Maria Golovin* and *The Medium* by Gian-Carlo Menotti, *Six Characters in Search of an Author* by Hugo Weisgall, and *The Scarf* by Lee Hoiby.

As in 1959, thirty young American composers were invited to attend rehearsals of the operas and to see how they were prepared for production. The 1960 tour is to include two weeks of performances in New York, and five weeks visiting such cities as Boston, Cleveland, Detroit, Chicago, Pittsburgh, Washington and Philadelphia, as well as several college and university communities. Five or six of the best operas from the two previous seasons will be presented on the tour.

Another Ford Foundation project is aimed at helping young composers to find an outlet for their works. Without an outlet, composers are generally forced to find teaching positions that allow them opportunity to compose only in their spare time. With the co-operation of the National Music Council, the Ford Foundation will place twenty-five young composers for a year

ASSOCIATED PRESS

"Praise Him in the Sound of the Trumpet," is the theme of the "jazz mass."

Viennese pianists Demus, left, and Badura-Skoda.

each in various secondary schools, not to teach, but to compose music for the school orchestras, choruses and bands. Each composer chosen will have an opportunity to write steadily for performances by varied musical groups whose abilities he will know intimately. It is hoped that the schools and the pupils will benefit from having music composed especially for them.

While aid to composers and musicians in the United States is given by endowed foundations and private philanthropists, the Government of Canada, through its sponsorship of the Canadian Council, is supporting music directly. Early in 1958 the Council announced a grant of $60,000 to the Canadian Music Council for support of the newly formed Canadian Composers' Center. The principal task of the Center's director, Jean-Marie Baudet, will be to assemble a complete library of all music written by Canadians deemed worthy of per-

Antonietta Stella, soprano, as Leonora and Carlo Bergonzi, tenor, in part of the hero Manrico, with baritone Leonard Warren cast as villain in scene from Verdi's *Il Trovatore*.

formance in Canada and abroad. Scores will be made available to orchestras and performing agencies, to broadcasting and recording companies, and the Council itself is planning a recording program. In the meanwhile grants have been made to Canadian symphony orchestras from coast to coast. These funds are to be used for increasing the membership of the orchestras, for financing additional concerts and for tours to smaller communities near the orchestras' home cities.

Shortly after the close of World War II the Reverend Geoffrey Beaumont, vicar of St. George's Church in London, composed a "jazz mass" which was performed in his church. In 1957 it was given in America at Providence, Rhode Island, and later in Boston, but it was not until two years later (April 5, 1959) that a performance in St. Paul's Episcopal Church, Norwalk, Connecticut, attracted national attention to the

work. It is officially called a "twentieth-century folk mass." According to the Reverend Anthony P. Treasure, rector of St. Paul's, the performance represented an effort to place the words of the Liturgy within a musical framework that could be understood by modern young people. In the "jazz mass" the Kyrie and Agnus Dei move above a beguine rhythm; waltz time is used for the Gloria. A bold melody, mostly improvised, runs through the Credo, the Sanctus, and Pater Noster; and the trumpeter swings out for the words: "Praise Him in the Sound of the Trumpet."

For the instrumental accompaniment the Rector of St. Paul's engaged the piano, bass viol, drums and saxophone players of the Martino-Fraturo Sextet, a Stamford, Conn., combo. Much of the improvisation was supposed to be on themes by Father Beaumont, but it is said that a discerning ear could pick out such popular tunes as

It's Almost Like Falling in Love, Bernie's Tune and *Lover, Come Back to Me*. The congregation behaved with decorum, particularly the young people. A few of the older members were less controlled and responded with tapping feet.

Father Treasure justified the use of jazz in church services by saying that "jazz is more akin to the ancient plain-song melodies than anything else." Some of the parishioners were less enthusiastic, and one choirboy said: "It was good, but it was just a little queer in the church."

A month after the performance in Norwalk the propriety of the "jazz mass" was discussed at the annual convention of the Episcopal Diocese of New York. A resolution was referred to the Cathedral Church Council which promised to study the matter and report later.

Van Cliburn, the Texan pianist who was catapulted into fame after he won first prize in the Tchaikowsky International Piano Competition at Moscow (see *1959 Annual,* article on music) was forced to cancel the rest of his 1958-59 season's concerts following an operation on an abcessed finger (February 27, 1959).

The middle finger of his right hand had been bothering him for twelve days, and he wore a bandage during several of his recitals. On the advice of five hand and plastic surgeons, Cliburn canceled all concerts until the following June, including one scheduled for March 16 at which he was to play for eighteen thousand students in New York's Madison Square Garden. After resting his hand for two months, Cliburn was permitted to practice again in the latter part of April. In June he made five appearances in Europe—in France, England, Italy and Spain.

Playing piano duets has for years been a favorite pastime among amateur musicians. Piano teachers encourage their pupils to play such duets. Yet while two-piano teams are familiar to concert audiences, four-hand playing on one piano has been more or less confined to the studio and the home. A few years ago two young Viennese pianists who had met at Vienna's Academy of Music started to play together purely for relaxation. They found they enjoyed it so much that they made several recordings. Then they decided to give public concerts. Joerg Demus, thirty, and Paul Badura-Skoda, thirty-one, made their American debut as a four-handed team in January of 1959. In some pieces Demus played the treble part and Badura-Skoda the bass, and in others they switched positions. The pedaling was done by the treble pianist, largely because the bass player is apt to overpedal to avoid thickness of tone. The players were seated on separate benches, and when they crossed each other's arms in difficult passages, they presented what one critic termed "the bewildering aspect of a two-headed Siva" (a Hindu god with many hands).

The playing was clean and remarkably free from blurred passages, even though the music was intricate and filled with rapid ornamentation. Any slips that may have occurred were not noticed by the audience, but Badura-Skoda very modestly pointed out that this was probably because the music they played was unfamiliar to most of the listeners.

On the evening of October 26 the Metropolitan Opera opened its seventy-fifth season with a brand new and beautiful production of Verdi's *Il Trovatore*. The principal singers were Leonard Warren as the Count di Luna, Carlo Bergonzi as Manrico, Antonietta Stella as Leonora and Giulleta Simionato (a newcomer to the Met) as Azucena. The opera was staged by Herbert Graf and the sets and costumes were designed by Motley (Elizabeth Montgomery). Roald Reitan from Tacoma, Washington, cowinner of the Metropolitan Opera Auditions, another newcomer to the Metropolitan stage, played a gypsy.

The Revival of

Ragtime

By JOHN S. WILSON
Jazz Critic, The New York Times

IN the past few years the gay, snappy beat of a new type of piano music has been heard: new, that is, to millions of people born since the 1920's. This is the music called ragtime, and it has had a strange career of ups and downs. It grew out of the cakewalk and the minstrel-show music of the nineteenth century, and until after World War I it was popular not only on this side of the Atlantic but in many strange corners of the world. Then people grew tired of ragtime and it was seldom heard and almost entirely forgotten for more than twenty-five years.

Its original downfall may well have been brought on by too much popularity. This gay, jubilant music drew on many sources—the syncopation of the Negro's banjo playing on the plantations and in minstrel shows; on Negro folk melodies; on the strutting spirit of the cakewalk. It took shape as a blend of the European idea of form and the African approach to rhythm.

Its pattern was generally somewhat like that of the rondo, with several strains, or tunes, formally arranged and repeated. Unlike jazz, this was composed music, written music that could be read by any musically literate person. Playing it was something else again, because its rhythm was unlike anything in European music.

Syncopation—the accenting of the normally weak beat—was, of course, a familiar device in European music but only as a briefly used means of conveying a feeling of nervousness or restlessness. Ragtime, however, was almost *all* syncopation. The right hand played a syncopated beat while the left hand provided a steady, regularly accented foundation. On top of this, as jazz historian Marshall Stearns has put it, "a good pianist improvises an endless variety of rhythmic suspensions, unusual accents and between-the-beat effects. In other words, the best ragtime incorporates the horizontal rhythmic flow of all good American Negro music. It also retains its European form. The blend is a rare and sophisticated piano music that can be well played only by a very few, highly gifted virtuosos. They were the fountainhead of the ragtime craze."

A focal point in the development of ragtime was the little town of Sedalia, Missouri. It was there that Scott Joplin, the greatest composer of rags (*Maple Leaf Rag* is one of his best-known pieces), lived and worked, and it was there that John Stark gave this young, original music permanent form by publishing the work of the leading writers of rags. From Sedalia, ragtime spread out in every direction. In St. Louis and Kansas City such stars of ragtime as Tom Turpin and Joseph Lamb could be heard. In Chicago, Jess Pickett's *The Dream Rag* was one of the hits of the World's Fair of 1893; and in New Orleans, Tony Jackson and Jelly Roll Morton softened its brittle bounce.

Wally Rose

James P. Johnson

Jelly Roll Morton

Joseph Lamb

Knocky Parker

In the East it enlisted the talents of James P. Johnson, Luckey Roberts, Eubie Blake and others.

For most of the first twenty years of this century, ragtime rode the wave of popularity. It was in demand in cabarets, in vaudeville, at band concerts, on player pianos, wherever people went in search of entertainment. And, of course, because of its popularity it was diluted and distorted. Tin Pan Alley ground out so-called rags that had little in common with the classic rags written by Joplin, Lamb and others but the word "rag" in the title. The average home pianist had more luck trying to play these simple pseudo-rags than in battling the complexities of the real thing. Soon the shoddy "rags" had all but buried the work of the genuine-rag composers and performers, and in the end the public became bored with their drab sameness.

Meanwhile the true-rag idiom and its pianists were being absorbed by another rising musical line, jazz. The joining of the two was most noticeable in the Harlem school of pianists headed by James P. Johnson, Willie "The Lion" Smith and Luckey Roberts. They brought their ragtime heritage into jazz with the development of "stride" piano. In this a striding effect is created in the left hand by the use of a single note on the first and third beats alternating with chords in the second and fourth.

By the middle 1920's rags had practically disappeared except for such perennial favorites as *Twelfth Street Rag* and *Maple Leaf Rag*—and they had been trimmed of all vestiges of their ragtime origins and were played in swing versions. The real ragtime pianists had died, retired or changed over to jazz. Ragtime remained an almost forgotten relic of the past until the late 1940's. Then the revival of interest in traditional jazz spurred a few pianists to explore the old rags once more.

Wally Rose, the pianist in Lu Watters' Yerba Buena Jazz Band (which had much to do with stimulating the traditional jazz revival), was one of the first to give the old rags a new hearing. Rose played *Black and White Rag* at the Yerba Buena Band's first recording session in 1941. During most of the 1950's only two pianists besides Wally Rose paid serious attention to rags. One was Ralph Sutton, whose vast admiration for the stride style of Fats Waller and James P. Johnson led him, quite logically, back to its rag origins. The other was Knocky Parker, an English professor by trade, who devotes his non-teaching time to the music of Jelly Roll Morton, rags and other elements that have gone into the making of jazz.

By themselves these pianists could do little more than reach the few people who found a fascination in what seemed to be a charming if old-fashioned form of music.

But several other factors came together to create a new interest in this music.

One factor was the popularity of recordings by so-called honky-tonk pianists, whose lively but mechanical performances were supposed to represent the piano style of the ragtime era. People who were attracted to them began to want to hear the real ragtime. Then, in addition to the recordings and performances of Wally Rose, Ralph Sutton and Knocky Parker, records were made of piano rolls played by some of the great names of ragtime—Scott Joplin, James Scott, Tom Turpin—giving an ear-opening sample of ragtime's beauty and stimulation.

With this steadily accumulating and widening foundation, the old rags and the ragtime piano style began to gain a new, fresh-eyed audience. The Tin Pan Alley trash had long been forgotten. Jazz—and particularly piano jazz—had moved great distances since the ragtime influence had flowed into it. The piano rags that are being recalled today are the ones that gave ragtime its validity. The style itself is no longer close enough to current jazz to be considered a subordinate—or even closely related—musical line. It seems certain that after its long period of eclipse, ragtime is finally about to gain the recognition as a unique and delightful musical idiom that

it seemed destined for until it was ruined by its own popularity.

The best evidence of the comeback of ragtime (and of the vitality of the rag men) lies in the recording companies' diligence in seeking out and recording the work of veteran performers. Among these are 76-year-old Eubie Blake (on 20th Fox Records), 66-year-old Luckey Roberts (on Period Records) and 62-year-old Willie "The Lion" Smith (on Grand Award and Dot Records). It is even possible that the concertos, choral works and symphonies in ragtime to which James P. Johnson devoted much of his creative energies may some day be heard. If these works should eventually find an audience, Johnson can be added to the long list of determined but often bitter artists who were ahead of their time. For he died in 1956—just as the curtain was about to rise on the ragtime revival.

Eubie Blake

Willie "The Lion" Smith

Ralph Sutton

Three Great

Ballet Companies

By P. W. MANCHESTER
Managing Editor, Dance News

THE ballet of the Moscow Bolshoi Theater is the largest and most famous ballet company in the world. Its fame and reputation are so firmly established that most people have forgotten that these are very recent. They also forget that what we think of as the Russian ballet actually stems from the Maryinsky Theater of St. Petersburg (now the Kirov Theater of Leningrad). It was from this theater that Sergei Diaghilev took the dancers who revolutionized the whole Western ballet world when the Russian ballet first appeared in Paris in 1909.

Before the 1917 Revolution, the ballet of the Moscow Bolshoi Theater was looked upon as a mere provincial troupe, even though it was an imperial company appearing in a state theater. It actually had a long history, beginning in 1773, when the State Orphanage of Moscow started ballet classes and trained dancers for the original company of the Petrovsky Theater, which stood where the Bolshoi does now. Yet it never enjoyed, inside Russia or abroad, the prestige of the St. Petersburg troupe which had the patronage of the Tsar.

When Moscow became the political and cultural capital of Soviet Russia the status of the two theaters changed. Dancers from the Maryinsky, then renamed the Kirov, were transferred to Moscow (Marina Semyonova and Galina Ulanova among them) and for a time danced in both theaters. By the late 1940's the Bolshoi completely overshadowed the Kirov, since it was the company which all official visitors were taken to see.

The present Bolshoi company is about two hundred strong. When it travels abroad, only about one half of the company leaves Moscow; the rest remain to continue playing in the Bolshoi Theater.

Bolshoi productions frequently take a year or more to prepare and rehearse, and almost all of them last a full evening. The twenty- or thirty-minute ballet, introduced by Michel Fokine with the Diaghilev Ballet, is practically unknown in Russia. All scores for the ballets are specially composed. The repertoire naturally includes the standard classics, though the Soviet versions of such works as *Swan Lake, Coppelia* or *The Sleeping Beauty* vary considerably, having been reworked by various choreographers, not always to their advantage.

In the early days after the Revolution

many attempts were made to create ballets that would interpret Soviet ideology. Few of these propaganda works found public favor, and today Soviet choreographers rely largely on the rich fund of Russian folklore—*The Forest Devil, The Stone Flower*—the narrative poems of Pushkin, such as *The Fountain of Bakhchisarai* and *The Bronze Horseman,* or classic stories as *Romeo and Juliet* and *Cinderella.*

Ballet in Russia was always isolated; revolution merely deepened this isolation. The new forms and techniques created by Diaghilev and his great choreographer, Michel Fokine, influenced all Western ballet thinking but they were never felt in Russia. Although Russian choreographers and dancers seem unaware of it, their works are still in the style of the late nineteenth and early twentieth centuries, when the Maryinsky Theater was in full bloom. To Western eyes Bolshoi productions seem leisurely, heavy, overweighted with huge ensembles.

The dancers receive their general education along with their dance training in the theater school. Normally training begins at the age of 8 or 9, and at 18 the most talented pupils graduate into the company. Some who do not quite achieve the high standard demanded of the Bolshoi or Kirov companies are sent to one of the many other state ballet companies in the Soviet Union.

It is usual for a Bolshoi dancer to retire, with a life pension, somewhere between the ages of forty and fifty.

Leading dancers of the present Bolshoi company include Galina Ulanova and Olga Lepeshinskaya, both nearing retirement. Others are Maya Plisetskaya, Raissa Struchkova, Nina Timofeyeva, Marina Kondratieva and Ekaterina Maximova (believed by many to be one of the great ballerinas of the future). Among the leading men are Yuri Zhdanov, Yuri Kondratov, Nicolai Fadeyechev, Boris Khokhlov, Alexander Lapauri and Georgi Farmanyants. The Bolshoi has so many dancers of high caliber that the list could be doubled and still not include all its top-rate dancers.

The second great ballet company is The Royal Ballet of the Royal Opera House, Covent Garden, London. This company was known as Sadler's Wells Ballet until it received its Royal Charter on January 16, 1957, in its twenty-sixth year.

Under the direction of Ninette de Valois it began as half a dozen dancers, all girls, who provided the dancing for the ballets in the opera productions that alternated with Shakespeare at the Old Vic Theater. In 1931 the governors of the Old Vic opened the rebuilt Sadler's Wells Theater in Islington, a north-London district. By then the little group had grown to a size at which it

The Royal Ballet

Margot Fonteyn held high above a circle of water nymphs in *Ondine.*

Margot Fonteyn with Michael Somes in *Birthday Offering.*

PHOTOS, DANCE NEWS

could daringly offer a whole evening of English ballet. Anton Dolin was the guest leading male dancer for its first two seasons; Alicia Markova was its first prima ballerina. By 1939 the company was about forty strong and headed by Margot Fonteyn and Robert Helpmann.

When war broke out, the theater, like all London theaters, was closed for a time. It reopened for a few months and then the blitz of 1940 closed it for the duration of the war. The New Theater became the wartime London home of Sadler's Wells Ballet. During the war years when there were no glamorous annual visits from the great prewar Ballets Russes companies, the modest English company became firmly established. When the war was over, it was invited to reopen the Royal Opera House, Covent Garden, in 1946, as the Opera House's first resident ballet company.

The production chosen for this occasion was *The Sleeping Beauty,* the great Petipa Russian classic. Ever since then this has been what might be called the signature ballet of the company. It opened the historic New York season in 1949 and is usually chosen to introduce the company on its first visit to a new city in a foreign land.

The repertoire of the Royal Ballet in-

cludes all those works that are usually looked on as being standard, i.e., *Giselle, Coppelia,* the full-evening *Swan Lake* (only the one-act version is in the repertoire of American and most other companies), Fokine's *Les Sylphides* and *Petrouchka* together with his version of *Firebird.* Ninette de Valois was an active choreographer during the formative years of Sadler's Wells, but her duties as director have long curtailed her creative abilities in that direction. Only her 1931 *Job* and 1937 *Checkmate* are still being performed.

Since 1935 the principal choreographer has been Frederick Ashton, the only chore-

PHOTOS. DANCE NEWS

Galina Ulanova prepares in her dressing room for *Romeo and Juliet.*

The Bolshoi Ballet

Vladimir Vasiliev and Maya Plisetskaya in *The Stone Flower.*

The colorful and exciting ball scene in the Bolshoi production of the classic tale of *Romeo and Juliet.*

403

The New York City Ballet

Janet Reed, the company's Ballet Mistress.

F. MELTON, NEW YORK CITY BALLET

FRED FEHL, NEW YORK CITY BALLET

A scene from Balanchine's Christmas ballet *Nutcracker*.

ographer today whose world reputation is on a level with that of America's George Balanchine. From his early *Façade* (1931) to his evening-length *Ondine* (1958), his works have been part of the basic structure of English ballet. He is one of the very few choreographers outside Russia who has created full-length ballets, beginning with his version of Prokofiev's *Cinderella* (1948) and continuing with Delibes' *Sylvia* (1952), Prokofiev's *Romeo and Juliet* for the Royal Danish Ballet in 1955 and the recent *Ondine* with score specially composed by Hans Werner Henze.

Younger choreographers in the Royal Ballet organization are John Cranko and Kenneth MacMillan. Present leading dancers are Margot Fonteyn, universally considered one of the greatest ballerinas of the day, Nadia Nerina, Rowena Jackson, Svetlana Beriosova, Anya Linden, and Michael Somes, David Blair, Philip Chatfield, Brian Shaw and Alexander Grant.

In 1946 a second company, known as Sadler's Wells Theater Ballet, was formed to give performances in that theater to take the place of the original company on its move to Covent Garden. An amalgamation of the two companies has been steadily taking place during the past two years and is now almost complete. As a result the company of well over a hundred dancers can be split up the same way as the Bolshoi.

Since 1946 the Royal Opera House, Covent Garden, has received a large subsidy from the British Government. The subsidy is administered by the Arts Council of Great Britain.

The school attached to the Royal Ballet is not free, for the state grant does not make any provision for this. However, many scholarships are available each year. Dancers may receive their full training and education in this school even though they may not ultimately be taken into the company.

The third great ballet company, the New York City Ballet, celebrated its tenth anniversary during the 1958-59 seasons. Its roots go back to 1934 when its director, Lincoln Kirstein, with George Balanchine and E. M. M. Warburg organized the School of American Ballet in Hartford, Connecticut. Students and guest dancers gave the first performance as the American Ballet Company in December of that year.

The company went on tour and then from 1935 to 1938 provided ballets for productions at the Metropolitan Opera House.

404

In the meantime Lincoln Kirstein had formed another group, known as Ballet Caravan, with the intention of establishing a repertoire of truly American works. Two ballets from this period are Lew Christensen's *Filling Station* and Eugene Loring's *Billy the Kid*.

In July 1946 the two companies merged as Ballet Society, which gave a few private subscription performances a year. In 1948, Morton Baum, chairman of the Executive Committee of the New York City Center, invited Lincoln Kirstein to incorporate his company with the opera and drama activities of City Center. Its first public performance there included three ballets which remain among the company's major works —*Concerto Barocco, Orpheus* and *Symphony in C*.

Though City Center is its home base for several seasons a year, the company has been an entirely independent body since early in 1949. The New York City Ballet has traveled extensively in Europe, the Far East and Australia, but, unlike the other American companies, it does not undertake long tours in the United States. The company is therefore in the position of being far better known abroad than it is at home, where it has been seen in only a few cities.

In New York the City Ballet has built up a large and loyal public for its very specialized type of ballet. This company is the instrument for the great creative talent of George Balanchine. Almost all other choreographers have created works to suit the particular dancers of a given company (Frederick Ashton for Margot Fonteyn, Fokine for Nijinsky and Karsavina, and Massine for Alexandra Danilova and himself). But Balanchine's main objective is that the dancers should interpret his individual vision. In this phase of his career he is concerned mainly with the mathematical designs of pure dance. Probably no other choreographer has ever lived who has had his sheer inventive skill in creating new steps and dance combinations. A "Balanchine dancer" must be both a willing tool and an exceptional technician. Balanchine has a particular affinity for the music of Stravinsky, who has composed scores for him, including *Apollo, Orpheus* and *Agon*.

For the sake of variety in program building, other choreographers (Jerome Robbins in particular) have created works for this company.

As though to emphasize that they are less important than the works they dance, leading dancers of the company are listed alphabetically. At this time they are: Diana Adams, Melissa Hayden, Allegra Kent, Maria Tallchief, Violette Verdy, Patricia Wilde, and Jacques d'Amboise, Tod Bolender, Nicholas Magallanes, Francisco Moncion and Roy Tobias.

Melissa Hayden leads the chorus in the rousing finale of *Stars and Stripes*.

MARTHA SWOPE, NEW YORK CITY BALLET

MOVIES
in Review

By PHILIP T. HARTUNG

Motion Picture Critic

The Commonweal; Scholastic Magazines

DESPITE the many jokes during 1959 about the motion-picture industry being a dying business, the facts disagreed.

It is true that Hollywood and the American movie business were changing—and have been changing for the past few years. The big studios are no longer as big as they were and now they make fewer films than ever before; but they have finally learned that TV is not necessarily a competitor. Practically all the big studios now work with TV and make some films especially for that medium. All of them have sold or leased many of their pre-1948 films to the networks. They all look forward to the eventual sale of their post-1948 movies and to the time when they can show new films on pay-as-you-see television.

Although fewer American movies were made during 1959, more blockbuster films were turned out. These elaborate films were in color, on wide screens, and were more expensive to produce but were also rewarded with greater profits.

Another change in Hollywood was the rise of independent producers, directors and stars who made pictures on their own and released them through the major companies. Produced with care and distinction, these "independents" were often among the year's best.

Theater owners suffered most from the small number of films (the number of motion-picture theaters dropped considerably during the past few years). However, their business was good in 1959, especially during the summer when the drive-ins flourished. There are now 4,500 of these popular drive-ins, more than one third of the United States movie theaters. The rise in attendance was no doubt due to the number of good films being released and the poor quality of summer television.

The film makers, however, have learned not to depend entirely on American moviegoers. They now hope to earn at least half of their gross profits from abroad where American movies are well liked.

But the true test of motion-picture production is in the movies themselves, and

Porgy and Bess: the famous Gershwin folk opera with Sidney Poitier and Dorothy Dandridge in the title roles.

no industry that turned out so many million-dollar pictures could be dying. Following the example set by Paramount with *The Ten Commandments,* which was made in 1957 for $13,000,000 and has already grossed more than $35,000,000, MGM released *Ben Hur* in 1959. This epic, made in Italy and Israel from the famous Lew Wallace story, was directed by William Wyler and starred Charlton Heston, Stephen Boyd and Haya Harareet. It cost $15,000,000 and may well break every box-office record.

An industry with such confidence in itself must be very much alive. Its policies have changed—but it is not dead. Even the lowly westerns, once the mainstay of the industry, turned out cheaply and quickly, were among the expensive pictures in 1959. Several of these attracted attention because of their good productions with top-ranking stars: Gary Cooper and Maria Schell in *The Hanging Tree;* Kirk Douglas and Anthony Quinn in *Last Train from Gun Hill;* John Wayne, Dean Martin, Walter Brennan and Ricky Nelson in *Rio Bravo;* Henry Fonda, Richard Widmark, Dorothy Malone and Anthony Quinn in *Warlock. The Big Country,* directed by William Wyler with an all-star cast, won an Oscar for Burl Ives as best supporting player. And one of the most unusual westerns, with stars made popular on TV, was *Yellowstone Kelly* with Clint Walker, Edward (Kookie) Byrnes and John Russell.

Two of the year's best outdoor pictures were more concerned with war than with the problems of the typical horse opera. John Ford, one of America's best movie makers, directed John Wayne, William Holden and others in *The Horse Soldiers,* about a Union cavalry raid into Southern territory during the Civil War. The exciting film *They Came to Cordura* took place during the 1916 expeditions into Mexico and was a bitter, realistic study of bravery and cowardice with an all-star cast led by Gary Cooper, Rita Hayworth, Van Heflin, Tab Hunter, Richard Conte, Michael Callan and Dick York.

There were modern war pictures of course during 1959. Some were comedies that had to do with men in uniform rather than with actual combat—like *The Perfect Furlough,* in which Tony Curtis chased after Janet Leigh and Linda Cristal in Paris; and *It Started with a Kiss,* in which Glenn Ford pursued and finally rewon Debbie Reynolds, as his wife, in Spain.

More concerned with actual fighting were *The Silent Enemy,* a British film in which Laurence Harvey portrayed the famous frogman Lionel Crabb; *Up Periscope,* in which James Garner played a United States Navy frogman on a dangerous mission; *The Last Blitzkrieg,* which had Van Johnson as a German spy; *Pork Chop Hill,* in which Gregory Peck played an officer in a realistic and grueling portrait of this desperate Korean battle.

Two of the most provocative war pictures did not deal directly with fighting at all. In *The Journey,* Yul Brynner, as a Russian major, detained Deborah Kerr, Jason Robards, Jr., and other travelers at the Austrian border during the Hungarian uprisings in 1956. One of the year's best pictures was *The Diary of Anne Frank,* beautifully produced and sensitively directed by George Stevens. Newcomer Millie Perkins played the role of the thirteen-year-old Jewish girl who hid for two years with her family and several other people in a crowded Amsterdam loft during the nazi occupation. The sorrows and joys, the perilous situation, the boredom and bickering were reflected in the entries the girl made in her diary and in the acting of the excellent cast led by Joseph Schildkraut who gave a magnificent performance as

Two chariots thunder to the thrilling finish of the spectacular race in the epic *Ben Hur*.

Anne's father. Also effective were Shelley Winters, Richard Beymer, Ed Wynn and all the other leads in this warm, human, inspiring drama.

The year brought other dramas based on best sellers. Lana Turner and Juanita Moore played two mothers and Sandra Dee and Susan Kohner their respective daughters in the very sentimental though handsomely made *Imitation of Life*. Orson Welles, Dean Stockwell and Bradford Dillman gave outstanding performances in *Compulsion,* a fictionized version of the Loeb-Leopold case. *Some Came Running* won neither critics nor audiences; but Frank Sinatra, Dean Martin, Martha Hyer and especially Shirley MacLaine received praise for their performances. The entire cast of *Anatomy of a Murder,* led by James Stewart, Lee Remick and Attorney Joseph N. Welch, were applauded but many critics found the courtroom scenes too sensational and realistic.

The Young Philadelphians with Paul Newman, *The Scapegoat* with Alec Guinness and a fine supporting cast, and *This Earth Is Mine* (based on the novel *The Cup and the Sword* by Alice Tisdale Hobart) with Rock Hudson, Jean Simmons and other popular players received mediocre critical notices but some audience en-

thusiasm because of their well-liked stars. *The Inn of the Sixth Happiness* won the acclaim it deserved for its moving story as well as Ingrid Bergman's excellent performance as a missionary in China.

Although several films changed the novels on which they were based, their producers were applauded for their courage in attempting to tackle difficult themes. Jerry Wald gave an outstanding production and cast to *The Sound and the Fury,* based on William Faulkner's portrait of a decaying Southern family. Producer Dore Schary brought top stars to *Lonelyhearts* which was adapted from Nathanael West's disturbing novel about the conflict between idealism and cynicism. *Green Mansions,* from W. H. Hudson's famous story, was finally brought to the screen by producer Edmund Grainger but proved a disappointment even with Audrey Hepburn and Anthony Perkins in the lead roles.

Miss Hepburn disappointed no one with her portrayal in *The Nun's Story,* based on Kathryn Hulme's novel. Many had misgivings as to the book's suitability for the screen, but critics and general audiences alike had only praise for Henry Blanke's fine finished production. Audrey Hepburn, as the nursing nun who felt after seventeen years that she must leave the convent, gave the finest performance of her career under Fred Zinnemann's first-rate direction. The entire cast, which included Edith Evans, Peter Finch, Mildred Dunnock and many others, was excellent in the beautifully photographed scenes that shifted from Belgium to the Congo. The whole of *The Nun's Story,* in spite of its offbeat ending, was done with dignity and inspiring reverence.

Several of the year's movies stemmed from plays. Of the two based on works by George Bernard Shaw, *The Doctor's Dilemma,* starring Leslie Caron and Dirk Bogarde, was the more interesting, witty and true to Shaw. *The Devil's Disciple,* in spite of its good cast headed by Laurence Olivier, Burt Lancaster and Kirk Douglas, was considered disappointing. Although Fredric March and Kim Novak gave good performances in Paddy Chayefsky's *Middle of the Night,* the film's realism and grim story failed to win popular or critical approval. Outstanding among the plays-into-films was *Separate Tables,* in which a fine cast portrayed lonely residents in an English seaside hotel. For his

Audrey Hepburn has a serious talk with Peter Finch in this scene from *The Nun's Story.*

performance as the bogus major in *Separate Tables,* David Niven won an Oscar in April as best actor, and Wendy Hiller also won one as best supporting actress.

Also from the stage was the year's best musical film: *Porgy and Bess.* Although this movie, based on George Gershwin's famous folk opera, was severely criticized for being so static, Samuel Goldwyn's production was excellent and the lovely Gershwin music came through in grand style. The Negro cast was headed by Sidney Poitier, Dorothy Dandridge, Sammy Davis, Jr., and Pearl Bailey.

The year saw few musical comedies—mainly because they were expensive and European audiences (on whom film makers relied for profits) did not usually care for them unless they were exceptionally good—like *Gigi. Gigi* was a standout; it won critical praise everywhere and its popular appeal at box offices won large profits for its makers. It also won nine Oscars (an all-time record) including best film of the year and best director for Vincente Minnelli at the April 1959 award ceremony.

Appearing in 1959 musicals were: Mario Lanza in *For the First Time,* a light and pleasant concoction photographed abroad; Bing Crosby, once more a priest, in *Say One for Me* with Debbie Reynolds and

On the Beach: Anthony Perkins, Gregory Peck and Fred Astaire face death by radiation.

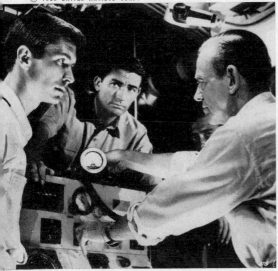

The Diary of Anne Frank: Millie Perkins as Anne, the girl whose diary became a legend.

Robert Wagner. It was a curious mixture of song and dance, comedy and religion. The best of the musical films was *The Five Pennies,* a handsomely made, semibiographical picture in which Danny Kaye portrayed band leader Red Nichols.

There were a few other 1959 biographical films. Rod Steiger was excellent in the title role of the realistic *Al Capone.* Susan Hayward gave another fine performance and won an Oscar for her portrayal of Barbara Graham, condemned to the gas chamber, in the fine and grim *I Want to Live!*

Going farther back in history, Robert Stack played the title role in the spectacular but plodding *John Paul Jones,* in which Bette Davis appeared as Catherine the Great. In *Tempest,* set in the same period in Russia, Viveca Lindfors played Catherine while Van Heflin as Pugachov led the peasant revolts against her. Anthony Franciosa, as the artist Goya, painted Ava Gardner in the fictionized biography called *The Naked Maja.* One of the most spectacular of the historical films, *The Big Fisherman,* went back to the first century. Although Howard Keel was

very effective as St. Peter, this long and occasionally tedious movie was mainly concerned with the routine romance of a young couple played by Susan Kohner and John Saxon.

Most of the year's comedies were light and breezy affairs like *The Mating Game, Count Your Blessings, Some Like It Hot* and *Ask Any Girl.* The best of these was *Pillow Talk* in which Rock Hudson, Doris Day, Tony Randall and Thelma Ritter were hilariously funny in a satire on modern romance and manners. Established comedians turned up in *Alias Jesse James* (with Bob Hope) and *Don't Give up the Ship* (with Jerry Lewis).

Unfortunately most of the films about young people were not particularly distinguished: *Gidget, Blue Denim, A Private's Affair, Senior Prom.* But they did win attention to rising young actors like Sal Mineo, Gary Crosby, Barry Coe, Christine Carere, Sandra Dee and Carol Lynley.

The year had its good share of adventure films with *Watusi* and two Tarzan features set in Africa, *Shake Hands with the Devil* in revolutionary Ireland, *North by Northwest* and *The F. B. I. Story* chasing around the United States, and *Third Man on the Mountain* taking James MacArthur high up in the Swiss Alps.

And there were fantasies that went to even more imaginative places: *The Seventh Voyage of Sinbad, tom thumb* (which won an Oscar for George Pal's special effects), Walt Disney's full-length feature cartoon *Sleeping Beauty* and his live-action films *Darby O'Gill and the Little People,* set in storybook Ireland, and *The Shaggy Dog,* set in storybook America with its tale of a boy who turned into a dog.

There were science-fiction films that were fantastic in their way and not meant to be taken seriously: *The Mysterians, First Man into Space, The Return of the Fly, The Man Who Could Cheat Death. The Mouse That Roared* was a very amusing and thoughtful political satire about a tiny Alpine country that conquered the United States and stole the world's most powerful bomb. Two films

that dealt with the future and what could happen when radioactive drift followed a nuclear war were meant to be taken seriously. In *The World, the Flesh and the Devil* Harry Belafonte, Inger Stevens and Mel Ferrer were the last people alive in the United States. Although this film was not as good as it should have been, its shots of deserted New York City were magnificent. Stanley Kramer's *On the Beach,* expertly filmed in Australia and well acted by a good cast including Gregory Peck, Ava Gardner, Fred Astaire and Anthony Perkins, carried the grim radiation fallout theme to its final conclusion: the death of everyone in the world.

No one could accuse the movie makers, even those who often indulged in escapist themes, of not being willing to tackle serious subjects. Nor could anyone rightfully say the motion-picture industry was a dying business, especially in a year that ended with announcements of new and bigger pictures in preparation.

Third Man on the Mountain: James MacArthur (left) is the hero of this outdoor adventure.

INDEX

e

f

r

s

t

X

y

Z